Comparative Health Policy

Comparative Health Policy

Fifth edition

Robert H. Blank

Viola Burau

and

Ellen Kuhlmann

First edition 2004
Second edition 2007
Third edition 2010
Fourth edition 2014

Published 2018 by
PALGRAVE

Palgrave in the UK is an imprint of Macmillan Publishers Limited, registered in England, company number 785998, of 4 Crinan Street, London, N1 9XW.

Palgrave® and Macmillan® are registered trademarks in the United States, the United Kingdom, Europe and other countries.

ISBN 978–1–137–54496–4 hardback
ISBN 978–1–137–54495–7 paperback

This book is printed on paper suitable for recycling and made from fully managed and sustained forest sources. Logging, pulping and manufacturing processes are expected to conform to the environmental regulations of the country of origin.

A catalogue record for this book is available from the British Library.

A catalog record for this book is available from the Library of Congress.

Dedicated to Hanne Lind Kristensen,

1967–2014

Contents

List of Illustrative Material

Boxes

Figures

Tables

Preface to the Fifth Edition

We wrote the first edition of this book to fill a glaring gap in comparative health policy. Although there had been numerous books about the health policies of specific countries and a handful of books that compared a few nations, our own research in a variety of countries convinced us that a more inclusive comparative coverage would be helpful in elucidating the issues and problems surrounding health care. Therefore, we pooled our shared knowledge of a diverse set of health care systems and wrote an introduction to the health policy of nine countries (expanded to ten in the third edition, with the addition of Taiwan). Based on numerous reviews in journals and on input from those who used the first four editions, we have extensively updated the text, statistical tables, and references to reflect the many changes that have taken place in the last several years. We have completely revised four of the chapters to better cover the comparative content and expand coverage of the international context of health policy and of global health issues. New coverage of the health workforce and primary care are supplemented with increased inclusion of low- and middle-income countries.

As in the earlier editions, to establish the extent to which the problems facing health care systems have common roots or spring from specific national circumstances, our assessment of health policy focuses on key themes, issues and tensions that run through the book. Thus, chapters are organized around these themes rather than looking country by country. How do the main types of health systems in the developed world address health care problems, and do diverse systems make a difference in policy outcomes? Is health policy in all developed countries converging due to globalization and other factors as some observers argue? This book, therefore, analyses what lessons can be learned about public/private mixes, policy and funding frameworks, health workforce composition, and acute and preventive services across disparate health systems. To accomplish this, the systems of developed countries –Australia, Germany, Japan, New Zealand, the Netherlands, Sweden, Singapore, Taiwan, the UK and the USA – are again central, but we have added more discussion of low- and middle-income countries where appropriate.

Throughout the book, we put health care in a broader social context and reveal its interdependence with factors often excluded from analysis. Health care, we argue, cannot be separated from other issues that impinge on health such as economic inequalities, the environment, migration and social services. Thus, we include analyses of the health care workforce, primary health care, long-term care for the elderly. We discuss an array of public health and broader public policy issues that cumulatively impact on health outcomes more than medical services per se. We also question whether the medical model and its heavy emphasis on technology is the most effective way to address the health of populations.

Chapter 1 introduces health policy and the impact of global trends of population ageing, technology diffusion and heightened public expectations on the health systems of developed nations. It also discusses the importance of comparative health care analysis and presents the typologies conventionally used to classify health systems. Chapter 2 looks at the institutional, historical/cultural and economic context of health care and proposes an integrated model of health that accounts for the variation across our countries. It also discusses differences over the definition of health, the role of alternative forms of medicine and the relationship between health status and the socio-economic milieu.

Chapter 3 shifts attention to the provision, funding and governance of health care and to the nature and scope of health reforms across the countries examined here. Our countries show considerable diversity, both among different health systems and across the sub-systems of each health system, and only a few countries neatly fit existing typologies. Chapter 4 continues and expands this discussion by examining priority setting in health care. It illustrates the problematic allocation and rationing issues facing all health systems and discusses how these countries have responded to these challenges. It also introduces health technology assessment and the evolving integration of information technologies into health care. Chapter 5 examines the composition and governance of the health workforce in these health systems. Although the face of medical practice has altered, doctors have retained considerable power and remain key players in health policy, but they are not alone. Therefore, the chapter examines the dynamics of staff and skill mixes, geographical imbalances and mobility of the health professions, and raises important tensions between high-income and low- and middle-income countries. The chapter also reveals the marginality of human capital in comparative health policy.

Chapter 6 moves the discussion beyond hospitals to primary health care and long-term care, including informal provision of care, which elucidates the interdependence of health with other care services as countries face the dual challenges of ageing populations and social transformation in an era of cost containment. Chapter 7 shifts focus from individual, patient-centred care to public health, with its emphasis on the health of populations, and examines the trends toward the globalization of public health. It discusses a range of international health threats including recent Ebola and Zika viruses as well as issues surrounding obesity and smoking policies and the environment. Overall, it illustrates that health outcomes for populations are more closely tied to health promotion and disease prevention efforts, income distribution, housing, social conditions and the environment than to medical interventions.

The concluding chapter returns to the broader themes introduced in Chapter 1 and begins by assessing the appropriateness of existing typologies of health systems. The discussion demonstrates the sustained importance of country-specific differences as well as the complexity of health systems. The chapter then moves on to discuss the possibilities and limitations of policy learning across countries that are inherent in comparative research.

In terms of the revisions for this edition we have benefited from constructive comments from colleagues whose valuable feedback has helped us sharpen our analysis. Some of the specific changes here are responses to suggestions raised in journal reviews which were mainly highly supportive of the earlier editions. Moreover, teaching in comparative health policy has offered a welcome test ground for new ideas and we are grateful to our students for their patience and input.

List of Abbreviations

ACA	Affordable Care Act (USA)
ACAP	Aged Care Assessment Program (Australia)
ACC	Accident Compensation Commission (New Zealand)
ACO	accountable care organization
ADL	activities of daily life
AIDS	Acquired Immunodeficiency Syndrome
AMA	American Medical Association
BMA	British Medical Association
BMI	Body Mass Index
BNHI	Bureau of National Health Insurance (Taiwan)
BRICS	Brazil, Russia, India, China and South Africa
CCC	Clinical Commissioning Groups (UK)
CDC	Centers for Disease Control and Prevention (USA)
CPF	Central Provident Fund (Singapore)
CT	computerized axial tomography
DAHTA	German Institute for Health Technology Assessment
DHBs	District Health Boards (New Zealand)
DHHS	Department of Health and Human Services (USA)
DRGs	diagnosis-related groups
ECDC	European Centre for Disease Prevention and Control
EHR	electronic health record
EMR	electronic medical record
EMRX	Electronic Medical Record Exchange (Singapore)
ER	emergency room
EU	European Union
FCTC	Framework Convention on Tobacco Control (WHO)
FDA	Food and Drug Administration (USA)
FFO	Fee-for-outcomes (Taiwan)
GATS	General Agreement on Trade in Services
GDP	gross domestic product
GMC	General Medical Council
GP	general practitioner
HCQI	Health Care Quality Indicator Project (OECD)
HIT	Health information technology
HIV	Human Immunodeficiency Virus
HMO	Health Maintenance Organization
HSPA	Health system performance assessment (WHO)
HTA	health technology assessment

IADL	instrumental activities of daily life
ICU	intensive care unit
IHR	International Health Regulations
IOM	Institute of Medicine (USA)
IPA	Independent Practice Association (New Zealand)
IPCC	Intergovernmental Panel on Climate Change
IQWIG	Institute for Quality and Efficiency in Health Care (Germany)
LMICs	low- and middle-income countries
LTC	long-term care
MBS	Medicare Benefits Schedule (Australia)
MHCs	Municipal Health Centres (Japan)
MOHW	Ministry of Health and Welfare (Taiwan)
MRI	magnetic resonance imaging
MSA	Medical Savings Account (Singapore)
NAFTA	North American Free Trade Agreement
NEHTA	National E-Health Transition Authority (Australia)
NGO	non-governmental organization
NHI	National Health Insurance (Taiwan)
NHIA	National Health Insurance Administration (Taiwan)
NHMRC	National Health and Medical Research Council (Australia)
NHS	National Health Service (UK)
NICE	National Institute for Health and Care Excellence (UK)
NIH	National Institutes of Health (USA)
NP	nurse practitioner
NPM	New Public Management
NRHA	National Rural Health Association (USA)
NZMA	New Zealand Medical Association
OECD	Organisation for Economic Co-operation and Development
PACE	Program for All Inclusive Care for the Elderly (USA)
PCCN	Primary Community Care Networks (Taiwan)
PCEHR	Personally Controlled Electronic Health Record (Australia)
PHO	Primary Health Organizations (New Zealand)
PHC	primary health care
PHCC	Primary Health Care Centres (Sweden)
PHS	Public Health Service (USA)
PHU	Public Health Units (New Zealand)
PET	positron emission tomography
PPO	Preferred Provider Organization
PPP	purchasing power parity
QALY	quality adjusted life years
SARS	Severe Acute Respiratory Syndrome
SDGs	Social Development Goals
SES	socio-economic status
SMA	Swedish Medical Association

TCM	traditional Chinese medicine
TTIP	Transatlantic Trade and Investment Partnership
UNAIDS	Joint UN Programme on HIV/AIDS
USAID	US Agency for International Development
UVB	ultraviolet B radiation
UVR	solar ultraviolet radiation
VPN	Virtual Private Network (Taiwan)
WHO	World Health Organization
WTO	World Trade Organization

Chapter 1

Comparative Health Policy: An Introduction

Health care has always been a controversial policy area, but lately it has become a major issue in all developed nations. Ageing populations, the proliferation of new medical technologies and heightened public expectations and demands, among other factors, have elevated health care to the top of the political agenda. Intensifying pressures on political leaders to meet rising public demands for expanded service conflict directly with the need to constrain health care costs and to manage scarce societal resources. Thus, despite major differences among countries as to how health care is funded, provided and governed, no government can escape the controversy and problems accompanying health care in the 21st century, although some seem to be coping significantly better than others.

Given the universality of the problems raised by health care, one must question whether what governments do about it – the policies they adopt – makes a difference. And if policies do matter, what approaches and strategies offer the most potential for resolving or managing the dilemmas? Does simply spending more money improve the health of a population? If not, what does? This book addresses these questions by examining health care policy across a collection of countries that have taken divergent approaches and instituted an array of mechanisms for covering the health needs of their populations. It also analyses trends within and across these countries to determine whether there is a convergence in health policy among developed nations, as claimed by some observers.

Health care as public policy

The term 'policy' has a wide range of meanings in current English usage. Politicians and parties present their intended actions as policies to be pursued and they defend past actions as policies to be extended. Political commentators often talk about a government's housing policy, crime policy or drug policy in general terms, while others debate a specific government action. Policy, then, can be used to refer to general statements of intention, past or present actions in specific areas, or a set of standing

1

rules to guide actions. Although all organizations have policies, at least in the latter sense, the focus of this book is on the policies of governments. 'Public policy' is defined here as a decision taken by the government or on behalf of it. Although usually viewed as an action, a decision not to act can also be a policy. All health policies, then, involve a fundamental choice by a government as to whether to undertake a specific action or to do nothing (see Howlett and Ramesh, 2009).

Only the government has the legitimate authority to make decisions that are binding and carried out in the name of the entire population. Other organizations, such as medical associations and nursing societies, often make decisions that affect many individuals as well as the health care system. While their decisions might indeed have a bearing on what the government ultimately does, they are not binding by force of law. Although, where appropriate, we discuss actions by private and voluntary organizations that impact on health care, the focus here is on governmental action or non-action.

It is useful here to distinguish between health policy, health care policy and health care politics. Health policy constitutes those courses of action proposed or taken by governments that affect the health of their populations. As we will see in Chapter 7, health policy overlaps with economic, social welfare, employment, and housing policy, among other areas. Health policy, then, is a broad term encompassing any action that has health implications. On the other hand, 'health care' policy is a narrower term that refers to those courses of action taken by governments that deal with the financing, provision or governance of health services. Although we use the term health policy throughout the book, given its prominence in Western countries, most attention is placed on health care policy. Only in Chapters 6 and 7 does this emphasis widen to health policy in the broader sense. Finally, 'health care politics' comprises the interactions of political actors and institutions in the health care arena. It will become apparent in Chapter 2 that politics is a crucial dimension of all attempts to frame health policy; but politics is very country-specific and it is impossible to cover systematically the intricacies of health care politics of each country here. While we do not purport to analyse country-specific health politics, however, readings that offer such detailed analyses of each country are found in the Guide to Further Reading at the end of this book.

It is also important to note that while health policy conceptually can be distinguished from other areas of public policy, it is highly interconnected with a wide range of social and economic policies. In fact, there are health dimensions in virtually all policy areas: among others, national security, immigration, environmental, housing, transportation, and labour policy. In Chapter 7 it will be argued that the health of a population can be as contingent on these policies as on prescribed health care policy.

Three types of public policy

Public policy can be categorized as one of three basic types: regulatory, distributive and redistributive (see Lowi, 1972). Regulatory policies impose constraints or restrictions on the actions of groups or individuals: they provide rules of conduct with sanctions backed up by the authority of government. Distributive policies are based on the notion of public goods, e.g. goods and services that benefit all individuals but which are unlikely to be produced by voluntary acts of individuals because they lack the resources. Public goods are defined differently by each society based on how broadly government responsibility is interpreted. Often, distributive policies provide advantages or benefits to specific segments of society. Considerable governmental activity revolves around the provision of public services, often without undue controversy until scarcity forces trade-offs to be made as to what groups get what goods. Redistributive policies, in contrast, are controversial in principle because they represent deliberate efforts by governments to alter the distribution of income, wealth or property among groups in society. The reallocation of resources through progressive taxes and other mechanisms occurs to some extent in all democracies, but it is the foundation of more egalitarian states. It should be noted that all policies create winners and losers, although the mechanisms by which gains and losses might occur are often subtle (Hill, 2009).

Health care encompasses all three types of policy. The regulation of the health care sector through fee schedules, licensing requirements, approval of drugs and other constraints on medical practice is extensive. In fact, despite their divergent types of health systems, health care is one of the most regulated sectors in all developed countries. The distributive policies of health care are most obvious in countries that have national health services, but occur to some extent in all countries through medical education, the funding of health care research, the provision of public health services and health promotion activities. Finally, redistributive health care policies are based on the concepts of need and entitlement and encompass a range of efforts by government to shift resources from healthy to non-healthy citizens. They are usually based on a society's conception of equality. Mechanisms for such policies include the use of general revenues to provide services to those who lack resources, means-tested social insurance schemes for the poor and programmes that redistribute societal resources from general revenues to the elderly, children or the indigent.

Health policy, then, is an amalgamation of these various types of policy as governments attempt to influence the provision of health care to their citizens. Of all areas of public policy, health care is one of the most contentious because it always entails conflicts, especially in the regulatory and redistributive modes. This is not surprising given its high emotional and economic stakes. In addition to the potential life/death stakes inherent in health policy, it is distinctive because the health care professions have, because of their specialized knowledge, a privileged status of experts in shaping and constraining it. Because of the centrality of health profession-als, a policy can be successful only if it has at least the tacit support of the medical – increasingly also of the nursing – community (see Chapter 5). Furthermore, since medical professionals largely define health need and the means necessary to meet it, any attempts by a government perceived as imposing undue constraints on the profession risk condemnation from these key stakeholders. The complexity of providing health care and the inherent uncertainty surrounding medicine further reinforces the power of the health care providers in influencing the delivery of medical services and thus shaping health care policy.

Negative and positive rights

Many of the most challenging dilemmas in democracies surface as gov-ernments struggle to find the proper mixture of policies in the light of conflicting interests. Because of the heavy emphasis on rights to health care in many countries, the distinction between negative and positive rights is important (see Heywood, 2002). Negative rights are those rights that impose obligations on governments and other citizens to refrain from interfering with the rights bearer. They relate to the freedom to be left alone to use one's resources as one sees fit. Under negative rights, each person has a sphere of autonomy that others cannot violate, but no one is further obliged to take positive action to provide that person with the resources necessary to exercise that right. The only claim on others is a freedom from intrusion. Health care as a negative right would allow patients with adequate personal resources or insurance to maximize their use of health care. Thus, negative rights are always in conflict with redistributive social welfare policies that deprive individuals of the free use of their resources.

In contrast, positive rights impose obligations on others such as tax-payers to provide those goods and services necessary for each person to exercise her or his rights. Although the level of positive rights is generally ill defined, this additional dimension requires the presence of institutions that guarantee a certain level of material well-being, through govern-mental redistribution of resources where necessary. Positive rights imply a freedom from deprivation, the entitlement to at least a decent level of human existence. The welfare state is based on this more expansive notion of rights. One question within health policy is whether all citizens have a positive right to health care and, if so, what it should entail. How far does a right to the freedom from ill health go in requiring societal pro-vision of health care resources to all citizens? What limits can justifiably be set on these entitlements to health care? For instance, could treatment be denied to an individual who causes his or her own ill health and who refuses to change his or her self-destructive behaviour despite repeated warnings? (See Chapter 4.)

Comparative health policy

Over the last several decades, comparative policy analysis has become a growth industry (see Marmor *et al.*, 2009a). Advances in information technology have expanded the availability and dissemination of data across many countries, while at the same time many policy fields increasingly have become globally oriented. A greater interest in information about policies in other countries has also been fostered by the perception of shared policy challenges arising from economic and welfare state crises. Deleon and Resnick-Terry (1999) refer to this development as the 'comparative renaissance'. The comparative perspective is now widely used in both the academic field of public policy analysis and in more applied policy studies (see, for example, Castles, 1999). Parallel to discussions about the insights generated by comparative analyses is a debate about the methodologies of cross-country comparison (for comparative politics see, for example, Peters, 1998; for comparative social policy see, for example, Hantrais and Mangen, 1996; Clasen, 1999).

This book places health policy in a comparative context to demonstrate the similarities and differences in approach among various countries as they attempt to resolve difficult health care problems. Although it can be risky to transfer policies that work in one country to another, comparative public policy is useful in expanding policy options and revealing the experiences of a wide range of applications. Øvretveit argues that comparative health research has a role in building relations among different communities 'by creating knowledge that helps people understand their differences and similarities' and that 'health managers can improve their services by sensitively adapting ideas that have worked elsewhere' (1998: 15). Marmor *et al.* (2009b) distinguish among three rationales for cross-national comparative health policy research: 'learning about national health arrangements and how they operate, learning why they take the forms they do, and learning policy lessons from those analyses' (2009b: 10). Comparative public policy is, therefore, a source of generalizations about public policy that, in turn, are valuable for understanding policy in any country.

In addition, comparative policy analysis can demonstrate that factors viewed as paramount in one country, such as the attitudes of its medical profession or the distinctiveness of its political customs, might produce divergent outcomes in other countries. For Immergut, the 'comparative perspective shows that some factors are neither as unique nor as critical as they appear, whereas others stand out as truly significant' (1992: 9). Ham (1997a) adds that an examination of international experience can illuminate both the difficulties faced by, and the wide range of strategies available to, policy makers. It can also elucidate the institutional context and the importance of the process by which decisions are made (Klein and Williams, 2000). Comparative studies, then, give us cross-cultural insights as to what works or does not work under an array of institutional and cultural contexts. Given the complexity of health care and the plethora of potential health care systems, only comparative studies can generate the evidence necessary to consider the full range of policy options.

Classifications of health care systems

At its base, health policy is, of course, a political matter. The most discernible dimension of the political context comprises the formal institutions that have been created for making public policy decisions. The institutional setting in which policy making takes place is termed the policy arena, which includes not only formal political institutions such as legislatures, executives and courts but also regulatory agencies, semi-public bodies and specialized committees and commissions. These institutions define the distribution of power and the relationships among the political players by setting the rules of the game regarding access and interaction within specific arenas. As such they give distinct advantages or disadvantages to various groups in society. Equally important to understanding public policy, then, are the informal practices and structures that have evolved within a specific formal institutional framework. These traditions and rules of the game define a special political logic in each country. They are also critical to an environment in which interest groups, political parties, bureaucrats and individual politicians vie for influence over policy.

Together these formal and informal political institutions shape how politics is conducted and create a strategic context for political conflict within the arena. 'Political factors help to determine whether a problem is defined as a public policy that requires action, they shape the way in which the problem is defined, and they intervene in the resolution of that problem.' (Immergut, 1992: 10) Although institutional variables are not the only ones to matter, variation in institutional conditions across countries yields distinctive opportunities for the actors involved in policy making in each country (Okma *et al.*, 2010). The health system represents a set of sector-specific institutions. However, while health politics is big business for governments, it often remains characterized by strong private-interest involvement by medical professionals.

Although no two political systems are identical, many share characteristics that allow us to develop *typologies* or ideal models. The use of typologies is central to the comparative shift in policy analysis and they have been used to conceptualize the institutional context in which policies are embedded. Seminal examples include: Castles' (1999) notion of 'families of nations', which describes different clusters of cultural, historical and geographical features of nations; Esping-Andersen's (1990) welfare state regimes, which identify distinct welfare state logics; and Lijphart's (1999) and Blondel's (1990) typologies of democratic and state regimes. Cross-country comparison generates an abundance of information and ordering this data through typologies simplifies it to facilitate our understanding and analysis of policy emergence, policy making and policy cycles.

Despite widespread variation among health care systems, at root they represent variants or blends of a limited number of types. As with political systems, the comparative analysis of health policy often uses typologies to help capture the institutional context of health care and contribute to the explanation of health policies across countries. Typologies have the advantage of allowing the inclusion of many countries in the analysis. They can also 'provide a basis for bridging the macro-micro link in comparative studies in such instances as when analyzing the outcomes of certain health policy constellations' (Marmor and Wendt, 2012: 18). While typologies can be valuable in simplifying a multifaceted set of cross-cutting dimensions, one must be cautious when interpreting them because they do represent ideal types of specific macro-institutional characteristics (Burau *et al.*, 2015). As will be demonstrated here, the real world of health care systems is considerably more complicated.

Early OECD typology of health systems

Because of their importance in the literature, several typologies that have been widely used to classify health care systems are reviewed here. An early typology developed in a series of studies by the Organisation for Economic Co-operation and Development (OECD) has been particularly influential (see Figure 1.1). This typology defines the health system as an ideal typical set of macro-institutional characteristics based on variations in the funding of health care and corresponding differences in the

Figure 1.1 *Types of health care system by provision and funding*

Sources: OECD (1987: 24).

organization of health care provision. This reflects the presumption that the public funding of health care (or lack of it) is the defining character-istic of the degree of public involvement in health care (Freeman, 1998).

As illustrated in Figure 1.1, the *private insurance* (or consumer sov-ereignty) model has the least state involvement in the direct funding or provision of health care services. This model is distinguished by the purchase of private health insurance financed by employers and/or indi-vidual contributions that are risk oriented. This system is also largely based on private ownership of health care providers and the components of production, although it might include a publicly funded safety net for the most vulnerable groups such as the poor, the elderly or children. The principal premise of this approach is that the funding and provision of health care is best left to market forces.

The second basic type of health system when it comes to state involve-ment is the *social insurance* (or Bismarck) model. Although there is signif-icant variation as to organization, this type is based on a concept of social solidarity and characterized by a universal coverage health insurance generally within a framework of social security. As a rule, this insurance is compulsory and funded by a combination of employer and individual contributions through non-profit insurance funds or societies, often reg-ulated and subsidized by the state. The provision of services tends to be private, often on a fee-for-service basis, although some public ownership of the factors of production and delivery is common. A variation of social insurance is represented by the Taiwan (see Box 1.1) and South Korean National Health Insurance (NHI) systems. By distinguishing between

---

Box 1.1   A new health care system

Taiwan is the most recent advanced economy to adopt a universal health insurance programme. The introduction of National Health Insurance (NHI) in 1995 created a single-payer national insurance programme financed through a system jointly financed by payroll taxes, governmental subsidies and individual premiums. In the past decade, it has increased the proportion of the population with insurance coverage from 57 per cent to 98 per cent. Moreover, it has improved the delivery and availabil-ity of health care services for its citizens while managing to contain cost increases. The NHI Administration (NHIA), the government agency that administers the NHI under the Ministry of Health and Welfare (MOHW) is by law is mandated to fund and operate the NHI on a self-sustaining basis. To do this, it has been given near monopolistic power over health care providers as the single buyer of and payer for health care services including drugs. This power enables the NHIA to control costs and provide Taiwan's public with affordable health care services (Blank and Cheng, 2015; Cheng, 2015).

finance and provision (highly centralized/largely private in the NHIs), Lee *et al.* (2008) argue for inclusion of a fourth type of health system, 'national health insurance'. Similarly, Kam (2012) suggests that East Asian countries do not fit the three existing categories and that there is a case for an East Asia welfare regime type or a hybrid of the liberal and conservative models. Although we see merit in this line of reasoning, in this book we will continue to treat these systems as a subset of social insurance.

The third type is the *national health service* (or Beveridge) model. This model is characterized by universal coverage funded out of general taxation. Although this model is most identified with the UK, New Zealand established the first NHS in its 1938 Social Security Act which promised all citizens open-ended access to all the health care services they needed free at the point of use. The provision of health care services under this model is fully administered by the state, which either owns or controls the factors of production and delivery.

This initial OECD typology was a descriptive categorization of how health care is organized in different countries, reflecting its origins in applied policy analysis. As Freeman (2000) observes, the typology emerged from a search, dominated by economists, for better solutions to common problems. This led to a focus on the internal workings of health care rather than on its political and social embeddedness. However, this situation changed with the wide use of the basic typology in the comparative analysis of health policy (see, for example, Ham, 1997a; Freeman, 2000; Burau and Blank, 2006; Burau *et al.*, 2015). The typology has been a facilitator for critical analyses of the health system as the institutional framework in which health policies are embedded and how the institutions of health care (among others) shape health policies (and politics). Scott (2001), for example, used the typology as part of her framework to analyse public and private roles and interfaces in health care across different countries. In contrast, Ham (1997a) in his cross-country comparative analysis focused on health reform.

These latter applications also have in common their consideration of other aspects of the institutional context of health care in addition to the typology of health systems. Freeman (2000), for example, explicitly includes the mechanisms by which health care is coordinated (health care governance). This inclusion clearly demonstrates that applying the typology of health systems to a wider range of cases has also led to its adaptation. As Collier and Levitsky (1997) note, this process is typified by the tension between increasing analytical differentiation needed to capture the diverse forms of the phenomenon at hand and avoidance of the pitfalls of conceptual stretching and applying the concept to cases that do not fit. The literature on comparative health policy has addressed this tension by adding new attributes to the definition of the health system.

Health care states

An analogous classification of health systems, based on a distinction among institutions related to the governance of consumption, provision and production, was offered by Moran (1999, 2000) who constructed four different types of health care states, three of which are especially relevant here. In entrenched *command and control* health care states, the governance of consumption consists of extensive public access based on citizenship and extensive control of resource allocation through administrative mechanisms. In contrast, in the *corporatist* health care state, funding through social insurance contributions makes for de facto public access to health care and gives public law bodies (such as statutory, non-profit insurance funds) an important role. This limits the public control over health care costs. The role of providers is even greater in the *supply* health care state, where funding through private insurance limits public access to health care as well as the public control of costs.

Moving towards more complicated models

A more elaborate extension of the typology was advanced by Wendt *et al.* (2009) who distinguish health care arrangements by the roles state, societal (non-governmental) and private actors have in the financing, provision and regulation of health care. The result is a rather unwieldly classificatory scheme of 27 types of health care politics. Three ideal types are based on uniform features across all dimensions of health care: *state health care systems*, in which financing, service provision and regulation are all carried out by state actors and institutions; *societal health care systems*, in which societal actors take on the responsibility of health care financing, provision and regulation; and *private health care systems*, in which all three dimensions fall under the auspices of market actors. Interestingly, they found a predominance of mixed types where consistent features are seen along two of the three health care dimensions, thus approximating an ideal type. Moreover, in six 'pure mixed types', there is no uniformity regarding financing, service provision and regulation, and, therefore, no resemblance to any ideal type. Wendt and colleagues suggest that this expanded typology offers a wide variety of combinations that 'provide a rich basis against which real cases can be evaluated and also point to the differences in real world representation that exist' (2009: 82). Although this meticulous classification scheme is thought provoking there are problems including the likelihood that many of the modalities, i.e. private regulation in conjunction with state-based financing and provision, do not exist in practice and that it defeats the primary goal of typologies to simplify reality and, thus, facilitate cross-national analysis.

In their analysis of the Wendt *et al.* typology, Böhm *et al.* (2013) assume that there is a hierarchical relationship between the three dimensions, led by regulation, followed by financing and lastly service provision, where the superior dimension restricts the nature of the subordinate dimensions, thus limiting the number of theoretically plausible types to ten. To test their argument, they classified 30 OECD healthcare systems using OECD health data and WHO country reports. Their classification results in five system types: national health service, national health insurance, social health insurance, etatist social health insurance and private health system (see Table 1.1).

Single variable ranking of countries

Yet another way of categorizing countries is to rank them on a single variable considered appropriate for the comparisons being made. For instance, one simple measure of state involvement that is often used to compare countries is the extent to which health care is publicly funded. Table 1.2 (for more details see Table 3.3) shows a country ranking on

Table 1.1   *Types of health care systems*

Regulation	Financing	Provision	Health system type	OECD countries
State	State	State	National health service	Denmark, Finland, Iceland, Norway, Sweden, Portugal, Spain, UK
State	State	Private	National health insurance	Australia, Canada, Ireland, New Zealand, Italy
Social	Social	Private	Social health insurance	Austria, Germany, Luxembourg, Switzerland
State	Social	Private	Etatist social health ins.	Belgium, Estonia, France, Czech Republic, Hungary, Netherlands, Poland, Slovakia, Israel, Japan, South Korea
Private	Private	Private	Private health system	USA

Source: Adapted from Böhm *et al.*, 2013.

Table 1.2   *Public expenditure on health care as a percentage of total expenditure on health care, 1975–2015*

	1975	1985	1995	2005	2015	%
Australia	73.6	70.6	65.8	67.0	66.7	–6.9
Germany	79.0	77.4	81.6	77.0	85.0	+6.0
Japan	72.0	70.7	83.0	82.7	84.9	+12.9
Netherlands	67.9	70.8	71.0	62.5	80.7	+12.8
New Zealand	73.7	87.0	77.2	77.4	79.7	+6.0
Singapore	69.9	n/a	n/a	38.5	37.7	–32.2
Sweden	90.2	90.4	86.6	81.7	83.7	–6.5
Taiwan	n/a	n/a	n/a	62.5	64.8	+2.3
UK	91.1	85.8	83.9	86.9	79.0	–12.1
USA	40.9	39.6	45.3	45.1	49.4	+8.5

Sources: Data from OECD (2016a); Taiwan Ministry of Health and Welfare (2013); Singapore Ministry of Health (2016).

that criterion, ranging from around 85 per cent in the Germany, Japan, and Sweden to just over 30 per cent in Singapore (see also Box 1.2). It should be noted that this ranking, as with many typologies, can tell us nothing about whether one system is better or worse than another; it simply illustrates how the countries array themselves on this

Box 1.2   The Singapore system: low in public funding, high on individual responsibility

Singapore is most unusual in its low level of public funding. The main reason for this is that in 1984 it instituted a compulsory savings scheme that shifted primary health financing responsibility from the state to individuals (Asher *et al.*, 2008). Funds are deposited in a savings account in each contributor's name that can then be drawn on to pay for health insurance or hospital expenses incurred by that person or his or her immediate family. The scheme is compulsory in the form of a tax on income, but because each account is private, it is deemed privately financed. This health care system is based on a unique interpretation of individual responsibility and is designed to provide incentives to reduce consumption and offer protection against 'free-rider' abuses while guaranteeing affordable basic health care through government subsidies. Individuals can also choose the level of subsidy they wish to receive in public hospitals: if they opt for a fancy ward the subsidy is low or non-existent whereas if they go for a less fancy ward the subsidy is higher. The key principle is that patients are expected to pay part of the cost of medical services that they use, and pay more when they demand a higher level of service (Singapore Ministry of Health, 2008).

dimension. Another use of this data is to trace changes, both for specific countries and collective patterns, and to compare the comparative rankings over time.

It must be stressed that while typologies are helpful for teaching and organizing purposes by allowing us to simplify a complex reality and focus on the most important aspects, they remain problematic and offer only an estimate of the real world of health care. Even in those cases where the health system of a country is dominated by one of the types, traces of numerous variants are identifiable. Most countries reflect mixes of characteristics in finance, provision and governance across the various types and there is often variation across time and space within a single country. The specific configuration of any health care system depends on a multitude of factors including the political system, the cultural framework, the demographic context, the distinctive historical background, specific events and social structures inherent to that country (see Chapter 2). Societal goals and priorities develop over time and shape all social institutions and values, which themselves are fluid and changeable (see Box 1.3). As aptly stated by Freeman and Frisina in their analysis,

---

Box 1.3 Transformation and the typology

Wendt *et al.* (2009) suggest that three forms of transformation are possible. The most radical occurs when a system moves from one type to another, for example when a state-based type develops into a private type. Such a 'system change' is expected to arise only in exceptional instances where radical turns in policy goals are accompanied by high levels of public support. A more common form of transformation unfolds along only one of the system's dimensions and does not culminate in a larger system change. An example of an 'internal system change' of this kind would be if the provision of health care shifts from state-based to private actors, but financing and regulation remain in state hands. Therefore, while the system witnesses a significant alteration, it remains predominantly state-based. A third, milder form of transformation is that of an 'internal change of levels' in which a shift within one or more dimensions takes place without leading to an alteration of the system's main features. Although the latter does not embody the same degree of transformation as more drastic forms, it does indicate a significant development within health care systems. Because of its modest nature, an internal change is the most likely transformation, particularly over short time spans which are the typical horizons of researchers and politicians. Moreover, such a change might be the antecedent to a more graduated form of transformation, especially if state, societal or private features are at risk of losing their dominant position within a given dimension.

although classification is the 'very stuff of the comparative analysis of health policy', a debate continues over:

> which characteristics should be taken to be definitive or constitutive of the health system; about whether or not these fall into typical clusters; about whether or not these types should be empirically or normatively defined; about which countries are instances of which types and about which countries best represent each particular type. (2012: 174)

It is also important to note that comparative health policy and these attempts to define classifications usually do not take health workforce policy into account and ignore the relevance of the structure, development and governance of the health workforce for the functioning of health care systems. While analyses of the health workforce have recently gained prominence (see Chapter 5), the system characteristics and typologies largely neglect the human resources dimension although Wendt and Kohl (2010) do include health human resources as a category next to finance, service provision and health status, and Cylus and colleagues (2015) include the health professions in a broader category of physical and human resources.

Countries selected for study

To provide a constructive cross-country analysis of health policy, we have selected ten countries for primary coverage in this book. The countries were selected to give the reader systematic exposure to the full range of health systems (see Figure 1.2). Although all three have moved away from the pure model in varying degrees, Britain, Sweden and New Zealand are examples of a national health service (in the following, when we refer to Britain or the UK we often specifically focus on the organization and policies of health care as they exist in England. Following political devolution in the late 1990s the health systems in the four countries of the UK have developed in different ways (for an overview, see Baggott, 2010)). Germany, Japan, the Netherlands and Taiwan are variations of the social insurance type, while Singapore, with its compulsory Medisave system, is a variant on that theme, but with a heavy private component.

Britain	Germany	USA
New Zealand	Japan	(Australia)
Sweden	Netherlands	(Singapore)
	Taiwan	

NHS	**Social Insurance**	**Private Insurance**

Figure 1.2   *Types of health care systems*

Finally, the private insurance type is most clearly represented by the USA and (historically) by Australia, although many systems contain some elements of the private marketplace. Additionally, these ten countries represent a wide spectrum of political, cultural and economic environments for illustrating the vagaries of health care.

Our country selection includes some, such as Germany, Sweden, the UK and the USA, that are frequently included in comparative policy studies, and others, such as Australia, the Netherlands and New Zealand that are less so. Also included in the coverage here are Japan, Singapore and Taiwan that offer valuable insights into health care policy commonly overlooked in the largely US/European-based literature. Individually, each of the countries has a unique contribution to make to the study of health policy. In combination, they serve as a good sample by which to analyse the dynamics of health care policy in the 21st century.

Obviously, even the relatively large number of countries covered here does not exhaust the vast array of variation in health care systems found across the world. All these countries are developed nations with Western-type medical systems. Even Japan, Singapore and Taiwan have highly sophisticated medical systems and affluent populations with high levels of expectations and demands. Missing from this analysis are cases from Africa, the Middle East, the Balkans, Eastern Europe and the former Soviet Union, which collectively represent over 4 billion people. Although inclusion of a selection of these countries would be illuminating, it would also be unwieldy and complicate the level of analysis. One of the drawbacks in trying to cover even ten countries is that it is not possible to provide a thorough analysis of any one of their health care systems. Regarding specific countries, then, the objective of this book is to be an introduction, not a comprehensive analysis, and to provide a context within which to study individual countries. To this end, readers with an interest in a specific country or countries should make use of the Guide to Further Reading at the end of this book which should provide a valuable basis for building on the foundational knowledge offered in the chapters. In addition, the Guide to Websites provides links to the most recent information and data on these countries.

It should be noted that the countries included in the analysis of the comparative health workforce in Chapter 5 departs from this country sample. Because there are no comparable data for Singapore and Taiwan at this differentiated level, the analysis draws on OECD data as the most complex and standardized source of workforce composition and mobility figures. Moreover, the addition of other countries here reflects the workforce situation in middle-income countries especially in the global South, and more generally, the relevance for comparative health policy. Likewise, because health workers are mobile across labour markets, it is important to have a better understanding about the low- and middle-income countries (LMICs) that are crucial for the mobility discussion.

Growing problems in health policy

Despite variation in health care across countries, there are several factors endemic to all developed nations that make health policy ever more problematic. In the wake of falling national incomes and increasingly scarce resources for social spending, all countries, no matter how much they vary politically or socially, face growing struggles in the financing and delivery of health care. Table 1.3 clearly demonstrates that while countries differ as to the percentage of their gross domestic product (GDP) they devote to health care, in virtually all cases it has increased appreciably over the last 25 years. This means that health care costs are increasing at rates exceeding that of economic growth, a pattern that is not sustainable over the long run. Recently, this has been severely exacerbated by the global financial crisis, which Mladovsky and colleagues (2012) characterize as an 'external shock' to health systems which need stable resources. A complicating factor is that, with the growing demand for health care, many countries are experiencing shortages of health personnel. This has resulted in imbalances and maldistribution of health human resources globally (Campbell *et al.*, 2013; WHO, 2015a; Global Health Workforce Alliance, 2016; see Chapter 5 for details).

The increase in health care costs, by itself, is not the problem. As Duff (2001) points out, an expansion of spending on other goods is welcomed

Table 1.3   *Health expenditure as a percentage of GDP, 1990–2015*

	1990	2000	2005	2015	% change
Australia	6.9	8.3	8.8	9.3	2.4
Germany	8.3	10.3	10.7	11.1	2.8
Japan	6.0	7.7	8.2	11.2	5.2
Netherlands	8.0	8.0	9.2	10.8	2.8
New Zealand	6.9	7.7	8.9	9.4	2.5
Singapore	2.8	n/a	3.8	4.6	1.8
Sweden	8.2	8.2	9.2	11.1	2.9
Taiwan	5.5	5.9	6.3	6.9	1.4
UK	6.0	7.2	8.2	9.8	3.8
USA	11.9	13.2	15.2	16.9	5.0

Sources: Data from OECD (2008a, 2012, 2016a); Singapore Ministry of Health (2016); National Health Insurance Administration (2015).

as contributing to economic well-being; why, then, should more consumption on health care be a problem? Furthermore, every country spends 100 per cent of its GDP on something, so if countries spend considerably more than others on health care that is their choice. However, the main reason we should care about growing health care expenditure is that the extra spending might not be providing as much value as if those funds were used for education, housing, environmental protection or other private or public consumption or investment (Fuchs, 2005: 77). In economic terms, the 'opportunity costs' might be too high when excessive money goes to health care and is thus diverted from more effective areas of spending.

A final cause for apprehension is the combination of ageing populations, rapid advances in medical technology and expanded public expectations and demands that aggravates the situation. Recent reform efforts in virtually all countries are largely a reaction to these major forces, and, although there is variation by degree across countries, these trends signify ominous signs for the funding and provision of health care in the coming decades. As noted by Saltman (2015), the future health policy landscape is becoming even more complex than in previous periods. The number of actors involved in the formulation and implementation of health policy in developed country health systems – governmental, regulatory, industrial, political, social, community, and individual patient and citizen – continue to expand. Simultaneously, the accelerating pace of innovation in clinical technology poses new policy challenges that existing health systems will have increasing difficulty in meeting.

Confounding the health policy context, in part driven by the shift towards sophisticated curative care over the second half of the 20th century, is the fact that the bulk of health care spending is concentrated on a relatively small number of patients. A minority of each population cohort, often chronically ill, disabled and/or indigent, generates enormous medical costs; approximately 10 per cent in each age group incurs 60 to 70 per cent of total health care costs each year for that group (Cohen, 2015). Table 1.4 demonstrates the extent of this concentration in the USA, but similar patterns have been documented in systems as diverse as Canada, France, New Zealand and Taiwan. In any given year, the top 1 per cent of users account for over 20 per cent of all health care expenditures; the top 5 per cent use over 50 per cent; and the top 10 per cent use almost 70 per cent. In contrast, only 3 per cent of payments go to those patients in the healthiest half of the population. In 2013, those in the bottom half incurred an average annual expenditure of $253 in medical costs compared with an average expenditure of $43,058 for those in the top 5 per cent and $95,200 for those in the top 1 per cent (Cohen, 2015). Likewise, only 5 per cent of beneficiaries of the US Medicare system account for nearly half of total Medicare spending (Medicare Payment

Table 1.4   *Distribution of health expenditures for the USA by magnitude of expenditures for selected years 1963–2013*

Percentage population ranked by expenditures	1963	1970	1980	1996	2002	2009	2013
Top 1%	17%	26%	29%	27%	22%	21%	22%
Top 5%	43%	50%	55%	55%	49%	51%	50%
Top 10%	59%	66%	70%	69%	64%	66%	66%
Top 30%	–	88%	90%	90%	–	91%	90%
Top 50%	95%	96%	96%	97%	97%	97%	97%
Bottom 50%	5%	4%	4%	3%	3%	3%	3%

Sources: Stanton and Rutherford (2005); Cohen (2015).

Assessment Commission, 2011). Thus, 90 per cent of citizens are collectively accountable for a very small proportion of health care spending.

It is possible, of course, that these figures reflect the fact that while a few people become seriously ill each year and use significant resources, they often leave and are replaced by others in succeeding years. Evidence, however, demonstrates that a small number of high-need patients consume substantial resources over a longer term (see Box 1.4). A systematic analysis of high users by Cohen (2015) found that most high users exhibit persistently high expenditures from one year to the next. Critically, the heaviest users of health care come predominantly from two groups: the elderly and those persons who engage in high-risk behaviour and cause or contribute to their own ill health. Chronic diseases, especially prevalent in the elderly population, generate a large proportion of health care spending (Goetzel *et al.*, 2007). While those over age 65 represented 14.7 per cent of the US population in 2013, they comprised 43.9 per cent of those individuals who remained in the top decile of users (Cohen, 2015). This concentration of the cost for health care is important because it necessitates the redistribution of significant resources from young to old and from those persons who live healthy lives to those who do not. This pattern raises questions of equity and fairness especially in times of distributing scarce resources (see Chapter 4).

The concentration of health care spending also has critical implications for health policy, particularly in designing strategies to control overall spending for health services. Specifically, it means that targets for cost saving must focus on the treatment of the high-user individuals, especially those with chronic conditions, since this is where the bulk of spending occurs. As noted above, the bottom half of the population accounts for

---

Box 1.4   High-need/high-cost patients

Just nine individuals in Austin, Texas, accounted for nearly 2,700 emergency room visits between 2003 and 2008. The cost to taxpayers through Medicare and Medicaid exceeded $3 million. Eight of the nine patients had drug abuse problems, seven were diagnosed with mental health issues and three were homeless. Although these 'frequent flyers' pose major problems for health care delivery, one could oversimplify the high-need/high-cost population and its needs. In fact, the population is socially and clinically diverse. Some have multiple chronic conditions that are stable with treatment and can persist for years, while others have extreme functional limitations. Some have severe, persistent behavioural health challenges. Others have conditions that are exacerbated by social factors such as lack of housing, food and supportive personal relationships (Blumenthal *et al.*, 2016).

---

only less than 3 per cent of health care spending, thus, even if such expenditures were cut in half, the savings would only be 1.5 per cent of total health care spending. In contrast, the costs in treating the top 1 per cent is over 20 per cent of health care spending. If these costs could be cut by just 7 per cent, it would generate more savings than slashing the costs of the bottom 50 per cent of the population in half. Importantly, a 15 per cent cut in the costs of the top 1 per cent would save more than the complete elimination of *all* medical spending for the bottom 50 per cent! (National Institute for Health Care Management, 2012). For Powers and Chaguturu (2016), high-risk care management of this small percentage of high users could substantially reduce costs and improve quality, but heterogeneity in their clinical needs will complicate efforts to develop integrated strategies. Importantly, the ageing of our population ensures that HNHC patients, many of whom are older adults, will account for an increasing proportion of users of health care systems (Blumenthal *et al.*, 2016).

Ageing populations

As illustrated in Table 1.5, demographic projections show that most countries will experience considerable ageing of their populations over the next 30 years. Although the ageing process is taking place earlier and more rapidly in some countries, all will experience it. The primary cause of the ageing of Western societies is the precipitous decline in fertility rates since the 1970s that has increased the proportion of elderly. This trend is exaggerated because the sharp upturn in birth rates after World War II produced a bloated age cohort in the baby boom generation, the first wave of which has reached retirement age. Even if life expectancy is

Table 1.5   *Percentage of population aged 65 and over*

	1960	1980	1990	2000	2020	2030	2040	2050
Australia	8.5	9.6	11.1	12.4	18.3	22.2	24.5	25.7
Germany	11.5	15.6	14.9	16.4	22.7	27.8	31.1	31.5
Japan	5.7	9.1	12.1	17.4	29.2	31.8	36.5	39.6
Netherlands	9.0	11.5	12.8	13.6	19.8	23.4	25.0	23.5
New Zealand	8.7	9.7	11.2	11.8	16.7	21.1	23.8	24.6
Singapore	n/a	4.9	6.0	7.0	18.5	21.0	26.0	27.3
Sweden	11.8	16.3	17.8	17.3	21.1	22.8	24.0	23.7
Taiwan	n/a	5.8	6.2	8.6	13.6	24.0	31.8	33.0
UK	11.7	15.0	15.7	15.8	19.0	21.9	23.7	24.1
USA	9.2	11.3	12.5	12.4	16.3	19.7	20.4	20.7

Sources: Data from OECD (2009) for all but Singapore (Singapore Ministry of Health, 2008) and Taiwan (Bureau of National Health Insurance, 2008).

unaltered, this wave of ageing baby boomers, along with declining fertility rates, guarantees an increasing proportion of the elderly.

The second factor contributing to the ageing of populations is increased life expectancy. Between 1950 and 1980, life expectancy at birth increased by 8.5 years for females and 6.0 years for males. These significant gains reflect improved social factors, health habits and the new capacities of medicine to reduce infant mortality and extend the lifespan. It is important to note that in the past gains in life expectancy have been under-estimated, meaning that there could be even more significant increases in the coming decades. Moreover, substantial differences in average life expectancy across OECD countries strongly suggest that further gains could be made in many countries. Ironically, these health-improving steps, together with continued low fertility rates, could exacerbate population ageing and complicate funding problems.

Within these ageing trends are two critical shifts in the population structure. First, within the overall trends towards older populations is the ageing of these elderly populations themselves. At present the most rapidly growing segment of those 65 and older is the 80-and-over cohort. As illustrated in Table 1.6, this proportion is expected to climb to over 30 per cent of the elderly in most countries, and over 40 per cent in Japan, by 2050. These increases are particularly significant for health policy because those over 80 are by far the heaviest users of health care.

The second trend within a trend relates to the sex composition of the elderly population. Because of their longer life expectancy, women outnumber men significantly in the elderly age cohorts. Furthermore, the sex imbalance increases with age, meaning that as the very elderly cohort

Table 1.6   *Percentage share of very old persons (80+) among the elderly, 1960–2040*

	1960	2000	2040
Australia	14.3	23.6	31.8
Germany	18.4	22.3	29.9
Japan	12.6	22.0	41.1
Netherlands	15.2	23.5	30.0
New Zealand	17.1	23.8	30.5
Sweden	15.9	29.0	31.5
UK	16.4	25.4	29.1
USA	15.2	26.4	33.3

Source: Data from OECD (2005b).

expands, the proportion of elderly women will grow. Even though this imbalance is projected to narrow over time, especially at the younger end of the elderly age group, women will continue to constitute a substantial majority of the elderly, particularly among the most elderly. As with the other trends, this has considerable impact on the nature of the health care needs of the population.

So, what does it matter for health care if the population gets older? It matters because currently a disproportionate share of health resources go to the elderly, particularly those over age 80. As illustrated in Table 1.7, in most countries the over-65 cohort accounts for at least double the

Table 1.7   *Percentage of health expenditures and persons aged 65 or more, 2003 and estimated 2020 and 2040*

	2003		Projections	
	% 65+	% Total expenditure	2020	2040
Australia	12.8	40.2	46.4	56.0
Germany	18.6	34.1	40.0	49.4
Japan	19.0	42.4	52.5	55.9
Netherlands	13.8	41.2	49.6	60.1
New Zealand	11.9	42.1	47.2	52.3
Sweden	17.2	54.2	59.6	63.3
Taiwan	9.9	25.8	36.9	44.0
UK	16.0	43.0	45.6	54.1
USA	12.4	48.8	56.9	62.9

Sources: Data from OECD (2006); Taiwan (Bureau of National Health Insurance, 2012).

expenditures relative to its proportion of the population, and in some cases (Australia and USA) almost quadruple. In the case of the USA with its extreme spending near the end of life, 12.4 per cent of the population now aged 65 and older consumes nearly half of total health care resources. Ironically, because of medical improvements and technologies that prolong life, and the concurrence of multiple and frequently chronic conditions, the cost of prolonging the life of elderly patients is considerably higher than that of younger ones.

Elderly patients use more acute care, are hospitalized about twice as often, have longer stays in hospital and are much more likely to be readmitted to hospital (see Chapter 4 for details). The cost of intensive care unit (ICU) care in the USA for a patient over age 65, for instance, is, per day, three to five times the cost for the average acute care admission. Moreover, the Clinical Advisory Board (2001) estimates that current baby boomers could outlive today's elders by seven to 15 years, thus requiring a doubling of ICU care by 2020. In the USA, the prevalence of Alzheimer's disease is expected to more than double in the next 20 years (Thacker *et al.*, 2006). How can health systems continue this spending pattern as the proportion of the elderly swells? Although improvements in health conditions might serve to delay the highest expenditure that occurs at the end of life for some people, cumulatively ageing populations will demand ever-greater health care spending.

As the projections in Table 1.7 illustrate, the estimated increases in health spending on the elderly are staggering in some countries, especially Sweden and the USA. Although it varies by country, the trend towards a heightened concentration of health care spending on the elderly is universal, with most countries registering over 50 per cent by 2040. The ageing population not only increases health care spending and shifts it towards the elderly, but it also has considerable potential impact on the type of health care provided. Obviously, the growing number of old people will generate a higher demand for long-term care and thus a proportionate increase in facilities and personnel in long-term care (see Chapter 6).

Several additional aspects of the ageing of populations are critical to an understanding of the full range of implications for health policy. Although attention here has focused on the increased expenditures generated by the growing proportion of the elderly, there is also the issue that as populations age the size of the productive sector decreases, thus raising concern over the capacity of society to support the new demands. The ability of any country to finance increased costs associated with the ageing population depends upon the relative size of the productive population (usually measured by dependency ratios of some type), as well as unemployment rates and productivity. As the workforce and the tax base is reduced through ageing and continued low levels of fertility, the pressures on the remaining working-age population intensifies.

Finally, just at the time where there is an increased need for long-term care-giving, social changes have undermined traditional, largely informal care mechanisms for the elderly. The decline in the extended family, increased mobility, and the trends towards more working women and fewer children have in many countries reduced the willingness and ability of families to care for the elderly. Although women continue to provide significant levels of long-term care for family members, coverage is saturated and as a proportion will decrease (see Chapter 6 for details). Therefore, the demands for formal long-term care services will intensify and such services will depend increasingly on public funds.

Medical technology and health policy

Another force impacting on all health systems is the rapid expansion of medical technology. Simply put, there are a lot more technologies available today for intervention – and many of these new techniques are very costly on a per-case basis. Vast improvements in surgical procedures, tissue matching and immuno-suppressant drugs are making repair and replacement of organs routine. Likewise, innovations in diagnostic machinery continue to push the boundaries. Computerized axial tomography (CT) scans and magnetic resonance imaging (MRI) have been followed by positron emission tomography (PET) and other specialized diagnostic/therapy machines including the super-costly proton particle treatment (see Box 1.5). Moreover, human genetic technology, stem cell research, neuroscience and pharmacology promise a dramatically expanding array of expensive diagnostic and therapeutic applications that will increase both the range of intervention options and the pressures on health care systems to deliver. These innovations can enhance care but they tend to cost appreciably more than former forms of treatment. Moreover, once in place there are strong pressures to use them to offset the investment.

This proliferation of innovative medical technologies and pharmaceuticals has been one of the most important drivers of health care spending growth, if not the most important (Aaron, 2003; Bodenheimer, 2005). New medical technologies account for up to one-third of the rise in annual health care costs (Zwillich, 2001). Diffusion of new technology into practice is associated with greater per capita utilization and higher spending. Medical technology affects outlays by adding to the arsenal of feasible treatments and by reducing the invasiveness of existing interventions, thus increasing the number of patients who might enjoy net gains from diagnosis and treatment. Although not every technological advance leads to increased expenditure, the net effect has tended to inflate costs due to extensions in the range and intensity of care. Thus, even relatively

Box 1.5   Does every cancer patient really need proton beam therapy?

Proton beam therapy is a type of particle therapy that uses a beam of protons to irradiate diseased tissue, most often in the treatment of cancer. Proton therapy is far more expensive than conventional therapy and requires a very large capital investment of US$150 million or more per machine. Supposedly proton machines will reduce side effects and allow for higher doses that will cure more patients, but, to date, there have been no controlled trials that demonstrate that proton therapy yields improved survival or other clinical outcomes compared to other types of radiation therapy (Emanuel and Pearson, 2012). The British NHS was faced with a dilemma when some overseas clinics providing proton beam therapy heavily marketed their services to desperate British parents. In 2013, the British government announced that £250 million had been budgeted to establish two centres for advanced radiotherapy, to open in 2018. Until now, the NHS has paid to have suitable cases treated abroad, mostly in the USA. Such cases rose from 18 in 2008 to 122 in 2013, 99 of whom were children, with the cost to the NHS averaging about £100,000 (NHS England, 2015).

inexpensive advances, such as antibiotics, which appear to reduce health care costs by treating common diseases at a lower cost than conventional treatments, add significantly to medical spending.

Baker *et al.* (2003) found that increases in the supply of technology tend to be related to both higher utilization and spending on the service in question. Thorpe *et al.* (2004b) found that a small number of medical conditions were associated with much of the increase in health care spending between 1987 and 2000, with the top 15 conditions accounting for approximately half of the overall growth in spending (see also Skinner *et al.*, 2006). Moreover, the problem of priority setting is destined to become more acute in the coming decade because we are seeing the rapid proliferation of costly 'last chance' therapies: technologies that represent the last chance for prolonging life for individuals. These are very expensive and typically yield what might be judged as marginal benefits relative to their costs (see Box 1.6).

Advances in technology enable the prolongation of life for persons with illnesses that until recently would have been untreatable – but at high cost. Moreover, while curative treatment may be beneficial to individual patients, the marginal gain in terms of length of survival and quality of life is difficult to judge (Lewis and Leeder, 2009). This uncertainty is complicated by the fact that most medical procedures have not been subject to controlled assessment to determine their effectiveness and how they compare in outcome to less expensive alternative approaches. Furthermore, as noted by Campillo-Artero (2011), often health technologies

---

Box 1.6   The cost of technology

After helping to develop some of the hottest new drugs, cancer specialist Leonard Saltz has come down with a bad case of sticker shock. The price tag for treating patients has increased 500-fold in the last decade. Ten years ago, doctors could extend the life of a patient who had failed to respond to chemotherapy by an average of 11.5 months using a combination of drugs that cost $500 in today's dollars. Now, new drugs can extend survival on average to 22.5 months, but at a cost of $250,000, not including pharmacy mark-ups, salaries for doctors and nurses and the cost of infusing the drugs into patients in the hospital. That kind of cost is unsustainable. 'Sooner or later the bubble is going to pop,' according to Saltz. The question is simple: how many exorbitant cancer drugs can society really afford to stack on top of one another? 'Absent a thoughtful national discussion, the answer is none,' says Michael A. Friedman, chief executive of City of Hope, a cancer centre in Los Angeles. 'We will quickly run out of resources, leading to de facto rationing.' The rising costs, he says, are 'utterly insupportable' (Herper, 2004).

---

do not reach their potential because they fail to change the behaviour of the health professionals that will use them.

Although medical technology is global and contributes to cost escalation in all health systems, there is evidence that policies adopted by countries can have a significant impact on the use of new technologies (see Chapter 4). Although all countries feel the impact of new technologies, many try to limit the diffusion of expensive new drugs, procedures and equipment by instituting controls and requiring physicians and hospitals to work within fixed budgets (Fuchs, 2005: 76). McClellan and Kessler, for example, found 'enormous differences in how quickly and widely treatments diffused into medical practice' (1999: 253), especially those high-technology treatments with high fixed costs or high variable costs per use. They also found more modest differences in the times it takes new drugs, procedures or devices to become available. Thus, while the approach of the USA reflects the view that new technologies should be made available quickly, other countries have been more cautious. The result is that medical spending growth across nations has diverged as some countries implement cost containment policies designed to curb the diffusion of medical technology and others fail to do so.

Rising public expectations and demands

The primary forces behind technological medicine come from the providers of the health care community who implant a demand in the public. Health professionals are trained to do what is best for their patients and, in some countries, this has produced a do-everything approach. Moreover, health care is big business with huge financial stakes. The health care industry itself is a powerful shaper of perceived needs and it benefits significantly from an ever-expanding notion of health care. Not surprisingly, any attempt to place limits on access to the newest technologies risks condemnation from practitioners, their patients and the public. Moreover, any limits on health spending will be strongly resisted by groups that are negatively affected. The pressure to use medical technologies past the point where they have no marginal value is very strong and the long-term spending growth trend is inevitable (Altman *et al.*, 2003).

These inflated public expectations and perceptions of medicine have produced an over-utilization of and reliance on technology (Ubel, 2001). Patients demand access to the newest technologies because they are convinced of their value. Popular health-oriented magazines, television shows and internet marketers extol the virtues of medical innovations. Physicians are trained in the technological imperative, which holds that a technology should be used despite its cost if it offers any possibility of benefit. Furthermore, third-party payment provides no disincentive against the over-utilization of medical technology. Any limits on the allocation of medical technologies, then, must come from outside the health care community itself and the public. The only agent with the power to enforce such limits on an inclusive scale is the government, but it can do so only within the context of escalating public expectations. Also, since it is natural for politicians to want to please their constituents and be re-elected, they are beholden to those interests with political power and to the claims of their constituents. Thus, they tend to over-promise and avoid proposing limits whenever possible.

The expectations and demands of the public for health care, then, are theoretically insatiable and they are fuelled by a medical industry that has much to gain by the continual expansion of the scope of medicine. Health care costs have increased partly because citizens expect and often demand higher and higher levels of medical intervention, levels undreamt of several decades ago. Moreover, patients have become less deferential and more informed as to their options through the internet and the social media (Scott *et al.*, 2005). This exaggerated view of health care often is nurtured by those who place heavy emphasis on the rights of individuals to health care with few limits. It also reflects the fact that every person is a potential patient or a family member of one who at any time might need health care. Furthermore, since World War II there has been a shift towards the notion of positive rights to health care that places a moral duty on society to provide the resources necessary to exercise those rights. The long-term effect, within the context of ever more sophisticated technological options, is that setting limits has become progressively more difficult politically as the population takes health care entitlements for granted.

Moreover, the proposition that one should limit the medical expenditure on a patient to benefit the community contradicts the traditional patient-oriented mores of medicine as practised in many countries. Thus, there are strong pressures for intensive intervention on an individual basis even in the last days of life, often despite the enormous cost for very little return in terms of prolonging the patient's life. In countries with more communal or collectively rounded cultures, this maximalist approach to health care is less rigid and the public more accepting of limits, but even in Taiwan the NHI reimbursement scheme has 'reinforced the perception of the goals of medicine by the public, relying increasingly on making office visits and taking medicines to get well and feel better, rather than working on a change to healthier life styles' (Wen *et al.*, 2008: 266).

Public expectations may be elevated unrealistically because of a tendency to oversell medical innovation and overestimate the capacities of new medical technologies for resolving health problems. At the centre are the mass media, which are predisposed to idealistically optimistic and oversimplified coverage of medical technology. Frequently, the initial response of the media, often encouraged by medical spokesmen, is to report innovations as medical 'breakthroughs'. Because most health care is routine and not newsworthy, the media naturally focus attention on techniques that can be easily dramatized. Overall, media coverage solidifies public trust in the technological fix and 'stimulates their appetite for new, expensive, high technology procedures' (Kassler, 1994: 126). Moreover, media coverage, along with a freedom of information climate that has emerged in many countries, has forced the rationing process out into the open. Users of health care are less willing to accept a gatekeeper role for their general practitioners, especially when they read in the papers of inconsistencies and problems in the health care system. Therefore, many politicians find it difficult not to join in the call for expanded access to new technologies, while the media seem to relish uncovering and sensationalizing cases where treatment is denied. Cases of denial of access result in dramatic news stories and tough questioning of those officials who venture to deny such care (see Box 1.7).

Arguments in favour of containing the costs of health care, while widely accepted at the societal level, are often rejected at the individual level. Thus, while a large proportion of the population in theory supports the need for cost containment, when one's own health or that of a loved one is at stake, constraints on the availability of health care resources are viewed as unfair: 'I know the government needs to control health care costs but not when my child needs an expensive new drug.' It is little wonder that elected officials are not willing to make decisions that jeopardize these emotionally held values. Again, it is important to note that although there are global forces working to increase public demands and expectations, these are stronger in some countries than in others.

Box 1.7   Media campaigns for treatment denied

In the UK, furious multiple sclerosis sufferers go to the media when the National Institute for Health and Care Excellence, the government's cost-effectiveness agency, threatens to ban a new drug because at £10,000 per year per patient it is too expensive for its relative benefits. One mother of two children with the disease is quoted as saying: 'My children are dependent on me – how can you put a price on that?' Should the government step in and fund the drug for these young children and, if so, where will the money to do so come from? Meanwhile, in New Zealand a 76-year-old man is denied kidney dialysis by the public hospital. The man and his family take his case to the media, accusing the health authorities of denying his rights to life-saving treatment. The media portray him as a victimized war veteran and include emotional interviews with family members. Unrelenting media pressure forces political officials to over-rule the hospital authorities and give him dialysis despite the hospital's argument that he was an extremely poor medical risk for reasons they could not disclose due to patient confidentiality. He received dialysis but died within five months due to heart failure. Were the politicians right in bowing to public pressure?

It has been observed that no matter to what extent health care facilities are expanded, there will remain a steady pool of unmet demands. Despite the policy statements of medical advocates, there is little evidence that additional facilities and money alone will resolve the health care crisis (see Chapter 4). Although wealthier countries devote substantially higher proportions of their resources to health services than poorer countries, the demand for services does not abate; instead, the public comes to expect a level of medical care that could not be imagined by citizens of less affluent countries. Moreover, as these expectations are met, demand for more health services heightens even though, internationally, there is virtually no relationship between health status and health spending beyond about US$1,000 or so per annum per capita. The upward trajectory in health status flattens out beyond this threshold and the marginal health benefits from additional health care spending become vanishingly small. Indeed, Lewis and Leeder (2009) conclude that wealthy countries are all on the 'flat of the curve'.

Policy convergence?

Against a background of these common policy problems, many comparative studies have highlighted the importance of policy convergence for understanding how health care policies are shaped (cf. Harrison *et al.*,

2002). Convergence implies that countries increasingly rely on a similar design of policies to pursue their goals (Schmid and Götze, 2009). Health policy convergence suggests that there are global trends in the formation of health policies, and that the objectives and activities of national health systems are becoming more alike. Moreover, observations of policy convergence have turned attention to international interdependence (Holzinger and Knill, 2005), the result of diffusion, which is defined as 'a pattern of successive or sequential adoption of a practice, policy, or program either across countries or sub-national jurisdictions such as states and municipalities' (Freeman, 2006: 367). Cross-national influence and the diffusion of policies are predominant topics in deliberations about health reform (Nolte *et al.*, 2008; Gilardi *et al.*, 2009; Okma *et al.*, 2010). Dobbin and colleagues (2007), for instance, offer four theories of distinct mechanisms explaining the diffusion of policies across countries: competition; coercion; emulation; and learning.

The convergence thesis, then, suggests that health policy across disparate country environments tends to become similar over time. Moreover, since all countries face similar demographic challenges and the proliferation of expensive technologies, the pressures towards convergence are extenuated. Based on an examination of trends across industrialized democracies, Chernichovsky (1995) contends that despite the diversity of health care systems, health system reforms have led to the emergence of a 'universal outline or paradigm' for health care financing, organization and management that cuts across ideological (private versus public) lines and across conceptual (market versus centrally planned) frameworks. Other authors point to medical knowledge and technology as drivers of health policy convergence. Field (1999) suggests that the means of medical production are becoming universal and that the social organization of medical work has become strikingly similar across systems, leading to health systems sharing more common elements.

Convergence is bolstered by globalization (Taylor, 2009), and by the development of an international health forum through the internet where people anywhere can obtain information as well as by the private sector that has a huge economic stake in health care (see Box 1.8). In addition, explicit efforts by international organizations such as the OECD, the World Health Organization (WHO) and the European Union (EU) help prepare the foundations for what Harrison *et al.* (2002) in their study of evidence-based medicine refer to as 'ideational convergence'. Moreover, some argue that the World Trade Organization's General Agreement on Trade in Services (GATS) could lead to homogeny of health services such as health insurance, hospital services, telemedicine and the acquisition of medical treatment abroad. These common driving forces, then, suggest a convergence in relation to the framing of policy problems and the intellectual underpinnings of policy solutions.

> ### Box 1.8   Market-driven convergence
>
> Cortez (2008a) notes that while attention has focused on 'policy' convergence in the public sphere, it is driven primarily by the private sector that pushes for convergence because it benefits from it. He contends that various methods, practices and standards in the health care industry are becoming more alike across countries through 'market-driven convergence'. For example, there are internationally recognized uses of many drugs, hospital quality standards are spreading and the expectations for doing business in health care are becoming more universal. Moreover, this trend is heavily promoted by the USA, and convergence is towards America's unique brand of health care. Although market-driven convergence presents concrete benefits including increased efficiency in health care markets, gains from trade, higher quality goods and services and enhanced patient choice, these benefits may disproportionately accrue to the private sector at the expense of already overburdened public health systems. Thus, 'policymakers should be wary of the risks of conforming with international, market-driven standards, particularly if it encourages their health care sectors to further privatize and commercialize' (Cortez, 2008a: 648).

There is, however, growing disparagement of initiatives such as GATS by those who contend they impose conformity at the expense of national and culturally specific health policy. Critics of GATS contend that it forces the privatization of health services, prevents governments from regulating health sectors and hinders a government's ability to determine the shape of its domestic health system in a democratic way. Although Belsky *et al.* (2004: 138) conclude there is 'little clear evidence of such adverse consequences', it is too early to tell what if any impact GATS and similar EU initiatives will have. While GATS at present does not appear to be significantly affecting health care services, Sexton (2001) contends that if current proposals are implemented, GATS could be used to overturn almost any legislation governing health services. Although the controversy surrounding GATS and its imposition on national autonomy and democratic legitimacy are bound to escalate, it is most likely that such concerns will be concentrated in LMICs which are most vulnerable to outside pressures to adopt models that are unresponsive to the health needs of their populations.

Similarly, much of the debate over the emerging Transatlantic Trade and Investment Partnership (TTIP) in the UK has concerned its potential impact on the NHS, with opponents arguing that including health care in the agreement could force the privatization of the NHS, or at least make it impossible to reverse. The fear is that market access means that monopolies must be abolished, including public services provided by the state or by a limited number of suppliers – like the NHS. The European Commission, in reply, contends that it will include well-established provisions to ensure governments have freedom to organize their health services as they wish and that there is no reason to fear either for the NHS as it stands today or for changes to the NHS in future resulting from TTIP (McKinney, 2016). Likewise, strong opposition to the North American Free Trade Agreement (NAFTA) has included concerns from some countries, like Mexico, over threats to their health care traditions. It is argued that under trade treaties, public–private partnerships threaten to diminish governments' regulatory ability in vital areas like health care and to shift risk from the investor or service provider to the public (Box 1.9).

Convergence theory remains intuitively attractive because similar problems potentially make for similar solutions, and under these circumstances it becomes more likely that health policies will converge. Ultimately there are a limited number of policy instruments available to address a certain policy problem, thus suggesting that function rather than politics informed by historical legacy or culture predominantly shapes health policies (Gibson and Means, 2000). Ideas travel around the world and influence national policy makers, although they are perceived in the context of national and system-specific experiences. Using diagnosis-related groups (DRGs) for inpatient services as an example, Schmid *et al.* (2010) show how cross-national influences as well as system-specific problems contribute to the implementation of innovative policy instruments. Although they are far from a uniform instrument and their use and implementation varies from country to country, the authors consider the spread of DRGs as an example of a convergent trend.

Box 1.9 Challenges of even more expansive trade treaties in Canada

While Canadians have repeatedly been assured that their health care system is beyond the reach of free-trade treaties, Canada's health care system is only partially shielded from their force. While the treaties provide some critical protection, the safeguards fall short of the full 'ironclad' exemptions for health repeatedly promised. The most serious free-trade threat is that, once entrenched, foreign health care insurers and companies can make use of NAFTA's tough expropriation-compensation rules. These provisions apply fully to Canada's health care sector and are backed up by NAFTA's notorious investor-to-state dispute settlement process. They risk making experiments with for-profit health care essentially irreversible. Despite the dangers that existing trade treaties already pose to health care reform, the federal government is promoting new and more expansive international trade treaties that would worsen this threat (Grieshaber-Otto and Sinclair, 2004).

Policy convergence is also encouraged by the fact that all health systems must fulfil similar types of functions, for example raising public funds to pay for medical care and organizing the delivery of these services. In contrast, Schmid and colleagues (2010) and similarly Rothgang *et al.* (2010) suggest that it is the specific, type-related deficiencies of individual health systems that lead to convergence. Since these deficiencies cannot be resolved by routine mechanisms, non-system-specific elements become integrated in individual health systems. Consequently, individual health systems progressively have a hybrid character and, overall, health systems are becoming more similar.

In contrast, critics of convergence theories argue that its proponents oversimplify the process of development and underestimate significant divergence across countries (Howlett and Ramesh, 2009). Moreover, most studies that have found evidence of convergence have failed to demonstrate that it is applicable across all domains, thus allowing for significant divergence in other areas (Blank and Burau, 2006). In their study of leadership and governance arrangements in seven developed health systems, Smith and associates (2012) came to similar conclusions. They analysed three fundamental functions (priority setting, performance monitoring, and accountability arrangements), and found that approaches to leadership and governance vary substantially and have been developed piecemeal. Although there might be practical consensus on the broad goals of the health system, there is considerable variation in approaches to setting priorities. Therefore, while one can selectively find evidence of convergence, it is by no means certain, inclusive or consistent and has not necessarily translated into similar health policies or policy directions across countries.

In their 36-year perspective of convergence patterns across 22 OECD countries, Leiter and Theurl (2009) found that convergence had taken place but the impacts are not equally pronounced for each dependent variable across health care systems and time periods. Moreover, the rate of convergence has in fact decreased over time. Using a similar cohort of 19 OECD countries for the period 1972–2006, Panopoulou and Pantelidis (2011) found a convergence in per capita health care expenditures for 17 countries, but when they tested for convergence of outcome using six different health measures, they found a divergence of the full panel of OECD countries for all but infant mortality, thus concluding that convergence in per capita health expenditures does not lead to convergence in health outcomes. Herwartz and Theilen (2010) found that international convergence of health care expenditure across countries depends on characteristics of the age structure of the population. Likewise, Vrangbaek *et al.* (2012) found evidence of convergence among four Northern European countries in the overall policy rhetoric about the objectives associated with patient choice, embracing concepts of empowerment and market competition, but less in the design of specific policies. Similarly, in their study of six countries, Okma and associates conclude:

> The seemingly common experience in reform goals and means can easily lead to generalized conclusions of [global] convergence. However, the health politics of the six countries in this study have not converged into one common direction. Each country has implemented change within the restraints of existing national institutions and political boundaries. While the goals and range of options considered were strikingly similar, the six countries diverged widely in the actual reform models and process of implementation. Ideas, interests and political institutions played important roles … In several cases, the introduction of market competition went hand-in-hand with increased government control, leading to increased 'hybridization' of health care systems. (2010: 78)

In agreement, Grignon (2012) contends that while there is considerable dispute about whether health care systems converge (see also Aslan, 2009; Paris *et al.*, 2010; Tuohy, 2012a), there is near-universal agreement that, when there is convergence, it is invariably slow. National institutions or characteristics of health care systems die hard. Health care systems are renowned for being resistant to 'real reform', namely reforms altering the basic rules through which individuals contribute to the financing of health care or through which care is delivered to patients. Grignon (2012) suggests that resistance to change does not mean inactivity, but despite over 1,300 reforms over eight years in 20 countries main institutions have survived essentially intact. As Okma *et al.* (2010) note, major change is rare and requires the confluence of political willingness to change, popular acceptance of the need to reform and the availability of reform options that fit the national context.

For Attia and Bérenger (2009), convergence in health care in the EU is evident at two levels: the generalization of medical coverage and the transformation of insurance schemes into universal national regimes. For instance, the reforms surrounding disease protection, adopted in the 1990s, have coalesced around two axes: the stake in competition among the providers and the stake in competition among health insurers. In the first instance, the reform of the UK NHS established a quasi-market for care where hospitals and health centres compete to offer their services. The mechanisms of quasi-markets served as reference to Spain where, since 1995, competition exists between the public and private establishments, a trend followed by Finland, Sweden and Denmark. The most significant example of the second is that of the German reform of 1992 under which the consumer can choose either public or private medical coverage thereby encouraging health insurance schemes to better manage their budget, offer competitive insurance services and, in the process, make the purchasers more responsible.

Overall, then, the literature on the convergence in health care systems reveals little consensus. Regardless of where they put emphasis, comparative studies of health policy largely agree on the coexistence of policy divergence *and* convergence (see Field, 1999; Hwang, 2008). While some authors identify a trend towards convergence (Hitiris and Nixon, 2001; Glennerster and Lieberman, 2011; Thomas, 2011), others find no signs for convergence at all (Globerman and Vining, 1998), while still others see a mixed picture (Blank and Burau, 2006; Wendt *et al.* 2009), finding convergence for some indicators and divergence for others.

It should also be noted that health policy is not static and that movement in one direction often is followed by a move in the opposite direction as political fortunes change or the public responds negatively to a change. For instance, New Zealand was widely cited as an example of NHS convergence towards market systems in the early 1990s when it initiated strong market reforms, but most of these reforms were repealed by succeeding governments. Finally, convergence theories beg the question of convergence to what: privatized health care, national health services, social insurance, national insurance, or some new hybrids? Tuohy concludes: 'mature health care states are hybridizing, resembling less closely the ideal types approximated by their founding models and increasingly incorporating elements of other models to produce distinctive national hybrids' (2012a: 612).

Conclusions

Health systems of all countries face major problems regarding the issues raised here. Thus, apprehension about health care expenditure growth and its long-term sustainability has risen to the top of the policy agenda in all developed countries. As continued growth in spending places pressure on government budgets, health services provision and patients' personal finances, policy makers have begun to launch forecasting projects to support policy planning. In their comparative analysis of 25 models that were developed for OECD countries by governments, research agencies and international organizations, Astolfi *et al.* (2012) found that while virtually all models accounted for demographic shifts in the population, the least understood influences on health expenditure growth are technological innovation and health-seeking behaviour.

Whether health care represents a crisis in a country depends on one's perspective, but certainly there is much variation in severity across nations on more objective measures as well. To what extent are these differences the product of health policies of the countries and to what extent are the problems beyond the direct control of policy makers? Put another way, what steps can governments take, if any, to maximize the chances of framing sustainable health care systems that can weather the ageing population, the proliferation of technologies, heightened public expectations and other forces driving up the costs?

What should be already evident from the discussion so far is that there are significant differences as to how well countries are doing in constraining costs, providing universal and quality care and protecting the public health. It has yet to be demonstrated convincingly whether universal, global forces are moving the health policies of industrialized, much less low- and middle-income, countries towards convergence. Even if that is the case, it is imperative to examine closely the variations and similarities of the health care systems of countries and to appreciate the implications for the provision of health care to populations. Chapter 2 begins this task by describing the political, cultural and historical context of the health systems of these countries to get a better understanding of how and why each country's health system has evolved the way it has. It presents three different sets of explanations for the divergent approaches to health care found in our countries. As such, the chapter provides a framework for studying the intricacies of the systems and the substantive issues introduced in the chapters that follow.

Chapter 2

The Context of Health Care

The health policy of any country at any point in time is the product of a multitude of factors, the most important of which are displayed in Figure 2.1. These factors include the intrinsic social, cultural and political fabric of a country, including its social values and structures, political institutions and traditions, the legal system and the characteristics of its health care community. For instance, policy-making authority might be highly centralized or widely dispersed across multiple levels. Moreover, in some countries unions and/or corporate structures are strong factors in determining social policy and might, in effect, have a veto power over proposed policy changes made by the government. Likewise, the influence of the medical industry and medical and nursing associations varies widely, as does the power of insurance providers in shaping health policy.

The practice of health professions can also be strongly affected by the legal system and its role in compensation claims and the definition of legal rights to health care services. Moreover, in some countries the courts can challenge and even negate government policies, while in others the government is supreme and its decisions are the law. Social values, too, are important forces, with some traditions emphasizing individual rights and entitlements and others putting heavy emphasis on collective or community good. The boundaries as to what is a 'public' good and what should remain in the private sphere also impact on health policy. Countries with stronger socialist roots are likely to define public goods and services much more broadly and to include universal coverage. Furthermore, in some societies like Japan and Taiwan, the extended family still plays an important role in health care while in others even the nuclear family has diminished importance in its delivery.

In addition to the values and institutions of a country, health policy is shaped by the composition of its population and by demographic patterns. Heterogeneous, multicultural populations require more complex health systems than more homogeneous ones. Likewise, older populations have different needs than younger ones. Populations can also be more or less stratified by class, economic status or other social groupings. As noted in Chapter 1, health policy and the way in which medical resources are distributed also reflect the current state of medical technology and the public expectations and demands that accompany it.

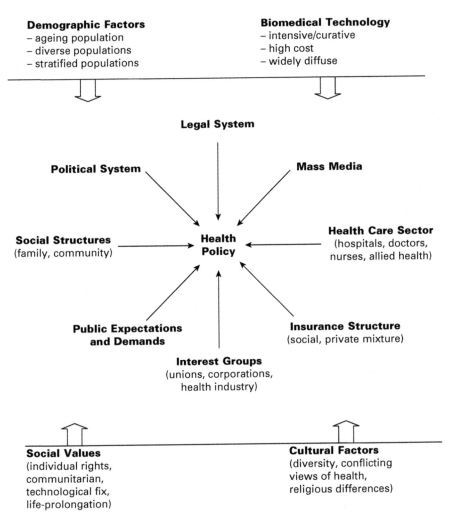

Demographic Factors
– ageing population
– diverse populations
– stratified populations

Biomedical Technology
– intensive/curative
– high cost
– widely diffuse

Legal System

Political System

Mass Media

Social Structures
(family, community)

Health Policy

Health Care Sector
(hospitals, doctors,
nurses, allied health)

**Public Expectations
and Demands**

Insurance Structure
(social, private mixture)

Interest Groups
(unions, corporations,
health industry)

Social Values
(individual rights,
communitarian,
technological fix,
life-prolongation)

Cultural Factors
(diversity, conflicting
views of health,
religious differences)

Figure 2.1   *Health policy context of developed nations*

The mass media and its coverage of medical stories clearly influence how the public perceives health care and health care policy. Countries with 'tabloid' traditions are likely to emphasize the more sensational aspects of medicine and those with more investigative traditions are likely to look for faults in the health care system. In general, however, the mass media has tended to dramatize medicine, heighten expectations and place more demands on health managers and politicians.

Public support for policy, of course, is an important factor in democratic societies and is critical in explaining how governments with similar problems cope differently. Interestingly, levels of public support for health services across countries seem to have little correlation with levels of

Table 2.1   *Public views of their health system, 2010*

	AU	GER	NE	NZ	SW	UK	USA
Works well, needs minor changes	24%	38%	51%	37%	44%	62%	29%
Fundamental changes needed	55%	48%	41%	51%	45%	34%	41%
Needs to be completely rebuilt	20%	14%	7%	11%	8%	3%	27%

Source: Thomson *et al.*, 2013.

health spending or any objective level of services provided (Table 2.1). Blendon and associates (2001), for instance, compared public satisfaction with one's health care system with the percentage of GDP spent on health care, and it found little relationship between higher spending and satisfaction. Spending more does not necessarily increase satisfaction levels.

Numerous statistical analyses have been offered to explain differences in aggregate health expenditure among nations and investigate the impact of institutions and other possible explanatory variables on these. Studies across developed and developing countries commonly find that the per capita income of a country is the single most important factor explaining health expenditure variation (Gerdtham *et al.*, 1998). Total health spending rises from around 2 to 3 per cent of GDP in the poorest countries to 8 to 12 per cent in the wealthiest, with the USA substantially higher (Musgrave *et al.*, 2002; Wendt, 2015; see also Dieleman *et al.*, 2016, for projected increases and remaining gaps). Since our ten affluent countries are all quite similar in wealth, however, we suggest that differences in spending reflect a combination of economic, cultural and historical factors. Wealth still might be the most important single factor but it is only one of many that must be considered. Moreover, statistical modelling studies cannot explain variation in how aggregate expenditure is distributed nor how the funding and provision of health services are organized.

Therefore, although health care on one level might reflect universal challenges for all countries, the political, historical and cultural context of health and health care varies from country to country as well as within countries. A main argument in this book is that variation in health policy from one country to the next can be explained only by understanding the unique combination of these variables and their interaction in each nation. This chapter examines three underlying and complementary explanations for country diversity: the institutionalist; the cultural; and the functionalist (or structuralist). First, institutionalist contextual factors, specifically the political structures and institutions of these countries and their legal systems, are surveyed. Second, attention is directed towards the historical and cultural context of health care. After discussing the defining cultural characteristics of each country, different approaches to defining health and the role of traditional medicine are examined. Third, functionalist explanations are presented. These include population size and diversity, the wealth of a country and social/economic determinants of health.

Institutionalist explanations: contrasting political systems

Although the political systems of no two countries are identical and each has a unique history and combination of formal and informal structures, the characteristics of political systems can be categorized along several overlapping dimensions (Lijphart, 1999). The major distinguishing factor is the extent to which political power is concentrated or dispersed. As a rule, *unitary* systems concentrate political authority in a central government while *federal* systems constitutionally divide powers among the central government and states, provinces or other sub-national units of government. Although the central government in a unitary system might choose to delegate specific administrative functions and responsibilities to lower units, final authority rests at the national level. In contrast, states in a federal system have constitutionally based powers that often include health policy. Unitary governments include Japan, New Zealand, Singapore, Sweden, Taiwan and the UK, while Australia, Germany, the Netherlands and the USA are examples of the federal model.

Another institutional configuration that relates directly to the continuum of centralization is the distribution of power within each level of government. For instance, many democracies, such as New Zealand, Taiwan and the UK, concentrate power in parliament where the distinction between executive and legislative power is obscured or virtually non-existent. Moreover, although many parliamentary systems have upper and lower houses (e.g. the House of Lords and House of Commons in the UK), in effect almost all power rests in the lower houses.

In stark contrast is the USA, with its deliberate constitutional separation of powers among a separately elected president, two houses of Congress and a relatively active judicial system. Despite a great deal of variation in dispersion of policy-making authority in parliamentary systems, when compared to the USA they all have considerably more concentrated bases of power. Figure 2.2 presents a rough distribution of our countries in terms of centralization of institutional power along these dimensions. This distribution corresponds closely to the findings of Lijphart (1999: 189) who classified Australia, Germany and the USA as

Singapore	Taiwan	UK		Japan	Germany	Australia
	New Zealand		Sweden	Netherlands		USA

Concentrated   **Fragmented**

Figure 2.2   *Institutional power in political systems*

'federal and decentralized'; the Netherlands as 'semi-federal'; Japan and Sweden as 'unitary and decentralized'; and New Zealand and the UK as 'unitary and centralized'. Singapore, a city-state in which all political power rests in the central government, is by far the most centralized of the countries discussed here.

The implications of these formal government types for health policy are significant. Where power is centralized, the government has the formal capacity to make more rapid and comprehensive policy changes. In the mid-1990s, Taiwan opted for a nationwide health insurance scheme that was implemented very quickly: NHI was submitted as a bill to Parliament in 1993, passed as law in 1994, and implemented in early 1995. With similar speed, Singapore put a complicated mix of private (but mandatory) savings schemes and public safety net funding in place (Okma *et al.*, 2010). Likewise, successive New Zealand governments have introduced almost unimpeded a range of major restructuring initiatives of the health system since the 1990s.

In contrast, the more fragmented the political authority, the higher the probability of deadlock and inaction, or at best more incremental change. The USA is the prime example of a system in which making even minor changes in health policy represents a long-term struggle. Even in a relatively narrow area such as payment of prescription charges for the elderly by Medicare where almost everyone agreed change was needed, little was accomplished after over two years of political wrangling (Abrams, 2002). Australia and the USA are both federal systems, but their approaches to health care are divergent. Although not as static as the USA, reform in Australia has been very restrained compared to that of neighbouring New Zealand.

Similarly, in Germany health policy making tends to be highly incremental, to the extent that health policy is often locked into 'reform blockades'. Because decision-making powers are dispersed among a multitude of mainly non-state actors (insurance funds and provider organizations) across federal, state and local levels, the federal government has little direct influence on health care. This is particularly pertinent in the case of medical reform (Bandelow, 2007). Furthermore, through their joint self-administration with insurance funds, doctors are at the heart of health governance, and it is difficult to address the relationship between economic and medical rationality.

Moreover, in fragmented political systems where competing political parties are able to control particular institutions, there is increased likelihood of being a divided government where one party controls one or several branches or levels and another controls the rest. Although this could contribute to a more deliberative policy-making process, it can also easily degenerate into stagnation and gridlock as has been common in US health policy. Conversely, it is expected that a centralized system such as the UK or New Zealand presents a policy arena characterized by more frequent and wide-ranging punctuated changes such as major restructuring, often to the detriment of programme stability. For instance, instability and insecurity were major charges made by opponents of the near-continuous reforms of the New Zealand health system in the 1990s (Martin and Salmond, 2001).

Judicial review

Another dimension that Lijphart (1999) sees as important in distinguishing among democracies is the strength of judicial review (the extent to which a high court can overrule elected representative bodies). Figure 2.3 demonstrates a range across our countries regarding the power of the courts to influence health policy. In recent decades, the German and American courts have become highly activist, invalidating many laws on constitutional grounds, thus earning the German courts the label of being an 'imperial judiciary' (Franck, 1996) and constitutional challenges to the Affordable Care Act in the USA.

In contrast, the Netherlands, New Zealand, Singapore, Taiwan and the UK do not have systems of judicial review of policy or administrative decisions. In these countries, the will of parliament is supreme and cannot be challenged or overridden by a high court. The remaining countries have provisions for judicial review, but for a variety of reasons the courts have exercised their power with restraint and moderation. The European Court of Human Rights eventually is bound to influence health policy in member countries, but its powers are still unfolding.

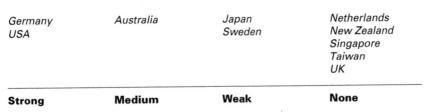

Germany USA	Australia	Japan Sweden	Netherlands New Zealand Singapore Taiwan UK
Strong	**Medium**	**Weak**	**None**

Figure 2.3　*The strength of judicial review*

Source: Adapted from Lijphart (1999: 226).

Legal systems

Figure 2.1 also suggests that the legal framework can have significant influence on health care. It can do this in many ways, ranging from regulating the medical professions, to influencing the distribution of health care resources, to constructing liability systems that impact on both. While some countries have opted for no-fault accident compensation systems and for sanctions by medical bodies, others turn to the courts to varying degrees to determine liability and the allocation of medical resources and to punish wrongdoers in the medical professions.

Given its emphasis on negative rights, the USA has the most extensive civil liability system, with health care being no exception. Many states are considered in crisis with medical malpractice insurance affordability or even availability, and doctors in some states have had work stoppages or slowdowns out of protest. When it comes to medical liability laws and culture, liability and premiums vary substantially by state and speciality. In Illinois and a cluster of states on the East Coast, including New York, Washington DC, Pennsylvania, New Jersey and Delaware, tort reform is virtually non-existent, litigation is commonplace with high per capita malpractice payouts and premiums for physicians are often debilitating, e.g. obstetricians and surgeons in New York City and Philadelphia pay over $100,000 per year (Roslund, 2014).

The medical profession's response is that medical liability awards for the pain and suffering, and punishment awards, which can reach tens of millions of dollars, must be capped (a usual figure given is $250,000). However, trial lawyers, consumer groups and the Obama Administration have argued that any attempt to limit awards runs counter to the rights of individuals to redress wrongs against them in a court of law and the real problem is the failure of the medical profession to discipline negligent doctors. Most observers agree, however, that the current system is inequitable and unsustainable because most patients who go to court lose and get absolutely nothing, while in some cases persons who have suffered little or no harm receive huge monetary settlements.

There is no doubt that the US liability system contributes to inflated health care costs, although the two sides offer widely divergent estimates. The system adds to the costs in two ways. The more limited direct cost increases come from the cost of malpractice insurance itself, most of which is passed on to patients and third-party payers. The indirect impact, however, is more profound, because virtually every medical decision is made under threat of potential litigation. This environment leads to what is termed *defensive medicine* where doctors order all available diagnostic tests and therapeutic measures, even those that are of marginal or no benefit to a patient, in order to avert a lawsuit (e.g. the doctor did not do everything possible) or, if sued, to provide documentation that all that was possible was done for the patient. In their analysis of the various components of liability system costs, Mello *et al.* (2014) estimate that annual medical liability system costs, including defensive medicine, are $55.6 billion, or 2.4 per cent of total health care spending. Therefore, although there remains debate over the impact of defensive medicine, it is significant and helps explain why US costs are so out of line with other countries (see Chapter 3).

Other countries have opted for alternative systems to deal with medical misadventure and compensation. New Zealand, for instance, created an accident compensation system specifically to avoid the problem of costly litigation. When an individual suffers harm under this system he or she is compensated by the Accident Compensation Commission (ACC) under a standardized formula. In return, legal remedies are severely limited, although in recent years the incidence of legal action has increased. Moreover, as more people have pursued medical misadventure claims, the ACC cost for health care has multiplied, as has compensation.

Although accident compensation systems are more successful in ensuring that all victims are compensated, often the compensation is small in comparison to the potential awards in a liability-based system. It makes sense that countries with national health services would want to avoid an unpredictable but costly liability system and opt for a predictable, less costly system even if critics argue it violates the rights of individuals to sue. That these health systems tend to be in countries with traditions of solidarity and community rather than individual rights gives them legitimacy they would not enjoy in the USA.

In the absence of civil liability, accident compensation systems normally are linked with stricter professional self-regulating systems for medical negligence. Medical societies are given responsibility to sanction and, where appropriate, prevent such members from continuing to practise. European countries in general have traditionally put emphasis on preventing medical malpractice and disciplining problem doctors through professional self-regulation. In Germany, for example, professional chambers at state level are responsible for licensing doctors, controlling medical ethics, organizing disciplinary processes and offering specialist training. The chambers are public bodies regulated by law (Moran, 1999).

However, the case of Britain shows the limitations of this approach. In recent years, there have been many high-profile cases of medical malpractice (Burau and Fenton, 2009; Fenton and Salter, 2009; Kodate, 2012). One involved a pathologist who had removed organs from the bodies of dead children during post-mortem examinations without the prior consent of parents. In another case, a general practitioner (GP) was convicted of murdering 15 of his elderly patients although a subsequent inquiry suggested that the actual number of victims exceeded 200. Both cases raise doubts over the ability of the doctors' professional body, the General Medical Council (GMC), to protect patients from medical malpractice. Mounting pressure from the government and the public, as well as the medical profession, led to substantial reforms of the Council, including reduction in size, increased lay membership, tightened fitness-to-practise procedures and the introduction of revalidation.

At the same time, liability claims in the UK have risen sharply. Claims against the National Health Service (NHS) for medical negligence rose by more than 20 per cent in just one year. More than 16,000 patients lodged claims during 2012–13, up from 13,500 the previous year and 5,470 in 2007–8 (Donnelly, 2013). Figures from the NHS Litigation Authority show that the service has put aside £22.7 billion for liabilities based on the number of claims it believes it is unlikely to be able to defend – a rise of 22 per cent in just one year following this dramatic rise in the number of patients taking legal action against hospitals and care homes. The NHS Litigation Authority is convinced that a major factor is the increased availability of the 'no-win, no-fee market' that enables claimants to litigate without financial risk and proves so lucrative for solicitors (Goldberg, 2012). Around one-quarter of costs are spent on legal fees, mainly to claimants' lawyers under a system which means legal firms can charge up to £900 an hour for their services if claims are successful. Despite divergent legal systems, then, the problems facing the UK are reminiscent of the malpractice debacle in the USA.

Cultural explanations: cultural/historical factors shaping health care

It is argued here that each country brings to health a distinctive combination of historical and cultural factors that are crucial in explaining its proclivities and characteristics. Political culture is the complex of beliefs, values and attitudes held by the public concerning the proper role of government. To focus on those elements of culture which influence health policy, one must look at beliefs concerning definitions of health, the role of the government in the health arena and the extent to which health care represents an individual right or a privilege granted by society. For instance, to what extent is health care a public as opposed to a private good and, if a public good, on what grounds should health services be distributed to individuals? To provide a basis for more in-depth comparison throughout later chapters, we will briefly examine one of the key defining cultural characteristics that shape health care across countries and then provide a summary of the most defining aspects of each country.

A crucial dimension of political culture focuses on how the individual in the society relates to the whole. What is the perceived role of the state as

Table 2.2 *Distribution by type of health political culture*

Communitarian	Egalitarian	Individualistic
Germany	Sweden	USA
Netherlands	New Zealand	Australia
Japan	UK	Singapore
Taiwan		

opposed to the citizen? Table 2.2 illustrates a rough distribution of these countries as to whether they are classified primarily as a communitarian, egalitarian or individualistic culture. Countries with communitarian traditions, based either in the family or other groupings, have designed various mechanisms to ensure the interests of the various communities. Germany, for instance, has a strong tradition of self-administration, the Netherlands guarantees empowerment of the various 'pillars' (social groups) to reach consensus, and Japan and Taiwan place strong emphasis on the family and on tradition itself (see details later in this section).

In contrast, egalitarian cultures such as those of New Zealand and Sweden, although having differing political systems, place emphasis on the entitlement to health care and on a societal commitment to provide health care on those grounds, whereas countries such as the USA and Australia with their 'rugged' individualistic roots tend to elevate individual rights above the welfare of the community. For them, it is difficult to limit negative rights to health care even for the common good. While rights and entitlements are often used synonymously, entitlements suggest a concern for equality that can be found only in the notion of positive rights, while the individualistic version of negative, self-centred rights lacks the social dimension found in egalitarian and communitarian societies.

Although they are placed in Table 2.2 as to their predominant orientation, some countries have tended to combine aspects of these types into unique hybrids. For instance, Singapore has merged traditional communitarian and common good features with a very strong view of individual responsibility for health and health care. Similarly, the UK culture combines a pragmatic approach to collective action with a very generous entitlement philosophy reminiscent of egalitarian cultures such as New Zealand and Sweden. In Japan, Taiwan and, to a lesser extent, Singapore, meanwhile, Western medicine has introduced a form of individualism foreign to these countries' communitarian roots and created friction between generations as well as among social classes, aptly illustrated by the discussion of traditional medicine later in this chapter.

Germany

Germany has a strong tradition of voluntarism, self-help and family support, embedded in Christian social teachings and the idea of 'subsidiarity'. The 1873 Social Health Insurance Act, the first of its kind, built on these traditions and incorporated them in a statutory system of social solidarity. The organization of health care in Germany is marked by rigid continuity and is shaped by numerous principles, among them social solidarity, freedom of choice for patients and nearly full coverage of services (Bäringhausen and Sauerborn, 2003). In the social insurance context, access to health care is an entitlement that individuals 'earn' by paying insurance contributions. This, together with a strong legalistic approach typical of Germany, turns access to health care into the right of individuals to a defined range of services. Patients literally have 'ownership' of health services. This helps to explain why the freedom of patients to choose their doctors remains a fundamental principle of health care provision. Not surprisingly, Germany is one of the few countries that does not operate a British-style GP gatekeeping system on a compulsory basis. The individualized right to health care also goes hand in hand with the expectation that the social health insurance system provides full coverage. In conjunction with the structural features of the health system, this makes cost containment and any restrictions of services covered by social insurance more difficult.

The Netherlands

Another example of a communitarian country is the Netherlands, which resembles Germany in that private initiative has been a guiding principle in the organization of society. Dutch society has traditionally been organized in separate segments or pillars that represent different religious and political orientations. Under the Roman Catholic notion of subsidiarity and its Protestant counterpart of sovereignty, the different segments in society should be empowered to provide for their members (Björkman and Okma, 1997). However, the process of 'pillarization' of Dutch society began to weaken in the 1960s and state intervention in health care increased, thus marking the modernization of the Dutch health system and a 'universalist turn' (Maarse, 1997). The introduction of insurance for exceptional medical risks in 1967 is indicative here. This insurance is compulsory for all employers irrespective of income and, together with relatively generous entitlements, such insurance has helped to establish a culture of care which gives preference to formal care. However, elements of universalism do coexist with the legacy of pillarization. The provision of health care continues to be predominantly in the hands of private non-profit organizations and health policy making still requires the consensus of many interest groups, yet the state can also take an interventionist role as illustrated by nurse prescribing and pharmaceutical regulation (Kroneman *et al.*, 2016).

Japan

Although for many Westerners Japan is an enigma, its health care context borrows much from Germany and has similarities to the Netherlands, because at its base Japan has a communitarian, extended-family-based culture with veneration for the elderly. For health care, this has meant that universal coverage is widely accepted socially as a given, although long-term care has until recently largely rested with the family, particularly women. However, during the last half-century, traditional Japanese values have come into conflict with the infusion of a Western, largely American, individualistic culture, thus causing significant distress, particularly among the older Japanese population. Japanese views of medicine are an amalgamation of Buddhist, Confucian and Shinto influence, combined more recently with Hippocratic and Christian influences. Although modern Western medicine took hold in the 19th century and the rapid progress of medical technology challenged the way medicine was practised, there remains a very strong paternalistic attitude on the part of doctors and a lasting reliance on traditional practice.

Taiwan

Like Japan, in Taiwan the family traditionally has been a major social force and continues to be an important factor in health care. However, over recent generations patients have developed a physician usage culture that includes consulting physicians even for minor ailments, visiting many physicians to find one that will do what the patient wants, and using the most popular doctors even if they do not specialize in what the patient really needs. The Taiwanese have readily embraced the Western medical model and its accompanying dependence on medical technologies in a culture looking for shortcuts to health improvement (Box 2.1). Until 2009, when it was invited to participate in the World Health Assembly, Taiwan's situation was complicated by its political isolation because professionals had received no formal technical assistance, nor participated in collaborative projects with international organizations such as the WHO or World Bank for over 40 years (Cheng, 2015). In public health areas, especially, activities such as information sharing and regional collaboration suffered.

Sweden

Perhaps the clearest example of an egalitarian type of culture is Sweden, which is notable for the early provision of medical care by the state

Box 2.1   Asking for problems?

In Taiwan, citizens on average visit a doctor almost 14 times per year (over 25 for those over age 65) even though they have one of the lowest physician/population rates in the world. Doctors in Taiwan see on average 128 patients per week. Accordingly, doctor visits are very short, averaging three to five minutes each. Because of this haste, medical errors are bound to occur at a high frequency, although statistics are limited since no one wants to publicize such self-incriminating data. In one report, however, computer error alone on prescriptions in one medical centre was 0.34 per cent (Chen *et al.*, 2008). If extrapolated to the entire country, there would be 96 million prescription errors a year. If Taiwan operated under a US-like liability system, the courts would be submerged in malpractice suits.

dating back to the 17th century (Glenngård *et al.*, 2005). Towns and cities employed doctors to provide public health care and municipalities also operated hospitals. In rural areas, the central state paid physicians to provide basic care. State involvement in health care was consolidated in the middle of the 19th century with the creation of county councils, which had primary responsibility for health care. However, a considerable expansion of health services only occurred after World War II, paving the way for the universal health care system as we know it today. The historical legacy of public involvement in health care is combined with the principle of equality, which is deeply embedded in Swedish society. People have a right to health care regardless of income and where they live (Håkansson and Nordling, 1997). The right to health care is part of people's citizenship and not an individually earned entitlement, as in the case of Germany and the Netherlands. Public funding and provision of health care are key features of the health system in Sweden, as is a strong emphasis on public health and concern for equity.

New Zealand

Although its national health system compares most closely with that of the UK and its political culture retains many features of its Commonwealth heritage, like Sweden New Zealand has a strong tradition of egalitarianism. This was clearly reflected in the Social Security Act of 1938 that promised an open-ended provision to all citizens based on need. It is also illustrated in the strong belief in the public consultation process and the view that elected officials are holders of the public trust, not above it. New Zealand's egalitarian foundation is also illustrated by the 'tall poppy' belief which holds that people who get too successful, wealthy or powerful must be cut back to size. New Zealand politicians embraced the new-right, market-centred philosophy in the 1980s and 1990s, but the public rejected attempts to restructure the health system in ways that were viewed as destructive to its egalitarian foundations. The result has been a series of rather bold attempts by governments of both parties to make major changes in the health care structure, only to pull back from more extreme and unpopular tactics once the public felt threatened and demanded a return to its more egalitarian roots.

Britain

In comparison to Sweden, the approach to collective action in the UK typically has been pragmatic rather than principled (Johnson and Cullen, 2000). This helps explain why following World War II a universal health service was introduced in what was traditionally a liberal state regime. Despite this, the NHS did not resolve the tension between laissez-faire liberalism and collectivism and instead a generous entitlement philosophy has coexisted with rationed service provision. The generosity of the NHS entitlement philosophy contrasts with both the failure of the earlier national insurance arrangements and the austerity of post-war Britain, and it is deeply entrenched in the public's mind. The NHS has always enjoyed high public support. Not surprisingly, reforms have focused on the organization of health services, and even the extensive changes under the Conservatives in the late 1980s were prefaced with the assurance 'the NHS is safe in our hands'. Universalism, together with a centralist political system, also generates expectations that health services are the same (or at least comparable) across the country. Concerns about inequities in access are prominent and are reflected in debates about the 'postcode lottery', whereby services vary significantly from one locale to the next.

United States of America

The USA is the prototype of an individualistic society. Although individual rights have some role in all the nations here, in the USA rights have been elevated to a status of supremacy over collective interests. Moreover, by rights Americans mean negative rights, and, consequently, they are hesitant to sacrifice perceived individual needs for the common good. Thus, there is no guaranteed universal coverage but also no limits on what health care individuals can buy if they can afford it. This cultural tenet goes a long way to explain why the USA expends so much more of its GDP on health care than other countries, without providing universal access. Cost containment measures such as Health Maintenance Organizations (HMOs) that attempted to set limits on individual care were widely attacked as counter to patient rights and led to calls for a

Box 2.2   Health care in the USA

American patients expect a higher standard of care. In contrast to Japan and Taiwan, where physicians spend little time with patients, such conduct is unacceptable in the USA. Moreover, compared to often austere conditions in hospitals elsewhere, amenities often include wireless internet services, satellite television, wide menu choices and tastefully decorated rooms. These extras have little appreciable impact on health but add to the costs, thus contributing to the inability to control health care spending. In 2014, over $3 trillion was spent on health care, an average of over $9,500 per person. Many observers warn that this trend requires drastic policy changes to put the brakes on spending growth, but given the egocentric US culture this is unlikely (Anderson *et al.*, 2006; Blank, 2012). Although Americans complain about high costs and deductibles, when their health or life is at stake they expect no expense to be spared and believe that medicine should not have a price tag.

'Patients' Bill of Rights'. Not surprisingly, there is also a strong aversion by the medical community to serve as gatekeepers and professional codes of ethics refuse to acknowledge the existence of scarcity of resources. The idea that limits on medical expenditures for an individual patient could be set to benefit the wider community contradicts the traditional patient-oriented customs of medicine (see Box 2.2).

Reinforcing the predominance of negative rights, US culture is also predisposed towards progress through technological means, resulting in an unrealistic dependence on technology to fix health problems at the expense of non-technological solutions. This demand for medical technology is reinforced by the dominance of medical specialists who quickly extend the indications for use of new innovations, thus leading to a very aggressive form of medicine, under which, for example, the USA carries out four operations for every one performed in Japan.

Australia

Although Australia shares the far South Pacific and a similar British heritage with New Zealand, the two cultures have diverged since independence in the 19th century, with the latter opting for a more egalitarian and collectivist political culture and Australia adopting a much more individualistic, US-type approach to defining the scope of public goods and the role of government in promoting equality. Australia's unique welfare state places it in a hybrid category value-wise, although the fragmented Australian health care system with its strong private component is closer to the USA than it is to New Zealand (Rix *et al.*, 2005). The decentralized Australian health delivery system reflects a rugged individualism needed to survive in a hostile environment as much as it does the fragmented federal system that defines Australian politics. Thus, while there has been an inevitable British influence in Australia, beginning with the first prisoner settlements, which continues to be reflected in some aspects of its health care system, the 'tendency to look to North America as a source of technology, of funding and organizational initiatives and the inspiration for new policies has continued to the present time' (Palmer and Short, 2000: 6). Australian culture, then, represents a unique combination of its European heritage with a heavy dose of individualism.

Singapore

Of all our countries, Singapore is the most difficult to classify as to cultural orientation, in part because, unlike other Asian countries, its history is short and it is thus a unique mixture of several blends of culture, East and West. Singapore has risen in the last 40 years from a Third World territory with appalling health and human conditions to a highly modern society that ranks high on health and economic measures. Singapore's approach to health policy is a distinctive combination of free-market principles and strict government control (Okma *et al.*, 2010). Its philosophy is to build a healthy population through innovative preventive programmes and promotion of healthy lifestyles that individuals have a civic duty to embrace (Box 2.3). Thus, the system deemphasizes high-cost curative technologies, thereby explaining the low rates of intensive medical procedures performed in Singapore relative to other countries and the low proportion of its GDP that it spends on health care. When

---

Box 2.3 Only in Singapore

A key principle of Singapore's national health scheme is that no medical service is provided free of charge, regardless of the level of subsidy, even within the public health care system. This mechanism is intended to reduce the over-utilization of health care services, a phenomenon often seen in fully subsidized universal health insurance systems. Patients are accustomed to cost sharing rather than depending on state funding. The cost-sharing formula has countered the 'moral hazard' generally associated with fee-for-service, third-party reimbursement. Singapore has deliberately avoided the costly 'levelling down' option of universal access regardless of ability to pay, in which the poor enjoy the same benefits as the rich. At the highest level of subsidy, although each out-of-pocket expense is typically small, costs can accumulate and become substantial for patients and families. At the lowest level, the subsidy is in effect non-existent, and patients are treated like private patients, even within the public system (Okma *et al.*, 2010).

hospitalized, each patient pays part of the bill with his or her own Medis-ave account, thus in theory giving him or her an incentive to be healthy, minimize the need for medical treatment and save on medical expenses. Singaporeans readily accept this social contract based on individual responsibility and co-payments because of their willingness to place the common good above self-interest, the absence of any tradition of state largesse, their 'spirit of self-help' and their pragmatic nature that under-stands that 'trade-offs are an inevitable fact of life' (Lim, 2004: 89). Thus, the Singapore value system represents a hybrid form of individualism often at odds with that of the USA and Australia.

Different approaches to defining health

A critical question for health policy, and one that varies across cultures, is what is meant by the term 'health'. There are several competing models, each of which has important implications for how we organize health care. The prevailing Western medical model defines health as the *absence of disease or illness*. People are healthy under this defini-tion if they are not suffering from an illness or disease. The goals of medicine, therefore, are to diagnose an illness and restore the health of the patient, who, by definition, is unhealthy. Intrinsic in curative medi-cine is the continual expansion of categories of disease to account for a broadening range of conditions deemed unhealthy. Moreover, such labelling of a condition as a disease tends to embed in medicine the notion that disease is the enemy.

A competing definition of health is the *coping* model where health is essentially an ability to adapt to the problems life presents us. Under this definition, individuals can be healthy even if they are ill so long as they have the personal strength and resilience to cope with life. In contrast, people without identifiable disease or illness are unhealthy if they are unable to cope. The tension with the Western medical model is mani-fested in a concern that the latter interferes with individuals' ability to cope with their internal states and environment.

The third definition of health promulgated by the World Health Organization (WHO) is 'a state of complete physical, mental and social well-being and not merely the absence of disease or infirmity' (1946). This ambitious ideal has been widely criticized because, if taken literally, it means that individuals are unhealthy if they are unhappy with their lot in life or even if they just feel unfulfilled. Moreover, in conflict with the coping theory, individuals with any defined disease, illness or disability cannot be healthy. Although this definition is so broad as to make it almost meaningless, it does incorporate the need to expand the definition of health beyond the situation where a person has a medically defined illness or disease. To the extent that it broadens ill health beyond the notion of biological dysfunction, the WHO definition is useful despite its operational problems.

One shortcoming of these definitions is their failure to establish the social and cultural dimensions of health and ill health explicitly. Health has both a personal and a public dimension. Although pain, suffering and regret are individual under the WHO definition, their effect on the lives of others might be severe. Moreover, health and illness are social constructs and culturally defined and must be considered within a cultural context. For Callahan (1990: 103), illness itself is as much social as individual in its characteristics because tolerability will depend on the kind of care and support provided by others and by the social meaning of the disease. Good health, therefore, requires social networks and systems that are complicated by these conflicting definitions of health.

Even within specific social systems health can be a very relative term. Seedhouse (1991), for instance, sees disease and health akin to the analogy of weeds and flowers. As with plants, what we perceive as undesirable in one case might be desirable in another. Pneumonia in an active 20 year old is undesirable and it is appropriate to say she is suffering from a disease. In contrast, pneumonia in a 90-year-old victim of a severe stroke might be welcomed as offering an easier death. Although in clinical terms pneumonia in both cases is termed a disease, the ambiguity of the disease label requires specification of the context. Increasingly, it is evident that health must encompass, not only the physical and mental aspects of personal well-being, but also the social facets.

Putting health into this broader context also raises the question of why we stress health in its narrow sense as freedom from disease. Although health must be highly valued because it is central to the completion of one's plan of life, health is better viewed as a means to broader goals and purposes in life. Good health is not a substitute for a good life, and good health does not guarantee a good life. Good health, by itself, cannot guarantee achievement of our goals, give us a reason to live, or maximize our potential to the highest order. Good health in the physical sense but without the other dimensions of health, then, is unlikely to ensure contentment. One area in which these ideas take form is in what is often termed 'alternative' or 'holistic' medicine.

Culture and traditional medicine

Although the Western medical model now enjoys dominance in the countries examined here, traditional values continue to shape how it is practised. Therefore, although most attention in this book centres on the analysis of the similarities and differences of these countries within that broader framework, it is imperative to examine features that might be unique to, or more influential in, certain countries. One topic that offers useful insights is the extent to which various forms of traditional medicine continue to be practised alongside Western medicine.

Until 1875, when Western medicine became the official form of medicine in Japan, kampo and acupuncture were dominant. Kampo means 'Han Method' in Japanese because the Chinese introduced the use of herbal products for medical therapy during the 7th to 9th centuries in the Han Dynasty. The Japanese health care system remains an amalgamation of modern Western medicine and traditional Eastern practices, and kampo is still an important feature of medical practice. The great majority of Japanese physicians (72 per cent of all Western-style doctors in a 2000 survey) use at least some kampo formulae in their practice. Moreover, almost all pharmacies have staff trained in traditional methods of prescription and most health insurance companies recognize and support its use (Kenner, 2001). From 1974 to 1989 there was a 15-fold increase in kampo medicinal preparations in comparison with only 2.6-fold increase in the sales of mainstream pharmaceutical products in Japan (WHO, 1996). Acupuncture and other holistic practices are also integrated into the Japanese health system, in part a reflection of its Shinto/Buddhist roots.

Despite initial opposition from the medical establishment, the Taiwan NHI included coverage for traditional Chinese medicine (TCM) in its comprehensive benefits package on an equal basis with Western medicine. Moreover, since the NHI is founded on a highly competitive public and private provider marketplace that offers virtually unlimited choice to the health care consumer with no formal referral requirement, people are free to choose any NHI-contracted hospital or clinic, including Chinese medicine, to receive inpatient or ambulatory care. Thus, a majority of Taiwanese patients still use TCM, in most cases in conjunction with Western medicine.

Similarly, while Singapore's health care services are grounded in Western medicine, it is common practice to contact traditional practitioners for general ailments. Thus, a wide variety of traditional practices continue to serve complementary roles (for implications of this clash of 'ethos', see Quah, 2003). Given the large proportion of Chinese in Singapore, TCM is an important part of Singapore's heritage and enjoys considerable popularity and is growing. Loh (2009), for instance, found that herb usage in children is very common (84.3 per cent) and that 80 per cent of parents admitted concurrent usage of TCM and conventional medicine for their children, raising concern over drug–herb interactions. Although its practice of TCM is largely confined to outpatient care, two acupuncture clinics are affiliated with public hospitals.

Perhaps because of their location in the South Pacific and close ties to Asia, the health care systems of both Australia and New Zealand have strong links to holistic medical practices. In Australia, for instance, where TCM has been practised since the 19th century, demand for and use of it has been growing steadily (Zhu *et al.*, 2009). For instance, 10 per cent of Australians get acupuncture treatment annually and nearly 85 per cent of general practitioners consider it to be safe and effective for primary care (Zheng, 2014). Recently, multidisciplinary clinics, where TCM practitioners work with medical doctors and allied health professionals, have become commonplace. As in Australia, alternative medicine is well established in New Zealand with schools of acupuncture, TCM and holistic healing. Many general practitioners are trained in acupuncture, and the use of herbal products, including New Zealand native plants, is common. Although Chinese and other Asian traditional approaches are available, the most unique influence on New Zealand health policy comes via Maori and Pacific Island cultures. Considerable effort over the past decades has been directed at accounting for cultural differences in the perception of health and health care between the European and Maori populations and to integrate this knowledge into the health delivery system.

In contrast with these systems, the dominance of the American Medical Association (AMA) and other mainstream medical organizations has marginalized the scope of alternative medicine in the USA. Although recently some insurance carriers and HMOs have begun to partially reimburse selected non-traditional treatments, this practice remains the exception. Moreover, unlike even Australia and New Zealand, few medical practitioners in the USA have training in acupuncture or other alternative regimes. The predominance of the medical model has resulted in a very narrow perception of health care among most Americans.

Although conventional medicine remains at the centre of the health service in Britain, there have been some efforts to integrate complementary and alternative medicine into the NHS (Saks, 2002). In 2000 a report by the House of Lords called for patients to have access to 'unconventional' medicine and to be given more adequate information about alternative therapies (Mills, 2001). Here, tighter regulation was identified as a key issue and the report argued that only those therapies that were properly regulated should be accessible through the NHS. In response, there have been moves to strengthen the regulation of alternative practitioners and to standardize the myriad training schemes in alternative therapies that exist. The Department of Health has also provided funding to develop the research capacity in alternative medicine as part of the drive towards evidence-based health care practice.

Functionalist explanations: population, wealth and economics

The third explanation for country-by-country variation is termed functionalist or structuralist because it centres on quantitative characteristics such as demographics and wealth. Problems facing a small, highly concentrated population like Singapore are on a different scale than those facing a large, diverse population like the USA, or even those of the similar-sized population of New Zealand that sprawls across two large islands. Moreover, we would expect that wealthier nations have an easier time meeting the health needs of their populations simply because they have more resources at their disposal (Musgrave *et al.*, 2002). This section examines these functionalist contextual factors for our countries.

Population size and diversity

Not surprisingly, health policy can be influenced significantly by a country's demographic characteristics. Moreover, because these characteristics change over time, such as the ageing or the diversification of the population through immigration, the health system must adapt to those changes. To some extent, the reform efforts of our countries over the last several decades represent attempts to deal with changing needs brought about in part by demographic trends, especially population ageing. One might expect, therefore, that some of the differences in health policy among these countries, described in the following chapters, can be traced to disparities in the size of the respective populations, their age and ethnic diversity, and their degree of social stratification in terms of the distribution of wealth.

Table 2.3 summarizes key demographic variables across our countries. Most obvious is the variation in the size of population. It is not surprising that the USA struggles to devise a workable health system for over 320 million people. The State of California alone is larger than half the countries examined here. Certainly, it can be argued that countries with smaller populations ought to be better able to design a workable health policy. Since the populations of New Zealand and Singapore are less than many metropolitan areas in the USA, perhaps it would be more appropriate to compare their systems with a smaller state like Colorado which has approximately the same population as New Zealand. Large population size might also be mirrored in efforts in the UK to decentralize decision making within the NHS.

Population size, however, is but one important variable for health policy. Population growth rates are also crucial because they point to future health needs and relate to the dynamic composition of the population. A high growth rate requires planning for expanded services and,

Table 2.3   *Population characteristics, 2015 (est.)*

	Population	% growth rate	Net migration	% over 65	% under 15
Australia	22,751,014	1.07	5.65	16.47	17.9
Germany	80,854.408	−0.17	1.24	21.45	12.88
Japan	126,919,659	−0.16	0.0	26.59	13.11
Netherlands	16,947,904	0.41	1.95	17.97	16.73
New Zealand	4,438,393	0.82	2.21	14.05	19.87
Singapore	5,674,472	1.89	14.05	8.88	13.14
Sweden	9,801,616	0.80	5.42	19.99	17.12
Taiwan	23,415,126	0.23	0.89	12.48	13.52
UK	64,088,222	0.54	2.54	17.73	17.37
USA	321,368,864	0.78	3.86	14.88	18.99

Source: Data from the *World Fact Book* (2016).

depending on where the growth is coming from (e.g. births, immigration), a change in types of services needed. In contrast, a low or negative growth rate might indicate difficulties in funding services even at the existing level. Singapore, Australia, New Zealand, Sweden and the USA display the highest growth rates, indicating a need for increased services to take care of the added numbers. In contrast, most of the European countries demonstrate smaller rates of growth, and in Germany and Japan negative growth rates, indicating shrinking populations. Combined with the ageing of their populations, these low growth rates signal difficulties in maintaining existing spending patterns without increasing the tax load on the dwindling proportion that is employed.

One way of counteracting low growth rates is to increase immigration rates, which several countries, such as Germany and the Netherlands, have done. Net migration per 1,000 population ranges from zero in Japan to over 14 in Singapore and 5 in Australia and Sweden. Again, it is crucial to know more details about the immigrants before estimating their impact on health policy. Are they skilled or unskilled, destitute or wealthy? Are they members of compatible cultures and religions or of those likely to cause friction with the existing community? Although diverse cultures and ethnic groupings can strengthen countries in the long run and even aid in the delivery of medical care, they can also place severe strain on the health and social service systems upon arrival (Moszczynski, 2008; Göpffarth and Bauhoff, 2015). Not surprisingly, growing levels of immigration in many industrialized countries have reignited debate about who deserves health care resources (Olafsdottir and Bakhtiari, 2015).

As noted earlier, distinct cultures can have vastly different views of health, health care and health service delivery. These differences are heightened when the values of a group conflict with those of the medical profession (e.g. female genital mutilation). With the clear exception of Japan, the countries examined here all reflect relatively high degrees of ethnic or religious diversity (Table 2.4), or, in many cases, both. While

Table 2.4   *Ethnic and religious composition, by per cent*

	Ethnic composition	Religious composition
Australia	Caucasian 92, Asian 7, Aboriginal and other 1.	Protestant 30.1, Catholic 25.3, Buddhist 2.5, Muslim 2.2, none 22.3, other or unspecified 10.6.
Germany	German 91.5, Turkish 2.4, other 6.1.	Protestant 34, Catholic 34, Muslim 3.7, none or other 28.3.
Japan	Japanese 98.5, Korean 0.5, Chinese 0.4, other 0.6.	Shinto 79.2, Buddhist 66.8, Christian 1.5, other 7.1.
Netherlands	Dutch 78.6, EU 5, Indonesian 2.2, Turkish 2.4, other 11.	Catholic 28, Protestant 19, Muslim 5, other or none 42.
New Zealand	European 71.2, Maori 14.1, Asian 11.3, Pacific Islander 7.6, other 2.7.	Protestant 32.7, Catholic 11.6, Hindu 2.1, Buddhist 1.4, other 3.8, unspecified or none 50.8.
Singapore	Chinese 74.2, Malay 13.3, Indian 9.2, other 3.3.	Buddhist 37.9, Muslim 14.3, Taoist 11.3, Hindu 5.2, Christian 18.1, none 16.4.
Sweden	Swedes with Finnish and Sami minorities; foreign-born or first-generation immigrants.	Lutheran 87, other (includes Catholic, Orthodox, Muslim, Jewish and Buddhist) 13.
Taiwan	Taiwanese (including Hakka) 84, mainland Chinese 14, Indigenous 2.	Buddhist and Taoist 93, Christian 4.5, other 2.5.
United Kingdom	Caucasian 87.2, Black 3, Indian 2.3, Pakistani 1.9, mixed 2, other 3.7.	Christian 59.5, Muslim 4.4, Hindu 1.3, other 2, unspecified or none 25.7.
United States	White 60.8, Hispanic 18.1, Black 12.5, Asian 5.7, Indigenous 1.1, mixed 1.8.	Protestant 51.3, Catholic 23.9, Mormon 1.7, Jewish 1.7, other 5.2, none 16.2.

Source: Data from the *World Fact Book* (2016).

religious diversity in some cases might be a significant factor beyond simply reflecting other cleavages in society, ethnic differences can be more divisive, particularly where newer immigrants are predominantly from lower classes such as is the case with South East Asian brides of young Taiwanese men. Different ethnic groups, therefore, not only challenge the health system because they may have specific health care needs, but also because they bring with them divergent views about the medical community, health and political authorities. The predicament is exacerbated, of course, when there are language difficulties.

Although most countries have a single principal majority, except for Japan they have substantial ethnic/racial minorities that might complicate the delivery of health care services. The problem can be aggravated where health services do not embrace diversity. An exception is the Chinese majority in Singapore, which seems to have been largely successful in integrating the Malay and Indian minorities into the health system. In contrast, blacks in the USA continue to be significantly less well served by the health care system than whites as measured either by access or health outcomes (Cooper *et al.*, 2012). Similarly, the Maori minority in New Zealand has traditionally had a difficult time assimilating into the health care system. Recently, the influx of asylum seekers migrating to Germany and other European countries have complicated health delivery and brought with them unique new health problems which the health care systems must resolve (Göpffarth and Bauhoff, 2015). Countries accepting large numbers of refugees are struggling to meet their health care needs, which range from infectious diseases to chronic diseases to mental health problems (Hunter, 2016). Moreover, access to health care for migrants is often problematic, involving the interaction of health and immigration policies (van Ginneken and Gray, 2015).

The comparative wealth of countries

As introduced earlier, the most obvious determinant of health care funding and provision across countries is wealth. Wealthy countries on average can put considerably more resources into health care simply because they have more discretionary funds. For example, pressures to enact the NHI came as Taiwan became more affluent. Unfortunately, very poor countries cannot compete with wealthier countries in health care spending and cannot afford the kind of medicine wealthy countries take for granted.

The most used comparative measure of wealth is the GDP per capita (see Box 2.4). In 2015, the average GDP per capita of all countries worldwide was $14,957, with a low of $400 in Somalia and a high of $145,000 in Qatar. Twenty-nine countries had per capita GDP below $2,000 and an additional 34 between $2,000 and $4,000. From the data presented

Box 2.4 Challenges in comparing wealth across countries

Although the comparison of countries by income gives us a useful measure of where the countries rank overall, results are dependent on how the figures are calculated. The GDP per capita figures in Table 2.5 are derived from purchasing power parity (PPP) calculations, i.e. the value of all final goods and services produced within a country in a given year, divided by the average (or mid-year) population for the same year. For comparison, one converts the GDP of each country in national currency terms to a common currency (in practice, the US dollar). Because estimates and assumptions must be made, the results produced by different organizations for a country tend to differ, sometimes substantially. Major disagreement exists over what method is most appropriate. Comparisons of national wealth are frequently made on the basis of nominal GDP and savings, which do not reflect differences in the cost of living in different countries. PPPs are the rates of currency conversion that equalize the purchasing power of different currencies by eliminating the differences in price levels between countries. Therefore, using a PPP basis is more useful when comparing differences in living standards between nations because it takes into account the relative cost of living and the inflation rates of the countries, rather than using only exchange rates, which may distort the real differences in income. Thus, GDP (PPP) per capita is often considered one of the indicators of a country's standard of living.

in Table 2.5, all our countries clearly are relatively wealthy; in fact, most cluster around $45,000, with Singapore the highest at $85,700 and New Zealand the lowest at $36,400. Although the variance in wealth among these nations might help to explain some economic limits on those nations near the bottom as compared to those at the top, overall

Table 2.5   *GDP per capita in US dollars, 2015*

Singapore	85,700
Australia	65,400
USA	56,300
Netherlands	49,300
Sweden	48,000
Taiwan	47,500
Germany	47,400
United Kingdom	41,200
Japan	38,200
New Zealand	36,400

Source: *World Fact Book* (2016).

the differences in wealth are relatively small, meaning that differences in health provision and spending that are found among them are not likely to be explained by wealth.

Social and economic determinants of health

Wealth itself, however, does not guarantee the best health, nor does it ensure health that is equitably distributed. In addition to the overall wealth of a country, there is evidence that the degree of inequality or disparity in social and economic conditions at the national level is a key determinant of population health. As noted by Taylor, 'economic growth and consequent wealth, on their own and without attention to distributive policies, do not assure countries of greater health... Social inequalities play through social determinants into inequities in health' (2009: 45). Despite overall wealth ranking, countries with greater inequality tend to have poorer health outcomes overall as well as a more unequal distribution of health. Social determinants are, thus, used as shorthand for the broad and complex array of social, political, economic, environmental and cultural factors that strongly impact on health status and equity. Health systems that do not consciously address these factors exacerbate health inequities (Rasanathan *et al.*, 2011).

Concern about inequities in the health status among different groups of people is not new, but the last two decades have seen an upsurge in the measurement and documentation of health inequities along a range of factors including gender, ethnicity, socio-economic status (SES) and education. This new understanding has shown that, even as average health status often improves, health inequities often continue to widen, thus putting health inequities at the forefront of the health policy agenda. As summarized by Roberts, 'To understand the performance of a nation's healthcare system, one needs to focus not just on national averages but also on the circumstances of those poor and marginalized groups who do relatively poorly in terms of key outcomes like health' (2015: 557). Moreover, success in reducing health inequities necessitates ensuring that the broad focus of primary health care and the social determinants of health are kept foremost in policy (Rasanathan *et al.*, 2011).

Navarro investigated the association between political economy type and socio-economic conditions in various countries and found that, compared with social democratic or Christian democratic political economies, liberal political economies had higher income inequality and unemployment, lower wage and salary levels and a higher proportion of people living in poverty (1999). Moreover, Navarro and Shi (2001) found that countries with liberal political economies had the largest income and wage differentials, the least redistributive impact of the state, and the lowest rate of improvement in infant mortality between 1960 and 1996. In their study of infant mortality rates in OECD countries, Navarro and associates at the International Network on Social Inequalities and Health found that political variables play an important role in defining how public and social policies determine the levels of inequalities. They found that political parties more committed to redistributional policies, such as social democratic parties, are generally the most successful in reducing inequalities and improving infant mortality (2003).

While our country data largely support this thesis, there are exceptions. For example, Japan ranks near or at the top for most population health indicators, even though it is a liberal political economy. As Boxall and Short (2006) point out, however, many features of Japan's political economy closely resemble those of social and Christian democratic political economies, it has a relatively equitable income distribution and high pension commitments and it practises 'stakeholder' rather than 'shareholder' capitalism. They also found that Australia runs counter to the hypothesis of the relationship between political economy, inequality and population health, but they suggest that its unique welfare state model may partly account for its exceptionalism in terms of population health outcomes.

Although there is considerable variation in health status across nations, often the variation among groups within a nation is even greater. For instance, in their study of 16 high-income countries, Nolte and McKee (2011) found that preventable mortality continues to fall in all countries, although the USA is lagging increasingly behind the others. In the USA, however, there are considerable disparities across states, suggesting that differences cannot be attributed solely to differences in the national health system (Kulkarni et al., 2011). Key factors are social and economic, which, in turn, might be reflected in differences in health by race, religion, class or ethnic background. Lower social class, as measured by income, education, or other SES indicators, is related to higher death rates overall and to those diseases that constitute the common causes of death (Fuchs, 2004; Fukuda et al., 2004). Moreover, social class disparities in mortality and morbidity continue to widen (Rainham, 2007). Inequalities in mortality from selected causes suggest that some variation may be attributable to socio-economic differences in smoking, excessive alcohol consumption and poor access to health care (Mackenbach et al., 2008).

If a primary goal of health policy is to improve the health status of the entire population, it is crucial to understand the economic and social determinants of health at the individual level as well. For instance, an Australian study found that the prevalence of chronic disease varies across the socio-economic gradient for many specific diseases and important disease risk factors (Harris et al., 2011). Therefore, any policy interventions to address the impact of chronic disease at a population level must account for these socio-economic inequalities (Glover *et al.*, 2004). A workable model of health, then, requires a shift away from the dominance of the medical care system towards this more inclusive model of health (see Chapter 7). Social problems are resolved primarily through non-medical means, signifying a need to shift emphasis away from the current practice of defining and treating them as medical problems.

The over-reliance on curative-oriented medical intervention presents at least two problems for improving health and health equity, both of which are complicated by over-reliance on doctors rather than exploring the right mix of skills and competencies of health care providers (Aiken *et al.*, 2014; Maier, 2015; OECD, 2016b). First, as noted in Chapter 1, there is convincing evidence that greater health expenditure does not correlate with population health or longer life expectancy, particularly when health care investments are aimed almost exclusively towards medical care. Therefore, 'responding to the (increasingly chronic) burden of illness with (increasingly expensive) technical fixatives is hardly a rational (or cost-effective) approach if the developmental goal that unites rich and poor countries is the social production of good health' (Taylor, 2009: 35).

A second problem is that health care systems, as currently commonly constituted, display a propensity to maintain and heighten health inequity (Mooney, 2009; Taylor, 2009). Health disparities or inequities are systematic, but potentially remediable, differences in one or more aspects of health across population groups defined socially, economically, demographically or geographically (Starfield *et al.*, 2012). Although the magnitude of inequity does vary across health systems, in all countries individuals across social strata differ as to their burden of morbidity and to the health care they receive. Importantly, many studies suggest that significant inequalities in health and health care are pervasive over time (Hernández Quevedo *et al.*, 2008). Without adequate attention to the underlying social conditions that cause ill health in the first place, health systems tend to aggrandize wider social inequalities, so that those who need health care most are those who are least able to access it, use it and benefit from it. Unfortunately, as noted by Lantz *et al.* (2007), health policy usually focuses on expanding access to personal medical services to the exclusion of expanding access to other services that affect an individual's health.

In 2008, the WHO Commission on Social Determinants of Health published its report stating that 'inequities are killing people on a "grand scale"' (WHO, 2008c: 1). Among the report's recommendations for action, improved access to (public, universal) health insurance was prominent (see Box 2.5). Indeed, over the past decade, acceleration of health spending in many developed countries has led governments to search for alternative financing structures, notably through increased private expenditures. However, some of the policy instruments used to reach

Box 2.5   Policy interventions to curtail health inequalities

Factors affecting health include health-related behaviours (smoking, alcohol abuse, diet, physical activity) that require individual action to reduce inequalities in health prevention; psychosocial factors (psychosocial stressors) that might be linked to higher prevalence among lower income groups due to tighter lifestyle restrictions; environmental determinants (social support, social integration), where more affluent individuals will inevitably have better access to health production factors, thus translating into better health; material factors (housing conditions, working conditions, financial problems); access to health care (easy access to high quality services), where the organization of the health system can determine the extent to which individuals are able to access health care in the event of need; and attitudes towards the distribution of health and health care. Although most European countries have explicit public health policies that address these areas, countries vary in their aversion to health inequalities, which might explain why some countries have higher inequalities than others (Costa-Font and Hernández Quevedo, 2012).

those goals, such as restricting eligibility criteria for public insurance and increasing reliance on unregulated private health insurance or cost-sharing arrangements, may have had the unexpected effect of erecting additional barriers to health coverage. Moreover, because the impact of these policies is generally not randomly distributed in the population, these transformations have raised concerns about their effects on both population health and inequalities in health (Quesnel-Vallée *et al.*, 2012). Wagner *et al.* (2011) argue for the need to expand health insurance coverage, so that all households can have access to needed care without risking financial hardship.

Health status disparities linked to SES are probably the result of a complicated mix of factors suggested by three distinct theories. The first, *natural and social selection,* contends that one of the key determinants of social class is health status. This theory assumes that persons with poor health, high-risk behaviour and social pathologies naturally concentrate in the lower social class. If good health is indeed necessary to pursue life goals and affords one the opportunity to succeed in meeting them, it should not be surprising to find that persons in poor health would tend towards a lower SES. Although this might explain the disparity at the margins, it is not generally seen as a major explanation.

A second theory, the *structuralist,* attributes class differences in health to structural factors such as the production and consumption of wealth. Lower SES persons generally exist in less healthy environments, both at home and work. For example, a recent study concluded that there is widespread evidence that the poor in the USA, UK and perhaps other countries as well, face a disproportionate burden of environmental risks (Huggins, 2002). They face more exposure to air pollution, poor water, ambient noise, sub-standard housing and overcrowding. In contrast, higher SES persons enjoy healthier homes, safer neighbourhoods, safer appliances and vehicles, and less hazardous jobs.

The third theory, a *cultural and behavioural* one, sees disparities in health among social classes as the result of differences in behaviour. Often the culture of the lower classes leads to multiple high-risk behaviours that, in turn, lead to poor health. Smoking, alcohol and drug abuse, violence, sedentary lifestyles, obesity, poor diet and other unhealthy behaviours are disproportionately present in lower SES groupings. Many observers have concluded that this last theory is the most explanatory, but most conclude that it must be accompanied by the structuralist theory because the behaviour occurs within this broader social context. As noted by Mechanic, SES is 'perhaps the single most important influence on health outcomes, in part through its direct influence, but more importantly, through the many indirect effects it has on factors that directly shape health outcomes' (1994: 149). These indirect factors are most apparent when one examines two components of SES: income and education.

Income

Income has been found to be a critical variable in determining health status at two levels. At a cross-national level, research consistently shows that the distribution of income has more to do with the health of the population than does the level of medical spending. The best health results are achieved in those societies that minimize the gap between the rich and the poor and that place heavy emphasis on the values of equity. Wilkinson (1997) suggests that healthy, egalitarian societies are more socially cohesive, they have a stronger community life and they suffer fewer of the corrosive effects of inequality. He also found that approximately two-thirds of the variation in mortality rates *within* the populations of developed nations is related to the distribution of income. This includes the UK where, despite universal access to health care, mortality rates among the working-class population increased as income distribution widened in the 1980s. In contrast, Japan has the most equal income distribution and the highest life expectancy despite relatively low levels of health care spending (Kawachi *et al.*, 1999).

At the individual level as well, low income is consistently related to ill health. Low-income families are more likely to assess their health status as 'poor' while low-income individuals are more likely to have preventable hospitalizations than high-income persons. The most likely explanation of these disparities is to be found in some combination of the theories above, but their implication for health policy is significant

(Schoenbaum *et al.*, 2011). The impact of any efforts to constrain health care costs will affect most severely those groups that are not only most likely to need the care but also least likely to have other options.

Education

Not surprisingly, given its close association with income, education is also significantly related to health status. For instance, although Mackenbach *et al.* (2008) found 'striking differences' among countries in the magnitude and even the direction of these inequalities, in Europe smoking and obesity are significantly more widespread among people with lower education levels. In their study of low- and middle-income countries, Ferri *et al.* (2012) found an important 'latent independent protective effect' of education even upon late-life mortality. Given the much higher absolute mortality rates among older people, efforts to ensure universal access to education should confer substantial health benefits for generations to come. Similarly, in their study in East Asian countries, Hanibuchi *et al.* (2010) found that class identification exhibited the strongest association with self-rated health. Moreover, individuals with less education have more frequent short-stay hospitalizations, a higher occurrence of chronic conditions with more limited activity due to such conditions, and significantly lower self-assessment of their health. One early study found that of all indicators, education had the strongest and most consistent relationship with health and was the single most consistent predictor of good health (Winkleby *et al.*, 1992).

Health status, then, is intimately related to various measures of SES, particularly education and income (Wilkinson and Pickett, 2006; Marmot *et al.*, 2008). These factors are critical in understanding the social and cultural context of health and require considerably more research on how they operate. The interactive model of health care attributes poor health outcomes to a broad range of social factors that are bound up in the SES construct. Although SES might have a direct impact on health, it is more likely that it operates indirectly through other factors. In addition to inequitable access to primary care, health promotion and disease prevention efforts, other critical factors include unemployment, violence, poor diet, breakdown of family support structures and inadequate housing (Muennig and Glied, 2010).

Unemployment and ill health

Unemployment too can influence health by reducing income level and standard of living. Moreover, the importance of work to one's wellbeing, over and above the financial aspects, is well documented (Winkelmann, 2009). The unemployed have lower self-esteem and experience significant psychological stress that is linked to higher levels of both subjectively and objectively assessed levels of physical and mental ill health. Heightened unemployment rates are associated with heightened death rates. One study concluded that 'increases in the unemployment rates in European Union countries are related to deteriorated health as measured by elevated mortality rates over the following 10 to 15 years' (Brenner, 2001: 3). Interestingly, the relationship was strongest in the UK, Sweden, Germany and Finland. Suicide and deliberate self-harm as well as smoking and alcohol and drug abuse are more prevalent among the unemployed, particularly the unemployed youth. At the community level, death rates have been found to increase during times of economic depression and joblessness and to decrease during times of economic growth (Modrek *et al.*, 2013). Although the full dynamics remain unclear, the assumption that employment is crucial both to mental and physical health is widely supported. Reduction of unemployment, therefore, has significant health benefits for the population as well as the individual (Kim *et al.*, 2012).

The family and health

The family has traditionally played an important role in integrating health-promoting routines into the daily lives of its members. It has also served as an important facilitator of self-esteem and a social setting that provides critical contributions to psychological and physical development. While reality has often fallen short of this ideal, the decline first of the extended family and more recently the nuclear family in Western nations has had adverse effects on health. Studies consistently find that marriage is associated with lower levels of mortality, better overall health status and healthier behaviour patterns (Stanton, 2003). Although the reasons for this are unclear, a likely factor is the 'social support' of having a wife or husband nearby. Another explanation is that both single men and women tend to have less healthy lifestyles including sleep deprivation, poor diet and work habits, and to be more prone to loneliness and depression. Stable family relationships, however, in whatever form, do appear to encourage good health practices and provide strong social links that reduce the likelihood of ill health. Thus, one would expect that, other things being equal, health outcomes would be better in those countries like Japan and Taiwan where close family structures remain a more resilient feature of society.

The context of health care

This chapter has placed health care in a more expansive context for each of our countries. We submit that one cannot understand the dynamics of a health care system without understanding the political and legal institutions and practices of the country and the cultural and historical environment from which it emerged. The size and mix of the population, its ethnic, racial and religious composition, and the level of economic equality, all help shape the health care system of a country. Each of our countries has its own character – a certain combination of features that sets it apart. Although far from an in-depth analysis of each country, this overview demonstrates that each provides a distinct setting for the emergence of its health care system over time. Interestingly, in their analysis of 92 countries covering the 1970 to 2005 period, Bergh and Nilsson (2010) found that economic globalization has a robust positive effect on life expectancy, even when controlling for income, nutritional intake, literacy, number of physicians and other factors, that holds even when the sample is restricted to low-income countries. 'For economic globalization, evidence suggests it is, indeed, good for living' (2010: 1200).

Chapter 1 suggested that there are strong forces that might be leading to a convergence of policies across countries. In this brief overview of the context of health policy in ten countries, although they are all affluent, developed countries they bring with them a divergent set of structural and value systems that are valuable for comparative purposes in the following substantive chapters. While these factors certainly cannot explain all the differences or similarities among these countries, they help delineate some of the anomalies that will arise out of the more in-depth analysis of these health care systems that follows.

Chapter 3

Funding, Provision and Governance

Health care is often thought of as a system, which consists of a range of sub-systems. Among these, the sub-systems of funding, provision and governance are central for understanding health policy comparatively. The sub-system of *funding* is concerned with raising financial resources and allocating monies to the providers of health care. Health care can be funded from a range of sources, from taxes and social insurance contributions to private insurance premiums and out-of-pocket payments by patients. Funding, however, is about more than the technicalities of raising and allocating financial resources. Funding is also a pointer to power, and control of funding is a major resource in health policy.

The sub-system of *provision* focuses on the delivery of health services. Health systems provide a range of services, and patients have varying levels of choice when using health services, for instance among individual doctors or different care settings. The delivery of health services is based on the health workforce comprising different professional groups (discussed in Chapter 5), in the hands of different types of providers including public and private, profit or non-profit, and hospitals, ambulatory or primary health care (PHC) and long-term care (LTC) providers (discussed in Chapter 6). The mix of providers makes the provision of health care more or less publicly integrated.

The sub-systems of funding and provision, in turn, form the basis of the sub-system of *governance*. Governance describes the modes of coordinating health systems and their multiple actors across, above and beyond the formal government, and including numerous levels and areas of governing. Governance is accompanied by many tensions among public and private, professional and organizational interests, self-governing professional provider groups, and the centre and localities. As governments tend to play an important role in health systems, governance can also be thought of as government capacity or authority. A systems-based governance approach is therefore particularly useful and, as Brown and Harrison note, 'capable of addressing the interdependencies of factors ... necessary for achieving sustainable solutions' (2013: 11; see also Greer *et al.*, 2015; Kuhlmann *et al.*, 2015a; Kuhlmann and Larsen, 2015).

In a comparative context, health systems are often grouped under specific typologies of health systems, as discussed in Chapter 1. The typologies present models of funding, providing and governing health care in the form of distinct ideal types (Burau and Blank, 2006; Burau *et al.*, 2015). The implicit assumption of many typologies is that certain models of funding are associated with certain models of provision. For example, the funding of health care from taxation is said to make for public provision of health care. As the analysis below shows, this is the case in the health systems in some countries. In others, however, individual health systems combine various models of funding and provision, and increasingly rely on a mix of several models of funding or provision (Blank and Cheng, 2015; Burau *et al.*, 2015). In addition to system characteristics, a range of external factors, such as austerity politics or transnational/global challenges, impact on funding and create dissimilar pressures for reform with distinct outcomes (Frenk and Moon, 2013; Penno *et al.*, 2013; Reeves *et al.*, 2014). This directs the attention to the country-specific political contexts in which health systems are embedded as discussed in Chapter 2.

For example, in Britain and Sweden, where health care is predominantly publicly funded and provided, government looms large in the governance of health systems. At the same time, the specific features of health governance reflect the fact that the wider political system and health governance in Britain is more centralized than in Sweden. Similarly, New Zealand's NHS favours a more hierarchical, integrated approach, with clear lines of accountability, and central government capacity to define objectives and monitor developments (Ettelt *et al.*, 2012). The factors that lead to differences among countries coexist with the common pressures across health systems including ageing populations, shortage of health workers, advances in medical technology and increasing demands from patients raised in Chapter 1.

This chapter provides an overview of the funding, provision and governance of health care and shows how they are shaped both by country-specific contexts and by universal pressures. An important aim will be to assess the relative usefulness of the typologies of the different types of health systems. Against this backdrop, comparison is largely limited to high-income countries for two reasons. Firstly, there is a severe lack of data that would allow for a more comprehensive comparative approach as outlined in Chapter 1. Secondly, emergent schemes of universal health care coverage in middle-income countries combine elements from divergent health care systems in various ways (Wendt *et al.*, 2013; Giovanella and Faria, 2015; Reich and Takemi, 2015), while low-income countries often also rely on international organizations and donors. An international overview of funding illustrates the sharply contrasting circumstances in resource-rich and resource-poor countries (Dieleman *et al.*,

2016; Evans and Pablos-Méndez, 2016). These conditions constrain comparative analysis across a range of high- to low-income countries. We will come back to the challenges in the final section.

Comparing funding of health systems

Funding offers a good starting point for looking at health systems comparatively and provides a first indicator of the relative size of health systems and the role of governments in health systems (Wendt, 2015). Table 3.1 ranks the countries by their per capita expenditure on health care. The USA ranks first and spends more than twice that of the NHS systems in Australia, New Zealand and the UK, and nearly twice as much as the most expensive social insurance system (the Netherlands). On the other end, Taiwan is the by far lowest spender followed by Singapore. All countries have increased spending within the five-year period, although Sweden and the USA are highest with the absolute increases more than three times that of New Zealand, Singapore and Taiwan. When looking at the relative increases, Sweden shows the highest percentage followed by Taiwan, while the Netherlands ranks lowest followed by New Zealand. Despite the variety in expenditure increases, the ranking of countries remains quite stable.

Table 3.2 provides the health care expenditure as a percentage of GDP. In 2015, most countries spent around 9 to 11 per cent of their GDP on

Table 3.1 *Per capita expenditure on health care in US dollars, 2010, 2015*

Country	2010	2015	Trend	Percentage of increase
USA	7,929	9,451	+ 1,522	19.2
Netherlands	4,671	5,343	+ 672	14.39
Germany	4,359	5,267	+ 908	20.83
Australia	3,607	4,420	+ 813	22.54
Sweden	3,544	5,228	+1,684	47.52
Japan	3,205	4,150	+ 945	28.24
New Zealand	3,020	3,590	+ 570	18.87
UK	3,036	4,015	+ 979	32.25
Singapore	2,273	2,752	+ 479	21.1
Taiwan	950	1,370	+ 420	44.21

Sources: Data from OECD (2016a); Singapore: WHO, 2015b; Taiwan (extrapolated from National Health Insurance Administration, 2015).

Table 3.2   *Health care expenditure as a percentage of GDP, 1975–2015*

Country	1975	1980	1985	1990	1995	2000	2005	2010[a]	2015
Australia	6.5	6.3	6.6	6.9	7.4	8.3	8.8	9.1	9.3
Germany	8.4	8.4	8.8	8.3	10.1	10.3	10.7	11.6	11.1
Japan	5.7	6.5	6.7	6.0	6.9	7.7	8.2	9.5	11.2
Netherlands	7.0	7.4	7.3	8.0	8.3	8.0	9.2	12.0	10.8
New Zealand	6.7	5.9	5.1	6.9	7.2	7.7	8.9	10.1	9.4
Singapore	n/a	n/a	n/a	2.8	n/a	2.9	3.8	4.0	4.6
Sweden	7.5	8.9	8.5	8.2	8.0	8.2	9.2	9.6	11.1
Taiwan	3.8	4.8	n/a	5.5	5.7	5.9	6.3	6.4	6.9
UK	5.5	5.6	5.9	6.0	6.9	7.2	8.2	9.6	9.8
USA	7.9	8.7	10.0	11.9	13.3	13.2	15.2	17.6	16.9

n/a = not available.
[a] Data for Australia and Japan are from 2009 and Taiwan from 2008.

Sources: Data from OECD (2008a, 2012, 2016a); Singapore (Singapore Ministry of Health, 2016); Taiwan (National Health Insurance Administration, 2015).

health care, while the USA was a high outlier at 16.9 per cent and Singapore the lowest at 4.6 per cent. Besides the overall level of funding, the sources of funding give an initial indication of the kinds of health system with which we are dealing. As Table 3.3 illustrates, all health systems, except Singapore and the USA, are predominantly publicly funded. Most

Table 3.3   *Public expenditure on health care as a percentage of total expenditure on health care, 1975–2015*

	1975	1980	1985	1990	1995	2000	2005	2010	2015
Australia	73.6	62.6	70.6	66.2	65.8	67.0	67.0	68.6	66.7
Germany	79.0	78.7	77.4	76.2	81.6	79.7	77.0	76.8	85.0
Japan	72.0	71.3	70.7	77.6	83.0	81.3	82.7	81.95	84.9
Netherlands	67.9	69.4	70.8	67.1	71.0	63.1	62.5	87.0	80.7
New Zealand	73.7	88.0	87.0	82.4	77.2	78.0	77.4	83.2	79.7
Singapore	69.9	68.0	n/a	n/a	n/a	26.0	38.5	36.3	37.7
Sweden	90.2	92.5	90.4	89.9	86.6	84.9	81.7	81.0	83.7
Taiwan	n/a	44.4	n/a	46.1	n/a	63.8	62.5	64.8	n/a
UK	91.1	89.4	85.8	83.6	83.9	80.9	86.9	83.2	79.0
USA	40.9	41.2	39.6	39.4	45.3	43.7	45.1	48.2	49.4

Sources: Data from OECD (2016a); Taiwan Ministry of Health and Welfare (2013); Singapore Ministry of Health (2016).

Table 3.4 *Sources of funding as a percentage of health care expenditure, 2014**

	Public funding		Private funding		
	Government	Social security	Out-of-pocket	Private insurance	Other
Japan	8.5	75.8	12.7	2.2	0.8
Sweden	83.4	0.0	15.5	0.6	0.6
USA	26.1	23.1	11.5	34.4	4.8

*or nearest year.

Sources: Data from OECD (2016a).

countries, especially the social insurance systems, reflect an increased public share over time, while the NHS systems in Australia, Sweden and the UK have faced a decline. Singapore demonstrates an even more dramatic decrease in public funding as a result of moving to the Medisave scheme, thus theoretically shifting to an individual funding base (Mossialos *et al.*, 2016). Although the public share in Singapore is again on the increase, in 2008 it did not even reach half of the share spent in 1975.

More fine-grained information is available for three different types of health care systems, including Sweden, Japan and the USA. Table 3.4 distinguishes between public expenditure by governments and compulsory social security schemes, and private expenditure from out-of-pocket payments, voluntary insurance and other private funds (non-profit institutions and enterprise funding schemes).

Looking at the public sources of funding, it is striking that countries seem to rely principally either on social security schemes, as in the case of Japan, or on government funding, as in the case of Sweden. The exception is the USA, where private insurance is the main source of private funding and the sources of funding are much more diverse. The reasons for these differences in the sources of funding are analysed in more detail in the following sections.

Models of funding health services

Three basic models of funding can be distinguished: the NHS model with a commitment to public funding; public funding through social insurance; and private insurance with an emphasis on individual responsibility. As introduced in Chapter 1, NHS models are the archetype of a publicly funded health system. Health care is predominantly funded from taxation and is available to every resident. Public funding results in universal access. Britain is a classic example of this type of public funding and significantly, co-payments are low (Boyle, 2011; Cylus *et al.*, 2015). In contrast, other countries are actively supporting the expansion of private health insurance. Australia is a case in point where about 45 per cent of the population has private insurance (Doorslaer *et al.*, 2008).

Social insurance, another form of public funding, is a hybrid and combines two contrasting principles of organizing health care: the insurance is paid for by independent institutions but is publicly mandated (Freeman, 2000). As noted in Chapter 1, Taiwan, with its national insurance plan, is an exception in that there is a single insurance plan under governmental control. Unlike private insurance, social health insurance is based on the principle of social solidarity. This represents a redistributive policy between high- and low-risk patients as well as between high and low earners. Dependants of employees (i.e. non-earning spouses and children) are also covered, thus in effect ensuring universal coverage of the population (Blank and Cheng, 2015).

The pioneer of social insurance was the German health system. Health care is funded by contributions that are largely paid equally by employers and employees as a fixed percentage of the monthly salary. Membership is compulsory for everyone with annual earnings below a certain ceiling. Social health insurance is administered by private, non-profit funds, which operate under public law. Employees earning above the ceiling and the self-employed also must be covered by an insurance plan, but can choose to stay with social health insurance or join a private health insurance scheme. Private insurance accounts for approximately 10 per cent. Other sources of private funding are co-payments. Co-payments for drugs were introduced in 1977 and have increased regularly, and with the health reforms from 2000 onwards the range of services under the reimbursement scheme are defined by the self-administered body of the statutory insurance system, the Federal Joint Committee, and subject to periodical revision (Advisory Council on the Assessment of Developments in the Health Care System, 2014; Busse and Blümel, 2014; Wendt, 2015).

Compared to national health services, social insurance funds generally are characterized by a closer interface between the public and the private sectors, but in some countries the role of the latter is much more marked. For example, in Taiwan social insurance accounts for 67 per cent of total health expenditure, while direct patient co-payments account for 21 per cent. Similarly, in Japan all 5,000 plus insurance plans are (to varying degrees) characterized by co-payments (Tatara and Okamoto, 2009).

Countries that predominantly rely on private insurance put considerable emphasis on individual responsibility, yet private funding generally coexists with public funding, particularly for designated groups such as the poor and elderly. The USA is the archetypal example of this system of funding and characterized by high complexity. Outside of programmes for the elderly and some disabled persons, the US health system is provided by thousands of largely for-profit insurance companies, except for Blue Cross-Blue Shield and a few other non-profit providers. In 2011, an estimated 45 million people had no insurance coverage, although the Affordable Care Act promised to reduce this by half (Hacker, 2011; for an overview, see Saltman and van Ginneken, 2013. Also see Box 3.1).

The importance of private insurance is not the only gauge of the emphasis on individual responsibility. For example, in Singapore, Medisave, the individual savings scheme managed centrally by the Central Provident Fund (CPF), relies on risk pooling even more limited than in ordinary private insurance schemes in the USA (Okma *et al.*, 2010). Unlike other compulsory savings plans, it largely rejects a cross-generational subsidy and instead is moulded around the life cycle where each person builds up her/his own reserves towards their own ill health (Reisman, 2006). Complemented by MediShield Life and Medifund, governmental funding has been gradually expanded, however, and the 2013 and 2015 reforms have even doubled it in some areas. The programmes now include, for example, long-term care (see Chapter 6) and screening, reduced out-of-pocket payment and expanded criteria for eligibility that have benefited low- and middle-income groups (Mossialos *et al.*, 2016).

Box 3.1   Medicare in the USA: public insurance in a private system

Medicare is a public insurance for the elderly with over 45 million beneficiaries, administered by the federal government and consisting of three parts. Part A is compulsory and covers hospital care funded through social security taxes paid by working citizens. Part B is voluntary and covers other costs including doctors' bills and outpatient hospital treatment and is funded by premiums paid by enrollees with substantial federal subsidies. Under the traditional programme, which covers 86 per cent of Medicare beneficiaries, payments to providers are determined by complex prospective payment systems that include a high level of control over the price component, but little leverage over the volume of services. The remaining beneficiaries are enrolled in the Medicare+Choice programme, under which private health plans are paid a monthly capitation payment for each enrollee based on the amount Medicare spends per beneficiary in the geographic area served by the plan. Under this system, the payment by Medicare to plans is fixed, and each health plan establishes its own methods for administering benefits and paying providers within parameters established by federal regulation. In 2003, the Medicare Prescription Drug, Improvement and Modernization Act became law and created Medicare Part D to provide drug coverage to the elderly, through private, stand-alone drug plans (Centers for Medicare and Medicaid Services, 2009b).

Control of funding and pressures for reform

As Figure 3.1 suggests, health care tends to be funded by a mix of public and private sources that reflect predominant types of funding and other, country-specific factors. National health services, with their commitment to universality of access, get most of their funding from taxes. Britain and Sweden are classical examples of this type of publicly funded health system while Australia and New Zealand combine tax funding and elements of private funding, with over 20 per cent of funds coming from private insurance and out-of-pocket payments.

Social insurance systems are hybrids and, except in Taiwan, money is raised from independent insurance funds that are publicly mandated and founded on the principle of social solidarity. Germany (together with Japan and the Netherlands) continues to be the classic example of this type of funding: social insurance contributions account for the bulk of health care expenditure, although even here increasingly there are elements of private/privatized funding (Wendt, 2015). The latter is even more prevalent in Taiwan, where social insurance coexists with strong elements of private funding from out-of-pocket payments (Blank and Cheng, 2015). Finally, health systems where private insurance dominates place strong emphasis on individual responsibility and rely more heavily on private funds. In Singapore, a highly individualized compulsory savings account is predominant, whereas the USA relies on a mixture of traditional private and public insurance (Wendt, 2015; Mossialos *et al.*, 2016).

As noted earlier, how funds are raised and allocated is a pointer to power. Different types of funding result in different types of control, and

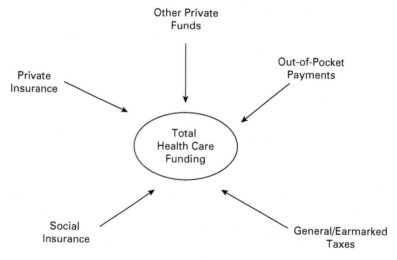

Figure 3.1   *Sources of health care funding*

different types of control lead to different types of pressures for reform. Public funding means public control and can be expected to be strongest in NHS systems, since they are chiefly funded by taxes. The prime example is Britain, where the total NHS expenditure is set by Treasury and is part of the government's spending reviews. Once the overall spending level has been set, the Department of Health determines the funds allocated to Clinical Commissioning Groups (CCC) as the providers of primary health care and purchasers of acute care and other forms of care. Public control of funding can also be more decentralized as in Sweden, where public control rests with the county councils (Anell *et al.*, 2012). On specific occasions, this may be supported through central intervention, underlining the national character of the health system. For example, on two occasions the Swedish national government has limited the level of taxes that can be raised by county councils (Glenngård *et al.*, 2005).

In national health systems, problems of controlling total expenditure are practically unknown. Instead, the central challenge is to meet the growing demands for health care within a fixed and tight budget. Health reforms over the last 20 years can be read as attempts to make limited resources go further and have focused on increasing micro-efficiency and competition. Although competition promises to provide more and/or better health services without spending more money, there are limits to this approach to reform: developments in Britain testify to this as the country became a victim of its own success in terms of cost containment. Beginning in 2000, an external review into the funding of the NHS provided powerful leverage for a sustained increase in NHS funding to match international spending levels (Ham, 2009). Between 1999 and 2005 this led to an annual growth rate 7.3 per cent above inflation and as Klein notes this was 'more than double the average in previous decades and unprecedented in the history of the NHS' (2006: 409) (for details, see Cylus *et al.*, 2015). Most recently, there is renewed concern that funding might decrease following economic pressures after 'Brexit' and the UK's opting out of the European Union.

In contrast with NHS systems, public control of funding is weaker in health systems that rely on social insurance and this typically manifests itself in problems of controlling total health expenditure. A classical case is Germany where health reform has long been viewed as an attempt to halt the 'cost explosion'. Pressures have increased from different sides. A progressively lower proportion of GDP goes to wages, reflecting larger profits by employers and wage increases below productivity as well as unemployment. Also, a greater share of wages is either exempt from contribution or exceeds the maximum ceiling up to which contributions must be paid. Moreover, traditionally, power over funding has been decentralized and fragmented. In part, this is typical of the organizational complexity of social insurance systems, but, in the case of Germany, is compounded by federalism (Busse and Blümel, 2014; Wendt, 2015).

Even social insurance schemes allow for some control of funding and, indeed, this seems to be a common trend when looking at recent reforms across countries. For example, Japan has a long tradition of successful public control, with all insurance funds and providers strictly regulated by the government and all health care payments made under a national fee schedule (Box 3.2). Moreover, like Taiwan (Blank and Cheng, 2015), all billing and payment is centralized through the payment fund of National Health Insurance, which reviews all bills submitted and has the power to reduce payments to minimize fraud. Similarly, in the Netherlands, the (income-related) contribution rates for social insurance schemes are fixed by the central government. In addition, private health insurance has also been subject to extensive regulation such as requirements for pooling and a standard insurance package for high-risk employees. The recent reforms continued this trend and integrated private insurance into a single, universal social insurance scheme (Schäfer *et al.*, 2010; Kroneman *et al.*, 2016; for a similar development in Germany see Wendt, 2015).

Systematic and effective public control of funding is weakest in health systems that rely on private insurance. The USA is a case in point. As seen earlier, expenditure is much higher than it is in all other countries and has significantly increased over time. Public control of expenditure is also undermined by the fragmentation of insurance funds and provider organizations, together with the federalist structure of the USA. In the 1980s, the government attempted to control Medicare/ Medicaid spending by initiating diagnosis-related groups (DRGs), a system under which

---

Box 3.2   Japan: low costs, high usage

In Japan, fees for all health care services are set every two years through negotiations between the Health Ministry and physicians. The negotiations determine the fee for every medical procedure and medication, and fees are identical across the country. If physicians attempt to game the system by ordering extra procedures to generate income, the government can lower them at the next round of fee setting. For example, the fee for MRI was lowered by 35 per cent in 2002. As the result of this strict fee structure, costs in Japan tend to be quite low compared to other developed countries. For instance, in 2009 an MRI of the neck region cost only US$98 in Japan compared to about $1,500 in the USA. At the same time, Japanese patients like medical technologies such as CT scans, and they receive MRIs at a per capita rate eight times higher than the British and twice that of Americans. Japan also has three times as many hospital beds and over four times as many hospital visits per capita as the USA (Tatara and Okamoto, 2009).

each category of treatment has a scheduled payment. After the initial stabilization of health care expenditures following the initiation of DRGs and managed care in the late 1980s to mid-1990s, costs rose rapidly again far exceeding general inflation rates. This is especially the case for Medicare/Medicaid where real growth can approach double figures annually, despite DRGs and passage of the Affordable Care Act (Blank, 2012; Saltman and van Ginneken, 2013; Wendt, 2015).

The country examples above focus on direct public control of funding, but more indirect controls also exist and Singapore offers an interesting example. Here, public control is directed towards influencing individual citizens' demands for and consumption of health care resources. The controls are so successful that in 2000, the WHO ranked Singapore as the most effective health system in Asia and sixth in the world, despite the country spending only 3.1 per cent of its GDP on health care (*Straits Times*, 2000). Participation in the Medisave scheme is compulsory and caps on contribution rates, together with very high co-payments, have given government firm control of expenditure. The highly centralized political structure of Singapore and widespread public approval of the regime ensures that government control is largely effective (Ham, 2010; Mossialos *et al.*, 2016).

Health care settings and patient choice

A common denominator of otherwise different health care systems is the dominance of hospital settings and medical 'curing' approaches, reflecting the allocation of health care resources and the powerful role of doctors (see Chapter 5). As Table 3.5 suggests, medical health services can be distinguished as to the specificity and the locality of care delivered. Primary health care (PHC) is less specialized than hospital (secondary) care, and long-term care (LTC) is less specialized than PHC. This distinction corresponds to different localities of care delivery. Typically, PHC

Table 3.5   *Types and settings of health services*

	Ambulatory settings	Hospital settings
Primary care	Services provided by GPs working in their own practices or in health centres.	Services provided by GPs in long-term care nursing homes.
Acute care	Services provided by specialists working in their own practices or health centres.	Services provided by specialists on wards or in outpatient departments in hospitals.

services are delivered in ambulatory settings (such as doctors' practices or health centres) whereas acute care services are delivered in (inpatient) hospital settings or in outpatient departments of hospitals. In contrast, chronic care services have traditionally been less medically oriented and are delivered in a range of LTC settings, from people's homes to day centres and nursing homes (see Chapter 6).

As Table 3.6 suggests, in most of these health systems hospital care accounts for the single largest share of health care expenditure, followed by ambulatory care. The Netherlands is an exception; here LTC is higher than ambulatory care (see Chapter 6). Germany has a slightly higher share of ambulatory care in relation to hospital care, reflecting the policy goals of strengthening ambulatory care (Advisory Council for the Concerted Action in Health Care, 2009), while in New Zealand expenditure reveals a priority of ambulatory care.

Patient access to different types of health care varies among countries, reflecting different levels of patient choice (Reibling and Wendt, 2012). Choice can mean different things, such as the ability to choose a generalist or a specialist doctor as the first point of contact or the ability to choose among different hospitals and ambulatory care settings. A broad distinction can be drawn among complete choice, extensive choice and the GP model, where choice is restricted. The level of patient choice reflects the way health services are organized, but also explicit decisions about the appropriate level of patient choice.

Taiwan offers virtually unlimited choice, which reflects the combination of a publicly funded NHI and the absence of formal referral

Table 3.6 *Expenditure on different settings of health care as a percentage of health care expenditure, 2014**

	Hospital	Ambulatory care	Long-term care
Australia	43.5	29.5	n/a
Germany	29.5	31.1	8.9
Japan	41.3	28.2	8.5
Netherlands	34.4	17.1	26.1
New Zealand	27.7	33.9	9.9
Sweden	38.6	24.2	18.5
Taiwan	39.6	34.1	n/a
UK	37.9	19.2	6.4
USA	33.8	30.7	5.4

* Or latest available data: 2013 for Australia and Japan, 2008 for Taiwan, 2009 for New Zealand.

Sources: Data from OECD (2016a); New Zealand data from OECD (2011); Taiwan data from Bureau of National Health Insurance (2008).

requirements. Thus, patients are free to choose any NHI-contacted hospital to receive inpatient or ambulatory care. Thus, the health service market in Taiwan is highly competitive, even more so than in the USA, and in practice all Taiwanese hospitals, regardless of ownership, behave as private businesses and keenly compete for patients. As patients tend to prefer larger hospitals, the expansion of choice has been at the expense of many small-scale hospitals (Blank and Cheng, 2015).

Next to Taiwan, Singapore offers the widest choice within the selection of our countries, but one that is restricted by the availability of sufficient Medisave funds. Patients with an active Medisave savings account are free to go directly to the hospital (private or public) of their choice and choose the level of subsidy they receive in public hospitals. In relation to PHC services, patients can choose among private practices and government-subsidized health centres. MSAs can also be used to buy private insurance or MediShield coverage (Asher *et al.*, 2008). Paradoxically, the high level of individual responsibility also limits choice when it comes to expensive or long-term care, because few patients are wealthy enough to afford such care and exercise free choice. Although Medisave contributes to the 'cultural rhetoric' of personal responsibility for health care, Barr (2001) argues that at its core the Singapore system of health funding represents a 'strict rationing of health services' by wealth.

The health systems in Germany and, to a lesser extent, Sweden also offer extensive individual choice. In Germany, patients are free to choose any doctor working in ambulatory care, but require a referral for hospital care. This leads to extensive choice as both generalists and specialists work in office-based settings. In Sweden, patients can choose between using a health centre or going directly to a specialist outpatient department in a hospital. However, in the case of the latter waiting times tend to be longer and co-payments are higher. Interestingly, patient choice has been broadened over the last two decades. In 2009, patient choice was further expanded; in fact, it became mandatory as did the right of accredited private providers to open practices (Anell *et al.*, 2012; Isaksson *et al.*, 2016). In contrast, in Germany efforts are mounting to strengthen gatekeeping mechanisms, although on a voluntary basis, through financial incentives for both doctors and patients (Reibling and Wendt, 2012; Busse and Blümel, 2014). Significantly, each county has developed its own model, reflecting a 'soft law in the shadow of hierarchy' approach to policy making, as Fredriksson *et al.* (2012) call it. Taken together, this reflects a strong commitment to equity and quality that contrasts with Britain and the Netherlands, where patients' choice often has been curtailed in the name of efficiency (Saltman, 1998: 164).

The GP model offers the lowest level of patient choice. Patients must register with a general practitioner (sometimes in their area) and it is the GP who refers patients to specialist out- and inpatient services in hospitals. This gives GPs a strong gatekeeping function. The GP model is widespread among health systems in industrialized countries (Reibling and Wendt, 2012). It even applies to countries like Australia, New Zealand and the Netherlands, which are committed to individualism, with significant components of private funding. In their comparison of seven countries, Schoen *et al.* (2007) found that a very high proportion (88 per cent) of Australians reported that they had a doctor or GP whom they regularly see. Under New Zealand arrangements, which unlike Australia provide incentives for patient enrolment, however, only 8.3 per cent of patients reported no affiliation with a single primary care provider (Jatrana and Crampton, 2009). Another multinational study reported that 69.8 per cent of UK patients but only 8 per cent of US patients had their regular physician for six years or longer (McRae *et al.*, 2010).

The boundaries between different types of choice have become increasingly blurred over recent years. As Reibling and Wendt, in a comparison of OECD countries, conclude, there is a diverging trend of reform, 'with some traditionally restrictive countries offering more provider choice and other countries limiting the choice of providers as a result of management reforms' (2012: 489).

Welfare mixes in the provision of health care

Health systems allow for different levels of patient choice, reflecting the ways in which health services are organized as well as specific decisions about the appropriate level of patient choice. This partly corresponds to the principles underpinning different types of health systems. The principles of equity, social solidarity and individual responsibility also inform the welfare mix in the provision of health care: who the providers of health care are (see Box 3.3).

The differences in welfare mix apply primarily to hospitals, whereas the situation in ambulatory care is more uniform. In most countries, doctors working in ambulatory care are independent practitioners, who either practise privately or who are contracted to provide publicly funded medical services. Reflecting their independent status, doctors are typically paid on a capitation or a fee-for-service basis, as discussed in more detail in the next section.

The provision of hospital care has traditionally been least mixed in national health services, where public hospitals provide most beds and where private hospitals are few. In New Zealand, for example, there are 80 public hospital facilities, which operate under the direction of 21 community-focused and elected District Health Boards (DHBs), the regional administrative tier of the Department of Health (New Zealand Ministry of Health, 2008). Public hospitals derive their entire income

---

Box 3.3   Welfare mix: mixed meanings and policies

As a concept 'welfare mix' refers to the diverse ways in which health services can be provided. Welfare mix is concerned with the division of labour between the public, private, voluntary and informal sectors. Because the provision of health care is always mixed to a greater or lesser extent, welfare mix is also a descriptor of how services are delivered in individual health systems. Finally, as a political programme, welfare mix challenges the notion that public provision is always best (Evers and Svetlik, 1993). For some, welfare mix is seen to serve better the needs of increasingly diverse societies. Others argue that a more mixed provision of health services is more cost efficient. Different health systems typically have different welfare mixes. Public funding through taxes often accompanies public ownership, leading to a highly publicly integrated provision of health services. Social insurance combines social solidarity with a commitment to individualism/subsidiarity. Public and private providers tend to exist side by side, creating complex and less well-integrated structures of health provision. The same is often true for health systems that predominantly rely on private insurance. In both social and private insurance systems, the welfare mix in health care provision comes naturally, whereas in national health services the welfare mix has been closely associated with market-oriented reforms.

---

from government funding agencies. A few private hospitals, primarily Southern Cross, provide acute health care services with costs met by individuals and/or private insurance. Significantly, only a few DHBs have contracted with private hospitals to provide services.

As part of New Public Management reforms (see Box 3.4) and their focus on the virtues of market mechanisms, the provision of health services has become more ambiguous in countries with NHS models. For example, in Britain health reforms since the late 1990s have placed a renewed emphasis on the private sector and aimed to increase its role in the NHS. This includes independent treatment centres for specialist operations, private GP practices, the expansion of contracting out of ancillary services such as medical supplies, and the so-called Private Finance Initiative (Taylor-Gooby and Mitton, 2008). As mentioned earlier, in Sweden, PHC provision is now open to private providers (Isaksson *et al.*, 2016). Therefore, countries with national health services are moving closer to the welfare mix that has traditionally existed in social insurance systems, such as those in Germany and the Netherlands (Reibling and Wendt, 2012; Busse and Blümel, 2014; Kroneman *et al.*, 2016). Market-based health systems, too, are characterized by high levels of welfare mixes, and, as compared to social insurance systems, private for-profit hospitals play an even more prominent role (American Hospital Association, 2009).

Box 3.4   New Public Management (NPM)

NPM is a management philosophy adopted by many governments since the 1980s to modernize the public sector by shifting emphasis from traditional public administration to public management. It is a broad term that draws on management techniques and practices drawn mainly from the private sector and describes the wave of public sector reforms throughout the world over the last three decades. Based on public choice and managerial schools of thought, NPM seeks to enhance the efficiency of the public sector and moderate the control that government has over it. The main, and controversial, assumption of the NPM reforms is that more market orientation in the public sector will lead to greater cost efficiency for governments, without having negative side effects on other objectives. NPM, then, reflected a change in attitude regarding public administration. Key elements include various forms of decentralizing management within public services (e.g. the creation of autonomous agencies and devolution of budgets and financial control), increasing use of markets and competition in the provision of public services (e.g. contracting out and other market-type mechanisms), and increasing emphasis on performance, outputs and customer orientation.

Medical payment and governance

How doctors are paid, which is linked to new forms of performance management and financial incentives, is an important element of governance (McDonald, 2015; Kirkpatrick *et al.*, 2016) and at the same time an indicator of professional power. Power here refers to the privilege of doctors to be rewarded in accordance with the medical treatment they provide. Systems of remuneration can either sustain or constrain this privilege, which in part can also account for variations in payments across countries (for an overview, see Fujisawa and Lafortune, 2008).

The fee-for-service system, under which doctors are paid for the individual services rendered to patients, supports this type of medical privilege most extensively. In contrast, with payment by salary there is little connection between the services rendered and the payment received by doctors. Between these two extremes is payment based on capitation, whereby doctors are paid a lump sum based on the number of patients registered with their practice. Typically, hospital doctors receive a salary, whereas office-based doctors are paid on either a fee-for-service or a capitation basis. In addition to the systems of payment, another indication of medical power is the role of doctors in the determination of fee schedules and payment structures.

As Table 3.7 illustrates, the payment of doctors is diverse and includes unexpected cases, such as salaried office-based doctors in public health

Table 3.7 *Types of payment for different types of doctor*

	Predominantly salaried	Predominantly capitation payments	Predominantly fee-for-service payments
Ambulatory care doctors	Singapore (public)	Britain Netherlands New Zealand Sweden	Australia Germany Japan Netherlands Singapore (private) Taiwan USA[a]
Hospital doctors	Australia Britain Germany New Zealand Singapore (public) Sweden Taiwan		Japan Singapore (private) USA

[a] The USA is undergoing a shift due to HMO movement but is still fee-for-service based.

centres (in Singapore) and hospital doctors paid on a fee-for-service basis (in Japan, the USA and in private hospitals in Singapore). Significantly, in most cases pay is not directly related to the volume of services, and even where this is the case there are limitations on payments. If power refers to the privilege of doctors to be rewarded by the medical treatment they provide, medical power is restricted.

Concerns for cost containment are likely to direct the attention to systems of remuneration, especially in countries where doctors are paid by the volume of services provided, including Australia, Germany, Japan, Taiwan and the USA. Classical examples of the fee-for-service system are Germany and the USA, which also illustrate its problems. In Germany, the Uniform Value Scale (*Einheitlicher Bewertungsmassstab*) lists the services that are reimbursed by health insurance funds, together with their relative weights for reimbursement which are measured in points. Since 2009, the monetary value of each point is fixed and there are top-ups for high quality care (Fujisawa and Lafortune, 2008). This constrains the total expenditure on ambulatory care, but not automatically the incentive to maximize the volume of services at the level of the individual practice.

The fee-for-service system in Germany remains problematic from the perspective of cost containment and has undergone several changes in recent years. Fee negotiations take place within legally set limits and doctors may be subject to utilization review, either randomly or if their levels of service provision are significantly higher than those of their colleagues; doctors are also made accountable if they exceed a fixed budget. This has been accompanied by measures to change the system of payment itself, including rewards for particular specialities (GPs in particular) and specific services (e.g. counselling rather than medical testing), together with blanket payments for certain sets of services.

The undesirable consequences of a fee-for-service system can be compounded by other factors. In Taiwan, for example, the combination of high levels of patient choice and cultural patterns that favour medical visits and pharmaceutical use has led to over-usage (Box 3.5). Outside of hospitals, the NHI pays providers on a fee-for-service basis, with patients free to choose among providers. Because NHI coverage is extended to virtually all physicians in all specialities, patients are in the position to pick and choose. Even after the introduction of measures to prevent duplication of services, the patient habit of doctor shopping persists. Moreover, medicines are prescribed in almost all visits and constitute over 25 per cent of the entire national medical expenditure (Wen *et al.*, 2008). The overuse of physician visits and prescribing of redundant medication are

---

Box 3.5   The culture of informal payments to doctors

One pattern that sets Taiwan apart from other developed countries is that Taiwanese physicians see almost twice as many patients per week as their US counterparts. Consequently, Taiwan has the highest average number of outpatient visits per capita in the world at 14 per year (over 26 for those over age 65). For generations, patients in Taiwan have developed a physician usage culture that includes consulting physicians for minor ailments, visiting many physicians to find one that will do what the patient wants, and finding and using the most popular doctor, even when he or she does not specialize in what the patient needs. A unique cultural factor is the practice of patients giving informal payments to physicians to get better service. In their study, Chiu *et al.* (2007) found that both before and after the introduction of the NHI, Taiwanese newspapers portrayed informal payments as appropriate means to secure access to better health care. Although the NHI reduced patients' financial barriers to care, it did not change deeply held cultural beliefs that good care depended on the development of a reciprocal sense of obligation between patients and physicians. Although illegal, physicians may also encourage the ongoing use of informal payments to make up revenue lost when the NHI standardized fees and limited income from dispensing medications.

common as result of a lack of gatekeepers (Blank and Cheng, 2015). In 2011, Taiwan tested a capitation model to see if it would help reduce these problems. In their analysis of the pilot programme after one year of implementation, however, Cheng *et al.* (2015) found only minimal impact on health care utilization with no compromise in health care outcomes.

A different approach to constraining expenditure in the fee-for-service system is the so-called system of 'bulk billing' adopted by Australia with the introduction of Medicare in 1984–85. In Australia, doctors' fees are not regulated. Under the bulk billing system of payment, however, a GP can choose to bill the government directly and receive 85 per cent of the scheduled fee, thereby avoiding administrative costs and delay. This also ensures that services are effectively free to the patient at the point of service. However, if the GP chooses not to bulk bill or chooses to charge patients a co-payment, the patient pays the bill and is reimbursed by Medicare for 85 per cent of the scheduled fee (Thomson *et al.*, 2013). Outpatient specialists set their patients' out-of-pocket fee independently, and 'many specialists split their time between private and public practice' (Mossialos *et al.*, 2016: 13).

Controlling doctors' pay in a fee-for-service system is further complicated where the health system is characterized by weak public and central integration. A case in point is the USA, where ambulatory care doctors are paid through a combination of methods, including fee-for-service payments, discounted fees paid by private health plans, capitation rate contracts with private plans, public programmes and direct patient fees. However, the growth of HMOs and other managed care schemes has resulted in changes in the methods of payment away from fee-for-service reimbursement. HMO doctors may be salaried, paid a fee for service, or paid a capitation fee for each person on their list. A variation of the HMO is the Preferred Provider Organization (PPO) in which a limited number of providers – doctors, hospitals and others – agree to provide services to a specific group of people at a negotiated fee-for-service rate that is lower than the normal charge. After a short period of successful price reduction through selective contracting, providers have now developed sufficient power to resist the control mechanisms (Wendt, 2015).

By contrast, in other countries ambulatory care doctors are paid predominantly on a capitation basis, allowing for much more direct control of doctors' remuneration. New Zealand is typical here, and indeed the country moved to capitation payments relatively recently, illustrating the advantages of this type of payment from the point of view of access. In New Zealand, capitation payments coexist with sizeable co-payments, but this is changing. Historically, government subsidies were paid on a fee-for-service basis targeted to low-income and high-risk people, but because the subsidy levels were not sufficiently tied to inflation and because GPs retained the right to set their own levels of co-payments, it resulted in a significant cost barrier to GP services for some people. In an effort to remove or reduce this cost barrier, in 2002 the government introduced the Primary Health Care Strategy to ease access to general practice services and transform publicly funded PHC payments from targeted welfare benefits to universal, risk-rated insurance premium subsidies (Howell, 2005). Yet, unlike hospitals, PHC is largely provided privately (Gauld, 2015).

For many years, Sweden was an example of one of the few countries where most of the ambulatory care doctors were public employees and paid a salary. This was manifested in the high degree of public integration of the health system, and doctors were firmly positioned in what is a very politically controlled health system (Garpenby, 2001). However, in 2003 a third of health centres and practitioners worked in privately run facilities (Glenngård *et al.*, 2005). Health reforms since 2007 have further facilitated primary care for private providers, who in many counties now can operate on par with public providers (Anell *et al.*, 2012; Isaksson *et al.*, 2016; see Chapter 6). This has also had knock-on effects for the remuneration of doctors working in ambulatory care, which has moved away from salaries and towards more mixed systems, combining capitation payments, payment by visit and pay for performance (depending on the individual county).

Unlike ambulatory care doctors, hospital doctors tend to be salaried employees, although in many countries they have the right to treat private patients who represent an alluring source of added income since services are often paid for on a fee-for-service basis and remuneration tends to be high. In Britain, for example, the right to practise privately was a key condition on which hospital doctors agreed to become part of the NHS when it was set up in 1948. Hospital doctors were initially opposed to a tax-funded health service, instead advocating the extension of the existing health insurance system, but they were won over by numerous concessions. Besides private practice and pay beds, they received large increases in salaries for those receiving distinction awards. In 2003, a new contract removed any limit on earnings from private practice and, not surprisingly, the British Medical Association (BMA) described the contract as a 'victory' (Boyle, 2011: 118). Recently, however, dissatisfaction with salary levels is growing, especially among junior doctors. This has provoked intensive debate and strikes (Rimmer, 2016a, 2016b).

There are some countries where hospital doctors are paid on a fee-for-service basis, but these are notable exceptions. In the Netherlands, for example, medical specialists have traditionally been independent practitioners who have 'bought' the right to practise in a hospital and who practise in partnerships. As such, they contracted directly with patients and insurance funds and were reimbursed on a fee-for-service basis separately from hospitals. This changed in 2000, after which doctors began to receive a lump sum directly from the hospital in which they practise. As a result, specialist medical services are now an integral part of the hospital contract and budget (Harrison, 2004), thus potentially providing leverage for hospital managers to exercise greater control over the practice of medical specialists (Trappenburg and De Groot, 2001). This trend has continued and, since 2008, the remuneration of medical specialists has been part of the hospital-wide system of payment based on DRGs (Schäfer *et al.*, 2010; Kroneman *et al.*, 2016).

The involvement of doctors in the process of determining pay is another indication of medical power (Table 3.8). In large part, salaries and capitation/fee-for-service payments are negotiated between doctors and the payers of health services, although there may be some restrictions, as in the Netherlands. Even where the government alone decides, the decision may be based on a broad range of evidence, as in Britain, or be limited in scope, as in Singapore. Significantly, doctors enjoy considerable power relative to pay determination compared to other groups of employees, although they can rarely act alone.

In the case of salaries, the process of pay bargaining involves pay negotiations where medical power depends on the relative strength of unions and employer organizations, together with the overall economic climate. An interesting exception is Singapore, where doctors working in public

Table 3.8   *The involvement of doctors in systems of pay determination**

	Salaries	*Capitation/fee-for-service payments*
Set by government	Britain (with review body as intermediary); Singapore (for doctors in public health facilities); Taiwan (hospitals)	Australia (de facto); Britain (with review body as intermediary); New Zealand (de facto); Taiwan (fixed-fee schedule)
Negotiated between doctors and payers of health services *Set by doctors*	Australia; Germany; New Zealand; Sweden	Germany; Japan; Netherlands (government approval required) Singapore (for doctors in private health facilities)

* The USA has been omitted from this table as the system of pay bargaining is too fragmented.

health facilities are paid based on the civil service pay scale, which is set by government with little input from the medical community.

The situation is more complicated in the case of capitation and fee payments, as they are the basis for many rounds of future remuneration. Negotiations of this type generally require extensive bargaining to reach an agreement. Countries operate different kinds of decision systems, ranging from payments set by government and negotiated with doctors to payments set by doctors themselves. Britain is an example of the first type, and Japan an example of a country where doctors' organizations have more direct influence and negotiate directly with the payers of health services. In relation to OECD countries, Ono *et al.* conclude: 'In countries where physicians work predominately in solo and group practices, there is almost always an element of fee-for-service payments and some capitation-based payments. In countries where physicians work in health centres, salaries play a much more important role' (2016: 145).

Health governance between centre and locality

The diverse ways in which funding and provision are organized lead not only to different policies and pressures for reform, but also to different politics, different relationships between the central and local governments, among government and provider organizations/payers, and among payers and providers themselves. Governance, for its part, does include the regulation of areas such as medical practice and pharmaceuticals, but it is broader than that. It is also concerned with modes of integrating and coordinating health systems and their multiple actors and stakeholder organizations. The need for, and usefulness of, more integrated and 'multi-level' and 'intersectoral' health governance approaches have been illustrated in relation to various areas of health policy and the levels of governance (Greer *et al.*, 2015, 2016; Kuhlmann *et al.*, 2015a).

This section focuses on central integration – the relationships among the different levels of governance. Some health systems are more decentralized than others, reflecting the respective political systems in which they are embedded. Over the last two decades, many health systems have attempted to decentralize governance. This indicates convergence, but offers equally strong indications of persistent differences, not least in terms of dissimilar types of decentralization (Greer and Massad da Fonseca, 2015). Saltman and Bankauskaite (2006) distinguish between fiscal, administrative and political decentralization. Illustrations of variations in the type of decentralization can be seen in the health systems of Sweden and Britain. In both countries, health care is publicly funded and provided, resulting in health systems that are characterized by a high degree of public integration and control. At the same time, important differences exist in relation to the levels of governance.

In Sweden, responsibility for funding and provision rests with the county councils, leading to decentralized health governance. Sweden has a strong tradition of sub-central government and, importantly, a type of sub-central government that defines itself by democratic decision making (Håkansson and Nordling, 1997). In addition, health reforms since the 1950s have systematically decentralized responsibility for health care to the regional level of counties (Saltman and Bergman, 2005). This contrasts with Britain where the publicly funded and provided health service is embedded in a highly centralized political system. The supremacy of central government is compounded by a tradition that sees local government, first and foremost, as a provider of services, described as 'command and control system' (Moran, 1999).

The differences in the degree of central integration can also help to explain differences in moves towards decentralization. In Britain, administrative decentralization is paramount and has occurred as part of the introduction of a quasi-market in health care that was inspired by the NPM paradigm. The present analysis focuses on developments in England, thus the political decentralization following devolution in Scotland and Wales is of less interest. The actors at local level are Primary Care Trusts and hospital trusts and, at regional level, health authorities which are not only creatures of central government but also continue to operate within a highly hierarchical system of health governance. Indeed, central control has increased following the introduction of the internal market. Most prominently the management of performance has become tighter as part of a more explicit 'quality turn' (Harrison, 2004). Not surprisingly, the autonomy of trusts and health authorities is confined to managerial responsibility.

The complex division of labour among different levels of governance has highlighted problems of accountability (Iliffe and Munro, 2000), and the relative balance between central and local levels is subject to reform concepts. For instance, under the previous New Labour government a 'new localism' gave PHC trusts extensive responsibilities and they received over 85 per cent of the NHS budget (Klein, 2006). Hospitals could apply for foundation status, which gave them greater autonomy, including in fundraising, and patients had free choice of provider (Hunter, 2008; Peckham *et al.*, 2008). Similarly, the health reforms introduced by the coalition government in 2012 included several elements of decentralization (Department of Health, 2012a, b, c): the new Clinical Commissioning Groups are smaller than Primary Care Trusts and enjoy greater autonomy; moreover, the same applies to hospitals which are to become foundation trusts. Yet, both commissioners and providers are to be held accountable at the national level by regulatory agencies. Taken together this illustrates a complex interplay between centralization and decentralization (Peckham *et al.*, 2008). As Klein (2010) argues, the dynamics within centre–periphery relations reflect salient tensions inherent in the NHS since its foundation, namely between equity and efficiency on the one hand and democracy on the other.

The case of Britain contrasts with Sweden, where political decentralization occurred in the early 1980s when county councils were given complete control over funding and delivery of services (Anell *et al.*, 2012). Since the beginning of the 1990s, this has been complemented by additional measures as part of moves to deregulate and privatize the health system (Fredriksson and Winblad, 2008). Here, decentralization was a genuine devolution of power that built on traditions of sub-central government, not simply a refocusing of central control as in the case of Britain. This further strengthened the directly democratic character of managerial decision making (Saltman, 1998). Ironically, at the same time, the central level has become increasingly involved. At policy level, specific action programmes have resulted in more direct intervention in service delivery and, at the level of supervision, the National Board of Welfare now has extensive powers to regulate provider organizations, based on national priorities and quality standards (Saltman and Bergman, 2005; Bejerot and Hasselbladh, 2011). There is still high variability among county councils, which can cause inequality in provision. For PHC, a recent evaluation found no signs of increasing inequality, however (Isaksson *et al.*, 2016).

Funding from social insurance results in institutional complexity and often limits the degree of central integration of health systems. For example, in Germany a statutory, joint self-administration of insurance funds and providers is at the centre of health governance, and this form of corporatism operates at different levels. At the local level, providers and insurance funds relate to each other through contracts, which specify the services to be provided and the prices to be paid, including the financing mechanisms. However, local contracts are embedded in a complex system of framework agreements at state and federal level (again between providers and insurance funds) and these, in turn, are embedded in federal legislation, the Social Code Book. Over recent years, these collective contracts have been complemented by specific contracts with individual providers, such as treatment centres comprised of ambulatory care specialists. Here, the insurance funds contract directly with providers without the involvement of the providers' collective organization. This development is part of the introduction of competitive elements in the health system. It has created different forms of contract law, including those for selective contracting between sickness funds and provider organizations to promote new provider models (Groene *et al.*, 2016) as well as a standardized remuneration system as part of the agreements on PHC/family physician-centred care provision (Gerlach and Szecsenyi, 2013).

Corporatism adds further institutional complexity. Corporatism is a unique approach to policy making and has several aspects to it. In the health care context, corporatism hands over certain powers of the state to corporatist self-governing institutions, including insurance funds and provider organizations. As corporatist institutions, they have mandatory membership and enjoy the right to raise their own financial resources as well as the right to negotiate and sign contracts with other corporatist institutions.

In Germany, institutional complexity is shaped by corporatism as a form of procedural subsidiarity and compounded by federalism, which taken together results in decentralized health care governance (Burau, 2007b). The introduction of competition is associated with the expansion of state intervention, including wide-ranging and detailed procedural management, an increasingly restrictive financial framework and tighter framework of statutory regulations. Interestingly, this is coupled with the strengthening of corporatism at the national level, where the powers of the Federal Joint Committee have been extended considerably. The mix of corporatism, federalism and decentralization has created both problematic 'governance gaps' (Kuhlmann and Larsen, 2015) and windows of opportunity for local innovation and policy making (Kuhlmann *et al.*, 2017).

Decentralized health governance can coexist with strong elements of centralism, as the Netherlands and Japan illustrate. In the Netherlands, the central government enjoys important powers in relation to the regulation of competition, including setting the income-dependent insurance contribution rate, the management of payments from the equalization fund and the definition of the basic health insurance package (Schäfer *et al.*, 2010). Crucially, corporatism is also confined to the national level. This more centralized form of corporatism is underpinned by a decentralized, yet unitary, political system, where municipalities and provinces often act as implementation agencies for national policy programmes (Kroneman *et al.*, 2016). Similarly, Japan combines central government control with strong elements of decentralization. Health governance is highly decentralized across 47 regional prefectures and thousands of municipalities, and provides a mixture of delivery levels reflecting a basic principle underlying national policies (Tatara and Okamoto, 2009). Despite this, the central government maintains strong control over all aspects of health care through the rigid and centrally controlled fee structure (Mossialos *et al.*, 2016).

Finally, levels of decentralization are not necessarily universal across the entire health system; they can also vary between different sub-systems. In Australia control over health funding is more highly centralized than control over provision. Over the past two decades, Australia has moved to centralize effective funding control through Medicare (Duckett, 2004b; Rix *et al.*, 2005) and this has reduced substantially the proportion of funding derived from private sources. Moreover, there has been a 'strong centralizing tendency' regarding funding within each of the Australian States and Territories in recent years (Dwyer, 2004; Mossialos *et al.*, 2016). This contrasts with Australia's strong tradition of decentralization and individual state autonomy in the provision of health care services that has included a robust and powerful private sector.

Health systems, governance and policy

Looking at the roles of centre and locality in health governance provides a compelling illustration of the complexity of health systems and the importance of contexts. Ultimately, health governance always happens at different levels: health systems as systems require direction from the centre while the provision of health care inevitably involves localities. The relative importance of diverse levels varies among health systems as well as among different subsystems within the same health system. The variation among and within systems reflects how health care is provided as well as the specific political contexts. For example, health governance is highly centralized in Britain, whereas it is more decentralized in the USA. This reflects the fact that the British central government is at the centre of the public funding and provision of health care, whereas in the USA mixed funding and provision inherently decentralizes governance.

The differences among countries also point to the importance of political contexts. As the comparison with Sweden confirms, however, public funding and provision alone do not guarantee centralized governance, but a unitary, centralized political system plays an important role. For instance, in the USA decentralized health governance is moulded by federalism. Differences among systems coexist with differences within a single health system. Japan, the Netherlands and Taiwan are cases in point: all three combine centralized governance of funding with decentralized governance of provision.

Executive and public integration provide further evidence of the complexity of health systems. The power of national governments and the power of governments over private interests are closely related and offer key indications of the relative authority of governments in health policy. This issue has been implicit throughout the chapter when discussing the sub-systems of funding and provision. The basic assumption is that public funding and provision result in public control – that is, government authority – because the government is the principal public actor in health

Public Control of Provision

		High	Middle	Low
Public Control of Funding	**High**	Britain Sweden New Zealand		Japan Netherlands Taiwan
	Middle	Australia	Germany	
	Low	Singapore		USA

Figure 3.2   *Public control of funding and provision of health care*

policy. Public control of funding can be measured in terms of the extent of public funding, the relative importance of taxes and social security as different types of public funding, and the power of government to control funding. Public control of provision can be measured in terms of the share of public provision of health care. On this basis, Figure 3.2 characterizes the health systems in different countries.

The overview of the modes of governance and the extent of government authority in different countries demonstrates the sheer diversity of health systems. All health systems are confronted with pressures from ageing populations, advances in medical technology and periodic economic downturns, and these pressures often manifest themselves in efforts to control and contain costs. However, the institutional contexts of health systems and the capacity of governments to address these pressures continue to vary greatly among countries. For example, public control of funding and provision is high in Britain and Sweden, whereas it is low in the USA.

Significantly, the picture is more complex than the typology of health systems introduced in Chapter 1 would suggest. The typology assumes that certain models of funding are directly associated with certain models of provision to the extent that high public control of funding goes hand in hand with high public control of provision and vice versa. This is true for health systems in some countries such as Britain (NHS centralised) and Sweden (decentralised type of NHS), Germany (social insurance), and the USA (private insurance), which are closest to the ideal types of NHS, social insurance, and private insurance system, respectively. In the health systems of the remaining countries, government authority differs between the sub-systems of funding and provision. For example, Japan, the Netherlands and Taiwan combine relatively strong (central) public control over funding with relatively low public control over provision, reflecting the predominance of non-public providers. This makes government authority over funding comparable to Britain and Sweden, but, relative to provision, government authority is closer to the USA.

Differences and similarities are specific to individual sub-systems of health care and as such point to the importance of country-specific political contexts. Examples include the semi-federal political system in the Netherlands that often helps to concentrate authority in the hands of central government, and the legacy of a private insurance system combined with federalism in Australia that weakens government authority over funding to some extent.

Acknowledging the uniqueness of individual health systems does not mean we must abandon cross-country comparisons. Instead, it requires removing the blinders of ideal types of health systems. This brings back the question of the place of middle- and low-income countries in relation to comparison and health system typologies centred on OECD/high-income countries. Available data and research largely focus on funding information (Dieleman *et al.*, 2016; Evans and Pablos-Méndez, 2016), while health system characteristics and multi-level governance are rarely addressed. More complex efforts to compare middle- and low-income countries, where they exist, are primarily concerned with a specific area or user group of health care policy and service provision, such as maternity care (Benoit *et al.*, 2015), drug policy (Tomson and Biermann, 2015) or primary health care (Gauld *et al.*, 2012; Groenewegen *et al.*, 2015). Although research shows that health policies and reform models in middle- and low-income countries do not fit well into health system typologies, individual elements of the typologies and system characteristics do recur in middle- and low-income countries. The resulting permutations create a policy and governance mix that is even more complicated than what we observed in our high-income countries.

A comparison of health reform policies and embedded funding schemes in South America impressively illustrates the huge variety of governance mixes, as shown in Table 3.9 (for details, see Giovanella and Faria, 2015). The total expenditure on health in many South American countries is in the range of 8 to 9 per cent of GDP, similar to that of our countries about a decade ago (except in Germany and the USA). Interestingly, the share of public expenditure on the total of health expenditure in all countries, except Paraguay, Venezuela and Brazil, is over 50 per cent, but the specific configuration of the different elements of funding – social security, focused public, Ministry of Health and private insurance – varies widely across the countries. Most countries combine at least three of the four components; Chile and Brazil are the only countries with a mix of only two components.

Table 3.9 *Health care expenditure and segments in South American countries, 2010*

Countries	Total spent on health as % GDP	Public as % of total spent on health	Social security	Focused public insurance	Ministry of Health	Private insurance
Argentina	9.0	64.4	++++	+	++	+
Bolivia	8.4	66.2	++	+	+	-
Brazil	6.5	47.0	-	-	+++++	++
Chile	7.9	59.5	+++++	-	-	++
Colombia	5.6	74.6	+++	++++	-	+
Ecuador	9.6	40.2	++	+	+++	+
Guyana	4.9	79.5	+	+	+	+
Paraguay	5.3	34.4	+	-	+++	+
Peru	8.1	56.2	++	+++	+	+
Suriname	5.3	51.7	++	++	-	+
Uruguay	9.0	65.3	++++	-	++	+
Venezuela	8.4	38.8	++	-	+++	+

Source: This table is reproduced from Giovanella and Faria, 2015: 207, Table 13.1.
+ ≤ 15%; ++ = 16–30%; +++ = 31–50%; ++++= 51–70%; +++++ ≥ 71%.

Brazil, where health care expenditure relies solely on funding from the Ministry of Health and private insurance, is a good case in point. This strategy has some similarities with a classic NHS model combined with higher individual risk management, yet the consequences are fundamentally different. While high-income countries even under austerity measures (at least to some degree) are able to buffer social inequality and assure the provision of universal coverage, such a funding scheme is a high-risk model in less well-resourced countries. The current political-economic crisis in Brazil reveals the potential threat to universal coverage where cuts in government funding combine with income cuts and many citizens can no longer afford out-of-pocket payments (Doniec *et al.*, 2016).

The example of Brazil and the funding schemes in South America suggest that 'removing the blinders' from health care state typologies is difficult and calls for a deeper understanding of contexts bolstered by sounder data and research. It needs a health system approach that looks beyond funding and explores the provision of health care and the mechanisms of governance, including the dominant actors. The lessons learned from cross-country comparison move beyond a mere assumption *that* context matters and show the way to explore *how* different contexts matter, and how health funding, provision and governance are embedded in health systems. Chapter 4 continues this pursuit by examining the implications of these health system characteristics for the allocation of health care resources, other than human resources, which are discussed in Chapter 5.

Setting Priorities and Allocating Resources

Chapter 3 demonstrated that health systems display variation in the sub-systems of funding, provision and governance that impact on health policy and health care. It also revealed that these sub-systems are dynamic and that many of them have undergone significant changes in recent decades. To understand their impact on health care, it is important to go beneath the institutional and structural dimensions and examine the goals, objectives and priorities of each health system. This chapter also examines the criteria that health systems use to allocate medical resources and the ramifications of these policies for their respective populations.

The goals of health policy

A successful policy is founded on goals and objectives that should be clarified early in the policy-making process. Two levels of goals are discernible. The first is broad stated goals that often function symbolically and are more in the realm of political rhetoric than reality. The second is specific programmatic goals that frame a specific policy. Both are critical in evaluating the success or failure of a policy. Although some goals can be specified and appraised with accuracy, others are more amorphous; generally, the broader the goal, the more difficult it is to measure. Analysis becomes even more problematic when the goals themselves conflict, are defined differently by the various participants, or they shift over time. Despite these problems, it is critical to examine the stated goals of health policy.

Ideally, a successful health policy in a democracy would provide timely, high quality services for all citizens on an equal basis. Moreover, it would be an efficient system with little waste and duplication and high levels of performance in all sectors. In addition to the goals of universal access, quality and efficiency, other objectives might include maximizing the choice of patients, ensuring high accountability of health care personnel and guaranteeing precipitous diffusion of the newest medical technologies. As will be discussed in Chapter 7, goals might vary as to whether they place the health of the population or the health of

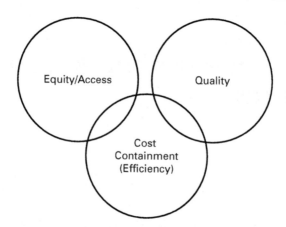

Figure 4.1   *Competing goals of health care*

individual patients foremost. Although, as discussed below, the goals of health care are numerous, Figure 4.1 displays the three goals at the centre of health policy.

For several decades following World War II, the predominant goals of health policy initiatives in developed nations were *equity* or *access* and *quality* of health care. Even though the actual policies varied significantly, the goals of access and quality shaped health care priorities. In large part, the disparity among countries could be explained by how much emphasis each nation put on subsidiary competing goals of freedom of choice for patients, autonomy of health care providers and insurers and assorted notions of common good or solidarity. The resulting mix of these policy goals has been shaped by distinctive national cultures, politics and institutional structures discussed in Chapter 2. In the USA, for instance, with the strong emphasis put on individual freedom, of both patients and the health care community, universal access and equity were not given the prominence enjoyed in other countries. In contrast, New Zealand and the UK, with their strong collectivist roots and tradition of common good, enthusiastically embraced comprehensive national health services based on the central goals of universal access and free care at the point of service.

Despite variation regarding universal coverage, health policy in all developed nations in the post-war period placed priority on ensuring that all citizens had access to an expanding array of medical interventions. New hospitals were built and many beds were added to existing structures, significantly expanded investments were made in medical education and biomedical research, the supply of medical personnel was increased, and the boundaries of medicine were extended through countless new medical specialities. Furthermore, new institutional mechanisms were initiated to ensure access to these resources, thus initiating the era of technological medicine as the new nucleus of health care. This post-war boom of medicine, in turn, was met by heightened expectations and demands from the public for greater access to an ever-expanding arsenal of costly medical innovations.

Equity and access: continuing problems

In its World Health Report 2000, the WHO reiterates equity as a pressing goal and calls for lowering (and ideally removing) all existing barriers to health care, especially those affecting financing and access to care, as well as preventive programmes (Costa-Font and Hernández Quevedo, 2012). Two types of access need to be addressed by health policies: financial access and physical or geographical access. Financial access can be furthered through restructuring health care funding and provision to provide universal access to at least a minimal level of health care for all citizens based on need. This entails either creating systems of direct public financing and provision of services or governmental regulation and coordination of private sickness funds with guaranteed coverage for those patients who fall through the gaps in the private system. Some, such as Germany and the Netherlands, chose to strengthen health systems that pre-dated World War II while others, such as the UK and Sweden, established new systems to meet these goals. Except for the USA, which did not establish a national system, all countries examined here have been largely successful in achieving universal levels of access, despite divergence in the means used to achieve that goal.

Until now, the USA is the only democracy that has not come close to achieving universal access. After a year-long, contentious battle over health reform, the Patient Protection and Affordable Care Act (ACA) was signed into law by President Obama on 23 March 2010, with the principal goal of addressing this longstanding deficiency in equity (Jacobs, 2011; Jost, 2011). This Act, along with the Healthcare and Education Reconciliation Act of 2010 (signed into law on 30 March), constituted the health care overhaul of 2010 (Box 4.1). Although the number of the uninsured has been reduced by nearly 9 million since its implementation, about 32 million Americans are still without health insurance with many more millions being underinsured or having large deductibles or co-payments (Majerol *et al.*, 2015). Moreover, undocumented immigrants technically are not eligible for public insurance or for private coverage obtained through exchanges under the ACA. Unless other policy actions are taken to provide for their coverage, or their immigration status is changed, they will eventually constitute a bigger percentage of the uninsured population (Zuckerman *et al.*, 2011).

Box 4.1   Moving towards universal access?

At its core, the ACA (often referred to as Obamacare) represents an ambitious attempt to provide some measure of equity in what has become the most unequal health care system in the developed world. Although the changes initiated by the ACA are significant, they fall well short of the transformation originally envisioned by those who favoured a 'public option' to compete with private insurers (Hoffman, 2010). Moreover, this 'patchwork' reform continues to face severe challenges before full implementation (Marmor and Oberlander, 2011). Most controversial was the individual mandate that required all Americans to carry health insurance by 2014. In a highly divisive case, the US Supreme Court upheld the mandate as constitutional, much to the dismay of critics (*National Federation of Independent Business v. Sebelius*, 567 U.S. (2012)). With the election of Donald Trump as president in 2016 and the control of both Houses of Congress in Republican hands, the future of Obamacare care is in doubt.

Although, unlike the USA, other countries have universal coverage, they too face problems of equity of access related to the presence of a tiered system in which persons with ample resources obtain services that are either unavailable or limited in the public system. For instance, New Zealand has a two-tier health system with elective surgery provided by both publicly funded state hospitals and by private hospitals. Derrett *et al.* (2009) argue that, despite the introduction of a prioritization system aimed at increased equity and fairness, the access to elective surgery remains inequitable. Moreover, the argument that private provision for better-off patients reduces the burden on the public system, thus allowing better access for the poor, has not been supported by the New Zealand case. Similarly, while universality is at the centre of the British NHS, often it is up to regional health authorities to determine which services to fund, thus opening the way to local variation, also referred to as the 'postcode lottery'. Waiting lists also limit access to elective surgery and buttress the tiered system (Baggott, 2010).

Geographical inequities

The second type of inequity became especially problematic as health care became increasingly specialized and capital intensive. Geographical inequities in health care, although intermittently reduced by regional reallocation schemes, remain challenging. Isolated, rural communities are consistently undersupplied in terms of skilled medical personnel and facilities in health systems as diverse as New Zealand and Taiwan. In many countries, the disproportionate number of physicians located in urban centres can be explained by an insufficient number of patients in many rural areas to justify huge technological investment. Simply put, health professionals go where the patients are, resulting in a concentration of health care facilities in core urban populations thus producing significant inequities, particularly in access to specialized care (Stukel *et al.*, 2005). Moreover, Semansky *et al.* (2012) argue that, historically, policy makers have designed reforms with more populous urban areas in mind and have not adequately considered rural contexts that differ from urban regions in terms of population density as well as geographical and topographical barriers that can hinder access to services.

Although most countries have created incentives to attempt to correct geographical imbalances of physicians, financial inducements and other policies have not resolved the problem (this is discussed in more detail in Chapter 5). For instance, Germany has one of the highest proportions of doctors per 1,000 inhabitants (see Table 5.1), but they tend to be concentrated in urban areas. In 1993 the freedom to set up practice anywhere was replaced by health workforce planning based on community needs, and the number of additional doctors per speciality and region was limited. Although the main aim of this policy was to limit the absolute number of doctors, one of its side effects was to make rural regions more attractive to new doctors (Burau, 2001). More recently, the regulation of the number of doctors in ambulatory care has become less standardized. Instead it is up to regional associations of insurance fund doctors to fine-tune supply and geographical distribution of doctors working in ambulatory care (Ozegowski and Sundmacher, 2012).

There are no legal restrictions on the ability of doctors to establish a practice wherever they wish in Australia, and consequently the doctor–patient ratios are much higher in the capital cities than in the remainder of each state (Davies *et al.*, 2006). In 2009, the Commonwealth government announced reforms to address major workforce shortages in rural and remote health services, including cash incentives to encourage doctors to work in some of Australia's most isolated communities. Under the new system, a doctor relocating from a major city to a regional centre could receive a grant. If that doctor moved to a very remote area, the grant could be considerably higher. Retention payments are also linked to remoteness, with bonus payments for doctors working in some of Australia's most inaccessible locations. Moreover, restrictions on overseas-trained doctors are lifted sooner if they move to rural areas to practise and more locum relief will be available for doctors in 'difficult locations' (FarmOnline, 2009).

Approximately 20 per cent of the US population resides in rural areas while less than 9 per cent of US physicians practise there (Association of American Medical Colleges, 2008). Despite incentive programmes, remote areas find it difficult to retain doctors. The fact that the USA is heavily skewed towards specialities compounds this problem since family practice doctors are the most common rural physicians. In fact, the more specialized a physician is, the less likely he or she will practise in a rural area (National Rural Health Association, 2009). The National Rural Health Association (NRHA) reports that 2,157 geographic regions designated as health professional shortage areas are in rural areas, compared with 910 in urban settings. The numerical increase in the number of physicians in the USA has not resulted in a proportional increase in physicians practising outside urban areas and has not alleviated geographic maldistribution.

Similarly, despite the overall success of the Taiwan NHI, Kreng and Yang (2011) conclude that the disproportionate amount of health care resources allocated to North Taiwan has resulted in considerable geographical disparity. Furthermore, by necessity large-scale hospitals are congregated in metropolitan regions, thus limiting access to health care services for patients in rural areas. Individuals residing in less urbanized areas are also less likely to use outpatient services compared to those living in highly urbanized areas (Lin *et al.*, 2011).

An important barrier to establishing physical equity is the fact that the delivery of health care services to rural areas is significantly more expensive on a per-case basis, in part because of the high cost of capital equipment needed to supply state-of-the-art medical care. Therefore, many specialized services and diagnostics can be provided efficiently only in urban regional centres with a critical mass of population. This problem is especially acute in Australia, New Zealand, Sweden and the USA, where significant minorities of the population live in remote areas. Even when patients from isolated geographical locations have equal financial access to the same level of medicine as their urban brethren, travel costs, relocation costs and costs in time produce substantial inequities in effective access. Only in the concentrated population of Singapore is this not a problem.

Medical tourism

A related equity issue is the increased global market for patients in the form of medical tourism (Cortez, 2008b). For example, more than 374,000 foreign patients sought treatment in Singapore in 2005, four out of five in private clinics and hospitals (Okma *et al.*, 2010). Moreover, growth in the number of foreign patients has been averaging 20 per cent annually because of the stepped-up efforts by Singapore Medicine, a government/industry partnership established in 2003 to turn Singapore into a leading medical hub. Pocock and Phua (2011), however, contend that the rise of medical tourism in South East Asia is problematic and raises concerns about its potential impact, namely the exacerbation of existing inequitable resource distribution between the public and private sectors. They argue that unless properly managed and regulated, the financial benefits of medical tourism for health systems may come at the expense of access to, and use of, health services by local consumers.

Quality care: what is it?

The goal of high quality health care, a hallmark of the 1950s and 1960s, has also proved challenging. The main difficulty in defining 'quality' is that we lack an objective means of measuring what 'quality' health care is (Steinberg and Luce, 2005). International comparisons seldom address this factor because it is much easier to compare cost figures, usage figures and other readily quantifiable factors. To address this gap, the OECD Health Care Quality Indicator (HCQI) Project was initiated to collect internationally comparable data reflecting the health outcomes and health improvements attributable to medical care delivered in OECD countries (see Kelly and Hurst, 2006). The project goal is to track health care quality by developing a set of indicators to provide international benchmarks of quality and give national policy makers an opportunity to compare the performance of their health care delivery systems against a peer group. Moreover, the Commonwealth Fund, in developing a set of criteria for evaluating health care systems, defines high quality by an inclusive range of indicators such as provision of preventive care services, management of chronic diseases, care coordination, patient-centred care, low instance of medical errors and low preventable death rates (Commonwealth Fund Commission on a High Performance Health System, 2009). Finally, the WHO (2000) initiated health system performance assessments (HSPAs) that include a few quality indicators (see discussion in Chapter 8).

Even within individual countries, however, quality is rarely monitored systematically because there is little agreement on what criteria should be used. Unfortunately, quality is often equated with the latest diagnostic technologies and with specialist services. This emphasis is deceptive because it assumes that quality can be measured simply by counting the number of diagnostic machines, medical specialists and intensive medical interventions. Quality as defined by technology is also of dubious value when compared to health outcomes (see Box 4.2). Moreover, when quality is defined this way it is likely to clash with the goal of access, which by necessity requires limitations on what levels of care are provided. While the goal of universal access presupposes some minimal level of care for persons in need, it cannot sustain unlimited amounts of resources expended on high-technology interventions for a few patients. Despite

---

Box 4.2   Does more high-technology medicine improve health outcomes?

Numerous studies confirm that the US health care system makes more extensive use of high technology than other countries. For instance, a study comparing care for heart attack patients in 17 countries showed that, while treatment in all countries has become more intensive, the USA has a pattern of early adoption and fast diffusion of new technologies. By contrast, other countries showed either a late start/fast growth pattern of technological diffusion (Australia and Belgium) or a late start/slow growth pattern (the UK and Scandinavian countries). The patterns of diffusion for new, very high-cost drugs were similar to intensive procedures (Docteur *et al.*, 2003). Despite this pattern, however, the USA consistently rates below the top 20 nations in health outcomes. One study found that the USA ranked near the bottom of industrialized nations for the survival rates of infants, despite high spending on neonatal care (Tanner, 2006). Similarly, the Commonwealth Fund Commission on a High Performance Health System (2009) ranked the USA last on all three indicators of healthy lives. Other studies have found that Americans aged 55 to 64 are much sicker than their British counterparts (Banks *et al.*, 2006) and that Canadians are healthier than their USA counterparts on almost every measure of health (Lasser *et al.*, 2006). Despite massive spending on the newest technologies, Americans have higher rates of diabetes, hypertension, heart disease, stroke, lung disease and cancer than other Western nations.

---

these dilemmas, quality, along with equity, was the most articulated goal of health policy until the mid-to-late 1970s and remains a critical objective.

Cost containment: strategies of constraint

In the 1970s escalating costs, in large part fuelled by the open-ended goals of access and quality, were aggravated by a global recession. One result was an unmistakable shift in emphasis from access and quality to cost containment to constrain unbridled health care spending. Ageing populations, boundless technological expansion and heightened public expectations solidified this goal in the 1990s. Moreover, its prominence was stimulated by an ideological shift towards neo-liberalism, which eschewed the welfare state and placed emphasis on efficiency of the market. Ironically, the emphasis on cost containment and system efficiency has forced evaluation of quality (an effort that was conspicuously absent when quality was the preeminent goal) by requiring that priorities be set in distributing health care resources in terms of value for money. For an excellent summary of the dynamics of health policy trajectories over the past 50 years, see Saltman (2015).

Cost containment strategies differ significantly across health systems. Objectives can be to slow the rate of increase in costs, to prevent costs from rising in real terms, or more rarely to reduce the costs of health care in real terms. The health care sectors to which a specific cost containment strategy is targeted also vary depending on whether health services are financed by the government on a direct budget basis, through public contracts with independent providers such as physicians paid on a fee-for-service basis or hospitals paid per item of service provided, or by the private marketplace. As seen in Chapter 3, countries with national health services, such as Sweden, the UK and New Zealand, as well as several without, such as Singapore, Taiwan and Japan, exercise direct budgetary control, while countries such as Australia, Germany and the Netherlands rely more on the second, contractual-based approach. Finally, the USA depends upon a less effective mixture of approaches, including those based in the marketplace. The capacity for successful cost containment policies, therefore, fluctuates considerably over time from one country to the next.

Sweden is a good example of a country with a national health service that has effective controls and where the general rule of 'public funding makes for public control' applies. However, in contrast to Britain and New Zealand, control over funding is decentralized, since health care is predominantly funded from taxes raised by the regional tier of government, the county councils (Glenngård *et al.*, 2005). 'Macro-level' measures of cost containment vary, because county councils decide on the rate of regional taxation, much of which goes to health care. Besides this, global budgets play an important role and county councils may allocate funds to districts using needs-based global budgets. Similarly, county councils or districts may fund health centres and hospitals using global budgets in conjunction with other forms of payment. In recent years, resource allocation models have become more mixed and combine fixed per-case payments with price/volume ceilings and quality components (Harrison, 2004).

Cost containment strategies can operate either by reducing *demand* for, or controlling the *supply* of, health care. Additionally, they can be carried out through a direct, regulatory edict or through indirect incentive systems aimed at providers and patients. Furthermore, depending on the system, major efforts can be initiated and implemented either by public agencies – national, state or local – or by the private sector. In general, European countries emphasize macro-management strategies such as global budgets to control their health systems, while the USA, with its aversion to centralized control, has opted instead to utilize financial incentives to influence the use of health care services. However, even in Europe this is changing with moves to micro-manage some aspects of medical care.

Demand-side strategies

Demand-side cost containment relies primarily on strategies designed to reduce consumer demand by increasing patient consciousness of the costs of providing care. Usually this is accomplished by requiring some form of cost sharing by the users of health care, either through user charges as a flat rate per unit of service (e.g. $50 per hospital night, $20 per doctor visit, $20 per prescription), some proportion of the cost (e.g., 20 per cent of outpatient costs, 30 per cent of inpatient costs), or some combination of these. Out-of-pocket costs are normally applied at the time of use with the explicit goal of discouraging user demand and, by extension, acting indirectly on physicians to reduce services on the knowledge that the patient must share in the cost. Another approach is to require deductibles or excesses (e.g., the first $100 per condition or the first $1,000 annually) that the consumer must pay, thereby allegedly discouraging demand.

The form of demand-side strategies varies significantly across countries. In Germany, for instance, co-payments are the most common form of out-of-pocket payments and have a long tradition, particularly in relation to drugs. Since the early 1990s, however, they have increased noticeably and in 2002 represented 12 per cent of total expenditure on health care (Busse and Riesberg, 2004). With increasing cost pressures, co-payments in other areas have been added, including charges for inpatient days in hospitals, rehabilitative care facilities, ambulance transportation and dental treatment. Indeed, Carrera *et al.* (2008) conclude that developments emphasize the role of the individual in contributing to the sustainability of health financing and thereby strengthen personal responsibility at the expense of solidarity. Since health reforms in 2007, health insurance funds can offer lower contribution rates to those members who accept a fixed co-payment on all treatments (Gerlinger, 2010). In 2003, Japan increased the co-payment rate of all care for patients insured by the Employees' Health Insurance from 20 to 30 per cent to put it in line with that of the National Health Insurance (Tatara and Okamoto, 2009).

In contrast, out-of-pocket payments have traditionally played a marginal role in the Dutch health system, reflecting entrenched expectations that all health care should be free at the point of use (Maarse and Paulus, 2003). However, this is different for the exceptional medical risks scheme that accounts for almost half of total co-payments (Exter *et al.*, 2004). Furthermore, under the unified social health insurance programme for acute risks, people must pay a flat-rate premium directly to their sickness fund (Schäfer *et al.*, 2010). Significantly, with the introduction of the unified insurance in 2006, the flat-rate premium has risen, whereas income-related contributions have been reduced (Bartholomée and Maarse, 2006). Moreover, insurance funds charge patients a flat-rate co-payment on all health expenditures except general medical services, although these can be waived if patients choose a preferred provider or follow preventive programmes.

Initially Taiwan's NHI did not include co-payments, but in response to rising expenditures it adopted a co-payment system, although it waives cost-sharing obligations for many groups (Box 4.3). For each outpatient care visit, an insured person must pay NT$50 (US$1.50) to NT$210 (US$6.75), depending on the type of facility visited. For inpatient care, there is also a co-insurance rate of 10 to 30 per cent depending on the length of stay, with payment capped at 10 per cent of per capita income. The co-insurance rate for drugs is 20 per cent, with personal payment for drugs capped at NT$200 (US$6.00) per visit. Furthermore, NHI beneficiaries are required to make a co-payment of 10 per cent of hospitalization costs with an upper limit of NT$24,000 (US$725) per admission, although those with a low-income certificate are exempt. Hospitals are allowed to bill patients directly for medical materials not covered by the NHI such as private or double rooms (Cheng *et al.*, 2006).

Out-of-pocket payments in Sweden exist in the form of direct, small patient fees (for an overview see Anell *et al.*, 2012). The payments are a flat rate set by the county councils; however, the national parliament sets ceilings on the total to be paid by patients annually (Burstrom, 2004). Separately, for drugs there are co-payments established by central government and uniform across the country. In Britain, out-of-pocket payments take the form of co-payments. Prominent areas of cost sharing

---

Box. 4.3   Is Taiwan NHI too nice?

To ensure access to medical care for those with the greatest medical need, the NHI issues a 'catastrophic illness certificate' that exempts all co-payments and co-insurance to patients with one or more of 30 catastrophic diseases, residents of remote mountainous areas and offshore islands, pregnant women and child delivery, children under 3, veterans and their dependents and low-income households. In 2013, chronic renal failure and cancer accounted for 45 per cent and 33.5 per cent of NHI's total annual outpatient care expenditures, respectively. Moreover, cancer alone accounted for 45 per cent of total inpatient expenditures. As of 2013, 3.7 per cent of Taiwan's population held the certificate accounting for 29.4 per cent of total NHI expenditures. For Cheng (2015), although it is important to remove financial barriers to needed medical care, the question of sustainability of the current generous co-payment exemption policy must be raised and eligibility for co-payment exemption should be reviewed through means testing to prevent reverse income redistribution from the middle class to the rich, who are presently entitled to this generous government subsidy.

include: drugs, where co-payments have risen sharply over time; dental services, where patients must cover 80 per cent of the costs up to a maximum; and ophthalmic services that have been widely deregulated (Boyle, 2011; for a good European comparison of cost-sharing arrangements, see Ros *et al.*, 2000).

A major assumption of demand-side cost containment measures is that use of services will decrease when market incentives are implemented that make a patient bear part of the costs. Studies have found that cost sharing through either supplementary insurance or deductibles does, indeed, reduce health spending. The European Observatory on Health Care Systems (1999) cites a study in the UK showing that, even with widespread exemptions, changes in prescription charges can have a major impact on the number of prescriptions dispensed. Even a modest increase in prescription charges from £3.75 to £4.25 per item in 1993 resulted in a reduction of 2.3 million prescriptions. Correspondingly, the Rand Corporation Health Insurance Experiment in the USA found that outpatient spending was 46 per cent lower among individuals enrolled in health plans that required 5 per cent co-insurance compared with those in free care plans, with the 25 per cent co-insurance plans producing even larger savings. Likewise, outpatient spending was 30 per cent lower and inpatient spending 10 per cent lower under individual deductible plans, while cost sharing reduced adult hospital admissions by up to 38 per cent as compared to free plans (Peterson, 2006).

Despite these findings of apparent cost savings, there are questions as to how genuine the benefits of a demand-side approach are, especially if the vestiges of inefficient usage remain (Box 4.4). In their study

---

Box 4.4   Overuse of emergency rooms

A major problem in some countries is the overuse of costly emergency room (ER) and specialist care for primary care matters. For many years now, primary care in the USA has been in decline and patients have adapted by seeking care elsewhere when they get sick. For instance, of the over 350 million annual visits for acute care, 22 per cent are managed by GPs, 10 per cent by internists, 13 per cent by paediatricians, 20 per cent by office-based specialists and 28 per cent by hospital emergency departments (Pitts *et al.*, 2010). Similarly, nearly 15 per cent of all ER visits in Taiwan are non-emergency and an additional 20 per cent would have been emergency-preventable with primary care (Tsai *et al.*, 2011). One of the biggest barriers to providing acute care in primary care practice is that many GPs have full schedules, making 'same day' scheduling, much less treatment of walk-in patients, extremely difficult (Pitts *et al.*, 2010). It is faster and simpler to refer these patients to a specialist or the nearest ER even though that is considerably more expensive for the health system.

of US seniors, Costa-Font and Toyama (2011) found that while user fees reduced the use of inappropriate medications, expected prescription quality improvements from co-payments are small. Furthermore, in their study of the impact of increasing co-payments on the utilization behaviour of elderly patients, Huang and Tung (2008) found that the increase in co-payment significantly decreases visit frequency, but that this in some cases can delay needed treatment and reduce the adequacy of health care provision to the elderly.

An important question, then, is whether the reduced use of medical resources resulting from co-payments leads to lowered levels of health for those individuals who forgo treatment due to cost considerations. In the Rand study, access to more services did not result in better health among consumers who were young, middle income and in good health. In contrast, access to more services did result in better health outcomes among the poor and those persons with initial clinical indicators of poor health. In other words, while many healthy people can reduce care without adverse health consequences, when truly ill people forgo needed services, health outcomes suffer. Part of this difference, however, might be explained by the fact that relatively young, healthy and affluent consumers can carry supplemental insurance to cover charges, thus undercutting the strategy of cost sharing. Unless prohibited from doing so, those using insurance resources will counteract the apparent cost savings.

Other demand-side approaches to cost containment include the exclusion of certain types of coverage or limited reimbursement for specific services. Moreover, some systems such as Australia and the USA allow extra billing while others have either prohibited or strictly limited this practice because of its impact on equity and its overall inflationary effect. While Germany, Japan, the Netherlands, Sweden and the UK forbid extra billing by office-based doctors working in ambulatory care, a clear example of extra billing is France. As in many other countries, French doctors in ambulatory care are self-employed, independent practitioners, and they are paid on a fee-for-service basis. Although most contract with the social insurance system, up to a quarter opt out of the negotiated fee schedule in favour of extra billing, referred to as 'Sector 2' (Freeman, 2000). Patients are then reimbursed by social insurance according to the national fee schedule, regardless of whether or not they choose a doctor who charges higher fees. Although they must pay for the extra billing themselves, over 90 per cent have supplementary insurance to cover extra billing and other co-payments (Freeman, 2000).

Overall, demand-side approaches have an adverse impact on access and place inequitable financial burden across groups in society. While the problems of inequity they raise hypothetically can be reduced by providing subsidies or a safety net for those unable to pay or by providing exemptions to the co-payments (e.g., New Zealand's policy on GPs), this entails a complicated administrative and monitoring system that, in turn, adds to costs.

Supply-side strategies

Supply-side cost containment measures are generally more effective than demand-side measures, especially when they entail the imposition of direct, central controls on payments to providers. Other than the USA, most countries emphasize strategies that control the supply side by strengthening the hands of insurers and/or by imposing direct, central controls on payments to providers and on the capacities of their health systems (see Table 4.1). For instance, during the 1980s, the Netherlands introduced a system of global budgeting to replace the daily rates paid to hospitals, thus joining the UK and New Zealand which already had mechanisms for capping hospital expenditures (Hurst and Poullier, 1993). Also, since 2002 Taiwan's NHI has operated under a global budget (Cheng and Chang, 2007). Similarly, in 2005 Singapore implemented a global budget policy for public sector hospitals and health care institutions.

Global budgets

Additional instruments of regulatory cost containment are fee and price controls, control over capacity of the system and control over wages and salaries. The most direct supply-side strategy is to tighten controls over reimbursement or enforce payment schedules. This is easiest to accomplish in an integrated system where the government has the capacity to set global budgets. Sweden and the UK are classic examples of integrated health systems where the government sets global budgets, in the former

Table 4.1   *Supply-side strategies*

Global budgeting	Centralized control	Move to ambulatory and home care
Singapore	Germany	Germany
New Zealand	Japan	New Zealand
Netherlands	Netherlands	UK
Sweden	Singapore	Australia
Taiwan	Taiwan	
UK	USA (Medicare DRGs)	

case at the regional level. In Britain, the total expenditure of the NHS is set by the Treasury, and is part of the government's three-yearly general spending review. Once overall spending has been set, the Department of Health determines the funds allocated to Clinical Commissioning Groups (CCCs) (Primary Care Trusts prior to 2013). In contrast, hospitals are funded through contracts. Cost-volume contracts were long predominant but have now been replaced by commissioning based on national tariffs for Health Care Resource Groups (Boyle, 2011). CCCs rely on standard contracts developed by the Department of Health. As such, the UK is based on a system of cost-per-case payments. As noted earlier, the situation in Sweden is more complex because funding arrangements vary among county councils. Some county councils use global budgets to pay hospitals and health centres, while others have introduced a purchaser–provider split. For example, contracts with hospitals are often based on fixed, prospective per-case payments that are combined with price/quality ceilings as well as quality components (Anell *et al.*, 2012). However, overall the mechanisms for allocating financial resources have become more mixed.

Another approach is that of Germany where cost containment policy means limiting insurance funds' expenditure to a level where it matches income so that contribution rates remain stable (Carrera *et al.*, 2008). To achieve this, the 1990s saw the introduction of sectoral budgets or spending caps based on historic spending patterns rather than any needs-based formula as in the UK (Gerlinger, 2010). At the individual hospital level, this has coincided with the abolition of the full cost cover principle and, initially, the introduction of fixed budgets calculated for each hospital which have subsequently been replaced by a system of fixed payments per case, or DRGs. Furthermore, since 1989 fixed regional budgets exist in ambulatory care meaning that the fees for individual services are not fixed, but vary depending on the total budget negotiated with the insurance fund and the total volume of services delivered within the regional association of insurance fund doctors.

Global budgets for hospitals are more effective than price or volume controls alone because they cannot be avoided by raising volume when prices are fixed or raising prices when volume is fixed. Usually, discretion is given to local managers to spend within the prospective budget. Budget caps work provided there is the political will to enforce them, but they can be politically risky because they make the central government liable for the failure of micro-decisions. In other words, global budgets allow hospitals to blame government policy makers for shortfalls in service due to inadequate funding levels. Because hospitals consume the bulk of health spending, however, budget caps become less effective when the government grants additional funds to those hospitals that overspend and require supplements to their budgets to keep operating.

One problem with global budgets is that they might achieve cost containment by forcing hospitals to cut corners, thus lowering quality of care. Because one cannot readily distinguish as to the quality or intensity of care, there are often no rewards for *good* economical treatment. Chang and Hung (2008), for instance, conclude that the implementation of the global budget in the Taiwan NHI enhanced cost containment, but at the expense of quality. Although they suggest this problem can be minimized through close auditing of quality and a more effective monitoring and review system, global budgets, in themselves, are not sufficient to protect consumers because their priority is to lower overall costs. In terms of the goal of containing costs, however, any form of prospective payment will succeed by relating rewards to planned workload and encouraging awareness of cost per case. In contrast, any system with open-ended retrospective reimbursement for hospitals such as traditional private insurance in the USA will have higher expenditures per capita (Lamm and Blank, 2007).

Although global budgets are more easily implemented if there is one central insurer, single-source funding is not essential. Germany and the Netherlands, for example, have been successful in securing cost control in systems composed of many payers. Germany has accomplished this by the combination of restraining the payment to providers and centralizing control of funding (Carrera *et al.*, 2008). The 1990s saw the partial introduction of a system of prospective payments in hospitals that in 2000 culminated in the gradual introduction of a comprehensive system of DRGs. In ambulatory care, a maximum ceiling for fees per doctor was introduced, coexisting with fixed sectoral budgets. At the same time, the autonomy of insurance funds in raising and allocating funds has been curtailed. Following the most recent reforms from 2009 (Leiber *et al.*, 2010), the government sets income-related contribution rates that are uniform across insurance funds. The government also determines the formula for allocating financial resources to individual insurance funds as well as the level of additional funding raised by individual insurance funds through flat-rate contribution rates.

In the Netherlands, cost containment has been achieved through a combination of integrated control over funding and measures of spending control. The income-related contribution rates of the two social insurance schemes are set by the central government. The additional flat-rate premium raised by individual insurance funds is also subject to regulation and may not, for example, vary by gender, age or health risks (Maarse and Ter Meulen, 2006; Schäfer *et al.*, 2010). This is complemented by regulated competition, both among insurance funds for employees and among providers for selective contracting with insurance funds, as well as by micro-level measures to increase efficiency.

Similarly, Japan has been successful in controlling a vast network of private insurance funds and local providers by instituting a strict uniform fee structure and prohibiting extra billing. In 2003 Japan began to introduce a diagnosis-based hospital reimbursement system as a financial incentive for university hospitals to decrease inpatient costs by capping the cost per day for each inpatient by disease category. The disparate policies of these countries show that control over medical spending can be accomplished without centralized global budgeting. Although direct price and quantity controls may be less effective than global budgets or direct caps, they can be applicable to all segments of health care, including pharmaceuticals, and thus are potentially more comprehensive.

Diagnosis-related groups (DRGs)

Lacking the centralized regulatory control over health care found in other countries, the USA implemented a prospective payment system in the mid-1980s in the one area it could control, the Medicare programme. DRGs were introduced to constrain costs of Medicare spending by setting prospective limits per diagnostic category on a fixed schedule. It was hoped that the private sector would follow this lead to reduce overall costs, but this did not happen. There is evidence, however, that this approach alone cannot constrain costs in the long run and that it has resulted in a 'revolving door' through which patients are simply readmitted for a new DRG when the previous one runs its course (Lamm and Blank, 2007). For instance, while hospitals under the DRG system initially were found to have reduced costs per day by 9.8 per cent and average length of stay by 6.5 per cent, the effect on total costs was offset by an 11.7 per cent increase in admission rates. Similarly, in the late 1990s after the one-time savings from managed care began to dissipate, health care costs in the USA resumed their escalation, surging to over 10 per cent annually.

Other supply-side strategies

Other supply-side approaches include controls over construction of hospitals, the purchase of expensive equipment and the number of medical students entering designated specialities. Encouragement of outpatient over inpatient facilities and a reduction in the oversupply of acute hospital beds are also likely to reduce costs, as is the shift from more expensive hospital beds to nursing homes or home care (see Chapter 6). The changes in Germany are an example of this strategy. Traditionally, the monopoly of office-based doctors over the delivery of ambulatory care has hindered the development of outpatient facilities. However, in the face of cost pressures, hospitals are now allowed to offer day surgery, pre-admission diagnostic procedures and post-discharge treatment. Furthermore, the role of the outpatient departments of university hospitals in the provision of highly specialized care has been recognized through special contracts with insurance funds.

Meanwhile, in the Netherlands there has been a reduction in the capacity for inpatient care while day surgery has expanded (Exter *et al.*, 2004). This shift went hand in hand with increasingly tight government regulation of hospitals. For example, the Hospitals Facilities Act regulated the number of hospital beds and specialist units. Moreover, all major investments in hospitals need the formal approval of the Minister of Health if any added facility is to be reimbursed through social health insurance. Interestingly, central planning for hospitals was abolished in 2008 (Schäfer *et al.*, 2010).

Throughout the 1990s, Sweden saw a substantial decline in the number of hospital beds, more drastic than in other countries (Glenngård *et al.*, 2005) while the position of ambulatory care was strengthened. The 1995 Primary Care Act acknowledged primary care as a separate level of care and defined it as the foundation of health care. Furthermore, between 2007 and 2010 there were reforms to strengthen primary care through the introduction of compulsory patient choice and by opening primary care to private providers (Anell, 2010). This is significant, because compared to other European countries primary care in Sweden was traditionally less developed in part because it did not have a formal gatekeeping function. However, concurrent with the reduction in the length of hospital stays, the number of patient visits in primary care has increased over recent years (Anell *et al.*, 2012).

Major cost containment efforts in Taiwan have been directed at pharmaceutical expenditures that constitute about 25 per cent of the entire NHI budget. The government has introduced many strategies including price adjustment based on prices of international products or existing drugs, delegation of financial responsibility to regional bureaus, co-payment for outpatient drugs, generic grouping, a global budget payment system for clinics and hospitals, and reduction in the flat daily payment rate of the drugs for clinics. Lee *et al.* (2008) found that a global budget alone without other direct financial incentives would not be able to control expenditures on drugs. They concluded that the most effective strategies were generic grouping, reduction of the flat payment rate and delegation of financial responsibility. Chen *et al.* (2007), however, found that while generic grouping significantly reduced the daily expense of the three classes of drugs they studied, in response to this price adjustment policy hospitals tended to expand the volume of drugs prescribed, thus undermining the capacity of this strategy to constrain overall pharmaceutical expenditures.

Ambulatory care settings seem to hold the promise of both tailored and cost-effective care (Saltman *et al.*, 2006). Both points are particularly relevant in the context of the British NHS where patient demand often remains unmet and where successive governments have been interested in making existing funds go further. This is epitomized in the vision of a 'primary care-led' health service where GPs have become key players, not only in the provision, but also in the organization of health services. Following the purchaser–provider split in the early 1990s, GPs were given the option of becoming 'fund holders' and receiving funds to purchase a range of diagnostic and elective procedures. The health reforms under the New Labour government in 1997 built on these developments and GP practices became so-called 'Primary Care Trusts'. As part of these trusts, GPs were responsible for the commissioning of all health care services in their locale while retaining responsibility for the provision of ambulatory health care services. The most recent reforms in 2012 very much keep the focus on primary care, and commissioning is now in the hands of generally smaller, and GP-led, Clinical Commissioning Groups (Department of Health, 2012c).

A final supply-side strategy to cost containment is the creation of competitive market conditions under which the more efficient providers thrive and the relatively costly ones are driven out of existence. One such approach entails separating the funding and provision functions and thus, it is assumed, facilitating competition among providers. In the UK internal market, introduced in the early 1990s, for instance, self-governing public hospitals, together with private sector hospitals, were envisaged as competing for contracts with the health authorities that funded secondary health. Because of the heated controversy surrounding moves to incorporate marketplace mechanisms, it is important to look at the role of market in health care in more depth.

The government and the marketplace

One trend over the last few decades across Western democracies is the inclusion of market or quasi-market mechanisms in health systems to provide incentives to improve efficiency (Cortez, 2008b). Under neo-liberalism, public sector monopolies provide few incentives for system efficiency and, in fact, are likely to contain perverse incentives that in effect penalize efficiency (see Heywood, 2002). Instead, it argues, one must turn to the marketplace to instil efficient use of resources. Despite this paradigm shift, evidence suggests that a totally free market in health insurance can produce neither equity nor efficiency (Wells *et al.*, 2007).

Generally, governments can take one of two main routes in regulating health care systems, although as Saltman (2002) suggests the two approaches often exist side by side. The first approach involves regulation in the more conventional sense of setting constraints on the public and non-public sectors. This detailed command-and-control type of activity is generally designed to supplant or override market forces and institutions. Among other approaches, this can be effected by specifying coverage of insurance policies, regulating membership and premiums, controlling the quantity and quality of prices, mandating set fee structures and schedules, fixing wage rates or controlling planning capacity. For example, as noted above, in Japan over 5,000 insurance plans and predominantly private providers are highly regulated by the government through the universal fee structure, centralized billing and payment, standard co-payments and prohibition of extra billing.

The second approach, generally termed pro-market or pro-competitive, places more emphasis on the promotion of control by the health care community itself. The aim here is to maximize autonomy for insurers, providers and consumers through the operation of traditional marketplace principles. The government's role is to provide a balance among the assorted stakeholders as it does in other areas of the economy. Under a pure market model, the health care system is, in effect, a large business that, if left alone to operate under the principles of supply and demand, will best serve the consumer public. For reasons discussed below, no system embodies the pure model. Even in the USA, providers, especially hospitals, face scrutiny and indisputable constraints because of regulation by local, state and national government.

Limits of market approach

A pure market approach cannot work because health care contains none of the self-selecting mechanisms needed to check market excesses. For an efficient, market-based health care system to function, several conditions are essential. First, all decisions must be that of the consumer. Second, consumers must know the value and costs of the goods they are contemplating purchasing. Third, consumers must pay the full cost and receive the full value of the goods they choose to buy.

Importantly, not one of these conditions is present in the market for health care services (see Box 4.5). First, no medical decision is solely that of the patient. Although some discretion is possible, ultimately the individual patient's choice is heavily conditioned and inhibited by providers. Second, most patients have a difficult time judging the value of the care they get. Therefore, health care professionals have enormous sway in deciding both the type and cost of care provided. The specialized knowledge required for the dispensation of health care, in conjunction with the emotional and often urgent nature of medical decisions, undercuts the patient's ability to be a rational shopper. Furthermore, it does not follow

---

Box 4.5   Distortions in the health care market

The market for health care contains many distortions, including: (1) the asymmetry of information between physicians and patients; (2) the clinicians' dual role as patient agent and independent business owner who profits by ordering or providing medical services; (3) the effect of insurance in reducing the apparent cost to patients, thus leading to the 'price-wedge' distortion or 'moral hazard'; (4) tax subsidies that have a similar effect on consumers' decisions to buy insurance; and (5) the monopoly power bestowed on certain professions and, in some countries, on health insurance plans that constrain competition (Wells *et al.*, 2007).

---

that more informed consumers of health care shop for lower cost. In fact, evidence suggests that more information often leads to higher costs because informed patients tend to be more demanding in terms of drugs, diagnostics and treatments (Ubel, 2001).

The major reason that patients are unlikely to be frugal consumers as assumed by market models, however, is the failure to meet the third condition. Third-party payment, whether public or private, ensures that the consumer who receives the value pays only a fraction, if any, of the costs. Without controls, health insurance is accompanied by overconsumption because neither the patient nor the physician has much incentive to economize when an amorphous third party is paying the bill. *Moral hazard* is a term used by economists to refer to the behavioural changes that occur when people can spend or risk the funds of others rather than bear the cost themselves (Howe, 2005). Unless there are strong incentives not to do so, people will generally want more when someone else is paying for the service (see Box 4.6). Nevertheless, it should be noted that, although

---

Box 4.6   How moral hazard works

You have just finished a meal with a group of six of your friends at a fancy restaurant, and the waiter rolls by with a cart of desserts at a price of £7 each. You are hesitant to order because you are full and do not think you can get £7 worth of pleasure from the dessert. Then in a flash of brilliance, you remember that you are splitting the bill seven ways, meaning the cost of the dessert to you will be only £1. Surely you will be able to get a pound's worth of pleasure? So you go ahead and order. Unfortunately, your friends, reasoning the same as you, all order a dessert too. As a result, each of you pays the full price for a dessert that none of you would have spent £7 on. 'Health care insurance, like the single check in a restaurant, distributes expenses across many people, creating an incentive to buy health care services that cost more than they are worth...' (Ubel, 2001: 31).

---

he does not dispute the reality of moral hazard, Nyman (2008) argues that the preoccupation with it is misplaced and that a portion of it generates reduced downstream costs.

Therefore, without strict controls and a restructuring of traditional market functioning, both equity and efficiency will be lacking. Although there are steps that governments can take to modify the market (e.g. move from retrospective to prospective payment systems), adequate regulation requires inclusion of bureaucratic controls to shape the diverse demands of the health care marketplace. While this does not negate a role for the market, alone it is insufficient to deal with the peculiarities of health care. A major aim of moves towards managed care in the USA and elsewhere is to curb moral hazard by limiting services that the insured person can access at the plan's expense.

Medical savings accounts

Other mechanisms designed to rein in moral hazard are co-payments, discussed earlier, and medical savings accounts (MSAs) as found in Singapore. Proponents argue that the MSA model has the potential to constrict health spending by exposing consumers to greater cost sharing. The theory is that if people are given the opportunity to accumulate their own funds to pay for health care, they are more likely to think twice before using health services since the cost will be drawn from their personal account. Therefore, MSAs have received considerable interest across a variety of types of health systems and have even been discussed as an option for European systems (Thomson and Mossialos, 2008). In the USA, the Health Savings Account provisions of the 2003 Medicare Prescription Drug, Improvement, and Modernization Act provides tax breaks for individuals who establish such accounts when coupled with a qualified, high-deductible health insurance plan. By 2008 over 6 million privately insured Americans had participated (Glied, 2008). In addition to Singapore and the USA, about 15 other countries have either adopted or considered MSA programmes to reduce the moral hazard and shift some responsibility for risk bearing to the individual. Despite these efforts, its appeal to consumers has been muted and some observers conclude there is little to recommend them to European policy makers. 'Since MSAs are essentially a variant of cost sharing, their introduction could set in motion a process of de-insurance that may increase choice for some, but is also likely to jeopardize important health policy goals' (Thomson and Mossialos, 2008: 4). In other words, what might work in Singapore will not necessarily work in other cultural and political settings.

Adverse selection and risk spreading

In addition to the asymmetry of knowledge and power between patients and health care professionals, the inability of health care consumers to

---

Box 4.7   Adverse selection

Adverse selection is related to the concept of moral hazard and is endemic in private insurance. It occurs when sicker people, or those who present a higher risk to the insurer, buy health insurance while healthier people do not buy it, or when sicker people buy more health insurance or more robust health plans while healthier people buy less coverage. Adverse selection puts the insurer at a greater risk of losing money through more claims than it predicted. If an insurance company does not limit adverse selection, it will eventually will go out of business. In an unregulated insurance market, through an underwriting process, the insurer tries to determine the risk it will face in insuring an applicant. It might then decide not to sell health insurance to someone who poses too great a risk, or to charge a riskier person higher premiums than it charges someone likely to have fewer claims. Additionally, a company might limit its risk by placing an annual or lifetime limit on the amount of coverage, by excluding pre-existing conditions or specific expensive health care products or services from coverage. Under the Affordable Care Act in the USA, companies are prohibited from using most of these techniques, while an individual mandate is designed to force healthy individuals to purchase insurance (Davis, 2016).

---

judge the value received, and the general failure of marketplace mechanisms to produce efficiency, *adverse selection* is a pervasive problem in private insurance (see Box 4.7). Moreover, although private insurance can spread the risk and the burden of payment, private insurers have an incentive to exclude, or at least raise the premiums of, high-risk individuals. Typically, private health insurance is most economical for people who are healthy, while health care is consumed mostly by sick people who are unable to obtain affordable private insurance in the marketplace. Income redistribution based on market principles is, thus, not possible without intervention that negates the very principles of supply and demand. To some extent, then, a social insurance mechanism is needed to resolve this problem.

Controlling the marketplace

There are ways of controlling the non-public sector, however. As noted earlier, although Japan's health care system is dominated by the private insurance sector, and providers compete for patients, all sectors are strictly regulated through a centralized national fee schedule. While universal coverage guarantees access to available health care, in large part the uniform fee schedule has been successful in restraining total health care expenditures and has a critical role in setting allocation priorities. It serves as an allocation mechanism by providing a financial incentive structure for the provision of selected services (i.e. primary care) by setting the fee allowed higher than the actual costs. In contrast, it can discourage medical applications deemed undesirable by setting the allowable fees lower than the actual costs.

In addition to Japan, other countries actively intervene in private health care markets with detailed regulations of the command-and-control type. The Netherlands has gone as far as integrating private health insurance into a unified, compulsory social insurance, where private insurers (on par with the other insurance funds) are mandated to provide basic insurance at set income-related premiums. In contrast, in the UK, where private insurance plays only a supplementary role, there is little regulation of the private insurance market, while in the USA regulation is widespread, primarily at the state level, but is uneven and historically ineffective in controlling costs. Although many health systems have undergone reforms aimed at increased reliance on market or quasi-market mechanisms, in all cases governments have maintained firm control. Germany, the Netherlands, New Zealand, Sweden, Taiwan and the UK have introduced or strengthened competition among the providers in their health systems without sacrificing cost control and universal coverage.

In Sweden, New Zealand and the UK, the so-called 'purchaser–provider split' was introduced as an effort to mimic market mechanisms and to stimulate competition among providers. In the UK, the initial internal market with its emphasis on regulated competition was transformed into a public contract model that aimed to build on long-term cooperation (Ham, 2009). For example, contracts were replaced by long-term service level agreements, and purchasers became commissioners; that is, organizations that are concerned not only with paying for services but also with planning. In contrast to the UK, the introduction of the purchaser–provider split has been less prevalent in Sweden, reflecting the high degree of decentralization in the health system.

Meanwhile, in Germany and the Netherlands, the introduction of market mechanisms has mainly focused on competition among purchasers rather than providers: that is, the insurance funds (Greß *et al.*, 2002). This was effected by allowing employees a free choice of insurance fund, thus breaking with the tradition of occupation-based health insurance. In Germany, the insurance funds compete for employees on the basis of the additional, flat-rate contribution rate raised by individual insurance funds (Leiber *et al.*, 2010). To mitigate the unequal distribution of health risks, the funds from this contribution rate are pooled centrally and allocated on the basis of a risk adjustment mechanism. Ironically, Australia has taken measures to bolster private insurance in light of the steady decline in the proportion of the population with insurance for private hospital treatment since the 1980s (Box 4.8).

> ## Box 4.8 Encouraging private insurance in Australia
>
> To increase the population coverage of private insurance, reduce pressure on public hospital waiting lists and services, and support and improve the viability of the private insurance industry, Australia introduced a series of measures under the Private Health Insurance Incentive Scheme. In 1999, anyone purchasing private insurance received a 30 per cent subsidy, paid either as a tax rebate or as a reduced purchase price of insurance. In 2000, Lifetime Health Cover was introduced, which applied a base premium to those purchasing insurance up until the age of 30. Those who have continuous private health insurance cover from age 30 pay the base rate. Those joining after 30 pay an age-related premium calculated at 2 per cent on top of the base premium for every year of age, up to the age of 65. Thus, the government's solution to the private health insurance problem was to secure a reduction in the cost of premiums (the 30 per cent rebate), limit the out-of-pocket costs faced by the insured patient (the introduction of no-gap policies) and encourage younger people to join and maintain their fund membership through Lifetime Health Cover.

Although cost containment, accompanied by market mechanisms, became a central tenet of health policy reforms of the 1980s and 1990s, it has proven to be an elusive and disputable goal. To the extent that cost containment measures weaken the health of the population or access to care, they provoke disapproval. On the other hand, it is evident that without successful initiatives to constrain costs, health care systems face severe funding crises. Because of these counter-pressures, priority setting in health care undoubtedly will prove to be an even more incendiary issue in the future. Central to this is the concept of rationing medicine.

Allocation and rationing: the need to set priorities

'All health care systems face problems of justice and efficiency related to setting priorities for allocating a limited pool of resources to a population' (Sabik and Lie, 2008: 1). As pressures build to expand basic care coverage to encompass intensive curative regimes, the goal of universal coverage is threatened. A fundamental issue facing all health systems, then, is how to accommodate these important, but often conflicting goals. Weale (1998) likens this dilemma to what logicians call an 'inconsistent triad': a collection of propositions, any two of which are compatible with each other but which, when viewed as a threesome, form a contradiction. 'Perhaps we can have only a comprehensive service of high quality, but not one available to all. Or a comprehensive service freely available to all, but not of high quality. Or a high quality service freely available to all, but not comprehensive. Each of these three possibilities defines a characteristic position in the modern debate about healthcare costs and organisation' (Weale, 1998: 410).

While most Western countries have opted to ensure universal coverage, but limit the range of services, the USA has a system that offers high-technology, comprehensive care, but without universal access. Those with first-rate insurance coverage enjoy ready access to specialized medicine with near complete freedom of choice, but at the cost of equity in the health system. In contrast, critics of national health systems argue that free availability comes only at a cost to quality, choice and rapid technological diffusion. Weale (1998) suggests that while the third option – sacrificing some comprehensiveness to achieve at least a core range of quality services available to all – was a possibility when drugs were few and treatments simple, that is no longer the case. It is simply not possible to meet the needs of all citizens without compromising goals. Largely, this is what allocation, rationing and priority setting are all about – balancing the competing goals and demands facing the health system. Ultimately this entails making hard choices among equally admirable goals and explains why priority setting in health care is such a politically charged topic (Sabik and Lie, 2008).

Priority setting decisions take place at three levels: allocation to health care; allocation within health care; and rationing at the individual level. The first level, macro-allocation, is a decision as to how much of its resources society is willing to devote to health care: 5 per cent of GDP, 10 per cent, 15 per cent, or an unlimited amount? It addresses what priority society places on spending for medical care as compared to education, housing, social welfare, national security and so forth. To what extent does increased allotment of resources to medical care improve the health of the population when the funding must come at the expense of these other areas? In other words, what are the 'opportunity costs' of putting more resources into health care? (See Chapter 7 for expanded discussion of this issue.)

Once this determination is made, the question shifts to how these resources are to be allocated among the myriad categories of spending within health care, to distinct forms of treatment and to specific disease categories. Should priority be placed on preventive medicine, health promotion and primary care, or on more intensive high-technology medicine? Should treatment of diseases of the elderly or care of young mothers and children be given higher priority? Similarly, should precedence be placed on extending life or improving quality of life; the marginally ill or the severely ill; high-incidence diseases or rare diseases; AIDS or cancer or heart disease? At some stage, allocation within health care requires consideration of trade-offs that can be more or less transparent, centralized or decentralized, fair or unfair, but always controversial.

Finally, if society is unable or unwilling through its allocation policies to meet the health care needs of all persons due to limited resources, rationing decisions at the individual level are unavoidable (Lamm and Blank, 2007). The ubiquitous nature of scarcity driven by the trends discussed in Chapter 1 makes it certain that the demands of individuals and groups will exceed the available resources, thus requiring the rationing of these resources (see Box 4.9). Collectively, it is impossible for doctors to offer all technologically feasible and clinically beneficial medicine to all patients. As noted by Fleck (2002), there can be no health reform without health care rationing and no fair health reform without health care rationing for all.

Types of rationing?

Rationing is generally defined as the denial of a treatment to an identifiable patient who would benefit from it. This could be any type of treatment, but most often it is an expensive procedure or drug. Whatever specific form it takes, rationing always results in the situation where potentially beneficial treatment is denied on cost grounds. Given that rationing is necessary, the question becomes one of how to implement it. How do we assure legitimacy and impartiality without compromising success? Furthermore, if resources are to be focused on the provision

---

Box 4.9   Rationing is essential in tax-funded health systems

It has become commonplace for decisions made by the UK's National Institute for Health and Clinical Excellence (NICE) to be greeted with public outrage (Harrison and McDonald, 2007). It comes as little surprise that the Institute's rejection of five appeals against its guidance restricting the use of four drugs for Alzheimer's disease has been branded 'blatant cost cutting' by the Alzheimer's Society. But this reaction says less about NICE's decision-making process than it does about the divide between patient expectations of the health system and understanding the necessity for rational spending. Public opinion surveys in the UK repeatedly show overwhelming support for a universal health system, but it is clear from reactions to decisions such as that of NICE that individuals do not connect the NHS ideal with the necessity for some form of rationing to make the best use of limited funds. Is this simply a misunderstanding? Not quite. One big barrier to resolving this problem is the government's unbending commitment to the mantra of patient choice. By encouraging patients to demand more from health services, it effectively ignores the fact that a tax-based system means that some form of rationing is essential (*The Lancet*, 2006).

of 'appropriate' health care, who should define it and how can it be determined? And, what are the criteria for rationing – total lives saved, life-years saved, or quality-of-life years saved? Because there are no unequivocal answers and because rationing is so entangled with problems of cost containment and efficiency, its implementation is always exceedingly divisive.

Although the term rationing provokes strong emotions, all health systems ration medicine because none can provide unrestricted health care resources for all their citizens (Maynard and Bloor, 2001; Ham and Robert, 2003). Furthermore, despite intensified pressures on health care systems today, rationing has always been a part of medical decision making. Table 4.2 illustrates the range of ways in which health care can be rationed. Whether imposed by an attending physician, a market system where price determines access, a queue system where time and the waiting process become the major rationing mechanisms, or a triage system (see Box 4.10) where care is distributed as to benefit as defined by the

Table 4.2   *Forms of rationing medicine*

Form	Criteria used
Physician discretion	Medical benefit to patient
	Medical risk to patient
	Social class, gender, ethnicity, or mental capacity
Competitive marketplace	Ability to pay
Private insurance	Ability to pay for insurance
	Group membership
	Employment
Social insurance	Entitlement
	Means test
Legal	Litigation to gain access and treatment
Personal fundraising	Support of social organizations
	Skill in public relations
	Willingness to appeal to public
Implicit rationing	Queuing
	Limited manpower and facilities
	Medical benefits to patient with consideration of social costs
Explicit rationing	Triage
	Medical benefits to patient with emphasis on social costs and benefits

Source: Adapted from Blank (1997: 93).

Box 4.10   Medical triage

Triage, meaning 'choice' or 'selection', is used when many patients simultaneously need medical attention and medical personnel cannot attend to all. The rule is to first treat persons whose condition requires immediate attention without which they will progress to a more serious state. Others, whose condition is not as serious and who are stable, are deferred. This sort of triage is often necessary in busy emergency departments. A second sort of triage is indicated in disasters where the most seriously injured may be left untreated, even at risk of death, if their care would absorb so much time and attention that the work of rescue would be compromised. As applied to rationing, triage means that some patients will not be treated if the use of resources on them would be futile and would divert resources from those patients who would benefit more.

---

medical community, medical resources have always been allotted with criteria that inherently contain varying degrees of subjectivity. Moreover, in many instances, rationing principles can be grounded in a value context that results in an inequitable distribution of resources based on social as well as strictly medical considerations.

Although a mixture of these types of rationing is present in all countries, each health care system accentuates specific forms. Countries with national health systems have an easier time using more explicit rationing mechanisms through their control of the supply of resources. This is because they usually have not explicitly defined their services, as is common in social and private insurance systems where the member has, in effect, a contract for specific services. Therefore, the services are purposely kept vague by the government so as to provide more room for manoeuvre. Moreover, in countries with socially determined health budgets, constraints in one area can be justified on grounds that the money will be spent on higher priority services in another area. By contrast, in the fragmented US system or Singapore's individual responsibility system it is considerably more difficult to refuse any services for specific patients because there is no certainty the funds will be put to better use elsewhere. The lack of a fixed budget, either for government funding or overall national health care spending, makes it impossible to say where money 'saved' from rationing will go, but it does not mean that rationing does not exist (Box 4.11).

Not surprisingly, rationing is more complex in social insurance systems where legislation and/or contracts explicitly spell out the coverage. In principle, this makes rationing easier as it merely involves excluding certain treatments and procedures from the list of reimbursable services. An obvious lever is the assessment of medical technology discussed below.

Box 4.11   Rationing in the USA: haphazard and uncoordinated

Americans resist direct, explicit limitations on medical care, but rationing occurs in less obvious ways on many levels. It begins with coverage decisions over the scope of benefits and eligibility, while at the programme level decisions are made about reimbursable providers and institutions. Related decisions include the use of formularies and payment tiers, gate-keepers to specialized services, access to primary care doctors and specialists and other managerial choices that influence coverage, access and treatment. Rationing also occurs at the direct service level when clinicians make decisions on patient priorities, time for each, need for referral, and expensive interventions. Other types of rationing that are not transparent to the public include: denial of access and services; selection based on subjective assessments of likely benefit or patient status; deflection when patients are sent elsewhere to avoid responsibility for care; deterrence when people are confronted by unresponsive phone systems, rude personnel and long waiting times; delay that makes it difficult to schedule an appointment in a timely fashion; dilution by offering less content in the service than is reasonable or needed; and termination when people in distress are told that no more can be done for them. Therefore, the inclination to see rationing solely as distribution of an unavoidably scarce resource misses the numerous policy and service decisions that determine what care people receive (Mechanic and McAlpine, 2010).

In the Netherlands, for example, the coverage of social health insurance has come under scrutiny and homoeopathic drugs have been excluded, while the standard dental package has been considerably reduced. However, the explicit way in which coverage is defined also makes rationing more difficult because it makes any exclusion of services highly visible and therefore potentially politically costly.

Supply-side rationing traditionally is practised by national health services and depends upon setting strict limits on medical facilities, equipment and personnel. Rationing in both the Netherlands and Germany has focused on measures such as reducing the number of hospital beds, setting sectoral budgets and contribution rates, and restricting the increase in the number of doctors. In these systems, the availability of resources inevitably affects clinical decisions, with GPs often serving as gatekeepers and deflecting patients from overloading the system.

In contrast, market-oriented systems depend on *demand-side* rationing which is even more contentious. The USA, for instance, begins with excess hospital capacity and an oversupply of accessible specialists. As a result, the system has the capacity to perform any available procedure, including those that the public system does not cover. Persons

| Taiwan | UK | Germany | Japan | Australia | USA |
| Sweden | New Zealand | | Netherlands | Singapore | |

No Price Rationing   **High Price Rationing**

Figure 4.2   *Degree of price rationing*

with adequate insurance or resources are unlikely to accept artificially imposed constraints on their access to medical specialists. Moreover, demand-side rationing in this environment is susceptible to constant personal appeals for coverage and is difficult to sustain politically.

An overlapping distinction is between *price* and *non-price* rationing (see Figure 4.2). Price rationing is commonplace in the USA where health care resources are denied only to persons who cannot afford them or who have inadequate third-party coverage. In contrast, non-price rationing, which is characteristic in public health systems, depends on limiting the availability of certain health services, and thus denies medical resources even to persons who have the means to afford them. Of course, one option open to patients in countries with strict non-price rationing is to go elsewhere (medical tourism) for treatment and pay for it out of pocket (Cortez, 2008a). Another option is to use the private sector if one is available domestically.

Another aspect of rationing is that some forms can be carried out only by government action while others fail to distinguish clearly between public and private sector choices. As one moves to the more explicit forms of rationing at the bottom of Table 4.2, a more systematic government role is required and thus it is no surprise that these types are found primarily in national health systems. Other forms of rationing, such as public relations and market, often occur outside the public sphere. A related question regarding the government role in rationing is where it is carried out: are these decisions made by government, by a department or ministry, by regional health authorities, or by individual hospitals? Are these decisions highly centralized or decentralized, bureaucratized or ad hoc?

Core or basic services approach

Rationing has also been proposed as a means of guaranteeing every citizen a basic level of health care and excluding treatments outside this package. The explicit trade-off here is between universal access to those services deemed basic on the one hand and unequal access to the full range of technically feasible services on the other. A basic level of health care often emphasizes primary care and restricts coverage of high-technology services such as organ transplants, fertility treatments and cosmetic surgery. Health systems such as those in Britain, New Zealand and Japan are more successful in providing universal coverage and maintaining lower per capita costs than the all-embracing US system, but only so long as they curb accessibility to high-technology medicine. Once they provide levels of medical care similar to the USA, they lose this advantage.

One approach to rationing, then, is to define a set of funding priorities or list of *core* services to be funded (see Sabik and Lie, 2008). In 1992, New Zealand set up the Core Services Committee with the objective of implementing a comprehensive core services strategy to ration health services. The Committee promulgated four principles for assessing a service: benefit; value for money; fairness; and consistency with the community's values and priorities (New Zealand Core Services Committee, 1992). After extensive public consultation and research on a range of specific treatment regimes, however, the Committee concluded that an exclusive list of funding priorities that denied specific treatment categories was untenable and opted instead to continue services already funded. Exclusion of treatment categories was not only politically volatile, but also raised questions of fairness and failed to account for variation among patients within each category.

Another approach was offered in the 1991 Dunning Committee report advising the Dutch government on priorities in social health insurance (Ham, 1997b). Like New Zealand, the Committee proposed a comprehensive approach that would include health technology assessment, the use of guidelines for the adequate provision of care and the identification of criteria for prioritizing patients on waiting lists. The aim was to provide politicians with tools to generate a basic health care package. Such explicit priority setting was considered necessary to continue guaranteeing access to essential care for all; however, since the Committee's report, initiatives have focused on assessing the cost-effectiveness of health technologies (and developing guidelines) rather than on choosing among services (Ham, 1997b). Again, this reflects strong professional and public resistance to the removal of certain services, such as contraceptives, from public funding (similarly, see Sabik and Lie, 2008).

Although the UK has not conducted a national inquiry into priority setting, in part because priority setting happens at the local level of the health authority (Locock, 2000), in response to a comprehensive review by a parliamentary committee, the government articulated its view on the issue. While explicit exclusion of certain services from the NHS was seen as unnecessary, it was felt that resources should be concentrated on the most effective type of treatments. This plea for 'evidence-based medicine' was echoed by developments in health technology assessment, particularly the creation of the National Institute for Clinical Excellence (NICE) in 1999 (later renamed National Institute for Health and Care

Excellence) that, ironically, is viewed by some to constitute explicit, national rationing (Syrett, 2003). At the same time, with its focus on national standards and transparency, NICE offers a counterweight to the predominant practice of local decisions on provision and coverage of service (Landwehr and Böhm, 2011).

Rationing by exclusion has been criticized as price rationing because those patients with the ability to pay can often obtain the services in the private market or elsewhere while those who cannot must do without. Other problems include 'co-morbidity inconsistencies', when one condition is included and the other not, and 'diagnostic creep', where doctors manipulate diagnoses to ensure they fall within the funded list (see Moynihan, 2016). Core service or other prioritizing schemes also can lead to political pressures to add dramatic lifesaving interventions for individuals, especially for those previously covered services eliminated from the list.

Other rationing strategies

Although not as transparent as these attempts to prioritize health care services, the universal fee structure of Japan has a clear prioritizing function through its control over the diffusion of new technologies. More expensive innovations are discouraged because the charge allowed for a new treatment is computed by comparing it to the cost of the nearest existing treatment. Rationing decisions are made through the incentive structure determined by societal priorities as reflected in the fee levels. Moreover, the government ensures equity in financing among the multitude of private and public plans and equality of service since providers are always paid the same amount for a service no matter what insurance plan the patient has, even if on public assistance. Although the system has problems with multiple diagnoses and increased volume to make up for fee constraints, overall Japan has created an effective system for eliminating the necessity of making patient-specific rationing decisions at the individual level.

In Germany, priority setting is both implicit and explicit (Landwehr and Böhm, 2011). In comparison to the Netherlands and Sweden it is implicit, in that there has been no formal review of the issue. At the same time, priority setting is quite explicit in that it is part of the contractual and fee negotiations between providers and insurance funds. For example, broad priorities can be expressed by defining the coverage of social health insurance through a positive list (as in the case of care by non-physicians) or through evaluating the effectiveness of new as well as existing diagnostic and therapeutic methods. Fine-tuning of priorities is also possible through defining the relative value of an individual treatment as part of the fee schedule.

These diverse efforts at rationing represent rather primitive initial attempts to face systematically the problems of setting health care priorities within the context of scarce resources. Although none of these efforts has been fully successful, they have helped lay the groundwork for fair and workable rationing approaches. Explicit priority-setting efforts must withstand pressures for dramatic, often lifesaving, interventions for specific individuals identified as needing them and face allegations that a narrowed core services agenda magnifies inequities between those with private insurance and those without. For Klein (2005), the legitimacy of any rationing scheme depends on better, more evidence-based methods of analysis. Moreover:

> Given conflicting values, the process of setting priorities for health care must inevitably be a process of debate . . . which cannot be resolved by an appeal to science and where the search for some formula or set of principles designed to provide decision-making rules will always prove elusive. Hence the crucial importance of getting the institutional setting of the debate right . . . the right process will produce socially acceptable answers – and this is the best we can hope for. (Klein and Williams, 2000: 25)

To attain legitimacy, rationing processes need to command the confidence of a public who do not know, or care, about the technical aspects but want assurance that decisions reflect social values and are transparent.

Rationing by lifestyle and age

Rationing by lifestyle

Any rationing of health care resources is complicated because, as noted in Chapter 1, with the advance of sophisticated curative medicine, health care spending has become concentrated in a relatively small number of patients in acute care settings. Typically, these high users of health care are likely to be persons with chronic medical problems who exert disproportionate leverage on medical resources by repeated use of hospital facilities. In addition to the elderly, high users of health care are predominantly identified as persistently ill individuals, many of whom have unhealthy lifestyles and who are often non-compliant. A few risk factors, including alcohol and drug abuse, cigarette smoking, obesity, sedentary lifestyles and unhealthy diets, are particularly evident among high users of medical care (see Table 4.3). In addition to having more frequent episodes of ill health, patients with these behaviours require greater repeated hospitalizations for each episode, thus increasing the 'limit cost' of the illness.

Table 4.3   *Lifestyle and self-inflicted diseases*

Lifestyle	Self-inflicted diseases
Alcohol abuse	Cirrhosis of the liver, encephalopathy, foetal alcohol syndrome, accidents, violence
Cigarette smoking	Emphysema, chronic obstructive pulmonary disease (COPD), chronic bronchitis, lung cancer, coronary artery disease
Drug abuse	Suicide, overdose, malnutrition, infectious diseases
Overeating	Obesity, hypertension, diabetes, heart disease, varicose veins
High fat intake	Arteriosclerosis, diabetes, coronary artery disease
Low-fibre diet	Colorectal cancer
Lack of exercise	Coronary artery disease, hypertension
High-risk sexual behaviour	Sexually transmitted diseases, AIDS, cervical cancer

Source: Adapted from Leichter (1991: 77).

Over the last half-century, data on the major causes of mortality show a shift from infectious diseases to degenerative chronic diseases linked with individual behaviour (Nolte and McKee, 2011). Behavioural causes now account for nearly 40 per cent of all deaths in the USA (Mokdad *et al.*, 2004) and even more in other countries like Taiwan with over 50 per cent (Wen *et al.*, 2008). As illustrated in Table 4.4, two factors,

Table 4.4   *Causes of death in the USA, 2000*

Cause	Estimated number of deaths	Percentage of total deaths
Tobacco	435,000	18.1
Obesity	400,000	16.6
Alcohol	85,000	3.5
Microbial agents	75,000	3.1
Toxic agents	55,000	2.3
Motor vehicles	43,000	1.8
Firearms	29,000	1.2
Sexual behaviour	20,000	0.9
Illicit use of drugs	17,000	0.7
Total	1,159,000	48.2

Source: Adapted from Mokdad *et al.* (2004).

smoking and obesity, alone account for 35 per cent of the 2.4 million deaths in the USA. Moreover, it has been estimated that 50 to 90 per cent of all cancers are promoted or caused by various personal and environmental factors. 'Better control of fewer than ten risk factors . . . could prevent between 40 and 70 per cent of all premature deaths, a third of all cases of acute disability, and two-thirds of all cases of chronic disability' (Sullivan, 1990: 1066). Likewise, as will be discussed in Chapter 7, the impact of obesity on health care spending is substantial and growing rapidly (Thorpe *et al.*, 2004a).

These data raise serious implications for rationing. First, they suggest that any efforts to reduce health care costs must be directed at high users simply because they collectively consume such a large proportion of funds. 'There are serious limitations to the effectiveness of any cost containment strategies that focus on the 90 percent of the population that collectively accounts for only one-third of the total US health care spending.' (Berk and Monheit, 2001: 17) Second, they demonstrate that considerable redistribution of societal resources is necessary if these individuals, many of whom are poor and/or on benefits, are to get the many health services they need. Third, they raise vital questions concerning the extent to which society can afford to support individuals who knowingly engage in high-risk behaviour. This is a particularly salient issue when these services include expensive interventions such as intensive care and organ transplantation.

Due to the high costs that risky behaviours generate, health systems are under heightened pressure to become more actively involved in personal lifestyle choices. Whether out of concern for fairness, paternalism, strict economics or a blame-the-victim mentality, momentum has led to aggressive efforts to effect changes in individual behaviour deemed dangerous for health. This is evident for smoking and drinking. Attempts to prohibit smoking in public places and discourage its use through high taxes are approached with near missionary zeal in many countries and similar anti-obesity programmes are emergent (see Chapter 7).

What should be done, however, when efforts to change behaviour fail and we are faced with patients who need treatment for self-imposed illness? Should smokers get heart transplants or bypass surgeries? Should alcoholics who drink themselves into organ failure be candidates for liver transplants? If so, should they go to the top of the organ waiting lists if they are the most urgent cases? Is it fair for those who try to live healthy lives to pay the enormous costs of those who do not? In other words, can it ever be fair to ration medical resources away from those individuals who cause or contribute to their own ill health? The answers to these questions, of course, are in part to be found in the cultural frameworks discussed in Chapter 2, but they also reflect the economic realities of limits.

Box 4.12 How much is too much?

Gregory 'X' is a 'frequent flyer', a label that many emergency rooms give to their regular visitors. Developmentally disabled and unwell in large part because he refuses to take his blood pressure medicine, between 1996 and 2001 he called '911' and was taken to the emergency room by ambulance over 1,200 times. His emergency room visits, ambulance rides and hospital stays have cost taxpayers over $900,000, with no end in sight. According to the staff, Mr X enjoys his notoriety and the treatment he receives, which he takes for granted – 'last year they told me my bill was a quarter-million dollars. I said so what? I'm sick. Take care of me.' Is there a moral obligation to treat such patients indefinitely or should society set limits? If so, who should implement these limits (Foster, 2001)?

In an age of scarce resources in which medical goods and services are rationed, the debate over lifestyle choice will increasingly focus on the extent to which this choice ought to influence rationing decisions. More than any other issue surrounding the rationing of medical resources, this aspect of lifestyle promises to be the most poignant. When should lifestyle criteria be expressly entered in the rationing equation? Who is responsible for establishing the criteria? What impact will this selection process have on the practice of medicine? What limits, if any, are there on the care of persons who continually harm themselves? (See Box 4.12 and consider what decision you would make in this case.)

Rationing by age

Another highly controversial aspect of rationing centres on the disproportionate use of health care resources by the elderly, especially those over age 80 (Reese *et al.*, 2010). The most common argument against considering age in making health care decisions is that such rationing amounts to age discrimination and is unfair because of the past contributions made to society by the elderly. In other words, society owes the elderly their 'just rewards'. Critics also reject economic arguments that greater savings are made from denying care to the old because younger people are relatively more productive to society or that more life-years are gained by giving preference to younger people. Moreover, opponents contest the view that elderly patients are less able to benefit from treatment and reject chronological age as a useful gauge of benefit, arguing that all patients should be assessed for treatment equally based on their physiology alone (Churchill, 2005).

In contrast, the 'fair innings' argument maintains that it is just that those who have already had more than their fair share of life should not be preferred to the younger person who has not. Williams (2000) suggests that we should not object to age being a criterion used in the prioritization of health care, because the alternative is too outrageous to contemplate – namely, that we expect the young to make large sacrifices so that the elderly can enjoy small benefits:

> This vain pursuit of immortality is dangerous for elderly people: taken to its logical conclusion it implies that no one should be allowed to die until everything possible has been done. That means not simply that we shall die in a hospital but that we shall die in intensive care. (Williams, 1997: 820)

Likewise, Callahan (1990) argues that even with relatively ample resources, there are better ways to spend our money than on indefinitely extending the life of the elderly beyond the 'natural lifespan'. For Callahan, a natural life span is one in which life's possibilities have largely been achieved and after which death may be understood as a sad, but nonetheless relatively acceptable event. To this end, we must abandon the notion that we should try endlessly through medical progress to reverse old age and instead accept ageing as a part of life, not just another medical obstacle to overcome. See Box 4.13 regarding kidney transplants and decide for yourself what is fair.

Box 4.13   Age, health and fairness in rationing kidney transplants

The current system for allocating kidney transplants to adults with end stage renal disease in the USA has emphasized fairness on a single principle: the longer a person has waited for a kidney, the more priority he or she must be given to receive one, with no consideration as to life expectancy before or after receiving a transplant. Thus, higher priority could be given to an 80 year old on dialysis with diabetes mellitus and extensive vascular disease who has waited longer than a more recently listed 30 year old with no comorbidities (Reese *et al.*, 2010). Although this system worked reasonably well when the number of older adults needing transplants was small, epidemics of obesity, diabetes mellitus and hypertension have led to rapid growth in the number of older adults with kidney failure. Consequently, the waiting list for kidney transplants more than doubled from 30,000 candidates in 1997 to over 83,000 candidates in 2009, while the proportion of recipients aged 65 and older increased from 6.5 per cent to over 16 per cent, with many centres accepting patients in their 70s or 80s (Reese *et al.*, 2010). Is it fair to take age and health into account when rationing scarce organs, given that many younger, healthier people will die by not doing so?

The older we become, the more health resources we consume. People who in earlier times would have died of one illness are often kept alive to suffer long-term decline in quality of life (see Box 4.14). Average per capita expenditure is approximately four times higher for the elderly than the non-elderly (Centers for Disease Control and Prevention, 2007) in part because of the concurrence of multiple and often chronic conditions. As noted in Chapter 1, the elderly use more acute care, are hospitalized about twice as often, stay longer in hospitals and are much more likely to be readmitted to the hospital. In the USA, nearly half of all ICU patients are over age 65, and the cost of ICU care for a patient over age 65 is three to five times more per day than the cost of resources utilized for the average acute care admission:

> Similar differences among age groups are reflected in the data on the top 5 per cent of health care spenders. People 65–79 (9 per cent of the total population) represented 29 per cent of the top 5 per cent of spenders. Similarly, people 80 years and older (about 3 per cent of the population) accounted for 14 per cent of the top 5 per cent of spenders. (Stanton and Rutherford, 2005: 3).

The debate will go on, but with the ageing of the baby boomers, unless something is done to change the skewed spending pattern, this burgeoning cohort will consume an inordinate proportion of health care resources. Simply put, health care costs cannot be controlled without using age as a criterion in rationing simply because the elderly are the prime users of technologies that increase the costs of medicine. Interestingly, although using age as a factor in rationing has been most widely

---

Box 4.14   Keeping the elderly alive but at what cost?

The cost of caring for ageing US citizens by 2030 will add 25 per cent to the nation's overall health care costs unless they actively work to stay healthy and preventive services are provided to help them (Centers for Disease Control and Prevention, 2007). Even if improved lifestyles and medical technologies can reduce the major causes of premature death, we will be left with a growing elderly population whose additional years of life may be dominated by non-fatal but highly debilitating conditions such as arthritis, osteoporosis and Alzheimer's disease (Stanton and Rutherford, 2005). The result could be longer life but worsening health, thus an actual decline in active life expectancy. Under these circumstances, health care becomes Sisyphean, where we conquer one disease only to throw ourselves into the arms of another disease as we attempt to fill this fiscal black hole by using resources that are desperately needed by other generations (Lamm and Blank, 2007).

condemned in the USA, in other countries such as the UK old age 'is a criterion for rationing health resources and it occurs at all levels of the National Health Service' (Williams, 2000: 198).

Whatever one's view as to whether the elderly are getting their fair share of the health budget or if they ought to get less than younger people because they have had their fair share earlier in life, there is no denying that the ageing population is a major problem for the distribution of health care resources and, in fact, in the redistribution of all societal resources. It is also clear that the problem will get progressively worse, particularly in countries like Australia, New Zealand, Taiwan and the USA that currently have relatively young but ageing populations. Any debate over setting limits to medical technologies and rationing health care must address the intergenerational redistribution of resources as well as the implications of any policy changes for the elderly. It is likely that as the issues raised here become understood by younger generations intergenerational tensions over health care will intensify.

Efforts to control new technologies

As noted in Chapter 1, the proliferation of biomedical technologies is a major factor in the escalation of health care costs. Although the patterns of introduction, diffusion and allocation of new technologies vary across countries, generally those with centralized funding and controls require that new technologies be accommodated within existing systems of resource allocation. Because trade-offs must be made between the innovation and current treatment for a specific medical condition as well as other existing conditions, there is a need to establish priorities. Analysis of marginal costs and benefits and comparison with existing treatments is critical, and a new procedure or drug can be rejected unless there is evidence it will have a major positive impact on health outcomes and/or reduce costs.

In contrast, in market-oriented systems new technologies are seldom rejected even when found to be ineffective and less so if they are efficacious and safe, but unaffordable. Since elimination of ineffective technologies alone is unlikely to restrain costs, countries face difficult decisions that involve sacrificing clinically useful technologies that might work but that collectively could impoverish the system while contributing very little to the health of the population. Thus, mechanisms are needed to engage in prospective assessment of technologies before they are widely diffused as well as compel discontinuation of those technologies that are ineffective, only marginally effective, or effective but too expensive to find social justification.

> ## Box 4.15 Lack of systematic assessment
>
> In the USA, assessment of new health policies is rarely systematic and typically undertaken by a haphazard collection of the curious, concerned or adequately funded. Moreover, often the objectivity of the investigators is difficult to assess, and studies are retrospective and include populations that are convenient from a sampling perspective but not relevant to broader policy making. 'Even though the concept of evidence-based decision-making is widely accepted in the clinical world, the approach has not permeated health policy' and this often leads to the 'discovery of unintended consequences years later' (Wharam and Daniels, 2007: 677).

Bodenheimer and Fernandez (2005) suggest that controlling costs while preserving quality requires a multifaceted approach. In addition to strengthening primary care and disease management programmes and reducing inappropriate care, medical errors and the use of hospital and emergency departments by high-cost patients, we need the dissemination of effective technology assessment mechanisms. Yet, in most countries, the history of health technology assessment (HTA) has been inconsistent and controversial (see Box 4.15). It has strong opposition from interests that see it as a threat to their autonomy and, conversely, reproach from others who feel that it has failed to provide critical assessment and thus stem the dissemination of dubious technologies and procedures.

Health technology assessment

HTA is well established in Australia, Britain, Sweden, the Netherlands and the USA, whereas in other countries it is still in its infancy (Banta, 2002; for an overview of European countries see Garrido *et al.*, 2008). In the Netherlands, when the implementation of the Dunning Report guidelines for the exclusion of some medical services from social insurance coverage proved too controversial, attention turned to HTA. An initial evaluation of the effectiveness of 126 existing technologies was undertaken as part of the investigative medicine programme run by the Health Insurance Funds Council (Ham, 1997b). In this shift towards evidence-based medicine, emphasis has been placed on the role of professional bodies and specialist associations. Interestingly, as Exter *et al.* observe, 'since the 1990s, such systematic evaluations . . . are used as an important tool to assist policy-making, including priority setting' (2004: 99). Here it is also indicative that the government created a specific programme to fund evaluation of health technologies. In sum, the Dunning Report has had a long-lasting effect on health policy and indeed its basic algorithm for health priority setting provides the basis for decisions taken on the basic health insurance package (Schäfer *et al.*, 2010: 99).

In 1987, Sweden was the first European country to establish a public agency, the Swedish Council on Technology Assessment in Health Care, which is responsible for promoting the cost-effective use of health care technologies (Garrido *et al.*, 2008). The Council reviews and evaluates the social, ethical and medical impact of health technologies and then distributes the information to front-line decision makers, including officials in the central government and county councils as well as doctors (Werkö *et al.*, 2001). In addition, the National Board for Health and Welfare has been commissioned to develop evidence-based guidelines for the treatment of selected chronic illnesses. Interestingly, the guidelines come in versions not only for health personnel and patients but also for policy makers and include guidance in priority setting (Glenngård *et al.*, 2005).

Similarly, in recent years, HTA in Britain has received heightened public awareness with the creation of NICE (Harrison and McDonald, 2007). NICE is responsible for evaluating new technologies and care guidelines regarding their clinical and cost-effectiveness at the request of the Department of Health. The Institute's guidance on the effectiveness of specific drugs has attracted public attention, among them Beta Interferon for multiple sclerosis sufferers, the flu drug Relenza and new types of drugs for breast cancer patients. The establishment of NICE accompanied the development of the National Service Framework, which set out patterns of care for specific diseases, disabilities and patient groups and the establishment of the Commission for Health Improvement (later replaced by the Healthcare Commission and absorbed into the Care Quality Commission in 2009) which, in turn, is responsible for monitoring and improving standards at the local level (Harrison and McDonald, 2008).

The Australian Health Technology Advisory Committee advises the government on the costs and effectiveness of targeted medical technologies. The Committee has representatives from the federal and state governments as well as the medical profession, insurance funds, hospitals and consumers. The Australian Institute of Health and Welfare also established a health technology division to monitor technological developments and advise the government on whether and under what conditions technologies should be used in Australia. Of the specific major areas studied, including MRIs, organ transplant procedures and laparoscopic surgery, recommendations have led to the introduction of these new techniques on a controlled basis (Palmer and Short, 2000). Additionally, in 1998 the Medical Services Advisory Committee was established to screen new medical procedures and services.

In the USA, assessment of medical technology has been pervasive in both the private and public sectors, but there has been little cooperation, coordination or even exchange of data among the many assessment endeavours. This situation led the American College of Physicians to conclude that the USA 'has no effective policies to restrain the spread of technology' (2008: 60). In a major study, the Institute of Medicine (IOM) likewise concluded that the USA must strengthen its capacity to assess clinical services (IOM, 2008). It recommended that Congress establish a National Clinical Effectiveness Assessment Program to develop standards and processes to provide 'systematic, reliable and unbiased information on clinical effectiveness'. It argued that although numerous stakeholders, policy makers and government entities have proposed that new investments be made in comparative effectiveness research, more attention is needed to ensure that health care decision makers can discern which evidence is valid and under what circumstances. To that end, the IOM recommended that the Program appoint an independent Priority Setting Advisory Committee to develop and implement a process for identifying high priority areas that merit systematic evidence assessment. It should be noted that such efforts have been proposed frequently in the past with little long-term success in the highly fragmented private/public environment of US health care.

HTA in Germany has tended to lag behind other countries. The German Institute for Health Technology Assessment (DAHTA) was first established in 2000 as part of the German Federal Ministry of Health and focused on the licensing of pharmaceuticals and medical devices or linked to the coverage specified in contracts with health care providers. In the case of ambulatory care, where regulation has developed furthest, the Joint Federal Committee (Gemeinsamer Bundesausschuss, G-BA) decides on the effectiveness of new technologies to be covered by health insurance as well as re-evaluating existing technologies based on the criteria of benefit, medical necessity and efficiency. Since assessments are sector-specific, historically HTA has been fragmented although developments in recent years mark a more systematic approach (Burau, 2007a; Sauerland, 2009). Examples are Disease Management Programmes for selected chronic illnesses that were introduced in 2004 and are based on evidence-based clinical guidelines and connected to mechanisms of financial reimbursement. Furthermore, the Institute for Quality and Efficiency in Health Care (IQWIG) in many ways resembles NICE in the UK and is responsible for evaluating clinical guidelines and providing information on quality (Busse and Blümel, 2014).

To date, the inclusion of quality management in Taiwan has been limited although there is increasing discussion of clinical guidelines and evidence-based medicine. While the Bureau of National Health Insurance (BNHI) has initiated a variety of quality monitoring and assurance programmes, including the Fee-for-outcomes (FFO) approach and the construction of hospital quality indicators, in comparison to other countries here Taiwan has trailed in this area. Moreover, HTA has been limited in Taiwan and the NHI has not made significant efforts to shape the diffusion of the latest sophisticated high-technology medicine (Lu and Hsiao, 2003). The ardent belief in the medical model, combined with the strong profit motive of providers in Taiwan, has resulted in the proliferation of new medical technologies with little substantiation as to whether they improve health.

In summary, HTA has become more critical in priority setting as the scarcity of resources increasingly conflicts with intensified demands and pressures for the dissemination of innovative techniques. Evidence-based medicine is currently a catch phrase for efforts to resolve health care dilemmas and provide a foundation for the allocation and rationing of health care resources, but it continues to lack clear definition and commitment in most countries.

Information technologies in medical practice

Another emergent debate over technologies in health care centres on the role of health information technologies (HIT) that facilitate the comprehensive management of health information across computerized systems and the exchange of this information among consumers, providers, government and quality entities and insurers. To date, most policy attention within HIT has focused on electronic health records (EHRs), which represent a systematic use of digital health information about individual patients or populations (Jha *et al.*, 2008).

EHRs have been touted by some as the most promising instrument for improving the overall quality, safety and efficiency of the health delivery system and moving an archaic, disjointed and inefficient system into the 21st century (Chaudhry *et al.*, 2006). Proponents argue that broad and consistent utilization of EHRs (and HIT in general) will moderate costs, improve quality, reduce medical errors, increase administrative efficiency, decrease paperwork and expand access to affordable care. Moreover, many public health benefits, including early detection of infectious disease outbreaks and improved tracking of chronic disease management and evaluation of health care, could accompany the use of HIT (Davis *et al.*, 2009). In contrast, critics of EHRs argue that the start-up costs in time and money are prohibitive and raise concerns over privacy and confidentiality and other potential unintended consequences of digital records. Thus, adoption of HIT and, especially, systems for sharing information across providers has been slow and erratic across countries (Schoen *et al.*, 2007).

New Zealand

New Zealand was among the first countries to adopt HIT, particularly in primary care, where it has one of the highest international rates of use.

Although GPs moved quickly into EHR use in the 1990s, until recently HIT in general has lacked government leadership or coordination (Gauld *et al.*, 2012). Consequently, most physician groups are unable to share records with one another and interoperability with hospital systems and after-hours facilities is limited. In 2009, however, the national IT Health Board was created to coordinate developments, including nationally consistent portable electronic patient records, with an aim for all New Zealanders to have access to a basic set of web-based health information by 2014. The IT Health Board also produced the National Health IT Plan in 2010 to facilitate a fully integrated health system and works with a range of agencies, including private vendors whose activities such as working towards common standards are coordinated under the aegis of the New Zealand Health IT Cluster (Thomson *et al.*, 2013).

Britain

Through reimbursement, incentives and locally led commissioning from private providers, EHRs are also used in all GP practices in the UK NHS (Gauld *et al.*, 2012). Despite this, as in New Zealand the use of HIT in secondary care is sporadic, largely because of huge cost overruns and delays in implementing a nationwide NHS HIT programme deployed in 2005. The goal was to have 60 million patients in a centralized electronic health record by 2010, but because of numerous setbacks and widening criticism, it was terminated as a sentinel programme in 2011, although EHRs in physicians' offices remain.

Germany and the Netherlands

In Germany, there has been a high uptake of relatively sophisticated HIT in primary care settings, including that used for disease management and referrals, although interoperability between hospitals and primary care settings remains limited. There is no national strategy for HIT, but the electronic health card introduced in 2011 was to be fully implemented in 2014. Patients can decide whether their medical data are saved on the card or not. Similarly, in the Netherlands, all GPs use EHR for health recording and for administrative purposes. Drug prescription, communication with specialists and performance measurement are facilitated by EHR systems, although, to date, hospitals have comparatively low levels of EHR use and poor interoperability (Gauld *et al.*, 2012). A National IT Institute for Healthcare was created to improve this situation and coordinate future developments, although in November 2011 the planned national electronic patient record system was tabled for the immediate future.

Australia

Australia has been active in the development of lifetime EHRs for all its citizens and has a near universal use of them in GP practices and more limited usage in the hospital sector. The national strategy on health information is managed by the Australian Health Ministers' Advisory Committee with accords in place among governments and other key agencies on developing, collecting and exchanging data to improve the health of the population and the delivery of health services (Thomson *et al.*, 2013). In conjunction, health system performance indicators are being adopted and monitored. Moreover, an intergovernmental strategy on HIT was approved and the National E-Health Transition Authority (NEHTA) created to improve the quality and efficiency of health care. Under the Healthcare Identifiers Act of 2010, a unique 16-digit health care identifier is assigned to each health care consumer and provider to improve communications in discharge, tests, referrals and prescriptions. Another major national EHR initiative, Personally Controlled Electronic Health Record (PCEHR), became available nationally in 2013.

Singapore

Singapore has a comprehensive HIT system that began as an effort to develop hospital administrative systems for admissions, discharges and billing processes. This was supplemented in 2004 with an Electronic Medical Record Exchange (EMRX) to provide an electronic platform for the sharing of medical documents, which, in turn, led to the advent of EHRs designed to permit the eventual integration of diverse sub-systems. Singapore also developed the Integrated Care Services (ICS) webportal to connect acute hospitals, primary care providers and the public with nursing homes and chronic disease facilities. A distinctive feature of Singapore's HIT services is a personal health record (PHR), which incorporates hardcopy personal health books that provide individuals with ownership of their health records and promote better continuity of care both at the institutional level and at home (Lim, 2006).

Taiwan

As a leader in HIT, Taiwan has four major systems. The foundation of Taiwan's NHI system is digitized patient records and claims, which are closely linked to the other three elements: online claim submissions, the NHIA virtual private network (VPN) and the smart IC card (Long and Chang, 2012). The incentive for Taiwan's providers to digitize their patient records and claims is that with online claim submissions and reviews they can receive reimbursement from NHIA more quickly. Moreover, the online claim submission saves substantial administrative costs on both sides. These first three components are connected through the VPN and comprise Taiwan's NHI management information system that allows NHIA to carry out real-time monitoring of utilization. There is evidence that this system contributes to reduction of duplications in diagnostic procedures and laboratory tests, as well as duplication or contraindications of prescription drugs (Chi *et al.*, 2012).

Japan

Despite numerous initiatives over the past decade, HIT is not widely used in Japan other than for billing purposes. In 2010, the government announced the New IT Strategy to encourage its use. The Strategy has four parts: (1) develop patient electronic medical records that can be accessed by all providers; (2) develop HIT and telehealth platforms to help link patients with doctors and nurses in underserved areas; (3) create a platform that can monitor prescriptions and adverse events in real time; and (4) create a claims database of all conditions and interventions to facilitate assessment of community needs and development of interventions (Thomson *et al.*, 2013). Despite these initiatives, there continue to be many political and cultural barriers to widespread HIT adoption in Japan.

United States of America

A RAND Health study suggests that the US health care system could save more than $81 billion annually, reduce adverse health care events and improve the quality of care if it were to widely adopt HIT (Hillestad *et al.*, 2005). Despite calls for action by the IOM and an Executive Order from President Bush in 2004 that established a ten-year plan to expand HIT, most medical records are still stored on paper, meaning that they cannot be used to coordinate care, systematically measure quality or reduce medical errors. As of 2009, less than a third of physicians' offices had high functionality EHRs and less than 2 per cent of hospitals had comprehensive EHR systems (Thomson *et al.*, 2013). To stimulate investment in HIT, the 2009 American Recovery and Reinvestment Act provides financial incentives of up to $27 billion over six years for physicians and hospitals tied to the attainment of benchmarks for the 'meaningful use' of HIT (Thomson *et al.*, 2013). Moreover, the President's Council of Advisors on Science and Technology concluded that the move to EHRs is critical to cost containment efforts (Executive Office of the President, 2010). EHRs also figured prominently in the Affordable Care Act as noted by then Office of Management and Budget Director Peter Orszag in describing the Obama Administration's strategy:

> In order to help contain cost growth over the long term, we need a new health care system that has digitized information ... in which that information is used to assess what's working and what's not more

intelligently, and in which we're paying for quality rather than quantity. (Charlie Rose–Peter Orszag Interview, 2009)

Despite these efforts, Rudin *et al.* conclude that the pace of innovation of HIT in the USA 'continues to lag' (2016: 815).

Trends in priority setting

National policies on priority setting are a pertinent area to test the concept of convergence discussed in Chapter 1 since the predominance of public funding means that resources are limited, thus making priority setting inevitable. Table 4.5 summarizes our findings that reconfirm the interrelationship between convergence and embeddedness suggested by Saltman (1997). Using Bennett's (1991) distinctions between

Table 4.5   *Substantive and procedural aspects of health policy convergence*

	Policy goals	*Policy content*	*Policy instruments*
Rationing/ priority setting	An issue in all countries, but limited agreement on its meaning.	Much variation. Demand vs supply, price vs non-price rationing.	Wide variation though some moves towards more centrally controlled instruments.
Increased dependence on marketplace	An issue in all countries, highly controversial in many countries.	Most countries have adopted some market features but there is no clear convergence.	Wide variation even among national health and social insurance systems.
Cost containment strategies	An important goal in all countries, but even at this level its importance relative to universal access and equity varies.	Some moves to co-payment, provider-payment mechanisms, etc., but persistent differences in weight given to demand vs supply.	Considerable variation and mixes of policy instruments used to contain costs.

Source: Adapted from Blank and Burau (2006: 69).

convergence by policy goals, policy content and policy instruments, our analysis shows that there is some convergence, but it is restricted largely to the procedural aspect of policy goals and does not appear to extend to content and instruments. Despite signs of convergence at the ideational level, policy content and the preferred policy instruments for implementing such policy continue to vary widely across these countries. By and large, countries continue to adopt different strategies to deal with similar problems.

While there has been a shift in goals in all countries towards cost containment, the disparate emphases on an array of demand- and supply-side approaches display significant diversity across these countries. Also, while the inclusion of efficiency or cost containment as a goal appears universal, there remain wide disparities among the countries as to the degree of access and equity in their respective health care systems. Similarly, although all countries have integrated some aspects of the market into their systems through recent reforms, the wide variation in both form and degree argues against the conclusion that they are converging to a market-driven health system. Far from it! Unlike the USA, other countries continue to maintain relatively robust regulatory controls over market forces.

Regarding the allocation and rationing of health care resources, about the only perceivable convergence is that it is increasingly evident in all countries that medicine must be rationed because, in the light of endless technological possibilities, no country can serve the health needs of their population to the fullest. Countries with global budgets or other supply-side controls are likely to depend on non-price rationing mechanisms and make tougher choices at the macro-allocation level. In contrast, countries that rely more heavily on price rationing forgo setting broad limits, thus losing any semblance of equity or systematic rationing policy. The result is that rationing in national health systems differs greatly from that in social insurance systems and, especially, market-dominated systems.

It should also be noted that health policy is not static and that moves in one direction are often followed by moves towards the opposite direction as political fortunes change or the public responds negatively to a change. Any discussion of convergence risks underestimating the political dynamics inherent in health policy. For instance, New Zealand was widely cited as an example of NHS convergence towards a market system when it initiated strong market reforms in the early 1990s, although most of these reforms were repealed by later governments.

In the end, all countries must face the issue of rationing of health resources for the high users of health care, particularly the elderly and individuals who engage in high-risk behaviours. Evidence, however, suggests that there is little consensus in our countries as to whether or how to do this. Furthermore, because controlling the diffusion of medical technologies is such a critical factor in cost containment and central to any debate over rationing, the uneven efforts at HTA in most countries must be strengthened. The process of making the explicit trade-offs required when a decision is made to fund expensive new technologies or drugs must be more transparent: where specifically will the money come from, and what other programmes might be negatively affected?

Chapter 5 continues the critical analysis of resource allocation and now brings the health human resources into focus. Here, the interests of the medical profession as an important player in the health policy process converges with the rationale of health workforce governance to maximize 'value for money' and get the 'right' skills at the right places.

The Health Workforce

Health policy has long reduced health workforce issues to the medical profession while neglecting the vast number of health care workers, and comparative health policy mirrors this problem. Efforts to be more inclusive have gained momentum since forecasts revealed a widening gap between demand and supply, and international organizations took action (European Commission, 2008; OECD, 2008a; WHO, 2008a; Vujicic *et al.*, 2012; Dussault, 2015), reminding us that there is 'no health without a workforce' (Campbell *et al.*, 2013). The lack of attention to the human resources of health systems turned from a workforce issue into a system and policy failure. Health workers build the backbone of every health care system. Shortages, maldistribution and mismanagement therefore challenge equity and quality of care in the established welfare systems of the global North, and threaten the implementation of universal health care coverage and the global Social Development Goals (SDGs) in low- and middle-income (LMIC) countries (Bowser *et al.*, 2014; Glinos *et al.*, 2015).

Meanwhile, data source and monitoring systems have significantly improved and planning instruments are more complex in almost all OECD countries (OECD, 2013, 2016b; Batenburg, 2015; Joint Action, 2015; WHO, 2015b). Unfortunately, a lack of information on even basic health workforce indicators persists in many middle-income and especially in low-income countries and this limits systematic comparison (Ranson *et al.*, 2010; WHO, 2012a, d; Cailhol *et al.*, 2013).

After an initial focus on shortages and the 'looming crisis' (OECD, 2008b) of the health workforce, policy and scholarly debate are now drawing a more nuanced picture. Major concern has shifted 'from worries of widespread shortages towards more specific issues related to ensuring the right mix of health workers, with the right skills, and providing services at the right places, to better respond to changing population health needs' (OECD, 2016b: 13; see also WHO, 2016b). These developments have turned the health workforce into a highly dynamic labour market segment and a contested policy arena, where professional development and inter-professional relationships are re-negotiated to strengthen population and health systems' needs. This is in stark contrast to the past, where reform models targeted the medical profession, attempting to improve efficiency through various forms of management controls which are summarized as new governance and New Public Management, as discussed in Chapter 3.

Since the mix of skills and staff has moved onto the health policy agenda, nurses are gaining greater attention (Box 5.1). Across countries there is growing evidence of the benefits of an expansion of middle-level groups and the professional development of nurses, including shifting tasks from doctors to nurses (Global Health Workforce Alliance, 2010; Afzal *et al.*, 2011; Fulton *et al.*, 2011; Aiken *et al.*, 2013, 2014; WHO, 2015c; Schoenstein *et al.*, 2016). Yet 'evidence' does not easily translate into workforce changes, and new roles of nurses vary among health care systems (Kroezen *et al.*, 2014; Maier, 2015; Tsiachristas *et al.*, 2015; Maier and Aiken, 2016). A most recent OECD overview of policy priorities reminds us that an introduction of new roles for nurses has to overcome the initial opposition from the medical professions, and that:

[the] opportunity to expand further the scope of practice of non-physicians, will depend, to a certain extent, on the future supply and attitudes of physicians. Experience shows that such extensions in scope of practice tend to be easier to implement in times and places where there are fewer physicians. (Lafortune *et al.*, 2016: 59)

Box 5.1   Nurses in health systems

Among the many practitioners involved in the provision of health care, nurses now play a particularly prominent role, clearly illustrating the changes underway in the health workforce. Traditionally, nursing was conceptualized and de-valued as a 'semi-profession' with lack of full self-governing rights, reflecting the relative dominance of the medical profession in health systems. Recently however, feminist analyses have focused on nursing and its 'professional projects' (Witz and Annandale, 2006; Wrede, 2012). This has been echoed by studies, which stress that the health division of labour is not necessarily fixed, but instead dynamic and in flux and in fact more resembles a 'negotiated order'. This 'order' of medical dominance is increasingly questioned from different angles, including skill mix and task-shifting policies, patient needs, increasing specialization of nurses either on the lines of medical specialities (like theatre nurses, intensive care nurses, etc.) or as nurses' own professional projects, like the nurse practitioners (NPs) or elder care and community nurses. In many countries, nurses are academically trained and some hold postgraduate and PhD degrees. Nurses have been able to establish new leadership roles and strengthen their positions in management, as for instance in hospital management and quality control. Although still in low numbers, they have entered high-level leadership positions and some countries have strengthened self-governing capacities and nurses' participation in health policy making (De Raeve *et al.*, 2016). While change is underway in all countries, the success of nurses' professional development is highly dependent on the institutional contexts and governance models (Maier, 2015).

It is important to recall here the connections between the health workforce and the regulatory mechanisms of professionalism and medical self-regulation, which are embedded in the institutions of health care systems. The understanding of professions has changed over time (Dent *et al.*, 2016). Early approaches defined professions by specific traits (such as formal knowledge, extensive training and high social status) and by a positive role in society. These approaches have been criticized for taking the self-image of professions at face value and for remaining largely uncritical. Instead, later approaches focus on the social organization of power. Freidson (1994), for example, defines professions as being primarily concerned with attaining and maintaining control. Control consists of autonomy (that is, control over the professions' own work) and dominance (that is, control over the work of others). Medical power is highly complex and has both an individual and a collective dimension, comprising the freedom of individual doctors to practise as they see fit, as well as the activities of doctors' professional organizations. Light (1995) distinguishes among clinical and fiscal autonomy, practice and organizational autonomy, and organizational and institutional control, and Elston (1991) adds cultural authority to her understanding of medical power. Cultural authority refers to the dominance of medical definitions over health and illness.

At the same time, recent comparative studies on new forms of leadership and clinical management reveal variety in the control of doctors and their role in governance (Kuhlmann *et al.*, 2013; Burau, 2016; Kirkpatrick *et al.*, 2016). This builds on earlier historical analyses that emphasized the diversity of the phenomenon called 'professionalism' and exposed the Anglo-American centredness of many ideas about professions and power (Johnson, 1995). Acknowledging diversity of the professionals has been an impetus for comparative research more generally, as well as for gender-sensitive approaches (Kuhlmann *et al.*, 2012). It has also promoted critical revision of professionalism (Plochg *et al.*, 2009) and an expansion of the model of professionalism to nurses, therapists and other healthcare workers who are seeking to gain a voice in the policy process (Nancarrow and Borthwick, 2016). A further important characteristic is the gendered nature of professions that shape health workforce governance and the negotiations of new roles (McMurray, 2011; Kuhlmann *et al.*, 2012; Newman, 2014).

With this backdrop, this chapter places the comparative analysis of health workforce policy in the context of the medical profession's role, combining health labour market data and policy analysis. Comparative health workforce data are still poorly developed despite significant improvements (OECD, 2016a, b), especially when compared to other areas like funding. The analysis draws on OECD data as the most complex and standardized source, meaning that Singapore and Taiwan are missing from the workforce composition and mobility figures. Instead, additional countries are added to reflect the workforce situation in middle-income countries especially in the global South, and more generally, the relevance for comparative health workforce policy. In contrast to other dimensions of health policy, such as funding and allocation of physical resources, the health human resources are increasingly mobile in a globalizing world and a single European Union labour market, thus crossing the boundaries of country-based health system typologies. Poor workforce conditions in one country (usually less well-resourced countries), therefore, impacts directly in the health workforce in others and calls for global health policy responses.

The chapter continues by describing comparatively 'who doctors are' and highlighting diversity *within* the medical profession. It then explores the role of doctors as collective actors in the policy process. The sections that follow turn our attention to the variety *among* the professions, first by providing an overview of the occupational structure, and then by discussing in more detail the skills mix. The chapter concludes by examining the 'right places' (OECD, 2016b), including geographical imbalances and mobility flows and discussing challenges and development in health workforce policy in comparative perspective.

Who doctors are

Health systems and health policy cannot be understood without doctors and vice versa. The power of the medical profession stems from the fact that health care is largely defined as medical care. Doctors are responsible for diagnosis and as such define patients' health care needs, although the boundaries are now more permeable for other healthcare providers as well as for patients' perceptions. Doctors also provide treatment, but this nearly always involves (either directly or by referral) other groups, such as specialist doctors, nurses, physiotherapists, physicians' assistants, laboratory technicians or dieticians. This puts doctors in a key position regarding the allocation of health care resources, including to some degree health human resources and the skills and competencies of other health care providers.

Because doctors are embedded in specific sub-systems of funding, provision and governance, professional autonomy will always be contingent and relative, and this too points to the complex relationship between doctors and the state. Significantly, professional autonomy and power are part of the implicit contract between doctors and the state (Burau et al., 2009; Burau, 2016; Kuhlmann et al., 2016). The state grants professional autonomy in return for doctors providing services central to the legitimacy of modern states. Medical practice, because of the specialized knowledge at its base, also gives legitimacy to the (potentially problematic) allocation of health care resources. Inherent in this inter-dependent relationship between doctors and the state are tensions, espe-cially between medically defined need and a patient-centred approach, between medical-curative definitions and the views of carers and other professional groups and sectors, and between an expansion of medically defined need and a finitude of financial resources.

While the notion of profession suggests a cohesion that allows for dom-inance and autonomy, even a cursory look at statistics reveals consider-able diversity among doctors across and within countries, for example in terms of the number of specialists or the percentage of female doctors. The analysis of statistics naturally remains on the surface, but, as an overview, it provides a useful starting point for comparison. Through highlighting similarities and differences, statistics raise 'why' questions which demand more detailed analysis. The number of doctors presented in Table 5.1 pro-vides a first indication of the diversity that exists across countries.

In many countries, the trend in the number of doctors per 1,000 inhab-itants since the early 1960s tells a familiar story of welfare state expansion

Table 5.1   *Number of practising doctors per 1,000 inhabitants, 1980–2015*

	1980	1985	1990	1995	2000	2005	2010	2015[2]
Australia	1.8	1.9	2.2	2.5	2.5	2.8	3.1	3.5
Germany	n/a	n/a	n/a	3.1	3.3	3.4	3.7	4.1
Japan	1.3	1.5	1.7	n/a	1.9	2.0	2.2	2.4
Netherlands	1.9	2.2	2.5	2.4	3.2	3.7	3.0	3.4[3]
New Zealand	1.6	1.7	1.9	2.0	2.2	2.1	2.6	3.0
Singapore	n/a	n/a	n/a	1.4	n/a	1.5	1.8	2.3
Sweden	2.2	2.6	2.9	2.9	3.1	3.5	3.8	4.1
Taiwan	n/a	n/a	1.1	1.3	1.3	1.5	1.5[1]	1.7[4]
UK	1.3	1.4	1.6	1.8	1.9	2.4	2.7	2.8
USA	n/a	n/a	n/a	2.2	2.3	2.4	2.4	2.6

n/a = not available.

[1] The figures for Taiwan for 2010 are from 2007.

[2] Figures for New Zealand, Singapore and UK from 2015; figures for Australia, Germany, Japan and The Netherlands from 2014; figures for Sweden and USA from 2013.

[3] This number includes doctors working in management, education or other non-patient care jobs, resulting in a 5–10 per cent overestimation of practising doctors (OECD, 2016b: 42).

[4] Cited in Cheng, 2015; based on Taiwan Ministry of Health and Welfare, Statistics and Trends in Health and Welfare, Taipei, 2013: 135, in Chinese.

Sources: 1980–2010, OECD (2008a, 2012); Bureau of National Health Insurance (2008); 2015 (or nearest year), OECD (2016a), Singapore Ministry of Health (2016).

together with a shift towards curative, specialized medicine. In most countries, the number of doctors has more or less doubled. A steady growth continued even after the economic crisis in 2008 when austerity measures came into force. Moreover, in some countries the increase was even stronger than in the past, for instance in Germany, New Zealand and the UK, while an adverse trend can be observed in the Netherlands. This is interesting and illustrates that the health care sector is dynamic and less tied to economic cycles than other labour market segments (Pavolini and Kuhlmann, 2016). A recent report from OECD shows on average a 20 per cent increase of doctors in OECD countries between 2010 (2.3 per 1,000 population) and 2013 (3.3 per 1,000 population), while the ratio for nurses also increased but to a lesser degree (15 per cent) (OECD, 2016b: 17–18).

Beyond the commonality of growth over time, the current number of doctors ranges from 1.7 doctors per 1,000 inhabitants in Taiwan to 4.1 in Germany. The countries fall into roughly four groups: Taiwan with less than 2 doctors per 1,000 inhabitants; Japan, New Zealand, Singapore, the UK and the USA with 2.3 to 2.8; Australia and the Netherlands with 3.3 to 3.4; and Germany and Sweden with about 4 doctors per 1,000 inhabitants. The variation is obvious and, while there is no ready explanation for it, it may reflect differences in the levels of health care expenditure. It might also reflect government restrictions on the number of doctors in the form of limits on the number of medical students or the number of doctors who can establish practices outside hospitals (Moreira and Lafortune, 2016). A more recent impact may stem from new skill mix policies and the task shifting from doctors to nurses. This is, for instance, relevant in the case of the Netherlands (Kroezen *et al.*, 2014; Maier, 2015) where the number of doctors decreased between 2005 and 2013, following recommendations of the planning body, a trend that is also observed for Switzerland (not shown in Table 5.1) (Lafortune *et al.*, 2016: 58).

Countries differ not only in terms of the number of doctors but also in the diversity of the medical profession itself, as illustrated by the gender ratio and the ratio of generalists to specialists. Here, the scope of countries is expanded and includes Chile as an example of a South American system with a mix of Bismarckian and NHS-style reform elements and marketization (Giovanella and Faria, 2015), Turkey as an example of a successful reform based on strong state-interventionist policy but with little recognition of the health workforce (Agartan, 2015), and Portugal as an EU country faced by austerity measures and high unemployment rates (Dussault and Buchan, 2014; Correia *et al.*, 2015).

Table 5.2 shows an increase in women doctors to the extent that the sex ratio is now more balanced, with an average of 45 per cent women doctors in OECD countries (OECD, 2015). The share of women

Table 5.2 *Female practising doctors, as a percentage of practising doctors, 2007 and 2015*

	2007	*2015*
Australia	34	39
Chile	n/a	40
Germany	40	45
Japan	17	20
Netherlands	36	52
New Zealand	38	44
Portugal	49	53
Sweden	43	47
Turkey	36	40
UK	40	46
USA	30	34

Sources: 2007: data from OECD (2009); 2015 (or nearest): data from OECD (2016a) and OECD Health at a Glance (2015, Table 5.5).

is growing in mature welfare states as well as in middle-income countries, whereas women form the majority in some countries like in Portugal. In Japan, however, women doctors account for just 20 per cent of all doctors. The traditional dominance of males in the medical profession in Japan has been resistant to change and many women report gender-based career obstacles (Nomura and Gohchi, 2012), although an increasing number of young women have entered medicine in recent years, and the proportion of women is significantly higher among younger doctors. Similar trends have been reported for Taiwan (not shown in Table 5.2), where female doctors counted for only 15 per cent in 2009, but doubled to 31 per cent of recent medical students (Cheng *et al.*, 2012).

An overall increase in female doctors can be attributed, to some degree, to cultural and economic developments that have changed the position of women in society and to more specific state-initiated measures that have strengthened the position of women doctors. Yet the variation among countries with similar socio-cultural conditions, like Germany and the Netherlands, challenges this assumption and may point to the relevance of the medical profession as a more conservative policy actor in Germany. On the other hand, similar proportions of female doctors in economically and culturally different countries such as Turkey, Australia and Chile are also puzzling. The comparison suggests that national health care governance models matter in sustaining or transforming the gender relations in the medical profession, but the making of inequality happens on many different levels (Kuhlmann *et al.*, 2012) and is increasingly subtle.

A recent example is the new contracts for junior doctors in the English NHS, which are accused as being discriminating against women, despite the equal opportunity law in England (Rimmer, 2016b).

Another indication of the diversity of the medical profession is the share of generalist and specialist doctors. As Table 5.3 illustrates, in most countries there are significantly more specialists than generalists, while Australia and Chile show a more balanced figure and Singapore a higher ratio of generalists. The strongest mismatch between generalists and specialists can be observed in the USA, which has prompted a debate over severe shortage of generalists and policy failure (McKinley and Marceau, 2012; Health and Human Services, 2013).

One possible explanation for a higher ratio of specialists in many countries is that in specialist practice and acute care the medical model of health and illness can excel. Another important factor is that in many countries the growth in the remuneration is higher in the group of specialists (Lafortune *et al.*, 2016: 55). Other factors, like the organization of care, also matter. For instance, in Sweden and Taiwan the number of specialists per 1,000 inhabitants is three to four times that of generalists.

Table 5.3   *Numbers of practising generalist and specialist doctors per 1,000 inhabitants*

	Generalist doctors		Specialist doctors	
	2007	*2015**	*2007*	*2015**
Australia	1.51	1.53	1.43	1.61
Chile	0.88 (2010)	0.97	0.55 (2010)	1.05
Germany	1.48	1.69	2.01	2.35
Japan	n/a	n/a	n/a	n/a
Netherlands	1.2	1.46	1.6	1.86
New Zealand	0.79	0.91	1.25	1.29
Portugal	1.78	2.17	1.88	2.22
Singapore	1.00	1.42	0.63	0.87
Sweden	0.62	0.65	2.02	2.16
Taiwan	0.20	0.34	1.30	1.38
Turkey	0.52	0.54	1.03	1.22
UK	0.73	0.8	1.75	1.97
USA	0.3	0.31	2.13	2.25

n/a = not available

* 2015 or nearest data. For most countries data from 2013.

Sources: Data from OECD (2015, 2016a); StatLink (http://stats.oecd.org/index.aspx?DataSetCode=HEALTH_STAT#); Taiwan Ministry of Health and Welfare (2013); Singapore Ministry of Health (2016).

In the case of Sweden, this reflects the fact that hospitals have long been dominant in the provision of health care, with patients having direct access to specialists in outpatient hospital departments. In contrast, the provision of ambulatory care has been patchy.

Data for Japan are unavailable in part because, unlike Western countries, in Japan the generalist–specialist distinction is almost meaningless. Thus, OECD data combines specialists and generalists. By tradition, all physicians are doctors of medical science and trained to become a specialist, but once they complete their training only a few continue to practise their speciality, with most leaving the large hospitals to practise in small community hospitals or open their own clinics without any formal retraining as a general practitioner. Significantly, there is no nationally recognized or formal system of speciality training or registration; rather numerous academic societies have established their own certification systems. Both physicians and nurses are licensed for life in Japan with no requirement for licence renewal or continuing medical or nursing education, and no peer or utilization review (Thomson *et al.*, 2013).

When looking at trends (Table 5.3), the proportion of both generalists and specialists per inhabitants has increased in all countries between 2007 and 2015 (or latest available year). However, for many years the share of specialists has grown quicker in most countries. In 2013, selected OECD countries (Australia, Belgium, France, Germany, Netherlands, UK) showed on average a proportion of 29 generalists to 62 specialists (and a small remaining proportion of non-classified physicians) (OECD, 2015); 'generalists' include general practitioners/family doctors and other, non-specialist physicians (Lafortune *et al.*, 2016: 55). Recent trends indicate a move to a more balanced increase or even adverse trend in most countries (Germany, the Netherlands, New Zealand, Portugal, Singapore, Taiwan).

In most of the countries, the proportion of generalists in relation to specialists has decreased. This trend was especially strong in Australia and Germany, showing a decline of approximately 10 per cent of generalists in relation to specialists over the last two decades. One important reason for a growing imbalance within the medical profession might be the fact that medical students are drawn to specialities or sub-specialities, which typically offer greater compensation, prestige and regular working hours (Davis *et al.*, 2009). While the trend is similar, the effects in the health workforce of the two countries are different: a nearly balanced proportion in Australia, and an increasing mismatch in Germany. Notably, the trend in Germany is in stark contrast to health policy reform and numerous incentives, which seek to shift provider power to generalists to reduce expensive specialist care and hospital admissions (Kuhlmann, 2006; Busse and Blümel, 2014). This may be a result of the strong policy power of the medical profession in Germany, which is dominated by the interests of specialists. Similarly, the relatively high proportion of specialists in Portugal, despite strong austerity measures and cuts on health care, also points to a strong position of the medical profession (Correia and Denis, 2016).

Interestingly, the Netherlands deviates from a general trend and demonstrates a significant increase of generalists between 2010 and 2011, which remained stable in the following years. This trend might be a result of stronger primary care policies (see Chapter 6) coupled with an overall more than double growth in the remuneration of generalists compared to specialists (Lafortune *et al.*, 2016: 55; on the payment of doctors, see also Chapter 3 of this volume). In contrast, the USA is heading towards a severe primary care workforce bottleneck due to decreased production and accelerated attrition (Schwartz, 2011). Furthermore, demand is fuelled by the 80 million Americans who will be retiring over the next 20 years and the expanded insurance coverage under the Affordable Care Act.

Importantly, the primary care workforce is shrinking. A third of GPs will leave medical practice over the next decade as baby boomer physicians retire. Therefore, by 2016 the number of adult primary care physicians leaving practice will exceed the number entering. Moreover, the projected shortfall includes surgeons as well (Sheldon, 2011). Addressing these national shortfalls without further disrupting the global workforce will be a challenge in the coming decades. The government has responded to national shortfalls by significantly increasing the number of domestically trained doctors (Merçay *et al.*, 2016). However, there is now a blockage for speciality training (generalists include family doctors and internal medicine in the USA), which has not been resolved (Moreira and Lafortune, 2016).

In summary, the variety of medical workforce data cannot be explained one to one as a health policy outcome. Yet the comparative lens brings health systems characteristics and policy approaches (especially strong primary health care with improved skills mix like in the Netherlands) that may target specific compositions of the medical workforce (see Chapter 6). The next section takes a closer look at doctors as collective actors in the health policy process.

Doctors as health policy players

Issues around the position of doctors in the health labour market are concerned with medical practitioners as individuals. In contrast, the political organization of doctors' interests directs attention to doctors as a group and how doctors relate to the policy process. The interests of doctors can be organized in different ways, through specialist scientific societies, professional associations or trade unions. An important indicator of power is the degree of cohesion (or fragmentation); that is, the extent to which a group of doctors speak with one voice, or at least with different voices complementing each other. This has become increasingly challenging as distributional struggles between diverse groups of doctors have intensified under pressures of cost containment. At the same time, countries offer dissimilar points of access to organized interests, reflecting the specific characteristics of their respective political and health systems (see Chapter 2). The power of doctors largely depends on how a state is organized and on how powerful it is.

As Figure 5.1 suggests, in most countries the political organization of doctors is relatively cohesive, with one organization acting as the main agent of doctors' interests. This normally goes together with a high membership among doctors. However, in some countries divisions between different types of doctors have led to the fragmentation of the political organization of doctors. These divisions affect the distribution of financial resources and intensify under policies designed to contain costs. The relative collective strength of doctors coexists with varying degrees of access to the policy process, which, as noted in Chapter 2, embodies one indicator of how the power of the state is organized.

In most countries, doctors must rely on lobbying the government from the outside. As Britain demonstrates, the extent of influence varies over time and the cohesion of interest organizations is only one factor; the government's chosen approach to policy making also plays an important role. At the same time, lack of cohesion is not necessarily a bar to influence, as the USA, Germany and the Netherlands demonstrate. The considerable influence of doctors in the USA reflects not only the economic power of the medical sectors, but also the weakness of the state in health governance. In Germany and in the Netherlands doctors are part of health governance settings and, therefore, often have privileged access to

| | | Access to policy process | |
		As outsiders through lobbying	As insiders through corporatism
Organization of doctors' interests	Cohesive	Australia, Britain, Japan, New Zealand, Singapore, Sweden, Taiwan	
	Fragmented	USA	Germany, Netherlands

Figure 5.1   *The organization of doctors' interests and access to the policy process*

the policy process although in the Netherlands this role is increasingly more controlled and publicly governed. Being insiders gives doctors considerable influence, although this may come at the price of becoming agents of cost containment.

In many countries, the political organization of doctors shows a considerable degree of cohesion. This reflects abundant country-specific factors, including the type of political system and the size of the country. Cohesion is expected to be most likely in small unitary countries such as New Zealand, Singapore and Taiwan. New Zealand, for example, has one primary medical association that has a high level of membership among doctors. The New Zealand Medical Association (NZMA) is a voluntary organization that claims membership of about 70 per cent of the country's doctors. As such, the Association has a broader-based membership than many national medical associations. As well as being a membership-based organization, the NZMA also acts as an umbrella for many other medical and health organizations and maintains formal links with affiliates, including the Royal Colleges and speciality organizations, and acts as the primary representative of the profession in dealings with the government (Marshall, 2003; New Zealand Medical Association, 2013).

Even in larger unitary countries the organization of doctors' interests can be cohesive. Britain is a case in point. The British Medical Association (BMA) is at the centre of the political organization of doctors' interests and a large majority of doctors are members. The BMA acts in a dual role as a professional organization and as a trade union. As a professional organization, it promotes medical education and professional development, whereas as a trade union it represents doctors' economic interests. This de facto monopoly puts the BMA in a strong position in principle, but also requires that it caters to a diverse range of constituencies within the medical profession. Thus, conflicts between GPs and hospital consultants have been particularly prominent within the BMA (Giamo, 2002).

Likewise, as Sweden demonstrates, a more decentralized political system is no bar to a cohesive organization of doctors' interests (Anell *et al.*, 2012). Although membership of the Swedish Medical Association (SMA) is voluntary, the association includes 96 per cent of doctors (SMA, 2016). The Association acts as a type of umbrella organization and the specific interests of its membership are channelled through seven professional organizations and 28 local bodies. The SMA coexists with a range of scientific societies and, while the Swedish Society of Medicine is the largest, the smaller specialist societies are more influential actors (Garpenby, 2001). The Medical Association and the Society of Medicine have different responsibilities, although on some issues the two organizations compete (Garpenby, 1999).

In comparison, the political organization of doctors can also be highly fragmented. The USA represents a clear case of fragmentation between generalists and specialists that has been exacerbated by federalism and the sheer size of the profession. Although less than half of all practising doctors are members of the American Medical Association (AMA), it remains a very powerful political lobby group with significant influence in Washington DC and the state capitals. However, many speciality medical groups have been established which concentrate on their own interests, often in conflict with the AMA. There are literally thousands of medical associations at the local, state and national level in the USA, and although the AMA is the single most influential, the voice of the medical community is considerably more disjointed than in other countries. Hence, the AMA Health Policy Group 'serves as the voice of organized medicine by making recommendations to the Centers for Medicare and Medicaid Services (CMS) on the relative values of physician services pursuant to the Medicare Physician Payment Schedule' (AMA, 2016).

The organization of doctors' interests may be divided, not only between different types of doctors, but also between different types of organization. For example, in Germany the Marburger Bund is the main professional organization and trade union for hospital doctors, but the situation surrounding ambulatory care doctors is more complicated. Most of these doctors cannot exclusively rely on private practice and instead have to provide services under social health insurance. However, this requires joining one of the regional associations of insurance fund doctors (*Kassenärztliche Vereinigungen*) that assume an intermediate position between doctors and the state. As public law bodies, the associations have the statutory responsibility of ensuring the provision of ambulatory care and organizing the remuneration of doctors, including control functions such as assessing the economic efficiency of the performance of individual doctors. At the same time, they represent the interests of doctors when the associations negotiate contracts and fees with insurance funds (Kuhlmann, 2006).

The tensions inherent in this dual role have become more prominent and intensifying distributional struggles have made it more difficult for the associations to integrate the conflicting interests of their membership (Burau, 2009b). The distributional struggles result from a combination of the increasing number of doctors and more extensive competition and government control. The heightened conflicts have also negatively affected the division of labour between the associations of insurance fund doctors and the two lobbying organizations for ambulatory care doctors. At the same time, the position of the associations of insurance fund doctors may be weakened, because insurance funds can now contract directly with individual groups of doctors (Gerlinger, 2010). In practice, there are numerous problems but collective contracting with the doctors' association remains strong.

The relative cohesion of the political organization of doctors is only one measure of collective power of the medical profession. A complementary measure of power is the role of doctors in the policy process, and different health and political systems provide distinct degrees and types of access. This demonstrates how the power of doctors is tied to the power of the state. In most countries, doctors' organizations have access to the policy process as outsiders, mostly through lobbying and limited informal consultation (Figure 5.1). Countries with tax-funded health services embedded in a centralist and a federalist political system, respectively, illustrate the vagaries of the influence of doctors.

In Britain, for example, the fragility of this outsider type of access became apparent in the late 1980s. Reform efforts in part were aimed at weakening the role of the profession in the governance of health care and this affected the influence of doctors in health policy, resulting in a widening rift between the government and doctors. Significantly, the medical profession was practically excluded from the policy review that led to a major reform in the early 1990s (Harrison, 2001). Similarly, Hunter (2008) and Kay (2001) see the conception and implementation of the GP fundholding scheme and its subsequent redefinition as practice-based commissioning as an indication of the weakened influence of the medical profession. This stands in sharp contrast to the former corporatist settlement that was characterized by a strong insider role of doctors in government (Giamo, 2002).

Most recent developments show that devolution may therefore affect the role of doctors in different ways. The English NHS is reinforcing the medical professions' role as an external (yet strong) policy player, while the Scottish Government illustrates a more participatory policy. Severe cuts in the English NHS and new policies, like the introduction of new contracts for junior doctors, or cuts in the public health workforce and finance, have generated strong resistance from doctors, including a series of strikes. In contrast, the Scottish Government did not introduce new contracts and has sought to avoid conflict with doctors. Furthermore, public health policy is more strongly promoted and based on regular reviews (BMA, 2016; Rimmer, 2016a; Watson and Lloyd, 2016).

In contrast to NHS systems, the strength of the health care industry, combined with a policy process that is typically driven by lobbying and where winning is often manifested in blocking change, can help to sustain the power of the medical profession. A case in point is the USA, where the medical profession has been more successful at maintaining its traditionally compelling influence over health policy (Rice *et al.*, 2013). The medical sector is consistently ranked among the best organized and financed sectors in influencing politicians at the national and state levels by the Congressional Quarterly Service (Blank, 2012).

In corporatist systems, a key characteristic is that doctors are an integral part of health governance and this often gives them access to the policy process as insiders (Kuhlmann, 2006). However, as the example of Germany shows, even as insiders the influence of doctors is variable. Together with the insurance funds, doctors form an organization of self-administration, which is responsible not only for negotiating contracts, but also for implementing health care legislation. Here, the Joint Committee is important, and its responsibilities include defining the benefits catalogue, clinical guidelines and measures of quality assurance. The role of doctors in the health system is highly institutionalized and codified in Social Code Book Five (Busse and Blümel, 2014). In addition, the federal structure of health governance offers doctors multiple points of access. Significantly, however, doctors are involved in a public role granted to them by the state, and are not principally involved as representatives of private interests. This can lead to the kinds of conflict of interest that can constrain the collective power of doctors. At the same time, the position as an insider in the policy process privileges doctors in relation to other health care providers. Moreover, they provide opportunity to shape, at least in some measure, the professional development of other groups (Wissenschaftsrat, 2012).

Professional self-regulation of medical work

Professional self-regulation has been the traditional approach to setting and ensuring standards of medical practice, and involves licensing and (by implication) education and training. Furthermore, self-regulation is a key indication of the 'professionalism' of doctors and is at the centre of the regulation of competitive practice in medicine. A typical example of professional self-regulation is the General Medical Council (GMC) in Britain, which is responsible for keeping a register of doctors and for regulating their education, training and professional standards. The regulatory ideology underpinning the GMC has traditionally been rather narrow and isolationist and the Council has tended to focus on protecting doctors from market competition on the one hand and from interference from the state on the other (Moran, 1999: 103). Similar arrangements exist in Australia, Germany and the USA. However, as recent scandals in Britain have demonstrated, these arrangements are not necessarily successful at securing the quality of medical work and have led to policy reform (Fenton and Salter, 2009). In other countries, by contrast, professional self-regulation is less prominent and the bodies regulating medical work are government agencies that include doctors, but not exclusively so. In Sweden, for example, the Medical Responsibility Board, a government agency that assesses and decides on complaints and instances of malpractice, consists of members drawn from different stakeholders in the health service, including county councils, municipalities, the unions of health professionals and the public, all of whom are appointed by the government.

Over the last decade, the federal government in Germany has expanded the scope of self-administration while at the same time circumscribing its activities (Busse and Blümel, 2014). For example, the Joint Committee is now responsible for evaluating the medical efficacy and economic efficiency of existing treatments. Doctors have become key agents of cost containment precisely because the system of self-administration is adaptable and depoliticizes the implementation of potentially problematic policies.

Medical care is at the centre of health reform, reflecting the centrality of doctors in the definition, provision and allocation of health care resources. Across countries measures to control expenditure at the macro-level have progressively been complemented by measures to control the allocation of health care resources at the micro-level, and it is these measures that can be expected to affect doctors most directly (Burau *et al.*, 2009; McDonald, 2012). Reforms directed at the micro-level have included changes to how doctors are paid (discussed in Chapter 3), restrictions on available treatment and quality management measures such as medical audit, clinical standards and evidence-based medicine, as well as performance measures. However, the picture that emerges here is ambivalent. These reforms have certainly put greater pressure on doctors to account for their practice, but the turn to quality and (medical) evidence provides an opportunity for doctors to appropriate the measures of control and even reinforce their leadership in the health care sector (Dent *et al.*, 2012; McGivern *et al.*, 2015; Denis *et al.*, 2016). In many ways, quality management marks the rebirth of medical practice, although under different, more closely defined terms.

Comparative research has revealed a general trend in which doctors adapt professional practice to new demands and the processes and outcomes are shaped by the institutional settings of health systems (Burau *et al.*, 2009; Kuhlmann *et al.*, 2013; Kirkpatrick *et al.*, 2016). It is important to keep in mind that medical power is embedded on all levels of governance and decision making when looking at the contemporary attempts to intervene in the health workforce composition, which are the theme of the following sections.

The health workforce composition

The 'right' composition of the health workforce is increasingly perceived as a key to efficient and sustainable health workforce governance and service provision. This shifts the focus from doctors and reform of medical practice towards questions about the right skills, jobs and places (OECD, 2016b), and this, in turn, brings comparison into play. Occupational statistics may give a first impression of the various ways in which health systems combine staff (and the related skills) and distribute health workers, thus raising questions about the conditions that may support or constrain the changes in the skill mix.

To begin with the most basic indicator, 'health worker density to population' (Table 5.4), the figures for doctors in our selected OECD countries range from 2.3 per 1,000 population in Japan and 2.6 in the USA to 4.0

Table 5.4 Workforce composition and development of doctors and nurses in selected OECD countries

Country	Health professionals Medical + professional nursing practitioners per 1,000 population	Doctors Practising per 1,000 population	Doctors Graduates per year per 100,000 population	Nurses Practising per 1,000 population	Nurses Professional graduates per year per 100,000 population	Nurses Associate professional graduates per year per 100,000 population	Ratios Nurses per doctor[2]	Ratios Professional nursing graduates per medical graduates[3]	Trend in skills mix[4] Ratio professional graduates to practitioners
Australia	14.9	3.40	15.45	11.52	74.81	27.82	3.4	4.8	1.4
Germany	17.0	4.04	12.15	12.96	55.33	9.80	3.2	4.6	1.4
Japan	12.8	2.29	6.0	10.54 (2012)	40.09	8.01	4.6	6.7	1.5
Netherlands	14.4	3.30	14.41	11.08 (2012)	37.5	24.28	3.7	2.6	0.7
New Zealand	12.9	2.83	8.47	10.07	43.96	4.38	3.6	5.2	1.4
Sweden	15.3	4.12	10.27	11.15 (2012)	39.99	n/a	2.8	3.7	1.3
UK	11.0	2.77	13.18	8.18	42.13	n/a	3.0	3.2	1.1
USA	11.1	2.56	7.26	11.1[1]	63.37	17.34	4.3	8.7	2.0

2013 or nearest data, if no other source is provided.

[1] OECD, 2016b, Figure 2.5; data include all nurses working in the health sector (including educators etc.) thus overestimating the number of nurses in patient care.

[2] OECD, 2016b, Figure 3.

[3] own calculations based on OECD, 2015.

[4] own calculations; a trend is roughly estimated by placing the ratio of professional nursing to medical graduates per 100,000 population in relation to the ratio of nurses to doctors per 10,000 population. Note: associate nursing graduates are excluded from this calculation.

Sources: OECD, 2015; StatLink.

in Sweden and 4.1 in Germany, while the remaining countries cluster in the middle range of 2.8 (UK, New Zealand) to 3.3 (Netherlands) and 3.4 (Australia). For nurses, the figures look different, placing the UK at the bottom with 8.2 practising nurses per 10,000 population followed by 10 in New Zealand and peaking with 13 in Germany, while Australia, Japan, the Netherlands, Sweden and the USA cluster around 11 to 11.5 nurses per 10,000 population.

The comparative analysis following Table 5.4 shows many things; the density and the aggregate numbers of doctors and nurses especially highlight variation. For instance, the UK and the USA invest little in their professional workforce: staffing levels (11 health professionals per 10,000 population) rank lowest among these countries and represent only two-thirds of the levels in Germany (17.1). Australia, Sweden and the Netherlands are also positioned at the upper end (around 14 to 15), while Japan and New Zealand rank lower (12.8), but still higher than the UK or USA. To some extent, the findings confirm a familiar picture of underfunding and understaffing in the UK (see the debates over cuts in the English NHS and the strikes of doctors; BMA, 2016; Rimmer, 2016a) and poorly developed universal coverage in the USA (Blank, 2012). This also seems to promote the argument that doctors acting as 'insiders' in the policy process can use their jurisdictional power to increase the overall number of health professionals, as in Germany, while an 'outsider' position of the professions, like in the UK and the USA, may reinforce the risks of understaffing.

The problems are more complex. Neither the level of per capita expenditure for health as shown in Chapter 3 (see Table 3.1) nor the level of public funding for health care (see Table 3.3) can convincingly explain the differences in the allocation of health human resources across countries. For instance, the highest level of expenditure in the USA corresponds with the lowest level of health professionals. At the same time, high levels of public funding as observed in Sweden, the UK and New Zealand can create very different results in relation to the health workforce. The analysis suggests that health workforce policy generates its own dynamics, which cannot be fully explained by traditional health system characteristics and indicators.

Variety is even higher when looking at the workforce figures of the selected middle-income countries, as shown in Table 5.5. The density of both doctors and nurses is by far lower than in the resource-richer OECD countries presented in Table 5.4, while Russia is an exception. Interestingly, in Russia the number of doctors is much higher than in most OECD countries and the overall number of health professionals (nurses and doctors) is higher than in the UK and USA and similar to New Zealand and Japan. The other selected countries exhibit far lower numbers of health professionals, ranging from 1.5 in Indonesia, 2.0 in India and South Africa, and 2.8 in Columbia to 3.7 in China.

Table 5.5 *Density and ratio of doctors and nurses in selected middle-income countries*

Country	Doctors + nurses per 1,000 population	Doctors per 1,000 population	Nurses per 1,000 population	Ratio[1]
China	3.7	1.65	2.01	1.22
Columbia	2.8	1.77	1.03	0.58
India	2.0	0.73	1.25	1.72
Indonesia	1.5	0.31	1.15	3.71
Russia	12.3	4.9	7.43	1.52
South Africa	2.0	0.76	1.21	1.60

Data are for the year 2013.

[1] own calculations based on OECD, 2015.

Sources: OECD, 2015; StatLink.

The findings illuminate that the health workforce remains poorly developed even in the new emergent economies like India and South Africa, while China and Columbia seem to make higher investments in their health workforce. In the case of India and South Africa, one reason might be a historically contingent connection of Commonwealth countries that provokes negative spillover effects of an understaffed NHS system in England. Overall, the figures from middle-income countries tell a story of severe shortage of health workers (except in Russia), which calls for greater attention in health reform models (Ranson *et al.*, 2010; Bowser *et al.*, 2014). The attempts to improve universal health care coverage will not be successful and sustainable without a qualified health workforce. This also calls for more context-sensitive health workforce policy, as the approaches developed in resource-rich OECD countries may not fit the needs of other countries, and this is true even more for low-income countries (WHO, 2012d).

The next section shifts attention from aggregate numbers to the composition of the health workforces. As shown in Table 5.4, all countries show a much higher ratio of nurses relative to doctors per 10,000 population, ranging from 2.8 in Sweden to 4.6 in Japan. The variation between countries is interesting for two reasons. First, it might suggest that overall low levels of professions, like in the USA and Japan, could be mitigated, to some degree, by a more nursing-centred health workforce. Second, it supports earlier arguments that shortage of doctors (Lafortune *et al.*, 2016) and a medical profession acting more as an outsider in the policy process might promote an expansion of nurses. By contrast, a well-funded health system with high staffing levels of doctors and partnership governance, like in Sweden and Germany, may block an expansion of nurses. Interestingly, in Sweden not only doctors but also nurses are acting more as 'insiders' in the policy process. Once again, however, a single factor does not explain the workforce composition; for instance, in the UK, both the density of doctors and the proportion of nurses are low.

Skills mix and task shifting

Changes in the skills mix and new roles for non-medical providers are important tools of health policy to use the health human resources more effectively and help mitigate shortages. The ratio of nursing graduates to medical graduates (Table 5.4) may serve as an indicator of health policy incentives and future developments in the composition of the health workforce. A relevant increase in the nursing graduates per 100,000 population in all countries, except the Netherlands, are a clear sign that action has been taken to change the skill mix (or more precisely, the staff mix) and expand on middle-level professional qualifications, following international recommendations (GHWA, 2010). The differences between countries are stronger in the group of graduates than for the ratios of medical and nursing practitioners, ranging from 2.6 in the Netherlands to 8.7 in the USA. The comparative picture suggests that countries with overall level density of health workers seek to establish a more nurse-centred health workforce, like the USA and Japan; to a lesser degree this also applies to the UK. In countries with high density of doctors such as Germany, Sweden and in part Australia, the results might indicate a policy shift towards improving the skills mix. The reasons for the adverse trend in the Netherlands are not clear and are in stark contrast to the policy efforts to educate nurse practitioners (NP) and to accelerate the shifting of tasks from nurses to doctors and expand prescribing rights in Europe (Kroezen *et al.*, 2014; Maier, 2015; Maier and Aiken, 2016; Moreira and Lafortune, 2016).

The composition of the future health workforce is not fully predictable from changes in the education and access to the profession, but placing the ratios of graduates in relation to the ratios of practitioners in the two professional groups may give a first impression of the direction of travel. Here, we can observe a workforce policy trend towards increasing the proportion of nurses, which is strongest in the USA and on a comparably high level in the other countries, except the Netherlands (this latter one might either be a temporary effect and/or an artefact of data collection).

Next to the quantitative changes shown in Table 5.4, the introduction or expansion of new roles for nurses such as NPs or other non-physician provider roles (for instance, expansion of tasks and education of physician assistants) is a qualitative indicator for change in the skills mix of the health workforces (Maier and Aiken, 2016). Table 5.6 summarizes the policy

Table 5.6 *Recent introduction or expansion of non-physician provider roles and health workforce and system characteristics, selected OECD countries*

Recent introduction or expansion[1]	No introduction or expansion[1]	Health workforce and system characteristics[2]
Australia		Density of doctors high and nurses in a middle range; nurses per doctors in a middle range; trend modest increase, doctors as outsiders in health policy with cohesive organization; self-governance of nurses; highly reliant on foreign-trained health workers
	Germany	High density of doctors and nurses; nurses per doctors in a middle to low range with modest increase; doctors as insiders in health policy with fragmented organization; lack of self-governance of nurses; mainly self-sufficient but growing number of foreign-trained health workers
	Japan	Density of doctors low and nurses in a middle range; nurses per doctors high with significant increase; doctors as outsiders in health policy with cohesive organization; primarily self-sufficient health workforce
Netherlands		Density of doctors and nurses in a middle range; nurses per doctors in a middle range with decreasing trend; doctors as insiders in health policy with fragmented organization; strengthening of nurses' self-governance; primarily self-sufficient health workforce
New Zealand		Density of doctors and nurses in a middle range; nurses per doctors in a middle range with significant increase; doctors as insiders in health policy with fragmented organization; self-governance of nurses; highly reliant on foreign-trained health workers
Sweden		High density of doctors and nurses in a middle range; nurses to doctors low with slowly increasing trend; doctors and nurses as insiders in health policy; self-governance of nurses; some reliance on foreign-trained health workers
UK		Low density of doctors and nurses; nurses per doctors low with moderate increasing trend; doctors as external policy players with cohesive organization; self-governance of nurses; reliant on foreign-trained health workers
USA		Low density of doctors and nurses in a middle range; nurses per doctors high with strong increasing trend; doctors as outsiders in health policy with cohesive organization; self-governance of nurses; highly reliant on foreign-trained health workers

Sources:

1 Schoenstein *et al.* (2016: 75), based on the 2012–13 OECD Health Systems Characteristics Survey.

2 Based on Figure 5.1, Table 5.4.

responses of our selected countries and the health workforce and systems characteristics they reflect. This analysis highlights that, regardless of the composition of the health workforce and the role of doctors in the policy process, most countries have introduced new roles (see also Maier, 2015). Germany and Japan are an exception, but here too the health workforce or system characteristics vary. The findings suggest, in a similar vein as the quantitative indicators, that no single factor can be identified that could predict the expansion of existing roles or the introduction of new ones.

At the same time, the exploration of changes in national contexts brings a combination of positive and negative factors into view that may interact in different ways. For instance, a medical profession strong in power and in numbers, like in Germany, may counteract policy efforts to establish new roles or even increase the numbers of nurses, because of both weak nursing power and, compared to other countries, weak pressures for change in a primarily self-sufficient health workforce. On the other hand, high density of doctors with a position as policy insiders may lead to new and expanded roles if these factors coincide with more moderate numbers of nurses who are also policy players, and heightened pressures for change due to reliance on foreign-trained staff, like in Sweden.

Unfortunately, comparative analysis of the mix of skills and new roles is limited to higher- to middle-level professions, because data on caring personnel are still lacking even for most of the OECD countries. The USA has a density of 7.64 caring personnel per 1,000 population, while the UK exhibits a ratio nearly twice as high, of 14.83 (OECD, 2015; StatLink). In the UK, density of caring personnel is higher in relation to doctors and nurses, while the USA shows a similar density of nurses and caring personnel. Thus, the strong differences in the levels of nursing graduates may reflect different policy directions: for instance, in the UK an investigation into health labour market groups at the basis, or a focus on middle-level groups in the USA.

A comparison of four large Western EU countries (Germany, Italy, Sweden and the UK) provides in-depth information on Europe. This research found an overall composition of around 45 per cent care assistants, 40 per cent nurses and health professionals with similar qualifications (midwives, etc.) and around 15 per cent doctors (Pavolini and Kuhlmann, 2016). Notably, this composition of the health workforce changed only slightly during the last decade: 'all groups expanded in absolute numbers in Western Europe, but the basis of the employment pyramid, the care assistants, grew faster than doctors and nurses' (Pavolini and Kuhlmann, 2016: 662).

Finally, what is known about the skills mix in middle-income countries? Table 5.5 demonstrates that global policy recommendations to expand the nursing workforce and to strengthen middle-level qualifications overall are poorly implemented (GHWA, 2010; Aiken *et al.*, 2014; WHO, 2015c). The ratio of nurses to doctors is mainly in the range of

1.5 to 1.7, with 1.2 in China. This is less than half of the ratios described for the OECD countries (Table 5.4); it is also less than half of the composition of doctors (0.55) and nurses (1.88) which the WHO uses to define a threshold for unmet health workforce needs (Cailhol *et al.*, 2013). The two outliers among our selected countries, once again, seem to confirm that numbers of doctors do matter when it comes to skill mixes (Lafortune *et al.*, 2016). We see a comparably high density of doctors, and a ratio of just 0.58 nurses to doctors in Columbia, and an opposite effect of 0.31 density of doctors coupled with a 3.7 times higher number of nurses in Indonesia (Table 5.5).

There are also other examples, however, as a comparison of five sub-Saharan countries reveals, including low-income countries except South Africa (Cailhol *et al.*, 2013). Health workforce shortage is serious in all countries, and worst in Lesotho followed by Mozambique and Burundi, but the numbers of nurses per doctor are in all countries far higher than in the OECD countries (calculated from Cailhol *et al.*, 2013). There are also various examples of task shifting and new roles introduced by the governments (Box 5.2; see also Henning *et al.*, 2015).

Box 5.2 Task shifting and new roles in sub-Saharan Africa low- and middle-income countries

Workforce changes and new policies were introduced as a response to increasing need for HIV treatment and are related to international funding programmes.

> Informal task-shifting was followed by attempts to legitimize expanded professional responsibilities and to standardize practices. In South Africa, the government authorized formal nurse-initiated antiretroviral therapy, after the STRETCH (Streamlining Tasks and Roles to Expand Treatment and Care for HIV) trial demonstrated the safety of such a policy. In Burundi, a ministerial circular authorized nurses to prescribe antiretroviral therapy, although under the supervision of a medical doctor. In Mozambique and Lesotho ... scopes of practice of non-physician clinicians and nurses were officially expanded, with HIV training provided by international implementing partners.

In relation to new roles, in South Africa 'two new cadres of health professionals were officially created' including 'clinical associates' who have some responsibility for HIV management, and a 'middle-level pharmacy cadre, called pharmacists' assistants ... with some initial resistance from the pharmaceutical bodies'. Also, Community Health Workers have played a significant role in supporting antiretroviral therapy and are 'now being integrated into so called "ward-based PHC outreach teams", working under the supervision of nurses and as part of the formal health system'.

Source: Cailhol *et al.* (2013: 52–65).

Geographical imbalances and health workforce mobility

Geographical factors matter in the health workforce in two ways: first, as imbalances caused by regional mobility within countries and, second, as mobility flows between countries. Given the centrality of the human resources to finance and quality, regional imbalances reduce the efficiency of health care systems. As discussed in Chapter 4, most countries show some disparities in the density of health workers in rural and in urban areas, especially those with large remote territories.

Although a mismatch between remote/rural and urban areas seem to challenge all health systems, there are important differences among countries, which may also result from factors that are other than geographical. Estimated from OECD data (Ono *et al.*, 2016), the USA shows the highest variety in the density of doctors, ranging from less than 2 per 1,000 population in some areas to over 9 in Washington DC, and remains high (around 4 doctors) even if the peak in Washington is excluded. In Germany, the mismatch is about 2.5 doctors per 1,000 population. By contrast, the density of doctors in countries like Australia and Sweden, challenged by large remote territories, varies by less than about 1.5 doctors per 1,000 population (similar to Canada). The Netherlands and Japan face little variation, and New Zealand has nearly no geographical imbalances, which might be partly explained by its small size. Comparing the variation in the USA, and to a lesser degree in Germany, with Australia and Sweden illustrates that geographical imbalance cannot be reduced to a 'natural' challenge, like remote territories. Moreover, health policy incentives to improve recruitment and retention in rural and remote areas matter, including a wide range of activities from higher salaries to improved career changes and working conditions as well as better infrastructures in rural areas (Bourgeault *et al.* 2016). This has been confirmed by Carson and colleagues (2015), who have described the variety of the rural health workforce in the North of Europe.

The boundaries between regional moves/within-country mobility and cross-country mobility are increasingly becoming fluid in a globalizing world. One example is an increase in commuters in border regions due to improved transport infrastructures and services. Other relevant examples are countries of the EU that have introduced a single market with free movement of health care workers (Greer and Mätzke, 2015; Hervey and McHale, 2015). Given the EU single market law and mutual recognition of degrees (Directive 2013/55/EU), the regulatory opportunities of national governments are drastically constrained. Moreover, the mobility flows are largely driven by fluctuating economic factors, which escalate the risks of new imbalances and mainly threaten less well-resourced health care systems (Buchan *et al.*, 2014; Glinos *et al.*, 2015).

To make things even more complicated, students are also increasingly mobile, since foreign studies are encouraged and supported by EU policy and international funding programmes (Moreira and Lafortune, 2016). This means that a purportedly small, but unknown proportion of the health care workers, that appear as 'foreign-trained' in the statistics, are foreign-trained students who are returning to their country of origin/citizenship (Merçay *et al.*, 2016). Table 5.7 provides an overview of the percentage of foreign-trained doctors and nurses in relation to the total medical and nursing workforce in selected OECD countries.

The comparative analysis reveals that countries make use of foreign-trained health professionals in very different ways. There are on average four categories: countries that are fully reliant on foreign-trained health professionals (New Zealand and Australia); countries with high ratios of up to one-quarter (US, UK, Sweden); countries with a self-sufficient health workforce with some substitution (Germany); and countries with self-sufficient health systems with a negligible percentage of foreign-trained professionals (Netherlands). In all countries, the percentage of foreign-trained nurses is significantly lower than doctors, but the mobility pattern described above is similar for both professional groups, with two exceptions. In the USA, the percentage of foreign-trained doctors is nearly four times higher than nurses while in Sweden it is about nine times higher. These differences in the percentage of

Table 5.7   *Mobility trends of doctors and nurses in selected OECD countries, 2000–14*

Country	Doctors, foreign-trained % of total[1]			Nurses, foreign-trained % of total[1]			Trend[2]	
	2000	2006	2012–14	2000	2006	2012–14	Doctors	Nurses
Australia	n/a	25.0	30.5	n/a	14.5	16.0	5.5	1.5
Germany	3.7	5.2	8.8	n/a	n/a	5.8	5.1	n/a
Netherlands	1.8	2.1	2.6	0.9	1.1	0.7	0.8	-02
New Zealand	38.0	40.7	42.6	14.7	22.8	24.5	4.6	9.8
Sweden	13.9	19.3	24.3	2.7	2.8	2.7	10.4	0
UK	n/a	29.9	28.3	8.0	13.4	12.7	-0.8	4.7
USA	25.5	25.1	25.0	n/a	n/a	6.0	-0.5	n/a

Sources:

[1] Merçay *et al.*, 2016: Table 4.1, Table 4.2.

[2] Our calculations based on Merçay *et al.*, 2016: Table 4.1 and 4.2.

foreign-trained doctors and nurses suggest that health workforce policy does matter, as there is no convincing 'natural' explanation of how a health care system can manage a more self-sufficient nursing workforce but fails to do so for doctors.

With a view on trends, an overall increasing mobility is obvious for both doctors and nurses. Interestingly, though, the UK and the USA as classic examples of a high share of foreign-trained workforce show a slightly reverse trend for doctors, while the percentage of foreign-trained nurses is on the increase (Maier *et al.*, 2014; Glinos *et al.*, 2015; Leone *et al.*, 2016; Merçay *et al.*, 2016) (see Box 5.3).

What do we know about the mobility flows *among* countries? First, health workforce mobility can have positive effects on health systems and services and help close temporary gaps in skills and competencies. Mobility can also promote knowledge exchange and shared learning across countries, especially relevant in the field of rare diseases, and it can expand individual career and life chances. Despite these benefits, frequently there are problematic effects of mobility flows from a health systems perspective, often labelled 'brain drain' or 'care drain' (Martineau and Willetts, 2006; Dussault and Buchan, 2014; Buchan, 2015; Glinos *et al.*, 2015).

Information on mobility flows is poorly developed and lacks standardization, and planning and research often relies on uncertain estimates. The most comprehensive data are available from the OECD (OECD, 2008a, 2016a, b) and for the EU (Wismar *et al.*, 2011; Buchan *et al.*, 2014; Glinos *et al.*, 2015; WP7 Joint Action, 2016). Basically, three

---

Box 5.3   Increasing domestic training efforts to reduce foreign-trained recruitment in the USA

The USA provides a striking example of how a substantial increase in domestic training efforts for nurses can reduce the need to recruit foreign-trained nurses. Between 2001 and 2012, the number of domestically trained nurses passing the certification exam more than doubled, from less than 70,000 to nearly 150,000. This increase was accompanied by a sharp decline in the number of foreign-trained nurses who passed the exam, dropping from a peak of around 23,000 in 2007 to only about 5,000 in 2012. In relation to doctors, there was little change until 2012, but with the number of domestically trained doctors continuing to rise, it can be expected that fewer foreign-trained doctors will become registered in the USA in the coming years.

Source: Merçay *et al.* (2016: 112)

patterns of mobility flows with distinct effects on health care systems can be identified:

1. First, migration/mobility from low-income to high-income countries driven by economic push–pull factors which risks the 'draining' health care provision from poor countries to the advantage of wealthier ones;
2. second, mobility among high-income countries; and
3. third, the specific situation of EU mobility which shows similarities with within-country mobility due to a common labour market.

An International Code of Ethics (Box 5.4) has been developed and signed by many countries to reduce negative effects of health workforce mobility for resource-poor countries (Merçay *et al.*, 2016).

The Code might be a first step, but it fails to effectively reduce inequality and prevent new mobility flows driven by financial hardship and austerity measurements in some countries (Glinos *et al.*, 2015; Merçay *et al.*, 2016). For Buchan, 'there is clear evidence that there is a very high proportion of

---

Box 5.4 The WHO Global Code of Practice on the International Recruitment of Health Personnel, key issues

The Code is signed by countries on a voluntary basis and sets up guidelines and comprises five key recommendations for member states.

- Ethical international recruitment: The Code discourages the active recruitment of health care workers from developing countries with critical workforce shortages.
- Equal treatment of migrant health care workers: The Code highlights the importance of equal treatment of foreign-trained health workers and their locally trained counterparts.
- Health workforce development and sustainable health systems: member states should develop strategies for workforce planning, training and retention, adapted to the specific circumstances of each country, to reduce the need for migrant health workers.
- International cooperation: The Code encourages collaboration between health workers' countries of origin and countries of destination to improve reciprocal benefit (e.g. discussed as 'circular migration' in the EU; WP7 Joint Action, 2016).
- Technical collaboration and financial support: developed countries should provide technical and financial assistance to developing countries experiencing a shortage of health workers.

Sources: adapted from Merçay *et al.* (2016: 104) and WHO (2010a).

doctors and nurses trained in some low-income countries now working in high-income OECD countries' (2015: 342). In his overview, Buchan draws on OECD data from 2010 and shows that:

> some of these countries have an 'expatriation rate' over 50 per cent – in other words, at least half of the active doctors or nurses trained in the country are now working in OECD countries. The OECD reports an expatriation rate over 50 per cent for countries such as Mozambique, Angola, Tanzania, and many small island states in the Caribbean and Pacific. In terms of actual size of expatriate workforce, India and the Philippines are prominent: 110,000 Philippine nurses and 56,000 Indian doctors worked abroad in 2000. (Buchan, 2015: 342)

Table 5.8 shows the principal countries of origin of foreign-trained doctors in three selected destination countries with traditionally high reliance

Table 5.8   *Mobility flows of doctors, selected countries*

Receiving country	Main sending countries*		
	European Union countries	High-income countries without EU	LMIC countries
Germany[2]	Romania Greece Hungary Poland		
New Zealand[1]	UK (2,608)	Australia (401) USA (373)	South Africa (720) India (468)
UK[1]	Ireland (1,859)		India (16,833) Pakistan (5,275) Nigeria (2,189) Egypt (1,718)
USA[1]			India (47,271) Philippines (11,973) Pakistan (11,779) Mexico (10,501) Grenada** (8,847)

* Absolute numbers per year in brackets, if available.

** Most doctors are US citizens training abroad in preparation for return to practice in the USA.

Sources:

1 Merçay *et al.*, 2016: 110, Table 4.3.

2 Merçay *et al.*, 2016: 117, Figure 4.9; based on 'foreign doctors'.

on foreign-trained doctors. Both the USA and the UK recruit primarily from LMICs, with India being the main sending country (O'Dowd, 2016). In the UK, we also find a mobility pattern, which is common in Europe and linked to outflows from countries hit by austerity measures, like Ireland.

The EU mobility patterns in some countries illustrate similarities with the 'draining' of low-income countries in other parts of the globe: outflows hit the resource-poorer countries at the Eastern margins of the EU and the crisis-hit countries with strong austerity measures (Southern Europe and Ireland) the most. One example is Germany. Although foreign recruitment is overall moderate in Germany, the direction of the mobility flow is problematic: Romania is the number one source of doctors, followed by Greece, Hungary and Poland (Glinos *et al.*, 2015; Merçay *et al.*, 2016).

When looking at nurses, data sources are less detailed and comprehensive, but there are some similarly problematic effects regarding the depletion of health labour markets of middle- and low-income countries (Campbell *et al.*, 2013; Maier *et al.*, 2014; Buchan, 2015; Leone *et al.*, 2016). In the UK, for instance, the annual inflow of nurses 'coming from European countries hit hard by the economic crisis also increased sharply in recent years, notably from Spain and Portugal', followed by Ireland and Poland (Merçay *et al.*, 2016: 117). In Portugal, like Spain, the outflow of nurses increased after the economic crises, with the UK and, to a lesser degree, France and Germany being major destination countries (Kuhlmann and Larsen, 2015; Leone *et al.*, 2016).

There is a general trend to replace previous recruitments from non-EU countries with intra-European mobility (Glinos *et al.*, 2015). This development is a combined effect of EU enlargement and the adoption of the Professional Qualification Directive (Directive 2005/36/EC) by the European Parliament in October 2007, aiming to facilitate EU mobility. The directive was amended in 2013 (Directive 2013/55/EU), and in January, 2016, a Professional Card was introduced, which covers five professions including three health professions, namely general nurses, pharmacists and physiotherapists. An expansion to other health professions may be possible in future (Merçay *et al.*, 2016: 116–17). At the same, action has been taken both globally and within the EU to mitigate the negative effects of migration flows (see Box 5.4; Glinos *et al.*, 2015).

Governing the health workforce

In recent years, all countries have acted to respond to the health workforce challenges and improve planning, governance and policy (Bourgeault and Merrit, 2015; Buchan, 2015; OECD, 2016b). Four major governance approaches can be identified from the comparative analysis which are linked to specific tools and strategies:

- governing inflows – preparing health workers;
- governing skills and competencies – allocating competencies;
- governing mobile health workers – allocating people to places; and
- governing recruitment, deployment and retention – managing health workers.

The two most important single policy levers for governing health workforce development are education and finance. Effective governance calls for complex interventions, however. All countries make use of mixed strategies, although the specific tools and mixes vary across countries.

The classic tool to govern the influx in professional groups is the numerous clausus (in effect a quota on certain groups). In relation to medicine, Australia and Germany have reduced the numerous clausus; Japan, New Zealand, and Sweden reflect a more rapid growth of intake while the UK reveals a slight reduction. Governing the inflow of health professions via numerous clausus policies can be a powerful tool, as for instance shown by the Netherlands (Batenburg, 2015). Yet 'in several OECD countries, numerus clausus policies are still based on weak evidence and opaque decision-making processes' (Moreira and Lafortune, 2016: 90), and workforce planning is therefore limited (Joint Action, 2015).

When looking at the governance of the skills mix of the health workforce, the comparative analysis demonstrates an overall strong trend towards developing new roles for nurses and the shifting of tasks from doctors to nurses or non-medical providers (Maier, 2015; Schoenstein *et al.*, 2016: 175). Some institutional contexts, like the corporatist settings in Germany and Japan, may block new roles for nurses and task shifting more than others. Supportive contexts for skill-mix changes include strong markets as in the USA or more systematic health workforce policy development as in the Netherlands. For instance, currently the proportion of NPs (or equal qualifications) is highest in the USA (5 per cent of the nursing workforce) and rapidly growing in the Netherlands (Moreira and Lafortune, 2016; Schoenstein *et al.*, 2016).

The governance of mobile health workers is most challenging because the right of citizens to free movement may clash with the needs of health care systems for a competent health workforce to ensure universal health care coverage for the population. The problems are most obvious within the EU where free movement is a legal requirement for member states. Mobility flows can be restricted directly – as in the case of foreign-national (and non-EU within the EU member countries) – or targeted through an array of incentives, ranging from classic increases in salaries and remuneration to non-wage based incentives, such as better work and career opportunities and better infrastructures. Direct restrictions to overserved areas are rarely used as governing tool, but are reported in

Germany, and to some degree, in the UK. Financial incentives to target mobility flows towards underserved areas, on the other hand, have been established in most countries, except Japan and the Netherlands (Ono *et al.*, 2016). In Japan, regional quotas of students' allocation to underserved areas have been very successful (Moreira and Lafortune, 2016). Quotas, restrictions and financial incentives seem to be the most popular tools to govern a mobile health workforce (Ono *et al.*, 2016: 162), yet their impact is limited.

A comparison of sending and receiving countries reveals that free movement seems to benefit both urban regions and high-income countries. Some action has been taken through global networks and within Europe, but the effects are not well monitored and global action needs to be flanked by national/regional governance incentives to counteract outflows (Bowser *et al.*, 2014). Examples from the low- and middle-income countries in Africa and Asia illustrate that improvement in health workforce governance can make a difference and reduce shortages (WHO, 2012a).

Finally, the governance of recruitment and retention brings the management of the health workforce and the role of the organization into perspective (Bruyneel *et al.*, 2014; Kroezen *et al.*, 2015; Leone *et al.*, 2016). Intervention strategies at the organizational level may be highly effective, but they lack monitoring and systematic evaluation, and this, in turn, limits the opportunity for comparison.

The health policy efforts to respond to changing needs of the population for health services through better governance of the health workforce are connected to the organization of care in various ways. This takes us to an expansion of the provision of care beyond the hospital, which is the theme of Chapter 6.

Chapter 6

Health Care Beyond the Hospital

Health systems for many years have been concerned primarily with the provision of medical care and focus on acute illness, and this in turn has promoted a focus on doctors and hospitals as well as on curing as opposed to primary health care (PHC) and long-term care (LTC). Transformations in societies, including demographic changes and 'ageing societies', and the changing spectra of illnesses have created a new demand for health care services beyond traditional hospital treatment. A needs-based health service provision, therefore, calls for substantive changes in the organization and delivery of care services (WHO, 2016b). Next to the expansion of health promotion and illness prevention (discussed in more detail in Chapter 7), the major policy goals include strengthening of PHC and the development of a new LTC sector. Less acute care, often including chronic illness and multi-morbidity, is typically characterized by considerable diversity in terms of the range of services, the user groups, the localities of service provision and the professionals involved. There are also important differences between high-income countries and middle-to-low-income countries, especially in relation to LTC. While LTC is a major policy issue in high-income countries, it is not a theme in low-income settings and there is still little activity in middle-income countries although pressures will increase in near future (Rhee *et al.*, 2015).

This comparative chapter discusses how countries respond to the demand for restructuring the organization of health care to promote and establish health care services beyond the hospital. The chapter takes two major trends into account: the shifts within medical/clinical care towards the strengthening of a more multi-professional, needs-based primary health care approach and the development of an emergent sector of LTC including a broad range of home care services, which blend health and social care in flexible ways. The latter also transforms the boundaries between professional/formal care providers and a wide array of informal care-givers from family members to household helpers, who are in some countries positioned in 'grey' labour markets of care assistants.

The chapter begins with analysing in comparative perspective the classic types and settings of medical practice, which are based on the two pillars of hospital and ambulatory care. Here, the argument is much the same as in Chapter 5, namely that doctors are powerful players in the health care system who can shape the transformations in the provision of care. The second section shifts the focus to care outside the hospital and a specific strategy of reform, namely primary health care, while the third discusses in detail how this model of PHC has been translated into policy and provision in different health systems, using integration and coordination as major goals. The next section expands the boundaries of provider organizations further into LTC, the most rapidly growing sector of health care and a switchboard between formal and informal care (Pavolini and Ranci, 2013; Gori *et al.*, 2016). LTC is regularly provided in the home of a patient with elder people as the main user group and the terms 'long-term care', 'elder care' and 'home care' often used interchangeably. We refer to a broad concept of LTC following the definition of the OECD (2011). After providing details on funding and provision in LTC, especially in relation to home care, the interface between formal and informal care provision is explored. Finally, policy trends and developments are reviewed comparatively from a health systems perspective.

Types and settings of medical practice

The settings of medical practice describe the institutions in which medicine is organized and relate to what Moran and Wood (1993) called the 'regulation of market structures'. This section focuses on the settings where different types of doctors work and the implications this has for the power of the medical profession. As Table 6.1 illustrates, hospitals

Table 6.1 *Types and settings of medical practice*

	Ambulatory settings (in either solo or group practice)	Hospital settings
Generalist/ specialist practitioners[a]	*Generalists only* Australia, Britain, Netherlands, New Zealand, Sweden, Singapore, Taiwan	*Mostly specialists* Australia, Britain, Germany, Netherlands, Singapore, Sweden, Taiwan, USA
Private/ public practitioners	*Mostly public* Sweden	*Mostly public* Australia, Britain, New Zealand, Sweden, Singapore
	Mostly private Australia, Britain, Germany, Germany, Japan, Netherlands, New Zealand, Singapore, Taiwan, USA	*Mostly private* Japan, Netherlands *Public and private* Germany, Taiwan, USA

[a] It is difficult to include Japan in this category as there is no clear distinction between generalist and specialist practitioners.

and ambulatory practices are the typical settings for doctors. Moreover, ambulatory settings can be differentiated into solo and group practices.

In most countries, hospitals are the only places in which specialist doctors practise. Examples of the few exceptions are Germany and the USA. In Germany, hospital work is often seen as transitional and used as a springboard to set up a specialist practice in ambulatory care. Similarly, in the USA many specialists practise in ambulatory settings. However, due to managed care, demand for GPs is mounting because of their increased role as gatekeepers and to encourage the use of primary care doctors in lieu of more expensive specialists. Despite an increasing demand for GPs in many countries (see Chapter 5), it is still in specialist practice where the medical model with its emphasis on acute illness and specialist knowledge excels, making hospitals the most prestigious setting where doctors work. A notable exception is Japan, which places heavy emphasis on preventive medicine and primary care in ambulatory settings.

Different settings are closely associated with different types of medical practice (ambulatory settings with general practitioners and hospitals with specialists), although there are exceptions. Hospital doctors are either public or private employees, depending on the ownership of the hospital. As providers of specialist care, hospitals are complex organizations that rely on the division of labour across a wide range of health practitioners. This means that specialists depend heavily on the work of others when they practise in hospital settings. As complex organizations, hospitals also need management structures to coordinate the different parts of the labour process. These management structures have been expanded over recent years in response to new management and governance reforms with stronger market logics (see Box 6.1).

There are limits to the managerialist approach and in many countries there has been revival of elements of professionally based management since the late 1990s, but under changed conditions. Doctors are increasingly involved in management as active players on all levels of decision making and often enjoy leadership roles (Kuhlmann *et al.*, 2013; Burau, 2016; Correia and Denis, 2016; Kirkpatrick *et al.*, 2016). In Britain, for instance, it is indicative that a medical specialist appointed junior minister was chairing a review of NHS reforms and proclaimed that future change should be clinically and locally driven (Hunter, 2008). In this respect, Primary Care Trusts and the notion of practice-based commissioning served as a focal point for the type of organizational change envisaged by the review. This was reconfirmed by the health reforms in 2012, which introduced GP-led Clinical Commissioning Groups (Cylus *et al.*, 2015).

The situation is different in countries where doctors work in smaller ambulatory settings as private practitioners. For instance, in Japan

---

Box 6.1   Management and governance reforms in New Zealand

Before the health reforms of the 1980s and 1990s, hospital boards were controlled by triumvirates, composed of medical staff, nursing staff and administrators, with medical staff predominant on most boards. In large part, the reforms were an effort to wrest control from these boards, which critics felt were self-serving, inefficient and unconcerned with cost control. Beginning in 1983 with the government's setting of hospital budgets and culminating in the replacement of hospital boards with Area Health Boards in 1989, a series of steps was taken to create a structure for hospitals that would enable them to 'avoid capture by the medical community'. The continual erosion of the influence of the medical community over decision making and the shift in authority to managers and outside consultants has been a contentious issue that at times has resulted in near open warfare between the parties. Moreover, since the introduction of capitation funding for general practice, regulatory control of general practice fees has become increasingly intense, to the discomfort of many GPs who have yet to adjust to the political implications of increased public funding of their services (Dovey *et al.*, 2011).

---

doctors pronounce the independence associated with solo practice, where doctors operate out of so-called 'clinics', most which have some inpatient accommodation, where they exercise discretion on admission and discharge (Ikegami, 2007). Like Japan, in Taiwan most general practice clinics are solo practices; less than 20 per cent are partnerships or group practices. Until the advent of the NHI made the practice illegal, physicians both prescribed and dispensed prescriptions in their offices.

In contrast, in other countries group practices are the most common settings. The significance of group settings is particularly apparent in Sweden where doctors work in multidisciplinary health centres where their role is not necessarily paramount. This reflects the fact that the provision of health care has long been dominated by hospitals (Harrison, 2004) and that the initiative to set up health centres came from political-administrative circles (including the Ministry for Health and Social Affairs) not the medical profession (Garpenby, 2001).

Operating in a group setting typically involves a larger number of professional groups and may improve the role of nurses (Ham, 2010; Groenewegen *et al.*, 2015). Yet group settings may also strengthen the position of doctors as demonstrated by the emergence of regional independent practice associations (IPAs) of ambulatory care doctors in New Zealand and Australia. The IPAs act as collective negotiators, contract and fund holders for doctors who are overwhelmingly generalists. In New Zealand, for example, IPAs emerged largely as a pre-emptive response by GPs to a perceived threat by regional purchasers that contracts would be introduced for publicly financed primary care services, thus undercutting the tradition of fee-for-service private practice (Smith and Mays, 2007). Although developments in contracting and alternative methods of funding and managing services were initially either resisted or treated with caution by many GPs, early successes in contracting, in budget holding for pharmaceutical and laboratory services and in establishing new services led to a progressive recruitment of IPA membership (Ashton, 2005). Similar developments can be observed in Germany, although there is still a coexistence of solo practices, various forms of group practices with different owners or employed doctors and larger medical centres (Kuhlmann *et al.*, 2017).

The variety of organizational settings illustrate that the practice of doctors is embedded in the specific context of hospitals and ambulatory care and their relative position in the sub-systems of funding, provision and governance. In the case of Germany, for example, hospitals have traditionally been less well integrated in health governance, reflecting not only the mix of public and private non-profit providers that is typical of social insurance systems such as those of Japan and the Netherlands, but also the absence of a system of self-administration. Instead, health governance has been fragmented into contracts between individual hospitals and insurance funds, and into coexisting competencies between the federal and state governments.

The fragmentation of health governance (also typical of other federalist countries such as Australia and the USA) strengthened the position of the provider side and left hospitals and hospital doctors relatively untouched by health reforms in the 1980s (Schwartz and Busse, 1997). However, this has been changing and the practice of hospital doctors is now much more strongly integrated in and controlled by joint self-administration (Burau, 2007b; Busse and Blümel, 2014). The funding of hospitals has moved away from prospective payments to payments based on DRGs and flanked by extensive measures of quality assurance (Sauerland, 2009). Since the 2000 health care reforms, the Joint Committee as the key body of the joint self-administration includes hospital care which remains under the authority of the federal states. Of further importance is the more flexible boundary among the different settings; e.g. hospitals are now allowed to offer ambulatory care services.

This trend shows similarities with national health services, where organizational integration traditionally has been stronger. Britain is an example of a system where the degree of integration of ambulatory care has increased since the early 1990s. As part of the introduction of the internal market, many GPs chose to become 'fundholders' and were given budgets to purchase diagnostic procedures and elective surgery for their patients. GPs thereby extended their managerial responsibilities beyond their own practice and moved closer to the mainstream of NHS management. The reforms under the New Labour government from the late 1990s took this development a step further. General practices became part of Primary Care Trusts (later CCCs), which were responsible not only for the provision of primary care but also for the commissioning of all other health services within a certain area (Peckham and Exworthy, 2003). This developed into a comprehensive system of 'practice-based commissioning' where GPs work within an organization that is directly funded by and accountable to government. The Minister for Health appoints the chief executives of CCCs and they are subject to government guidance in the same way as hospital trusts (Hunter, 2008; Department of Health, 2012d; McDonald, 2015).

In summary, the traditional pillars of health care provision – hospital and ambulatory care settings – are becoming more diverse and the boundaries more permeable. However, the ambulatory care settings still demonstrate important differences, which are further explored in the next section in relation to primary health care.

Primary health care as reform model

Primary health care is part of ambulatory care and as such, is relevant in all health care systems and integrated in funding schemes and the policy of universal coverage (Chapter 3). PHC is not only a way of organizing ambulatory care, but also a reform strategy for better health care provision for all citizens (Starfield, 2012). While the organizational component is variable and context-dependent, the agenda for reform is universal, shared globally and accompanied with high-level international support. With this backdrop, PHC is an interesting example for comparison, which may illustrate how national policy contexts and the institutions of health care impact on the implementation of reform concepts (Gauld *et al.*, 2012, 2014).

The importance of primary health care was first raised by the WHO in 1978 and again stressed in the 2008 World Health Report (WHO, 1978, 2008d). As an agenda for reform, it has spread globally, following broadly similar goals and values of 'better health care for all' (Saltman *et al.*, 2006; Kringos *et al.*, 2010; Gauld, 2015; Groenewegen *et al.*, 2015). PHC reforms have common features in otherwise highly different institutional settings. Moreover, implementation is driven by similar goals to respond more effectively to changing health care needs of citizens and to create better coordinated and integrated services. The emergence of a global reform agenda of PHC was closely tied to the Alma Ata Declaration of the WHO in 1978 that defined health broadly as a state of well-being and identified PHC as a key to achieve this goal (WHO, 1978). Significantly, the Declaration defined PHC mainly as a range of *principles* related to the overall system of health care, including equity, community involvement (and by extension, decentralization), prevention and health promotion. The 'Health for All by the Year 2000' strategy subsequently translated the principles into targets, which the WHO Regions adapted to their respective contexts (WHO, 1981).

The tide of the WHO reform agenda turned in the late 1980s, when the focus shifted away from PHC and towards health care systems reform based on market principles, and when the International Monetary Fund, the World Bank and the OECD emerged as new influential players while the role of the WHO diminished. In the late 1990s, the singular focus on market-based health care system reforms was superseded by a more context-sensitive approach to developing health care systems. This was also associated with a comeback of WHO, but now as only one player among many in global health policy (Green *et al.*, 2007).

These developments provided a springboard for the revival of a global reform agenda of PHC from the early 2000s onwards. Here, the argument was that the principles underpinning the initial primary health care reform agenda were still relevant, but needed to be adapted to the changed context of health. This revival was strongly affirmed in the 2008 World Health Report (WHO, 2008d), which was concerned exclusively with PHC. The core strategies identified by the Report – notably universal coverage, people-centred care and public health policies – echo some of the principles of the initial agenda. The global reform agenda of PHC can be summarized as follows:

- Primary health care must be oriented towards chronic diseases and altered patient expectations towards services;
- This requires systematic changes that encompass all components of the care process;
- Service provision must be targeted towards integrated concepts of provision and coordinated across different levels of health care (Gauld *et al.*, 2012).

Interestingly, in relation to high-income countries, developments at global and local levels are characterized by temporal decoupling. There was no significant reform at local levels in the early 1980s when the global agenda was at its zenith, but heightened activity since the 1990s when the global agenda took a backseat. Reforms have continued since a modified version of the global agenda re-emerged in the early 2000s.

Table 6.2   *Indicators of integrated primary health care policy*

Model of integration	Level of integration
Within medical model	Across primary health care organizations
Under the leadership of doctors	Across health care sectors
Across different professional groups	Across policy sectors

Green *et al.* (2007) suggested that the WHO agenda initially had less appeal to high-income countries. These countries tended to adopt a narrow definition of PHC as a specific level of service – rather than a set of principles – and on this count, they saw themselves as already high achievers (Gauld *et al.*, 2012).

Yet primary PHC came into the health reforms of high-income countries through the back door, notably in the context of market-oriented policies, where PHC promised to square the circle between efficient and high-quality health care, thus becoming a proxy for integrating health care services and people-centred care and for controlling doctors (Saltman *et al.*, 2006; Kringos *et al.*, 2010). To this end, PHC emerged as a 'meta-concept' of improved coordination and integration, increasingly including inter-professional collaboration (Samuelson *et al.*, 2012) and issues of skill mix and task shifting (Wismar *et al.*, 2017). This has made PHC appealing for the highly specialized and often fragmented health care systems of high-income countries. Low-income countries, by contrast, may primarily benefit from the focused and structured approach and the inclusive model of a wide range of service providers. The level and the model of integration are, therefore, useful indicators for comparing PHC policy and provision, as shown in Table 6.2.

Integration and coordination in primary health care

Primary health care has the capacity to transform health care systems and at the same time, more than other parts of the health care system, tends to be influenced by the general institutional design of this policy field. In international debates of PHC reforms, Britain is often treated as an archetypical example of what PHC should look like as the health care system has a strong and longstanding GP gatekeeper model and PHC was a feature since the introduction of the NHS in 1948 (Cylus *et al.*, 2015). Yet the British model was narrowly focused on the provision of general medical services, which also have been rather separate from the remainder of the health service (Peckham and Exworthy, 2003). The introduction of Primary Care Groups in 1997 marked a radical change in PHC policies. The commissioning role of PHC was extended and institutionalized, and thereby strengthened integration within but also beyond the medical model. Nevertheless, policies in England remained narrowly concerned with developing GP-led primary health care organizations as the backbone of integration, thus giving preference to integration that focuses on the individual patient rather than the local population overall. More recently, the models of PHC became more diverse (Sheaff, 2013) and integrated in relation to the professional groups, especially nurses (Cylus *et al.*, 2015). Acceleration of 'the development of nursing roles in primary care' is among the key recommendations for PHC (House of Commons, 2016).

The Swedish health system is another archetype of a health care system with a PHC tradition, but it was more strongly guided by the principles of integration, public responsibility and equity than in the UK. 'Sweden developed in the post-war era a system of carefully planned allocation of primary health care centres (PHCCs) with a multi-disciplinary team of health professionals, operated directly by local public authorities' (Isaksson *et al.*, 2016: 4). Physicians were predominately salaried employees, and the general size of a team was four to ten GPs, nurses, physical therapists and dieticians. The PHCCs typically offer basic medical diagnosis and care, public health and preventive services and counselling. In 2010, a health reform for the first time opened PHCC for private entry, and there now 1,100 public and private facilities in Sweden (Mossialos *et al.*, 2016: 157). However, a recent evaluation found that in most regions the 'main form of primary care provider is still a relatively large multidisciplinary health centre offering a wide range of health-related services, including maternity care, child care and psychological counselling' (Isaksson *et al.*, 2016: 7). At the same time, contradictory expectations of providers, funders and patients are embedded in the model and may cause tensions at the micro-level (Andersson Bäck, 2016).

For many years, health policy in Germany represented a typical counter-model to the global primary health care agenda with its strong emphasis on medically oriented ambulatory care that includes specialists in addition to generalists. The tide turned from the 1990s onwards, when various policy initiatives aimed at integrated health care started to set the focus on PHC. Significantly, however, this occurred without any significant changes to the organization and governance of health services themselves (Burau, 2009b; Kuhlmann *et al.*, 2017). In 2009, PHC was for the first time used explicitly as a blueprint for organizational restructuring of ambulatory care (Advisory Council for the Concerted Action in Health Care, 2009: 140–1). The new model builds on the well-established scheme of family physicians with some integration of other

ISBN	9781137544957
Customer P/O No	MEDWC9565/1
Title:	Comparative health p... Viola Burau, Ellen
Format:	P (Paperb...
Author:	Blank, ...
Publisher:	Palg...
Fund:	MF...
Location:	
Loan Type:	
Coutts C...	
Order...	

Qty
1

Hand Notes:

Budget/Fund Code	MEDWC
Classification	WA 540.1
Loan Type/Stock	6 x owls
Sequence Code	INPROCESS
Site / Location	WHITECHAPL
Shelfmark	WA 540.1 BLA 2018
Cutter 1	BLA
PL Category	General
Order Date	11/17/2017
Order Type	orders
PL Intellect. Level	Adult

Customer Number: 21036007   ISBN: 9781137544957

Barts/London School of Med Whitechapel L

P11IS9A9N

Processing

than medical providers. Integration across sectors and policy areas and, excepting some regional pilot projects, among professional groups, however, has remained weak and does not question individualized medicine. PHC did achieve transformative potential primarily *within* the medical profession and in relation to organizational settings (Gerlach and Szecsenyi, 2013; Advisory Council on the Assessment of Developments in the Health Care System, 2014; Groene *et al.*, 2016). Change has largely been incremental within German corporatist partnership governance, although recently integration of a range of professions is increasing and supported by legislative reforms (Kuhlmann *et al.*, 2017).

The Netherlands, by contrast, provides an interesting example of more radical and comprehensive policy innovation to strengthen PHC in a system with strong tradition of ambulatory care and physician-centred provision (Kroeneman *et al.*, 2016). Most of this care is delivered by GPs working in their own practice and includes a range of services from classic ambulatory care to the management of chronic illnesses and preventive services, thus nearly all new health problems are managed within PHC settings (Tsiachristas *et al.*, 2011; Gauld *et al.*, 2012). Reimbursement is based on capitation for registered patients and fee-for-services. Care is provided by middle-to-large teams with a median number of three different professional groups in addition to GPs (Groenewegen *et al.*, 2015) and coordination supported by numerous guidelines and other efforts. As Gauld *et al.* (2012) argued, collaborative and coordinated approaches have been supported and improved significantly, while leadership remains fragmented.

Next to these examples of longstanding PHC/ambulatory care services, there is a wide range of innovation policy. In Australia, a range of policy reforms have introduced incentives to improve the inclusion of preventive services and a wider range of professional groups as well as the management of chronic illnesses and care for older people and Indigenous groups. Since 2007, policy reforms aim to develop larger GP clinics, yet no comprehensive coordination structure has been developed (Gauld *et al.*, 2012). They conclude that the initiatives 'to promote GPs working alongside other professions have generated a complex system that does not function in an integrated manner' (2012: 46). PHC has enhanced organizational transformation with some improvement of integration, although this can be constrained by the wide variety of organization types (Rodwell and Gulyas, 2013).

New Zealand introduced its Primary Healthcare Strategy in 2001, aiming at strengthening primary care, improving access and reducing inequalities in health through the development of 80 Primary Healthcare Organizations (PHOs). The PHOs are non-governmental, not-for-profit organizations contracted by their local DHB to manage capitation budgets devolved under contract and to purchase/commission a range of PHC services for their enrolled populations (Gauld, 2008). The reforms have promoted a multidisciplinary provider mix. In relation to hospital care and PHC, integration is less well developed but since 2008 the Government 'is promoting creation of larger family medicine centres that offer minor surgical services' (Gauld *et al.*, 2012: 47).

Similarly, in Taiwan Primary Community Care Networks (PCCNs) are the product of recent PHC reform initiatives. A PCCN consists of a group of clinic physicians whose medical jobs are categorized as family care as most GP clinics are solo practices. In turn, the clinics must cooperate with at least one hospital for their patients' secondary or tertiary care (Lin *et al.*, 2011). Overall, integration is poorly developed, however. There is a lack of integration between sectors and providers and of preventive services alongside poor involvement of the public and the medical associations in decision making (Gauld *et al.*, 2012). At the same time, traditional Chinese medicine (TCM) is widespread in Taiwanese culture and to some extent integrated in PHC (Cheng *et al.*, 2012), thus bringing in elements of illness prevention and health promotion.

Japan shows a more traditional model with PHC mainly delivered by doctors with a specialization working in solo practice (Ikegami, 2016). Reimbursement schemes have tended to favour doctors working in PHC, although there is an overall strong policy focus on hospitals (Gauld *et al.*, 2012). Integration of other than medical providers is poorly developed and organizational transformations are weak (Schoenstein *et al.*, 2016). Similarly, in Singapore private GPs and private payments of patients dominate PHC provision, while government-funded PHC is provided by doctors at polyclinics with subsidized patient fees but significant co-payments (Gauld *et al.*, 2012). The ratio of 1,400 private GP clinics against 18 multi-doctor public clinics (mainly providing services for low-income patents) illustrates the low public priority of PHC (Mossialos *et al.*, 2016: 145). At the same time, Singapore has a strong tradition of preventive services, and established a range of initiatives targeting improved coordination between services, yet there is little integration in relation to provider groups and the public (Gauld *et al.*, 2012).

The USA, as a strongly market-oriented system, has a long tradition of PHC, which allows the patient to choose between a medical provider, usually a GP, and a range of non-medical professionals such as NPs or physician assistants (Marcum *et al.*, 2016). PHC promoted new, more integrated organizational models (Box 6.2) and recent reforms have emphasized preventive services (Gauld *et al.*, 2012). However, coordination among the various services is poorly developed, and no coordinated leadership system exists (Gauld *et al.*, 2012).

> ## Box 6.2   Primary health care models in the USA
>
> In the USA, the 'patient-centred medical home' model, in which a patient can receive targeted, accessible, continuous, coordinated and family-centred care by a personal physician, has gained interest as a means of strengthening primary care. Another movement generating considerable momentum among both public and private payers is the creation of 'accountable care organizations' (ACOs), which are networks of providers, including hospitals and physicians, that agree to take responsibility for providing a defined population with care that meets quality targets. In exchange, they share in the savings that constitute the difference between actual and forecasted health care spending for their population (Thomson et al., 2013). Despite this, a recent evaluation found, that 'for at least one type of primary care provider – the RHC – there are substantial costs associated with ACO participation during the first two years' (Hofler and Ortiz, 2016: 1).

Table 6.3 summarizes the policies of integration and coordination in comparative perspective, using the matrix introduced in the previous section (Table 6.2). Interestingly, integration within the medical model is the dominant pattern in many countries, but importantly, differences exist in terms of the substance of the PHC model and the extent to which PHC connects with other models. The substance of the model varies among multi-professional teams in Sweden, multi-professional provider choice in the USA, GP-led PHC in the UK, New Zealand and Australia, ambulatory care with multi-professional teams in the Netherlands, specialists in addition to generalists in Germany, and more classic medical provider models of GPs in Taiwan, Singapore and Japan.

Table 6.3   *Comparing integration and coordination in primary health care in selected high-income countries*

	Model of integration	*Level of integration*
Australia	• Integration in a GP-led model of PHC with strong organizational change and multidisciplinary teams; • Integration of professional groups with new roles of nurses	• Some integration and improved coordination across providers and sectors, inclusion of preventive services and public health; • High variety and lack of comprehensive coordination

(Continued)

	Model of integration	Level of integration
*England/ UK**	• Integration within medical model predominant with focus on GP-led PHC; • Some integration across professional groups with a focus on nurses and new roles	• Integration across PHC organizations by merging GP practices into PHC trusts; • Some integration across health care and policy sectors, as primary care trusts have commissioning responsibility for public health and collaboration with social care
Germany	• Integration within medical model with focus on medial leadership and organizational restructuring; • Limited integration across professional groups, especially for nurses, but few regional pilots aim at shifting tasks from doctors to medical assistants	• Integration across PHC organizations to better connect generalist and specialist doctors; • Some integration and improved coordination but fragmentation of care sectors and weak public health; • Fragmented coordination with different social insurance schemes
Japan	• Some integration within a medical model with some organizational integration with hospitals; • Lack of professional integration	• Integration between medical providers to connect specialized PHC and hospital physicians; • Lack of coordination between sectors and policy fields
Netherlands	• Integration within a medical model with strong organizational change and multidisciplinary teams; • Integration across professions with new roles of nurses	• Integration and coordination across sectors with strong public health and patient involvement; • Little coordination of policy and fragmented leadership
New Zealand	• Integration in a multi-professional provider model with strong organizational change and large centres; • Integration across professions with new roles of nurses	• Some integration across providers and sectors; • Little coordinated leadership

Singapore	• Some integration within a medical model with little organizational change; • Lack of professional integration	• Lack of provider integration but strong integration of public health; • Some integration across sectors but lack of public integration with hierarchical leadership
Sweden	• Multi-professional teams with strong public responsibility and some organizational change; • Integration of professional groups with strong role of nurses	• Integration and coordination between organizations, sectors and policy fields through local authorities; • Coordination of leadership with some variety through privatization
Taiwan	• Integration within medical model strongly based on family doctors; • Lack of integration of professional groups, but some integration of TCM providers	• Some integration between medical providers but lack of integration between sectors and policy areas, and of preventive services; • Lack of coordination of leadership
USA	• Multi-professional provider model, although GP leadership is strong, and improved organizational integration; • Integration across profession with new roles of nurses	• Little integration between medical providers, sectors and policy areas; • No coordinated leadership

* As a result of devolution, variety is increasing within the UK; more recent information refers to developments in England.

There are also important differences in relation to the level of integration, ranging from strong integration and coordination between sectors and policy fields with coordinated leadership in Sweden towards little integration of public health and lack of comprehensive coordination and leadership in Japan, Singapore and Taiwan. Most of the countries in our sample are clustered between these two poles, however. Across countries, the focus lies on the integration among primary health care organizations, but variations exist relative both to the concrete organizational forms and the extent to which there are additional levels of integration and improved coordination between sectors and policy fields. Most striking is an overall lack of leadership and coordination mechanisms in most countries.

Interestingly, in low-income countries PHC plays a more prominent role as a 'hub of coordination' (WHO, 2008d: 55) and shared decision making than in many high-income countries, while at the same time there is a stronger local and community-based focus in relation to both policy making and the organizational settings (Box 6.3). For instance, developments in a district in Congo over the last 30 years illustrate the robustness of a PHC-led organizational model even under conditions of a sharp economic decline, inter-ethnic strife, a massive influx of refugees and two successive wars (WHO, 2008d). PHC services continued to expand with growing numbers of centres and improved quality of services. 'The continuity of the work under extremely difficult circumstances can be explained by team work and collegial decision-making, unrelenting efforts to build up and maintain a critical mass of dedicated human resources' and effective use of local capacity (WHO, 2008d: 31).

Looking at middle-income countries, a particularly interesting case is the development in Russia and the former Soviet Union countries, where PHC meets with a mix of new market politics and established public health care provision stemming from the Communist area. Here, integration of PHC emerged within a medical model with elements of general practice added onto an existing system of polyclinics. Rechel (2015: 244) argued that the Soviet model of administration, under which PHC was managed by the central district hospital, has persisted in countries like Azerbaijan, Kyrgyzstan, Tajikistan and Uzbekistan, but also in rural areas of Russia and Ukraine. As a consequence, evaluation of pilots found that PHC enjoys overall low priority, implementation is scattered and is narrowly defined by GP services (Kringos *et al.*, 2009). Only few

---

Box 6.3   Primary health care as robust model and hub of coordination in low-income countries

Primary-care teams cannot ensure comprehensive responsibility for their population without support from specialized services, organizations and institutions that are based outside the community served. In resource-constrained circumstances,... the classic image of a healthcare system based on PHC is that of a pyramid with the district hospital at the top and a set of (public) health centres that refer to the higher authority. ... The coordination (or gatekeeping) role this entails effectively transforms the primary-care pyramid into a network, where the relations between the primary-care team and the other institutions and services are no longer based only on top-down hierarchy and bottom-up referral, but on cooperation and coordination.... The primary-care team then becomes the mediator between the community and the other levels of the health system. (WHO, 2008d: 55–6)

comprehensive PHC models exist, and Moldova is one of the pioneering cases: in rural areas PHC is built on a family physician model and in urban areas on health centres (Rechel, 2015).

In China, another example of a BRICS country (as Brazil, Russia, India, China and South Africa, all 'emerging', are called) shaped by communist politics, PHC has become an important hub for system innovation (Mossialos *et al.*, 2016: 33) and integrated PHC approaches have been established, including a wide range of providers. The health reforms in 2009 mentioned PHC as one of five pillars of reform. Lin and Zhao describe the model of PHC as 'establishing a comprehensive network of basic health services through a three-tier rural network and urban community health services, with Chinese medicine integrated into these service delivery networks' (2015: 141). Hu *et al.* (2016) argue that people prefer hospital settings rather than PHC, because they perceive higher quality in hospitals. Patients in rural settings are encouraged to use village clinics, but they are also entitled to use upper-level GP services in hospitals (Mossialos *et al.*, 2016: 33). In China, the major constraints of PHC development are severe shortage of doctors and other higher-qualified health professionals. Under these conditions, most PHC services are provided in rural areas by low-qualified village doctors (not-licensed GPs) and community health workers, while GPs usually work in urban areas (Mossialos *et al.*, 2016: 33). Therefore, the boundaries among professions are more flexible and service provision is strongly linked to the community level.

Another example of PHC serving as 'coordinator' of an integrated service network and 'promoter' of inter-sectoral coordination are developments in South America (Giovanella and Faria, 2015: 216). Here, the model of PHC is described as more integrated in relation to the professional groups and local stakeholders and comprises a wide range of attempts to improve coordination across sectors. In their report on health systems in South America, Giovanella and Faria (2015) place the development of participatory decision making in PHC in the wider context of emergent new democratic institutions in the region.

In summary, the development of PHC in middle- and low-income countries shows similarities with the range of models found in high-income countries – from GP-led services to multi-professional teams and non-medical providers. Yet the PHC models seem to be more polarized in middle- and low-income countries, while high-income countries cluster in the middle with various forms of mixed models and levels of integration and coordination.

Long-term care

In most OECD countries, LTC services have rapidly expanded and moved up on the policy agenda, but unlike PHC no uniform reform model and coherent strategic response exists. Moreover, the policies and services are highly diverse, with much the same applying to the demand for LTC and the needs of the user groups. The OECD defines LTC as 'a range of services required by persons with a reduced degree of functional capacity, physical or cognitive, and who are consequently dependent for an extended time on help with basic activities of daily living (ADL)' (OECD, 2011: 1). Characteristically, a personal component of care is frequently provided in combination with basic medical services and can be combined with 'lower-level care related to help with instrumental activities of daily life (IADL)', such as housework and transportation (OECD, 2011: 1).

User groups reflect the support required at different stages of the lifespan, ranging from severely ill infants to adults at the end of life. Other beneficiaries include people with mental illness and disability, physical disability, drug-related disorders, and progressive illness. Care is also located in different settings, such as residential care and nursing homes, day hospitals and sheltered housing, as well as people's own homes. The professionals involved include nurses, community nurses, mental health nurses, care assistants, home helps, counsellors, physiotherapists and other therapists. Moreover, funding schemes range from inclusion in tax-based systems to the development of new statutory insurance-based models and subsidiarity of family care and self-payments (Carrera *et al.*, 2013; Campbell *et al.*, 2016; Fernández and Nadash, 2016; Mossialos *et al.*, 2016).

The diversity of care in the LTC sector reflects the varied yet interlocking needs of people who require long-term care (Rummery and Fine, 2012). At the same time, care services are often locally specific and even tailored to individuals, so it is difficult to identify the typical, let alone generalize (Burau and Kröger, 2004). Although care services outside hospitals are central to the health of individuals, they can be remote from the health system.

We focus here on care for older people who represent the largest user group of LTC and, in the face of ageing societies, have attracted considerable attention in health policy terms (Olivares-Tirado *et al.*, 2011; Pavolini and Theobald, 2015; Gori *et al.*, 2016). We refer to home care as an umbrella term for a wide range of services provided to elder people regardless of location, thus including various forms of resident care as well as care in one's own home. Although home care is related to health systems, it traverses the boundaries between health and social care, and between formal and informal care. It primarily involves nurses rather than doctors and, most importantly, principally women as informal care-givers.

LTC policies are pushed by demography and costs, but are shaped by country-specific factors. Key factors include how the funding and provision of health care is organized, where health systems draw the boundary between health and social care, and cultural assumptions about the appropriate relations among the generations and between women and men, what Pfau-Effinger (2004) calls 'gender cultures'. LTC (as well as public health discussed in Chapter 7) also demonstrates that many services now central to health are at the margins of health systems and, unlike other areas of health care, the medical profession is less directly involved.

Compared to other sectors of the health system, international statistics on LTC are meagre and often non-existent. Our comparative analysis looks at trends in institutionally based care, for which more adequate statistics are available. While information is improving for OECD countries (OECD, 2011; Ranci and Pavolini, 2013; Pavolini and Theobald, 2015; Campbell *et al.*, 2016), there is a lack of standardized definitions of 'disability' and 'need' for care (Wittenberg, 2016: 15), which limits the opportunities for comparison. Furthermore, with few exceptions, middle- and low-income countries largely remain a black box regarding LTC policies.

Expenditure for LTC services is a relatively robust indicator for comparison and an indication of different policy models and priorities, while 'life expectancy' can reveal differences in demand. Table 6.4 provides a first comparative overview of LTC (including recipients in institutions and at home) expenditures as share of GDP and of total health care expenditure, differentiated for funding schemes and provider groups. The comparison reveals enormous differences in LTC expenditure, which cannot be explained by life expectancy. Sweden and the Netherlands spend more than one-quarter of their health care expenditure on LTC, while in Germany, Japan and the UK the share is in a range of 14 to 18 per cent. In the USA and Australia only 2 to 5 per cent is allocated to LTC! There are also important differences in relation to the share of public and private funding and of residential homes, ambulatory and hospital-based LTC providers, which cannot easily be explained by health system typologies.

The percentage of LTC recipients 65 years and over in relation to the total population in Table 6.5 offers a further indication of the relative size of home care services and reveals a relatively low proportion of institutional care in relation to care provided at home, which is, except in Australia, more than double.

When looking at the supply side of institutional care there is no uniform trend in the last two decades. As Table 6.6 reveals, Australia, Germany and Japan have increased the beds in residential LTC facilities over time, while other countries show little change. Sweden is the only country that faced a sharp decline, yet the share of LTC beds is still higher than in other countries. This suggests that institutionally based care continues to be important, despite relevant shifts in policy to encourage older people to live in the community. Similarly, Campbell *et al.*, in their comparative

Table 6.4 Life expectancy and estimated spending on long-term home care as a percentage of GDP and total health expenditure, 2014

Country	Life expectancy		% LTC expenditure as share of GDP	% LTC expenditure as share of total health expenditure	Share per funding		Share per LTC provider		
	Men	Women		Total	public	private	residential	ambulant	hospital
Australia	80.3	84.4	0.2	2.3	2.1	0.2	n/a	--	2.3
Germany	78.7	83.6	1.5	13.8	9.4	4.5	8.9	2.6	--
Japan	80.5	86.8	2.1	18.2	16.6	1.6	8.0	5.6	4.6
Netherlands	80.0	83.5	3.0	27.2	27.2	--	24.1	--	3.0
New Zealand	79.8	83.4	n/a	n/a	n/a	n/a	n/a	n/a	n/a
Sweden	80.4	84.2	2.9	26.2	24.2	2.0	18.5	7.7	n/a
UK	79.5	83.2	1.8	18.0	12.0	5.9	6.4	3.8	0.5
USA	76.4	81.2	0.9	5.4	3.2	2.2	5.4	n/a	n/a

Source: Data from OECD (2016a).
All financing schemes.

Table 6.5   *LTC recipients aged 65 years and over in different LTC settings as a percentage of the total population, 2014*

	LTC recipients in institutions	LTC recipients at home
Australia	6.4	8.1
Germany	4.1	8.9
Japan	2.8	n/a
Netherlands	5.3	13.1
New Zealand	4.8	12.2
Sweden	4.5	11.8
USA[a]	3.3	n/a
[a] Data from 2011.		

Source: Data from OECD (2016a).

Table 6.6   *Number of beds in residential LTC facilities per 1,000 population, 2000–14*

	2000	2005	2010	2014
Australia	4.5	5.2	7.8	7.9
Germany	8.2[a]	9.2	10.3[b]	11.2[c]
Japan	4.2	5.1	5.5	6.2
Netherlands	10.6	10.4	10.4	10.6[d]
New Zealand	n/a	n/a	8.0	8.3
Singapore	2.1	2.3	n/a	n/a
Sweden	16.9	15.2	14.2	12.8
Taiwan	1.9	2.0	1.8	n/a
UK	n/a	9.0	8.4	8.5
US	5.4	5.3	5.4	5.1
[a] data from 2001; [b] data from 2009; [c] data from 2013; [d] data from 2012.				

Sources: Data from OECD (2016a); Singapore Ministry of Health (2008); Bureau of National Health Insurance (2012).

analysis, found that 'high HCBS [home and community-based] spending does not necessarily go with low institutional spending – if anything, the opposite is true' (2016: 60).

A more specific indication of shifts in supply is the number of LTC beds per 1,000 population aged 65 years. Table 6.7 shows a decrease in supply in most countries, especially large in Sweden. In contrast, Australia, and to a lesser extent Germany, increased facilities, while in Japan supply remained relatively stable.

Table 6.7   *Number of beds in residential LTC facilities per 1,000 population aged 65 years and over, 2000–14*

	2000	2005	2010	2014
Australia	36.2	40.4	57.6	53.5
Germany	49.2[a]	49.3	50.5[b]	53.1[c]
Japan	24.2	26.4	24.1	24.9
Netherlands	78.4	74.5	67.8	65.5[d]
New Zealand	n/a	n/a	61.9	57.5
Sweden	98.5	88.4	78.9	66.2
UK	n/a	56.4	51.6	48.7
USA	43.6	42.8	41.1	35.4

[a] data from 2001; [b] data from 2009; [c] data from 2013; [d] data from 2012.

Source: Data from OECD (2016a).

In terms of both funding and provision, home care is marginal in all countries, in some more so than in others, and trends in institutional supply of LTC are not uniform. The next section analyses in more detail the LTC policy models for home care.

Policy, funding and provision of home care

Home care is an important area of heath policy but often not fully integrated in the institutional fabric of health systems, thus creating distinct features in the funding and provision of services. Funding is relevant in two respects – the security of funding and the relative level of public funding – which give an indication of the extent to which LTC, especially home care, is an integral part of a health system (Campbell *et al.*, 2016). Funding models range from taxes and social insurance contributions to out-of-pocket payments and private insurance. The first two bases of funding provide secure funding, whereas out-of-pocket payments are a much less reliable source. Home care funding is typically highly mixed because funding from public sources is often insufficient and a substantial amount of services are funded from private, out-of-pocket payments (Pavolini and Theobald, 2015). Diverse approaches to funding create different types of access. In countries with tax funding, patients tend to have direct access to services. In contrast, in countries with social insurance funding patients often need a medical referral to access services, since service is provided as an earned right rather than a need.

The provision of home care reflects the level and security of funding, but is influenced by other factors. This includes policies explicitly aimed at substituting together with cultural expectations about the role of the family in care-giving. Substitution policies refer to a set of policies that are intended to replace institutionally based care with care in the home and related settings. Subsidiarity assigns primary responsibility for welfare to the individual and to the family and resonates with a gender culture that builds on part-time caring by women and full-time paid employment by men. In terms of the provision of formal services, priority is given to non-governmental, non-profit organizations.

A bundle of diverse factors creates variety of home care funding and provision. Major characteristics of funding are summarized in Table 6.8, while Figure 6.1 provides a comparative picture of the predominant types of home care provision in our countries.

Table 6.8   *Funding home health care**

Predominantly tax-based funding	*Predominantly social insurance contributions*	*Predominantly private funding*
• Australia • Britain/England • New Zealand • Sweden	• Germany • Netherlands • Taiwan (NHI)	• Singapore • USA

* Japan is difficult to categorize because home health care is funded equally by taxes and social insurance contributions.

Predominant Type of Provision

Level of Provision		Public	Non-profit
	High	Sweden	Netherlands
	Low	Britain	Australia, Germany, Japan, New Zealand, Singapore, Taiwan, USA

Figure 6.1   *The provision of home health care*

Only in Britain and Sweden are home care services provided publicly and firmly integrated into the health system. This situation is typical of national (centralized or community-based) health services, which are mainly tax funded and characterized by a high degree of public integration (see Chapter 3). This does not necessarily guarantee a high level of service provision, however, as the case of England demonstrates (Glendinning, 2013). Home nursing services are provided publicly with GP-led Primary Care Trusts responsible for organizing the provision of services. The Primary Care Trusts are intended to commission home help services which should help to better integrate the provision of home-based care services across the health and social care divide. However, the level of service provision is low, not least reflecting lower overall spending on health care in Britain/England compared to other countries (see Chapter 3), as well as the hollowing out of entitlements to tax-funded home care. Instead, home-based health care over the last decade has focused on acute care needs, while other care needs have been redefined as social care for which older people must pay depending on the local authority areas (Lewis, 2001). Family care is only partly shared with the state, and, consequently, the availability of social care service is uneven.

This contrasts with Sweden where services for older people with long-term care needs have long been well developed and social preferences for home care, together with the need for de-institutionalization, were recognized very early (see Gough, 1994; Trydegård, 2000; Anell *et al.*, 2012). A crucial factor is that home care is embedded in a gender culture that combines ideas of universal access to services with ideas of individual independence from the family as a source of financial and care support. Recent financial constraints combined with an emerging ideology of 'welfare mix' have put a strain on the system (Burau *et al.*, 2007). Private providers have come to play a significant role in the delivery of home care; between 1993 and 2010 the number of publicly funded hours of home care delivered by private providers increased from 2 per cent to 19 per cent (Meagher and Szebehely, 2013). The overall commitment to tax funding, female employment and universalism remained unchanged, however (Theobald, 2003; Lyon and Gluckmann, 2008).

Other policy models in predominantly tax-funded systems illustrate that the development of home care services also can be impeded by strong liberal elements in the health and welfare system. For example, the Australian government and state/territory governments jointly fund the Aged Care Assessment Program (ACAP) to conduct client assessments in relation to five dimensions of need: physical, psychological, medical, cultural and social. The core objective is to comprehensively assess the care needs of frail older people and to assist them to gain access to the most appropriate types of care, including approval for government-subsidized residential and community care services. The legacy of strong liberal elements remains present, even when there are moves towards greater public involvement as in New Zealand. Under the national 'Ageing in Place' programme in New Zealand, home care services progressively have been publicly subsidized (Miller *et al.*, 2008) and expenditure increased significantly. At the same time, eligibility and level of service are determined by needs assessment, although since 2005 asset testing has been gradually phased out (Miller *et al.*, 2008). This is typical of a care regime that combines very limited universality with means-testing and where privately paid and charitable services complement family care (Campbell *et al.*, 2016).

In the Netherlands, as in Sweden, home care traditionally has been viewed as an important part of welfare provision. It is covered by a separate type of health insurance that was introduced in the late 1960s and covers a range of exceptional medical risks (Knijn, 1998). The insurance is compulsory for all employees irrespective of income and is supplemented by central government funds and out-of-pocket payments. This represents a strong element of universalism in a health system with relevant elements of private insurance and provider organizations. A mixed provision of services, which is dominated by non-profit providers, coincides with a high overall level of service provision comparable to Sweden (Knijn, 1998). Interestingly, the Netherlands historically had a higher proportion of people living in institutions than any other European country and it was only in the 1980s that policies focused more explicitly on substitution (Loo *et al.*, 1999). Recent data indicate a marked shift from residential to non-residential care, which is likely to be reinforced in the future and forms one of the four pillars of the 2015 policy reform (Maarse and Jeurissen, 2016).

Public funding of home care has traditionally been less well established in social insurance systems, reflecting an implicit focus on the working population, together with a communitarian orientation that reveres self-help by individuals and communities (see Chapter 2). Here, the principle of subsidiarity underpinning German social policy is indicative. In Germany, LTC insurance was introduced in 1995 as a fifth pillar of the social welfare system with its own funding and governance procedures (Theobald and Ozanne, 2016). In Japan, in 2005 the government revised the Long-term Care Insurance Act to better promote the development of an integrated community care system and the establishment of community integrated support centres in all municipalities (Tamiya *et al.*, 2011).

Even under new insurance schemes, the legacy of subsidiarity can be influential. For instance, Japan imposes a 10 per cent co-payment for all services under LTC institutional provision and charges further costs based on income level (Campbell *et al.*, 2016). In Germany, high security of the new funding arrangement and comprehensive provision (including cash benefits that older people can use to pay informal care-givers) contrasts with the limited levels of funding available. Thus, many older people must depend on out-of-pocket payments and/or unpaid care-givers (Theobald and Hampel, 2013; Theobald and Ozanne, 2016).

Other countries largely rely on private funding of home care. In Singapore, for instance, users are expected to pay for home care services out of their Medisave accounts or through the private or public insurance they can purchase with those accounts (Teo *et al.*, 2003). Health care services for the elderly in Singapore are mostly run by voluntary welfare organizations, although government financial assistance is available. All Singaporeans over 60 are entitled to a subsidy of 75 per cent of the fees charged at polyclinics (Mehta and Briscoe, 2004). Medisave has been expanded gradually to cover chronic conditions, and in 2014 further chronic diseases were added to the Community Health Assist Scheme (Mossialos *et al.*, 2016: 150).

Like Singapore, Taiwan customarily depended on informal, largely family, care-givers, but the rapid urbanization and changes in family structures have led to a decrease in the number of family members who can take responsibility for caring for their elders, thus requiring the hiring of carers or entering care facilities (Hsiao and Huang, 2012). In 2008, the government initiated a ten-year, long-term care plan to create a more integrated service delivery system and to lay a foundation for the establishment of a long-term care insurance programme (Nadash and Shih, 2012). Nevertheless, the family still plays a dominant role in home care in Taiwan (Wang, 2011).

As expected in a market-based health care system, in the USA public sources of funding are minimal, commonly means-tested and highly fragmented. In recent years, largely to reduce costs, Medicare has initiated programmes targeted at home care to encourage people to stay at home. All Medicaid beneficiaries are now eligible for home nursing care if they meet certain conditions. At the same time, 'with its severe means-testing the US leaves a substantial burden on individuals and families' (Campbell *et al.*, 2016: 61).

There seems to be growing awareness of the need to bring LTC policies to the agenda of middle- and low-income countries, as demographic changes are likely to increase future demand for such care (Rhee *et al.*, 2015; Ikegami, 2016). With few exceptions, however, there is no substantiation of a systematic response and data on home care especially remain extremely limited (Brodsky *et al.*, 2003; Muiser and Carrin, 2007). However, this is bound to change with the increased interest in the advantages of home care.

The comparative view shows that, notwithstanding the substantive differences and continued insecurity of funding and the limits on funding, some countries have witnessed the wholesale introduction of new schemes over the last two decades. In Germany and Japan this took the form of the extension of social insurance and in Australia it took the form of a tax-funded programme. Even in the USA, states participating in the publicly funded PACE programme include a home care component. Private, non-profit providers can also be part of a universal system of service provision, resulting in the high level as demonstrated by the Netherlands. However, this the exception to the rule. In many other countries, the provision of home care is highly mixed and less well integrated into the health system, thus reflecting either a strong legacy of informal care (as in Germany, Japan, Singapore and Taiwan), health systems with a strong liberal element (as in Australia and the USA) and/or weaker demographic pressures (as in New Zealand). Germany (together with Japan, Singapore and Taiwan) is a fitting example of a country where the development of home care services has been impeded by a deeply embedded gender culture that gives preference to informal care.

The interface between formal and informal care

The interface between formal and informal care and the underpinning cultural expectations about the role of women in care-giving is an important part of health care provision, as most home care continues to be provided by unpaid care-givers. Under the banner of a greater welfare mix, the objectives of reforms are to integrate care-givers more explicitly into formal care arrangements (Schneider *et al.*, 2016). In those countries where family bonds and/or collectivist values are traditionally strong, the care-giving responsibilities of families are extensive. The inverse applies to countries where values of individual independence dominate and care-giving in the hands of paid professionals is more accepted. These clusters of values and cultural traditions coincide with different types of care regimes (Burau *et al.*, 2007), as shown in Figure 6.2.

Sweden is the classic example of a public service care regime where equality and individual independence are the key and which is characterized by high female employment. The overall commitment to this principle remains strong, although recent years have seen a much more explicit concern with the role of the family in care-giving (Meagher and Szebehely, 2013). In other public service care regimes, the attitude towards the role of women in care-giving is more ambivalent. In the Netherlands, for example, ideas of family care coexist with a strong emphasis on formal care.

In contrast, Britain is an example of a care regime with increasingly strong liberal elements and where means-testing tends to prevail (Baldock, 2003; Means *et al.*, 2003). It is assumed that families take on caring responsibilities of their elderly family members. Among the means-tested

Value Orientations

		Individual Independence	Family Responsibility
Care Regime	Public Service	Sweden	Netherlands
	Means tested		Australia, Britain, New Zealand, USA
	Subsidiarity		Germany, Japan, Singapore, Taiwan

Note: Japan and Singapore do not easily fit into (European) types of welfare regime. However, with Germany they share an explicit emphasis on family responsibility.

Figure 6.2   *Value orientations in informal care and welfare regimes*

care regimes, Australia is an example of a country that has been most active in the expansion of public support for families. Similarly, the US government is now beginning to accept some responsibility for long-term care of the elderly, although by and large it continues to be the duty of the family to arrange and fund this care through private insurance or personal resources. Germany is the archetypical example of a subsidiarity care regime that places great importance on the family as an organizing principle of society (Theobald and Hampel, 2013; Theobald and Ozanne, 2016). If self-help is no longer possible, then it is the responsibility of the family to take over from the individual, followed by voluntary organizations, and, only if all else fails, will the state then step in. The subsidiarity model is under pressure from demographic developments, however, as the example of Japan (similarly Singapore and Taiwan) illustrates. In Japan, a strong filial duty to care for elderly family members often falls on the daughter-in-law. In some cases, a woman might be caring for two sets of parents simultaneously, which seriously limits labour market participation. Health policy, therefore, needs to establish incentives that enable collaboration across the formal–informal division of care (Matsushige *et al.*, 2012).

Many countries have experimented in one way or another with a more explicit integration of informal care into the health system, thus acknowledging the importance of informal care (Burau *et al.*, 2007; Ranci and Pavolini, 2013). From a comparative perspective, the interesting question is what form this formalization takes and how policies define the interface between formal and informal care. Twigg (1989) presented a typology for understanding the range of relationships that exist between welfare agencies and informal care-givers. She distinguishes among care-givers as resources, when they are taken for granted; care-givers as co-workers, when they are treated instrumentally to ensure the continuation of their caring activities; care-givers as co-clients, when agencies are concerned with the needs of care-givers; and superseded care-givers, when agencies aim to replace them with paid formal care staff.

Sweden and the Netherlands are examples of countries that have traditionally favoured formal care, whereas Japan, Singapore, Taiwan and Germany are examples of countries that explicitly expect women to take on caring responsibilities. This attitude also exists, but more implicitly, in liberal welfare regimes in countries like Australia, Britain, New Zealand and the USA. Despite these differences, many countries – except Singapore, Taiwan, New Zealand, and the USA – have begun integrating informal care into the formal system of funding home care. In this regard, payments for informal care-givers have become vital. Although payments are largely symbolic (rather than reimbursements for a service), they are important indicators of a turn towards welfare societies.

With their traditionally strong preference for formal care, recent developments in Sweden and the Netherlands underline the aptness of the emphasis on informal care and the move towards a welfare society. In Sweden, informal care-giving has increased as the public supply of some secondary services such as help with domestic work and personal care has fallen. The availability of family care now also plays a part when assessing the need for care services (Ciarini, 2008; Meagher and Szebehely, 2013). The Netherlands adopted a more systematic approach and financial support for informal care-givers came as part of the introduction of a personal budget (a cash benefit) in 1995 (Burau *et al.*, 2007). The notions of autonomy and independence resonated with the criticisms of the self-help movement against paternalistic service provision; and carer organizations opted for care budgets as an opportunity to compensate informal care-giving (Kremer, 2005). The number of recipients of personal budgets has increased steadily (White, 2011). Similarly, in Germany the introduction of LTC insurance extended the commitment to unpaid informal care. The demands made on the families of older people are now being addressed by a range of support mechanisms, aiming to sustain informal care (Theobald and Hampel, 2013).

By comparison, the emphasis on informal care has typically been implicit in liberal welfare regimes and explicit support of informal care-givers has been weak. Significantly, in Singapore, the USA, Taiwan and New Zealand, public payments to informal care-givers do not exist. In the first two countries, this reflects strong private elements in the provision and funding of home care. Among liberal welfare regime countries there are, however, examples of schemes paying family members for home care work. Indeed, Australia has a long tradition of this type of payment and the Department of Families, Community Services and Indigenous Affairs administers two allowances for care-givers (Australian Department of Health and Ageing, 2006a). The corresponding schemes in Britain are more recent and are embedded in moves to promote consumerism in quasi-markets (Glendinning, 2008). The introduction of 'individual budgets' combines various measures that have emerged from the late 1990s onwards, including direct payments (Boyle, 2011).

Policy trends and developments

The final section of this chapter contrasts key trends in the organization of health care. The transformations in the types and settings of medical practice in many countries reveal shifts away from a solo-practice model with narrowly defined medical care towards more comprehensive care provision. In turn, this creates a need for negotiating the dominant position of both doctors and medically defined care in a changing organizational landscape and growing relevance of PHC. In this situation, the model of PHC may serve as a host for innovation in the provider organizations, integrating a wider range of professionals and services and improving coordination and leadership. The transformative capacity of PHC and the policy strategies and challenges may vary among countries, however.

Within high-income countries, transformations seem to be more comprehensive in NHS systems with more coordinated leadership, both in the decentralized Swedish system and the more centralized governance systems in England/the UK, compared to fragmented and diverse organizational settings like Germany (see also Gauld, 2015). The Netherlands shows the strong transformative capacity of the PHC model despite a classic GP-based organizational model. This suggests that multi-professional provider teams might embody stronger transformative capacities than organizational change aimed at better coordination among medical providers. This is what Contandriopoulos *et al.* (2016) described with the metaphor of nurse practitioners as 'canaries in the mine of primary care reform' and Groenewegen (2008) more generally related to nurses as 'grease in the PHC machinery'.

A further important policy level of the PHC model is improvement of coordination and development of a more coherent leadership approach. Interestingly, coordination seems to be a policy lever for innovation in low-income countries, while it is more challenging in high-income countries with complex forms of stakeholder involvement and corporatist models of partnership governance as well as in middle-income countries with emergent market systems. Lack of qualified health care staff (Chapter 5) is a further challenge to effective PHC, and may be one of the most serious barriers in middle-income countries and emergent economies along with underdeveloped universal coverage and funding schemes (Chapter 3).

The situation looks different in LTC, however, where no uniform model of innovation is available and the differences between high-income and middle- and low-income countries are much more clear-cut than in PHC. While LTC has not been a relevant policy concern in middle-income countries (Rhee *et al.*, 2015) – and even less in resource-poor countries – it is the most dynamic and fastest growing sector of care provision in high-income countries, where demand and pressures for innovation are stronger than in less well-resourced countries due to overall higher life expectancy and eroding of the family-based caring system. Variety and gaps in the implementation of funding schemes and accessible services for the citizens are even clearer among resource-rich countries, as for instance poorly developed LTC with higher levels of informal care-giving in Southern and Eastern EU member states (Pavolini and Theobald, 2015; Campbell *et al.*, 2016).

Regardless of policy trends in the provision and funding of services, however, home care remains overwhelmingly informal women's work. Most countries acknowledge the centrality of informal care, although this takes different forms, reflecting differences among care regimes and gender cultures. Policy responses range from the gender-blindness of liberal welfare traditions (USA) and gender-specific expectations in male-dominated, collectivist societies (Japan, Singapore and Taiwan), to the ideology of the welfare society (Sweden), the revival of subsidiarity (Germany) and symbolic payments to care-givers (Australia, Britain, Germany and the Netherlands). As Wittenberg reminds us, 'relatively small changes in the availability of unpaid care may have relatively large impacts on demand for formal care services', because unpaid carers provide so much work (2016: 9).

The comparative approach reveals different policy challenges not only among countries but also between PHC and LTC. Consequently, there is no uniform direction of travel in responding to changing needs of the population and innovating care provision beyond the hospital. Moreover, the comparative view across countries and sectors suggests that the shift towards needs-based services has created new demand for innovative policy and for developing more coordinated and integrated, yet context-sensitive, policy responses. Also, the move away from hospitals to a broader range of services embodies new challenges for research and comparative health policy. While the typologies and classic indicators of health systems remain relevant, they do not fully explain the variety in PHC (Groenewegen *et al.*, 2015), even more so in the highly diverse and emergent LTC sector and its fluid boundaries with informal care (Burau *et al.*, 2015; Pavolini and Theobald, 2015; Campbell *et al.*, 2016).

Chapter 7

Public Health

Until now the focus of this book has been on health care policy. We have been concerned with hospitals, doctors and other health care professionals and the funding, delivery and governance of health care services. Largely, the book has centred on the care of individual patients. Chapter 5 demonstrated the wide range of settings and activities in the delivery of modern medical care. Chapter 6 extended this to integrate health care with non-health arenas by demonstrating that it is not possible to disengage health care from social care. The health of a LTC client is as dependent on personal care as it is on medical care, perhaps in many cases more so. Even this more inclusive picture of health care, however, might be criticized for underestimating what are its most important dimensions for some observers: health promotion and disease prevention, which together are often termed public health. Due to the breadth and rather amorphous nature of public health, this chapter is more of an overview of the policy concerns facing our countries than the comparative analysis within previous chapters. Mackenbach and McKee found in a recent comparative analysis of 30 European countries that public health policy does not appear to be strongly influenced by institutional features, while the 'predominant political influence has been the rise of levels of democracy in countries in the Central and Eastern parts of the region' (2015: 1298). Examples from our countries, nevertheless, are used throughout the discussion to demonstrate the wide scope of public health issues facing all countries.

The biggest advances in human health and longevity in the 20th century were the products of improved hygiene and clean water supplies, vaccines to prevent viral infections and antibiotics to combat bacterial infections. Historically, such endeavours constituted the backbone of public health, although as we will see in this chapter public health is much more expansive today. Simply put, public health is concerned with the health of the entire community. Although public health can be defined in many ways, common denotations of the term include health promotion, disease prevention, primary care, community health and population health. Public health encompasses a wide range of activities including the management of diseases that threaten the health of the population, the assessment of the health needs of specific populations and health education and promotion.

Global public health

The move to public health necessitates the inclusion of international organizations into the health care equation. Increasingly, health care has become a global matter as illustrated by many examples ranging from communicable diseases, to obesity, to environmental health. In all areas of public health, national boundaries become less consequential as health threats assume global proportions. Moreover, with infectious disease in the context of rapid and extensive world travel, there is a need for systematic, concerted cooperation by the international community. In public health, therefore, increased attention has turned to the role of international health organizations and agreements among countries to deal with these health perils. International health, or global health, then, is a field of health care with a primarily public health emphasis that deals with health issues across regional or national boundaries. Additionally, public health experts recently have become interested in global processes that affect human health (Crisp, 2010; Keefe and Zacher, 2011; Skolnick, 2011; Craddock and Hinchliffe, 2015; Iha *et al.*, 2016). The impact of globalization on health, for example, illuminates the complex and shifting sociological environment within which the determinants of health and disease express themselves.

The most visible of the myriad of international organizations that have a health remit is the World Health Organization (WHO). The WHO is a specialized agency of the United Nations that is concerned with global public health (for details on the WHO see Youde, 2012). The WHO was established on 7 April 1948, is headquartered in Geneva, Switzerland, and is a member of the UN Development Group. The WHO played a leading role in the eradication of smallpox and its current priorities include: communicable diseases, particularly HIV/AIDS, malaria and tuberculosis; mitigation of the effects of non-communicable diseases; sexual and reproductive health; nutrition, food security and obesity; and substance abuse. The WHO is accountable for the World Health Report, a leading international publication on health, the World Health Survey, and World Health Day.

The World Bank is another major intergovernmental agency tied to the UN that is heavily involved in international health and loaning money to poor countries on advantageous terms not available in commercial markets (Harman, 2012a, 2012b; Loewenberg, 2015). In addition, three subsidiary agencies of the UN Economic and Social Council are committed to international health programmes. The UN Children's Fund (UNICEF) has made the world's most vulnerable children its top priority and devotes most of its resources to those aged under 5 from the poorest countries. The UN Population Fund focuses on family planning programmes, while the UN Development Programme concentrates on AIDS, maternal and child nutrition and maternal mortality. In conjunction with WHO and the World Bank, it also sponsors the Special Programme for Research and Training in Tropical Diseases.

In addition, substantial work in global health is performed by a multitude of non-governmental organizations (NGOs). Services provided by international health NGOs include direct health care, community potable water and alleviation of endemic and epidemic infectious diseases and malnutrition. Examples of NGOs dedicated to global health are CARE, Médecins Sans Frontières (Doctors Without Borders), The International Committee of the Red Cross, the Red Crescent, Oxfam, Partners in Health, Project HOPE and Save the Children. In addition, many bilateral agencies, which are governmental agencies in a single country, provide aid to developing countries. Although the largest of these is the US Agency for International Development (USAID), most developed nations have a similar body. However, this aid is mainly channelled towards the development of new medical interventions and often fails to address the immediate health problems facing the most vulnerable populations. Research policies in high-income countries lead them to invest in health research aimed at boosting national economic competitiveness rather than reducing health inequities. This pattern diverts funding away from research that is needed to implement existing interventions and strengthen health systems (Pratt and Loff, 2012).

Global health challenges

Although great strides have been made in conquering health scourges of the past such as smallpox, numerous novel threats to public health continually unfold. They include events such as terrorism, wars and natural disasters (for example, the Great East Japan Earthquake, tsunami and nuclear power plant disaster of March 2011) as well as longer-term health threats like viral and bacterial infections and high-risk behaviours. For instance, in the first half of 2006 among the many WHO Epidemic and Pandemic Alerts and Responses announced were anthrax, avian influenza, Ebola haemorrhagic fever, E. coli outbreaks, hepatitis, influenza, meningococcal disease, plague, severe acute respiratory syndrome (SARS), smallpox, tularaemia and yellow fever. Although many of these diseases are endemic to Third World countries, developed nations are at mounting risk due to immigration, air travel and the global economy. Even diseases that were once presumed to be vanquished, such as tuberculosis, have re-emerged on the public health agenda.

Until the mid-twentieth century, health care centred principally on public health approaches. Few medical technologies or lifesaving procedures existed and hospitals were primarily charity institutions for those who could not afford a personal physician. Because the leading causes of premature death were infectious diseases such as tuberculosis, typhoid and cholera, attention was focused on ameliorating the conditions under which they spread across populations. To contain the spread of a contagious illness, public health authorities relied on many strategies including isolation and quarantine. Isolation of people who have a specific illness physically separates them from healthy people and restricts their movement to stop the spread of that illness. It allows for the focused delivery of specialized health care to people who are ill and protects healthy people from getting sick. People in isolation may be cared for in their homes, in hospitals or at designated health care facilities. In most cases, isolation is voluntary; however, governments have broad authority to compel the isolation of sick people to protect the public.

Quarantine, in contrast, applies to people who have been exposed and may or may not be infected but are not yet ill. Separating exposed people and restricting their movements is intended to stop the spread of an illness, and quarantine has proven to be highly effective in protecting the public from disease. Although governments generally have wide authority to declare and enforce quarantine within their borders, often it is problematic politically because of its severe human rights ramifications, particularly when targeting specific social groups, and its potential adverse economic impact. The political dangers of quarantine are illustrated clearly by calls to segregate AIDS victims in the mid-1980s before the mechanism of HIV transmission was understood.

Protecting the public health also entails a wide range of monitoring and inspection mechanisms designed to prevent the spread of disease through food and water supplies, environmental threats and risky workplaces. As highlighted in Box 7.1, because of the transportation of food across long distances, often across national boundaries, the threat of contaminated food products can occur far from the origin of the product or processing facility and affect widespread populations. The case of 'mad cow disease' in the 1990s and the more recent threat of the spread of bird flu through humans highlight the need for continued attentiveness. Moreover, threats of biological terrorism and the emergence of even more aggressive strains of viruses clearly require proactive vigilance regarding public health and funding. Public health strategies, then, run the gamut from quarantining individuals suspected of having communicable diseases deemed to be threats to the public health, to regulating the workplace for health and safety, to reducing unemployment and economic disparities, to reducing greenhouse emissions and the depletion of the ozone layer. Moreover, these strategies stress the importance of the public health workforce which is essential to guarantee basic healthcare services especially in situations of disaster (e.g. current wars in some Arab and African countries) and pandemics, like Ebola or most recently Zika.

Box 7.1   E. coli threats to public health

Less than a week after the US FDA lifted its warning on spinach grown in California, a brand of lettuce grown there was recalled over concerns about E. coli contamination. Pathogenic Escherichia coli bacteria or E. coli can proliferate in uncooked produce, raw milk, unpasteurized juice, contaminated water and meat. The lettuce scare came amid other government warnings that shipments of beef could cause grave health risks including paralysis, respiratory failure and death. Epidemiologists also warned consumers to stay away from some bottled carrot juice after a woman was paralysed and two people in Toronto died, apparently due to botulism poisoning. Although most healthy adults recover within a week without long-term side effects, young children, senior citizens and people with compromised immune systems are vulnerable in extreme cases to kidney damage or death. The outbreaks have sparked demands to create a new federal agency in charge of food safety. 'This recent outbreak must be a wake-up call to get our food safety house in order, because right now it's in pure disarray', according to US Senator Schumer. 'We need to have one agency take charge to ensure the next outbreak isn't far worse.' (Konrad, 2006)

The SARS epidemic

Although public health is often viewed as a remote and esoteric field in which people are regarded as mere statistics, the spread of SARS in 2003 highlights the importance of public health and the fact that, since infectious diseases do not respect borders, international cooperation is essential (Tirado *et al.*, 2015). SARS is transmitted via droplets from infected individuals who, by coughing, transmit the virus to close contacts. Although this epidemic dissipated after several months, during that time it caused a great deal of concern and huge economic costs. SARS began in China but was quickly spread around the world. Although researchers eventually found evidence of the virus in the civet cat that is eaten as a delicacy by some Chinese (Ross, 2003), most SARS victims contracted it after being in proximity to an infected person. Although the number of persons killed by SARS was small by epidemic standards, it demonstrated how vulnerable to the rapid spread of communicable diseases we are in an age of air travel and concentrated medical facilities where, ironically, many of the victims became infected.

China's handling of the disease was viewed as reprehensible by many observers. When the first SARS cases appeared in southern China in March, Beijing denied it and tried to suppress the news, thus allowing the disease to be spread beyond its borders by unsuspecting victims. In contrast, and as might have been predicted given its strong community-centred culture, Singapore instituted an aggressive home-quarantine system in response to SARS. Whereas health officials in Toronto, Canada, simply asked citizens suspected of SARS exposure to self-quarantine, Singapore took more extreme steps to enforce quarantine, including the use of video cameras and electronic bracelets to monitor the movements of those suspected of incubating the disease. It also passed a bill requiring quarantine-breakers to be fined up to $5,000 without being charged in court. The Health Minister also warned that the government might name and shame quarantine-breakers. Although criticized by some Westerners as draconian, Singapore's tough approach was commended by the WHO (Greenlee, 2003). In the end, SARS was controlled but only after more rigorous public health policies were adopted. The WHO credited old-fashioned quarantines with breaking the back of the outbreak (Wong, 2003).

Soon after the passing of the SARS story, in early 2004 the media began to report the spread of avian influenza across South East Asia. Although 'bird flu' differs from SARS in that its transmission is from infected birds to humans, public health experts feared that it might mutate to enable it to spread from human to human. Another continuing public health threat is anthrax. Although its manufacture and use as a weapon for bio-terrorism has generated the most anxiety, humans can become infected with anthrax by handling animal products or eating undercooked meat from infected animals. Anthrax raises the possibility of investigation of terrorist suspects alongside investigation of the outbreak of the infectious disease and a likelihood of public panic and the inundation of public health officials with reports of suspicious white powder (Howse, 2004).

Global public health resources again were challenged by what began as 'swine flu' in Mexico in April 2009. Within a week cases were identified as far away as Israel and New Zealand. Many flights from, and trading transactions with, Mexico were halted and individuals potentially exposed to the virus were isolated and quarantined in some countries. Renamed H1N1, in part to stop the unnecessary slaughter of millions of hogs that occurred in Egypt and elsewhere, the WHO raised the alert level to a 5 (out of 6), declaring that 'a pandemic was imminent'. Although the virus was less virulent than anticipated, it caused major disruptions and served as another forewarning of the potential global threat of infectious diseases and a fear that a full pandemic could be a massive killer despite our advanced medical technologies (Bennett and Carney, 2010). On 19 May 2009 WHO Director-General Margaret Chan repeated her warning that this new virus had great pandemic potential and could pose a grave threat to humanity even though the fatality rate was low with no major outbreaks outside North America, and on 10 June WHO for the first time in history raised the alert level to 6, an international pandemic. 'This virus may have given us a grace period but we do not know how long this grace period will last. No one can say whether this is just the calm before the storm.' (CBS News, 2009)

Tay *et al.* (2010) describe the ambitious public health control measures implemented in Singapore to contain H1N1 and mitigate its social effects. Containment strategies included the triage of delirious patients at frontline healthcare settings, admission and isolation of confirmed cases, mandatory quarantine orders for close contacts and temperature screening at border entry points. After sustained community transmission became established, containment shifted to mitigation. The 2009 H1N1 pandemic was also the first test of the revised International Health Regulations (IHR) that were adopted in 2005 and took effect in 2007. The new IHRs marked a move away from the disease-specific approach of the earlier version to an approach focused on whether a public health event constitutes a 'public health emergency of international concern' (Bennett and Carney, 2010: 106).

One of the by-products of a pandemic is the disruption of the global economy. Mackey and Liang (2012) note that the lack of a formal system to review trade restrictions imposed during international public health emergencies creates disincentives for surveillance and reporting, thereby undermining protection efforts. The 2003 SARS outbreak exposed major weaknesses in global governance that caused uncoordinated public health and economic responses. While the new IHR demonstrated improvement, it fails to allow for management of public health emergencies in a way that balances threats to health and those to economies and trade. Mackey and Liang (2012) contend that the creation of a joint WHO–WTO committee to adjudicate these conflicts might better achieve that balance (see also Mackey and Liang, 2013).

Ebola

Ebola causes severe fever and muscle pain, weakness, vomiting and diarrhoea eventually shutting down organs and producing inexorable internal bleeding, with patients often dying within days. Between 2013 and 2015 this dreaded tropical virus killed over 11,000 and triggered a global health alert. Although in early 2016 the epidemic was declared over, with Liberia the last country given the all-clear, in two years it had destroyed the economies and health systems of the three worst-hit West African nations. From one Guinean infant in December 2013, the epidemic quickly spread into neighbouring Liberia and Sierra Leone, causing more deaths than all other Ebola outbreaks combined. The WHO came under fire for its slow response to the epidemic which killed over 500 health care workers and which local health care systems were underequipped to handle. The fears of a global pandemic increased after three health workers were infected in the USA and Spain. Western countries eventually rallied to contain it, sending thousands of troops and medics to Africa in 2014 and developing numerous promising potential vaccines and treatments, but not before it devastated the mining, agriculture and tourism industries in Liberia, Sierra Leone and Guinea. The Ebola case also reiterated the fact that international travel, development, habitat encroachment, large-scale global trade and war and civil unrest mean that future outbreaks of deadly diseases are likely. For Jonathan Ball, 'Whilst we can try to develop vaccines and treatments for some, it won't be possible to mitigate against all threats with these types of intervention. We can't simply think job done, move on.' (quoted in Dosso, 2016)

Zika virus (ZIKV)

The pandemic of Zika virus infection throughout South America, Central America and the Caribbean and threatening the US is the most recent of four unexpected arrivals of important arthropod-borne viral diseases in the Western Hemisphere over the past 20 years. It follows dengue, which entered this hemisphere stealthily over decades and then more aggressively in the 1990s; West Nile virus, which emerged in 1999; and chikungunya, which emerged in 2013 (Fauci and Morens, 2016; Rubin *et al.*, 2016). ZIKV infections have been known in Africa and Asia since the 1940s, but the virus's geographic range has expanded dramatically since 2007. Between 2007 and March 2016, local transmission was reported in an additional 52 countries and territories, mainly in the Americas and the Western Pacific. ZIKV infections acquired by travellers visiting those countries have been discovered at sites worldwide (Broutet *et al.*, 2016). Although *aedes aegypti* mosquitoes are the principal vectors, other mosquito species might contribute to transmission. A major concern associated with this infection is the apparent increased incidence of microcephaly in foetuses born to mothers infected with ZIKV (Mlakar *et al.*, 2016). ZIKV is widespread in Brazil and some questioned whether 2016 Olympics should be cancelled because of it (Axon, 2016).

The continuing AIDS epidemic

Although a 2012 report of the Joint UN Programme on HIV/AIDS (UNAIDS) reported remarkable progress in combating acquired immunodeficiency syndrome (AIDS) (Box 7.2), it remains a critical global health problem with an estimated 34 million persons infected with the human immunodeficiency virus (HIV), which causes AIDS. Each year around 2.7 million people become HIV infected and 1.8 million die of AIDS (WHO, 2012c). Although HIV continues to be a health problem in developed nations, the worst affected region is sub-Saharan Africa, where more than one out of five adults are infected in some countries (see Table 7.1). Moreover, since 2001, the number of new HIV infections in the Middle East and North Africa was up more than 35 per cent and

> ### Box 7.2   UN report on AIDS
>
> In November 2012, UNAIDS reported over a 50 per cent drop in new HIV infections across 25 low- and middle-income countries and a decline of AIDS-related deaths globally by over 25 per cent between 2005 and 2011. It contends that these data show that acceleration of domestic investments in AIDS by the governments of countries most affected is working. More than 81 countries increased domestic investment by at least 50 per cent between 2001 and 2011. Most progress is being made in reducing new HIV infections in children and half of the global reductions in new HIV infections in the last two years have been among newborn children. Impressive gains were also made in reducing tuberculosis (TB)-related AIDS deaths in people living with HIV. In the last two years alone, a 13 per cent decrease in TB-related AIDS deaths was observed. In conclusion, the UNAIDS report stated that eradicating AIDS was in sight, owing to better access to drugs that can both treat and prevent the incurable HIV. An aim to eventually end the worldwide AIDS epidemic is not 'merely visionary' but 'entirely feasible' (UNAIDS, 2012).

Table 7.1   *AIDS percentage rates for adults (15–49),*
selected countries, 2014

Swaziland	27.7
Botswana	25.2
Lesotho	23.4
South Africa	18.9
Zimbabwe	16.8
USA	0.6
UK	0.3
Australia	0.2
Netherlands	0.2
Our other countries are 0.1 or less	

Source: The World Factbook (2016).

evidence suggests that the epidemic is spreading rapidly in Eastern Europe and Central Asia, where the number of persons living with HIV increased by 250 per cent in the last decade (Foundation for AIDS Research, 2016).

There are many policies that can be implemented to reduce the impact of AIDS, beginning with the prevention of HIV transmission. Circumventing sexual transmission involves encouraging safer sexual behaviour through delayed first sex, partner reduction, increased male circumcision and condom use. Likewise, the spread of HIV through drug injection can be slowed by outreach work, needle exchange and drug substitution treatment, while transmission from mother to child can be drastically cut through use of medicines and the avoidance of breastfeeding (UNAIDS, 2010).

Although there is no vaccination or cure for AIDS, patients who take a 'cocktail' of antiretroviral drugs daily can expect to recoup their health and live for many years (UNAIDS, 2010). Accordingly, in most developed countries, AIDS has been redefined as a chronic disease. Although antiretroviral therapy has saved 14 million life-years in poorer countries since 1995, an estimated 6.8 million people are eligible for treatment but do not have access. Moreover, of the 34 million people living with HIV, about half do not know their HIV status: if more people knew their status, they could come forward for HIV services. However, while AIDS prevention and treatment regimens are now well recognized, they have been less successful in reaching key populations including sex workers, men who have sex with men and people who inject drugs (UNAIDS, 2012).

Again, despite recent gains, access to prevention tools such as HIV education, condoms, clean needles and programmes to prevent mother-to-child transmission are inadequate in many countries. Other major obstacles include weak infrastructures and shortages of health workers in the worst affected countries (UNAIDS, 2010). Political or cultural attitudes, such as opposition to condom promotion, sex education and needle exchanges are also significant impediments. Another common problem is stigma and discrimination of people known to be living with HIV who are often shunned or abused by community members and even health workers. In addition to causing personal distress, this social environment discourages people from seeking HIV testing, treatment and care.

AIDS funding has come from individual governments, multinational organizations and private organizations. Over the last two decades, efforts to fight AIDS have accelerated, with increased funding from the USA and other developed countries and heightened spending by affected countries. The USA accounts for 48 per cent of all international assistance for HIV and together with the Global Fund for AIDS, Tuberculosis and Malaria provides the lion's share of investments in HIV treatment (UNAIDS, 2012). However, the amount of funding available remains short of what is needed for a fully effectual response. In 2011, US$16.8 billion was available and the need for 2015 is between US$22 and 24 billion (UNAIDS, 2012). Furthermore, major international organizations, such as the WHO and UNAIDS, do not provide funding but rather coordinate and monitor global HIV and AIDS treatment, care and prevention efforts. The WHO routinely issues guidelines to help countries achieve the highest attainable standards, while UNAIDS monitors the global epidemic through an annual reporting system and the release of annual reports on the global AIDS epidemic and other HIV and AIDS issues.

Regrettably, while infectious disease control is one of the earliest and most important functions of the modern state, it still receives at best only modest attention and then only in reaction to a crisis (Greer and Mätzke, 2012). Recently, however, there has been increased activity in Europe. Martin and Conseil (2012), for instance, provide a useful overview of the current state of policies and laws governing pandemic influenza prevention and control in Europe and the concept of harmonization across European states, including an overview of supranational initiatives and powers created to enhance coordination of national pandemic disease policy. The European Centre for Disease Prevention and Control (ECDC) has been established by the European Union (EU) to act as a hub for disease control, drawing on networks across the continent to achieve what other political systems do with large agencies (Greer, 2012).

Framing a public health policy

Generally, disease prevention activities focus on the health of communities or populations rather than individuals, but De Ferranti (1985) makes a valuable distinction between patient-related and non-patient-related preventive care. Patient-related approaches are generally defined as primary care, take place in a clinical setting and include immunization, health education between patients and GPs, and cancer, cholesterol and prostate screening programmes. Non-patient-related preventive approaches include such disparate activities as improved sanitation and water systems, promotion of health and hygiene, provision of adequate housing, control of pests, food safety and the monitoring of disease patterns (epidemiology).

Although an integral part of health care, public health – including routine primary care services for well patients, health education, disease prevention, immunization programmes and health promotion activities – consistently receives only negligible shares of health care budgets. OECD countries, on average, spend only 3 per cent of their health care budgets on prevention and public awareness campaigns (OECD, 2005a). In the USA, it fares even worse with less than 1 per cent of the health care budget devoted to public health. Furthermore, the effects of the current global economic crisis on the spread and control of communicable diseases are unknown and there are few specific national policies and programmes aimed at mitigating its health impacts (Rechel *et al.*, 2011). Preventive services as compared to acute care are also more susceptible to budget cuts resulting from the economic crisis with services targeted at vulnerable and hard-to-reach population groups at special risk. Despite recent shifts towards a more public-health-oriented approach in many countries, even the most attentive countries would be well served to put a significantly larger proportion of their health care budgets into such efforts (Fry, 2010; Ham, 2010).

Although there is a general agreement that it is more humane and cost-effective to avoid a condition of ill health in the first place than to have to treat it later, modern health systems continue to emphasize curative approaches – treating the ill rather than keeping people healthy. In part this is because prevention deals with statistical future lives while curative medicine deals with identifiable patients who need help now. When a patient is facing imminent death, the individual, his or her family and society are willing to pay heavily for any innovation that offers even a small promise of saving his or her life. In contrast, we are less likely to demand innovations that will save many more lives in the distant future, because while promotion/preventive programmes also ultimately help individuals, it is difficult to identify who they might be (Jacobson, 2012).

Moreover, despite convincing evidence that the most significant advances in the health of populations comes from outside medicine, many forces, particularly the medical professions and the health care industry, have strong economic interests in maintaining or increasing funding for treatment (see Box 7.3). In combination with patients, and a public easily swayed by optimistic media coverage, they have aggrandized curative medicine at the expense of public health. Human-interest stories and favourable media coverage inherently follow technological breakthroughs in treatment, not public health efforts. Television dramas

---

Box 7.3 Confusion over the meaning of 'public health'

For MacIntyre (2011), the Australian national health reform agenda appears to have omitted public health. Despite huge national investment to avert a crisis in human resources for health, including the creation of Health Workforce Australia, the need for a public health workforce has been ignored. The National Health and Medical Research Council (NHMRC) commissioned the Nutbeam report in 2008 to improve the effectiveness of research funding for public health, but no concrete changes have resulted:

> Having read the various documents on national health reform ... I am left wondering why public health is such a notable omission ... I get the sense that the powers that be believe that "public health" and "primary care" are one and the same thing ... Perhaps it is as simple as politicians and the public thinking that "public health" means provision of acute health care in public hospitals and through Medicare, but I believe there is confusion even among relatively well informed stakeholders. (MacIntyre, 2011: 38)

exalt those who save individual lives such as trauma teams and surgeons, not public health nurses or epidemiologists. In combination, these forces represent formidable obstacles against a meaningful reallocation of scarce resources from curative medicine to public health strategies. If the goal of the health care system is to improve the health of the population, however, public health programmes, particularly those that produce healthier lifestyles, are critical. The public's health is the product of a complicated mixture of dynamic, adaptive and complex systems of agencies, infrastructure, relationships and interactions, and must be the focus in improving health outcomes and reducing health risks in a population (Ehrlich *et al.*, 2009; Van Wave *et al.*, 2010).

Does prevention save money?

Many observers contend that a shift towards disease prevention and health promotion would not only enhance health but also save money. As noted by Gostin *et al.*, while there is 'powerful intrinsic value in making health care services accessible', we could achieve better health outcomes at a lower cost 'by shifting priorities toward health promotion and disease prevention, mediated principally through primary care and population-based services' (2011: 1781). Similarly, Maciosek *et al.* (2010: 1656) conclude:

> We find that greater use of proven clinical preventive services in the United States could avert the loss of more than two million life-years annually. What's more, increasing the use of these services from current levels to 90 percent ... would result in total savings of $3.7 billion, or 0.2 percent of U.S. personal health care spending.

Other observers, however, are more sceptical of the savings from preventive strategies (Cawley, 2007; Cohen *et al.*, 2008). Many studies of programmes for hypertension screening, reducing high blood cholesterol and cancer screening tests demonstrate that the net costs per year of life saved are exceedingly high (Russell, 2007). The low per-unit cost of some population screening procedures obscures their true cost, which is the cost of achieving the desired outcome for the few who will benefit. Even though the cost of a single application is minimal, if the condition is rare, a huge number of such procedures are needed to identify and prevent one case.

The fact that population screening does not always save money should not detract from the advantage of rebalancing health care budgets towards disease prevention and health promotion (Goetzel, 2009). The investment in better health itself is a worthwhile goal even if the immediate costs are high (Cubit and Meyer, 2011). The rationale behind spending more on public health, then, is the inherent value we place on the health it confers on the population, not its monetary savings. Commitment to public health is a measure of concern for the future. Public health, then, is ultimately a question of what kind of society we want, and there is a close connection between democracy, equity and social security on the one hand and good public health on the other (Raphael and Bryant, 2006). Any investment in preventive/promotion programmes shifts benefits from present patients to statistical persons who will enjoy healthier lives in the future because of these investments. Moreover, by postponing the time at which we become victims of a chronic disease, prevention allows people to live healthier and more active lives, even though it might not necessarily extend their lifespan or save money (Donato and Segal, 2010).

Difficulty of changing behaviour

There is one important caveat regarding preventive/promotion strategies that deal with behaviour-linked illnesses that today represent major contributors to ill health. Even though some of the linkages between lifestyle and health remain speculative, to be successful prevention must change behaviour. Moreover, even where evidence of danger is convincing, such as smoking, alcohol abuse, obesity or even gambling (Adams *et al.*, 2009), there is considerable debate over how effective preventive measures alone can be in altering such behaviour. To effect necessary behavioural changes requires investment of considerable resources for research to better understand the linkages between social and personal factors. Despite these limitations, health promotion is a definitive element of health care reform.

Tenbensel *et al.* (2012) found that since 2003 there has been an increasing interest in initiatives that address health promotion and population health outcomes. Furthermore, ageing populations and the resulting changes in disease structures necessitates movement towards chronic care facilities and less expensive forms of institutional or home care as opposed to costly hospital care (Cubit and Meyer, 2011). Such moves are politically challenging, however, because they are often justified on the grounds of cost-effectiveness and frequently viewed as threats to the medical establishment. Moreover, they give the appearance of sacrificing the lives of identifiable patients for a more nebulous aggregate population. Also, because of the unpredictable nature of disease, few members of the public can distance themselves from the plight of individual patients and their need for immediate and often costly support in time of ill health.

Public health responsibility and funding

While public health continues to be underfunded compared to acute care medicine, all countries here have wide-ranging public health programmes, although, as with other areas of health care, each country brings with it a unique orientation for organizing public health services. For instance, while Singapore has a highly centralized and vigorous public health policy, in most countries the non-medical aspects of public health especially are delivered by locally administered agencies. The major responsibility for public health often falls on states, municipalities or other sub-national units, although in recent years some governments, such as Australia, have attempted to provide central coordination and increased national funding to the localities to strengthen public health.

Next to Singapore, New Zealand has the most centralized framework for public health, with responsibility vested in the Ministry of Health, but even there many public health activities are carried out through local programmes. Public health is the responsibility of 12 regional Public Health Units (PHUs), owned by the DHBs, and a range of local and non-governmental organizations. PHUs focus largely on communicable disease control, environmental health, tobacco control and health promotion. Policy priorities for population health, such as targets for immunization, cardiovascular screening and smoking cessation, are set by the government and pursued by a mix of DHBs, PHOs and PHUs (Gauld, 2013).

In Britain, the central government, health authorities and GPs share responsibility for public health (Baggott, 2010). Within the central government, public health falls under the remit of the Department of Health, although only since 1997 has there been a separate minister devoted to public health. Until recently, Primary Care Trusts were responsible for delivering public health and reducing health inequalities within the framework set by the Department of Health. Although GPs traditionally focused on the demands of individual patients, they increasingly have been integrated in public health initiatives. Following health reforms in 2012 and the introduction of Clinical Commissioning Groups, local authorities assumed increased responsibility for public health at the local level supported by 'Health and Wellbeing Boards', which bring together a wide range of local actors to coordinate public health initiatives (Department of Health, 2012b).

In contrast to Britain, responsibility for public health in Germany has always been more decentralized, reflecting its federal structure. As in Australia and the USA, public health traditionally has been the responsibility of the states (Busse and Blümel, 2014; Gerhardus *et al.*, 2016). The range of services covered varies from state to state, as does the structure of the local public health offices responsible for the delivery of services. However, since the 1970s an increasing number of public health activities, particularly health promotion and disease prevention, have become part of social health insurance and responsibility has shifted from the public health offices to ambulatory care doctors. Subsequently, the provision of public health services has become more standardized since doctors are now legally obliged to deliver public services as part of the benefits catalogue within the health insurance system. However, the focus of ambulatory care doctors on individual patients continues to undercut the public orientation of measures of health promotion and disease prevention.

Sweden resembles Germany in that the responsibility for public health is decentralized and rests with county councils and municipalities as service providers (Glenngård *et al.*, 2005; Anell *et al.*, 2012), although population-based measures are more highly integrated into the delivery of primary care services. Health centres employ school nurses to provide health education to children and doctors provide one-to-one health education on diet and alcohol consumption, operate well women clinics, and immunize children. Complementing this at the national level is the National Institute for Public Health, which is responsible for national programmes of health promotion and disease prevention. As in other areas of health care provision, the National Board of Health and Welfare is responsible for supervising and monitoring what transpires at the level of county councils and municipalities.

Compared to Sweden, the responsibility for public health is even more decentralized in the Netherlands. Following the 1989 Public Prevention Act, some core responsibilities for public health services, including health monitoring and dealing with contagious diseases, were delegated to local authorities. The activities of local public health agencies are only loosely prescribed, but typically focus on the young, elderly and minority groups and include health promotion and education, vaccination and public health research projects (Schäfer *et al.*, 2010; Kroneman *et al.*, 2016). The considerable autonomy at local level has resulted in substantial diversity in the delivery of public health services (Okma, 2001). In response to concerns about inequalities in access to public health services, a 1998 commission recommended that local authorities present an annual review of their public health activities. It also recommended that the Ministry of Health define a basic set of services that all local authorities must provide. The activities of the local authorities are overseen by the Inspectorate of Health, which has responsibility for monitoring the quality of health services and health protection measures (Exter *et al.*, 2004).

As in the Netherlands and Sweden, a large share of the responsibility for public health services in Japan falls on local governments and to a lesser extent the county-like prefectures (Matsuda, 2013). Each of the municipalities has a division responsible for health and the employment of public health nurses. In 2005, approximately 3,200 municipalities were reduced to 2,300 in a policy aimed at strengthening the financial basis of local governments and reducing administrative costs. In addition to basic environmental services such as water supply and waste disposal, under the Community Health Law of 1994 these primary local governments administer community health activities, including maternal and child care, immunization, health education, health screening and examinations for those over 40.

As decentralized as the organization of public health is in these countries, it is even more so in the federal systems of the USA and Australia. As noted earlier, the USA is a federal system with responsibility for many functions falling on sub-national units. Moreover, the US Constitution explicitly gives states the authority to protect the health of their residents. Each of the 50 states has a public health agency or department. In addition, there are 3,066 counties that have public health responsibilities as well as tens of thousands of cities, towns and other municipalities, all of which undertake some public health activities, many quite extensive. At the federal level, the Centers for Disease Control and Prevention have primary responsibility for monitoring and policy making in disease prevention, but they must rely on compliance from the state and local agencies to implement their guidelines.

Although all sides in the debate over the USA Affordable Care Act (ACA) cited the importance of public health, important public health investments, including smoking cessation, reproductive health, HIV and other preventive services were stripped from the final bill, while major increases were provided for cancer research. Despite this, Pollack (2011) concludes that the ACA, which establishes a Prevention and Public Health Fund to support preventive services and the public health infrastructure and requires all insurers to cover evidence-based preventive services, will have a positive impact on public health. In contrast, Gostin *et al.* (2011) conclude that while the ACA included promising public health provisions, it failed to make population health a focus of the reform.

Public health in Australia too is a small, highly fragmented component of the health system that has been funded poorly and unsystematically (Lin and Robinson, 2005) although there have been many recent efforts to increase national coordination. For instance, the Commonwealth Population Health Division has a formal responsibility to keep Australians healthy by helping them avoid illness and injury. The Australian National Preventive Health Agency was established in 2011 to develop strategic partnerships across all sectors, to provide technical advice and assistance, and to promote health and reduce health risk and inequalities (Healy and Dugdale, 2013). The Commonwealth invests in population health activity through a combination of Public Health Outcome Funding Agreements and direct grants to states/territories and community organizations, as well as through supporting population health activity undertaken by GPs and their divisions. Despite these varied activities, however, Commonwealth support for public health accounts for only about one-third of public health expenditure with the bulk coming from state and local governments.

Health promotion policies

The health promotion efforts in our countries have varied in their intensity, form and focus and to some extent their approaches and commitment reflects the general health goals predominant in each country. In Germany, New Zealand and Sweden, where the prevailing culture is more communitarian and egalitarian, health promotion strategies have focused on social factors and are more oriented towards broader approaches to health determinants (see Raphael and Bryant, 2006). In contrast, more individualistic countries such as Singapore and the USA tend to stress individual factors. Another variation is the extent to which health promotion is directed towards the population at large or at specific groups such as smokers, pregnant women or children. Furthermore, some countries have tended to target promotion policies at specific diseases or issues while others have taken more comprehensive approaches. In all cases, health promotion strategies reflect the organizational variation in public health activities in general, with some countries displaying rigorous national programmes and others largely delegating it to assorted sub-units.

Although health promotion is but one aspect of public health, it has received more attention recently as the links between individual behaviour and health have been elucidated. Even those countries that lack well-established health promotion policies realize that promoting healthy lifestyles is not only an effective way of improving the health of their populations, but also a crucial strategy for reining in escalating health care costs. Not surprisingly, then, countries across the full range of health systems have instituted programmes for health promotion and disease prevention, although their form and comprehensiveness vary greatly.

Germany

In Germany, the fragmented structure of public health and its medicalization over past decades have tended to work against a national strategy for health promotion. While health promotion has traditionally been the remit of the states, an increasing range of public health responsibilities have been integrated into the services offered by ambulatory care doctors. The Prevention Law makes a further boost by allocating a certain (yet small) amount of the total budget of the statutory health insurance funds to health promotion and disease prevention (Busse and Riesberg, 2004; Busse and Blümel, 2014). At federal level, responsibility for health promotion falls under the Ministry of Health, although the Federal Centre for Health Education is responsible for initiating and coordinating national health promotion campaigns. Long-term campaigns include AIDS, drugs and sex education, healthy eating and smoking cessation, whereas topical campaigns have been concerned with encouraging organ and blood donation.

The Netherlands

As in other European countries, Dutch patients have virtually universal access to a wide range of health services through publicly mandated insurance schemes. These services are supplemented by programmes for vaccinations, screening for cancers and pre- and postnatal screening, most of which have expanded over recent years. Policy initiatives have focused on promoting healthy lifestyles, reducing alcohol and tobacco consumption, and targeting new diseases such as HIV/AIDS, as well as health problems related to socio-economic status (Okma, 2001). The National Contract for Public Health stresses the need for cooperation among local and national levels as well as different sectors of health care provision.

Sweden

Although by international comparison Swedish citizens enjoy good health and long life expectancies, there have been concerns about health inequalities among certain social groups and, in 1991, a national strategy for public health was published that stressed the importance of cooperation among different levels and coincided with the creation of the National Institute of Public Health, which is responsible for national programmes. In 2000, this was strengthened by a publication of national public health goals, which reiterated the need to reduce health gaps among different social groups (Ministry of Health and Social Affairs, 2001). These developments culminated in a government bill on public health objectives in 2003 that is committed to ensuring social conditions that ensure good health for the entire population (Glenngård *et al.*, 2005). The policy was updated in 2008 and there is now a clearer focus on individual choice and responsibility together with greater emphasis on target groups, particularly children, young people and the elderly (Anell *et al.*, 2012).

Britain

In Britain, the 1992 White Paper, *The Health of the Nation*, provided the first national health promotion strategy (Baggott, 2010). It identified priorities for health promotion and set specific targets in relation to heart disease, strokes, cancers, mental illness, sexual health and accidents. The underlying stance was that individual behaviour is the key factor responsible for poor health. This strong individualist orientation was not surprising considering the New Right orientation of the government at the time and was moderated after the Labour government came into power in 1997. The revised strategy, encapsulated in the 1999 White Paper, *Saving Lives: Our Healthier Nation*, combines health promotion focused on the individual with an acknowledgement that social factors such as poverty contribute to poor health. A central feature of these initiatives is that they rely on collaboration among a wide range of actors, from central government and health authorities to local government and voluntary organizations and private businesses.

New Zealand

As a prime example of an egalitarian country, it is not surprising that New Zealand has adopted a broad health promotion approach that emphasizes social factors. In 2002, the New Zealand Ministry of Health launched *Achieving Health for All People* to provide a framework for comprehensive health promotion action under the New Zealand Health Strategy which emphasizes the importance of a population health approach for the improvement of health and the reduction of inequalities. A key theme of this initiative was that 'public health action is not the responsibility of public health services alone, or even of health services as a whole. It is about the organised efforts of society' (New Zealand Ministry of Health, 2003: 12). The Health Promotion Forum is a national umbrella organization representing over 200 groups nationwide that provides national leadership and support for good health promotion practice. In their analysis of the government's attempt to reorient the health sector towards population health, however, Tenbensel *et al.* (2008) question the governmental capacity to adequately address nationally determined population health policy priorities at the local level.

Japan

Likewise, Japan launched its broadly based First National Movement for Health Promotion in 1978 and the second wave in 1988. A key measure taken in the first movement was the creation of Municipal Health Centres (MHCs) in every municipality to coordinate health promotional activities. The second wave was dubbed 'Active 80 Health Plan' because its purpose was to promote a life span of 80 years. After more than 20 years since its inception, these health promotional activities have begun to bear fruit, as reflected in the third wave of the national health promotion movement, 'Healthy Japan 21'. In this wave, emphasis was placed on the prolongation of the 'healthy life span', meaning a lifespan without disability. This new focus reflected the problems facing the country with the world's longest lifespan.

Taiwan

In Taiwan, public health is a Department of Health, not an NHI, responsibility, with services provided through local agencies. The NHI provides few incentives for citizens to improve their health through behavioural changes. Furthermore, because health promotion falls under a governmental budget separate from NHI, there is little integration of medicine and health promotion. Thus, health promotion receives minimal attention and is isolated from the activities of the NHI. Moreover, the extremely heavy workloads of GPs mean that their limited time with each patient offers little opportunity for health promotion. Finally, the private dominance of health care provision has meant that health promotion does not have high priority since it tends not to be a money maker (Wen *et al.*, 2008).

United States of America

Although the delivery of most health promotion activities in the USA occurs at the sub-national level, the US Office of Public Health and Science serves as the health secretary's primary advisor on matters involving the nation's public health and oversees the Public Health Service (PHS). In turn, the Office of Disease Prevention and Health Promotion is mandated to provide national leadership for disease prevention and health promotion. Unfortunately, many federal programmes have a crisis orientation and do not lend themselves to approaches that require a longer-term perspective (Radin, 2010). Like the UK, the USA has a very individualist orientation in its health promotion initiatives. Therefore, much health promotion has been centred on screening and prescription of drugs to reduce cholesterol and high blood pressure. In 2010, however, the US Department of Health and Human Services unveiled *Healthy People 2020* which set the national health objectives for the decade, including the creation of social and physical environments that promote good health as well as promoting quality of life, healthy development, health equity and healthy behaviours. It also highlights the social determinants of health and health disparities and takes an expansive view of the impact on health resulting from constructed and natural environments. Concomitant with *Healthy People 2020*, the National Health Promotion and Prevention Council provides a vehicle for implementing a 'health in all policies' strategy across government agencies (Fielding *et al.*, 2012). Similarly, the US Preventive Services Task Force offers recommendations for strengthening health promotion efforts (Centers for Medicare and Medicaid Services, 2010).

Singapore

This heavy emphasis on individual responsibility in health care is also reflected in the ambitious health promotion activities of Singapore. In 1992, Prime Minister Goh Chok Tong launched the National Healthy Lifestyle Programme designed to educate Singaporeans about the importance of leading a healthy lifestyle and to encourage them to participate in regular exercise, eat healthily, avoid smoking and manage stress. The Programme takes an integrated approach that includes creating a supportive social and physical environment to encourage individuals to practise healthy behaviour. Between its inception in 1992 and 2001, the percentage of Singaporeans aged 18 to 69 years who exercised regularly increased from 17 to 20 per cent and those smoking dropped from 18 to 14 per cent (Singapore Ministry of Health, 2008). However, because the diet of Singaporeans had not improved and is still linked to high cholesterol and blood pressure, the 2002 National Healthy Lifestyle Campaign focused on the promotion of healthier food choices (Singapore Ministry of Health, 2008).

While strengthening public health research has become an important objective for most international health organizations, there has been less support for public health/health promotion research in Europe. Although all EU countries have strategies for public health, Conceição and McCarthy (2011) found 'little coherence' in public health research programmes. Moreover, while the European Commission has country contact points for both EU research and health programmes, they do not coordinate with national health research programmes.

Despite historic neglect, largely out of necessity, health promotion is enjoying heightened attention by many governments. This trend would represent going full circle back to the roots of health care if not for the fact that the resources being put into health promotion remain but a minute fraction of what is put into acute care. Also, because health is so tied to lifestyle choice, the success or failure of these health promotion initiatives is heavily dependent on the capacity to alter individual behaviour. Smoking-related illness and an obesity epidemic are forcing public health institutions to consider a variety of methods to influence behaviours of target groups including broadened use of 'sin taxes' (Green, 2011). This trend has been reinforced by the ongoing global economic slowdown that has driven governments to consider a variety of methods to generate funds for infrastructure. Consequently, public health approaches progressively conflict directly with the notion of the right to live one's preferred life free from government constraint. This tension is starkly illustrated in policies aimed to reduce obesity and tobacco use.

Obesity and health

As noted by the WHO, obesity is increasing at an alarming rate throughout the world: in every region of the world, obesity doubled between 1980 and 2008. Today, half a billion people (12 per cent of the world's population) are considered obese (WHO, 2012b). The highest obesity levels are in the WHO Region of the Americas (26 per cent of adults) and the lowest in the WHO Southeast Asia Region (3 per cent). Similarly, the 2006 International Congress on Obesity warned that an 'obesity pandemic threatens to overwhelm health systems around the globe'. The WHO's latest projections indicated that by 2015 approximately 2.3 billion adults would be overweight and more than 700 million would be obese (WHO, 2012b). Once considered a problem only in high-income countries, being overweight or obese is now dramatically on the rise in most countries (see Table 7.2). At present, 65 per cent of the world's population live in countries where being overweight or obese kills more people than being underweight (see Box 7.4).

Obesity is defined as a condition of excess body fat (generally the term overweight applies to those persons with a Body Mass Index

Table 7.2   *Comparative obesity rates, 2012*
(% over age 18)

USA	30.6
UK	23.0
Australia	21.7
New Zealand	20.9
Germany	12.9
The Netherlands	10.0
Sweden	9.7
Singapore	6.0
Taiwan	4.0
Japan	3.2

Source: WHO (2012b).

Box 7.4   A double burden of disease

Many low- and middle-income countries are now facing a 'double burden' of disease. While they continue to deal with the problems of infectious disease and under-nutrition, at the same time they are experiencing a rapid upsurge in chronic disease risk factors such as obesity and overweight, particularly in urban settings. It is common to find under-nutrition and obesity existing side by side within the same country, the same community and even within the same household. This double burden is caused by inadequate pre-natal, infant and young child nutrition followed by exposure to high-fat, energy-dense, micronutrient-poor foods and lack of physical activity (WHO, 2009a).

(BMI) between 25.0 and 29.9 and obese to those with a BMI 30 or above). Obesity is a major risk factor for numerous debilitating and life-threatening disorders, including cardiovascular disease (mainly heart disease and stroke) that is the world's number one cause of death, killing 17 million people each year. Moreover, it is a major cause of diabetes, which has rapidly become a global epidemic. The WHO projects that, largely because of obesity, deaths from diabetes will increase by more than 50 per cent worldwide in the next 10 years (2009a). Moreover, risk for these diseases heightens progressively as a person's BMI increases.

The European Commission has warned that obesity is now 'an urgent public health issue' that requires coordinated action by the EU and member states. It reported that up to 27 per cent of European men and 38 per cent of women are now considered obese and that obesity-related illnesses account for as much as 7 per cent of total health care costs in the EU (Haddon, 2006). In the USA, the situation is even grimmer: 60 million Americans adults are obese and over 9 million children and teens ages 6–19 are overweight (Lang and Rayner, 2005). A National Health and Nutrition Examination Survey estimated that 65 per cent of adults are either overweight or obese, up from 47 per cent in 1980 and 56 per cent in 1994. Moreover, based on current trends, it is predicted that by the year 2025 levels of obesity alone could be as high as 45 to 50 per cent in the USA (Box 7.5) and between 30 to 40 per cent in Australia, the UK and other EU countries (Haddon, 2006).

Box 7.5 US obesity rates to soar by 2030

If Americans stick to their eating and exercise habits, future historians will look back on the early 21st century as a golden age of svelte. Using a model of population and other trends, a report released by the Trust for America's Health and the Robert Wood Johnson Foundation projects that unless Americans change their ways over half will be obese by 2030. The 'F as in Fat' report highlights the current glum picture of the obesity epidemic, in which 35.7 per cent of adults and 16.9 per cent of children aged 2 to 19 are obese. For the first time, the report builds on state-by-state data from the Centers for Disease Control to project obesity rates. In every state, that rate will reach at least 44 per cent by 2030. In 13 states that number will exceed 60 per cent. The report projects 7.9 million new cases of diabetes a year, compared with 1.9 million new cases in recent years. There could also be 6.8 million new cases of chronic heart disease and stroke every year, compared with 1.3 million new cases annually now. The increasing burden of illness will add $66 billion in annual obesity-related medical costs over and above today's $147 billion (Begley, 2012).

Obesity and children

Of great concern is the skyrocketing rate of obesity among young children and adolescents in many countries. Worldwide, in 2010 over 40 million children under the age of 5 were overweight (WHO, 2012b). These data reflect significant upturns in obesity over the last several decades (Lang and Rayner, 2005). For instance, the percentage of overweight children aged 5 to 14 years in the USA has doubled in the last 30 years, from 15 to 32 per cent. By 2000 it was estimated that 6 million American children were obese enough to endanger their health and this number is mounting. Of the 14 million overweight children in Europe, 3 million are considered obese.

The tracking of obesity from childhood to adulthood is well substantiated and findings suggest that obese children are much more prone to chronic diseases that have a detrimental impact on their health in adulthood. Overweight children 5 to 10 years of age are 9.7 times more likely to have two risk factors for type 2 diabetes and 43.5 times more likely to have three risk factors (McConahy, 2002). As with adults, all diseases are exacerbated in children who are obese. It has been posited that the children of this generation may be the first to die before their parents because of health problems related to weight. Health expert Jay Olshansky states:

> within the next 50 years, life expectancy at birth will decline, and it will be the direct result of the obesity epidemic that will creep through all ages like a human tsunami . . . There has been a dramatic increase in obesity among the younger generation and it is a storm that is approaching. (Reuters, 2005)

Similarly, Brian McCrindle, a childhood obesity expert, warns the resulting 'wave of heart disease and stroke could totally swamp the public health care system' (NBC News, 2006).

Causes of obesity

Recent studies demonstrate that the social environment and individual behaviour are crucial factors in the obesity epidemic (for a discussion of the many factors, see Sassi *et al.*, 2009). Increases in overweight and obesity are attributable to numerous factors, including a shift in diet towards increased intake of energy-dense foods that are high in fat and sugars but low in vitamins, minerals and other nutrients. For the past 30 years, behavioural changes in Western societies, and more recently Japan, Singapore and Taiwan, have led to the expansion of high-calorie, fast food diets and all-you-can-eat buffets. Reinforcing this shift are trends towards more sedentary jobs and the replacement of physical activity with television, the internet and video games as primary recreation activities for many families. In addition, today's youth are considered the most inactive generation in history, caused in part by reductions in school physical education programmes and unavailable or unsafe community recreational facilities (Get America Fit, 2012). As noted by Sassi and associates (2009), we must remember that overweight and obesity are social phenomena. The behavioural choices leading to such conditions, typically nutrition and physical activity, tend to be shared among members of the same families, social networks and peer groups. A complicating factor for policy makers is that the prevalence of obese individuals varies with age, education, income and marital status. Individuals in lower SES groups, as well as those individuals with low educational attainments, are more likely to be obese (Costa-Font and Hernández Quevedo, 2012).

Although the cause of obesity is multifaceted and varies by individual, clearly in many cases chronic overconsumption of food plays a fundamental role. When this type of overeating becomes compulsive and out of control, it is often classified as a food addiction, a label that has caused much clinical and scientific controversy (Davis and Carter, 2009). Food addiction, which more accurately may reflect addiction to specific components of food, can be described in much the same way as other addictive behaviours (Taylor *et al.*, 2010). Davis and Carter (2009) conclude there is compelling evidence that highly palatable foods eaten in abundance have the potential to cause the same alterations in the brain as conventional substance dependence and thus justify its inclusion as an addiction disorder. Like drugs, foods induce tolerance over time, so that increased amounts are needed to reach and maintain satiety. Likewise, withdrawal symptoms such as distress and depression often occur during dieting, and there is a high incidence of relapse. These symptoms parallel to a remarkable extent those described in the *Diagnostic and Statistical Manual of Mental Disorders*, fourth edition (DSM-IV), for substance abuse and dependence, leading some to argue that food addiction should be considered a psychiatric illness (Volkow and O'Brien, 2007; Davis and Carter, 2009).

In making the argument for overeating as an addictive behaviour, it is clearly not appropriate to include all cases of excessive food consumption. For some individuals, overeating is a relatively passive, habitual event that occurs almost without awareness, in the form of liberal snacking and large portion sizes. For others, however, it can be compulsive and excessively driven. Davis and Carter (2009) suggest that there is sound clinical and scientific evidence that binge eating disorder is a phenotype particularly well suited to an addiction conceptualization. Neural imaging studies have shown that specific areas of the brain, such as the caudate nucleus, the hippocampus and the insula, are activated by food as well as drugs, and that both cause the release of striatal dopamine (Taylor *et al.*, 2010).

Costs of overweight and obesity

Whatever the ultimate cause, however, obesity has many negative health and social ramifications. Mortality and morbidity rates are higher among overweight and obese individuals than average weight people. A person who is 40 per cent overweight is twice as likely to die prematurely as a person of average weight. Thus, overweight/obesity is the number two cause of preventable death in the USA and the fifth leading risk for global deaths. Obesity is also a known risk factor for heart disease, stroke, hypertension, sleep apnoea, osteoarthritis and some forms of cancer (Thorpe *et al.*, 2004a). At least 2.8 million adults die each year by being overweight or obese. An estimated 80 per cent of type 2 diabetes, 70 per cent of cardiovascular disease, 30 per cent of gallbladder surgery and between 7 and 42 per cent of certain cancer burdens are attributable to overweight/obesity. It is also a major cause of hypertension, osteoporosis, varicose veins and joint replacement surgery (WHO, 2012b).

Obesity, then, has negative economic consequences for societies and individuals. The medical care costs of obesity in the USA alone are staggering. In 2008 dollars, these costs totalled about $147 billion (Finkelstein *et al.*, 2009; Get America Fit, 2012). Regardless of how one calculates the costs, obesity and the conditions related to it comprise an increasing share of health care expenditures and add significant pressures on health systems. Moreover, bariatric surgery, mainly stomach banding devices, is one of the fastest growing areas of health spending, particularly in the UK and USA (*Worldwide Market...*, 2007). In addition to its direct costs there are indirect costs for individuals, including ill health and reduced quality of life and for society though loss of productivity due to high rates of sick leave and premature pensions.

Not surprisingly, there has been a spate of studies analysing the costs of obesity and impact on health care systems (Costa-Font and Hernández Quevedo, 2012; Pelone *et al.*, 2012). In their macro-analysis of the costs of obesity in Europe, Von Lengerke and Krauth (2011), for instance, found that excess per capita direct costs ranged from €117 to €1,873, depending on cost categories and comparison group (normal weight, non-obese). They warned, however, that while on average higher costs for obese individuals were found across most studies, there was considerable variation within sub-group analyses. They suggest that findings such as higher health care costs in severely obese groups with higher socio-economic status and lower lifetime long-term care costs in obese groups due to reduced life expectancy may generate hypotheses both on under- and overuse of services (2011). In their systematic review of the direct costs of obesity worldwide, Withrow and Alter (2011) observe that obese individuals have medical costs that were approximately 30 per cent greater than their normal weight peers.

In their study, Wang *et al.* (2011) used a simulation model to project the probable health and economic consequences from a continued rise in obesity in the USA and the UK. These trends project 65 million more obese adults in the USA and 11 million more obese adults in the UK by 2030, consequently adding 6 to 8.5 million cases of diabetes, 5.7 to 7.3 million cases of heart disease and stroke, 492,000 to 669,000 additional cases of cancer, and 26 to 55 million quality-adjusted life years forgone for the USA and UK combined. The combined medical costs associated with treatment of these preventable diseases are estimated to increase by $48 to 66 billion annually in the USA and by £1.9 to 2 billion annually in the UK by 2030 (Wang *et al.*, 2011: 815).

Policies and strategies to combat obesity

Given the variations found in terms of the priority they place on health promotion, one would expect similar disparities across countries in their response to obesity. As noted above, although obesity is a global problem that transcends national boundaries, its prevalence varies significantly from country to country. Moreover, in their content analysis of the submissions to the New Zealand Inquiry into Obesity and Type 2 Diabetes, Jenkin and associates (2011) found 'stark contrasts' between the ways the food industry and public health sectors framed obesity (Box 7.6). Similarly, although there are many approaches to combating obesity, in their survey of obese individuals Thomas *et al.* (2010: 420) found

---

Box 7.6   Conflicting views on obesity

While the food and marketing sectors regard obesity as an economic burden to the health system with its health impacts limited to those who are obese, the public health sector sees obesity as an epidemic affecting both the overweight and obese. There is also disagreement over the main causes of obesity. Specifically, the industry frames obesity as a consequence of poor lifestyle choices attributed largely to lack of knowledge, and cultural or character deficits. It argues that a lack of physical activity rather than increased food consumption is the dominant cause of obesity. In contrast, public health groups view obesity as a natural response to an environment characterized by the ubiquitous marketing and availability of low cost, energy-dense/nutrient-poor foods. On the matter of potential solutions, the industry stresses education as a key strategy while public health advocates argue for government regulation of food and marketing industry activities and a revamping of national obesity strategies and policies to address wider determinants of health. Finally, while the industry espoused the individualism of 'market justice', public health appealed to the communitarian ethos of 'social justice' (Jenkin *et al.*, 2011: 1028).

that respondents favoured interventions that focused on encouraging individuals to make healthy lifestyle changes such as regulation of junk foods, physical activity programmes and public health initiatives. They found substantially less support for interventions perceived to be invasive or high risk (gastric band surgery), stigmatizing (media campaigns) or commercially motivated (commercial diets). Moreover, Maher *et al.* (2010) argue that while obesity is constructed as a broad public health crisis, within this crisis individuals are viewed as responsible for their own bodies and body sizes. In terms of childhood obesity, regrettably, one result has been to impute maternal responsibility for the weight of their children, thus deflecting attention from broader social factors.

This section examines a sample of a range of policy strategies designed to deal with obesity. Because of the magnitude of its problem, the USA has taken the lead, although Australia and New Zealand offer good examples of the range of strategies available (including food policy and collective/individualized public health strategies). Singapore offers a rather radical example of compulsion that is unlikely to work in other countries while Japan has taken a more measured approach to the emerging problem. Again, the importance of the cultural context of health policy is apparent in these diverse responses.

Although the Australian government took note of the problem in 1995 by convening the National Health and Medical Research Council on the Prevention of Obesity, by 2000, 17 per cent of men and 20 per cent of women were classified as obese, with a further 49 per cent of men and 27 per cent of women overweight, ranking it second in the world behind the USA (Nathan *et al.*, 2005). In response, the National Obesity Taskforce was established to develop a national approach to address the problem and identify initiatives needed to prevent obesity (Lin and Robinson, 2005). By 2005, Australia dropped its ranking for obesity to sixth but when those figures are combined with the proportion of overweight people, Australia still ranks fourth in the world behind only the USA, Mexico and the UK. The federal government aims to halve the number of overweight children by expanding the Healthy Schools Program that provides grants for initiatives such as improving school menus and launching a national physical activity campaign aimed at children and adolescents. In the State of Victoria, for instance, the Kids – 'Go for your life' (K-GFYL) initiative is a health promotion programme to reduce the risk of childhood obesity by improving the sociocultural, policy and physical environments in children's care and educational settings (de Silva-Sanigorski *et al.*, 2010).

Singapore has been one of the most proactive, and some might say draconian, countries with a strong commitment to reducing the prevalence of being overweight or obese. Since it introduced the school-based 'Fit and Trim' programme that includes rigorous exercise for overweight children and recommendations on food sold in canteens, levels of obesity among students have dropped and fitness has improved. The government also has initiatives to mobilize its adult population, of which about 6 per cent are obese, to adopt healthier lifestyles. Singapore holds a month-long fitness campaign each September aimed at getting the entire population to eat better and stay active. Moreover, Singapore health authorities are also deliberating nutrition labelling and regulations to reduce trans-fat in the food supply (Tan, 2011). Despite these efforts, a trend towards overweight citizens is attributed to a shift in diet towards Western fast foods. In response to studies that show that many Asians have more fat as a proportion of total body weight than Caucasians of the same age, sex, and BMI, and in response to the recommendations of the WHO, the Health Promotion Board lowered the BMI score for obesity among Asians to compensate for these differences.

Although the Japanese are not nearly as overweight as Americans (24 per cent as compared to 65 per cent), there is concern over changes in eating patterns. Men in all age groups have grown heavier in the past two decades, with the highest rate of obesity (34 per cent in 2003) among men in their 40s (Inagaki, 2006). Healthy Japan 21, a ten-year national plan for health promotion and disease prevention established by the Ministry of Health, Labour and Welfare, covers nine focus areas, including nutrition and physical activity, that explicitly set goals for decreasing obesity in adults and school children. Early detection of overweight students and education on healthy body weight take place in most primary and secondary schools in Japan (Matsushita *et al.*, 2004).

More than half of New Zealand adults are obese (17 per cent) or overweight (35 per cent). Obesity in New Zealand increased by 55 per cent between 1989 and 1997 and was predicted to increase to 29 per cent of all adults by 2011 if no changes were instituted. In response, the New Zealand Health Strategy targeted the reduction of the rate of obesity as one of the 13 priority areas for population health. DHBs are required to report annually on progress towards each of these priority areas. As part of a four-year bid to reduce its escalating obesity levels, in 2006 New Zealand banned fatty, sugary foods and drinks from school shops (Associated Press, 2006). At the launch of the NZ$67 million anti-obesity campaign, then Prime Minister Helen Clark said that over 30 per cent of children are either overweight or obese and that improving nutrition and encouraging more active lifestyles is the first step in fighting this epidemic. Imminent steps include introducing healthy food, drink and exercise policies into all government agencies. A labelling system for food and drinks was implemented for the 2007 school year, and although the government will not regulate to bring about change, school boards are required to develop policies that promote and achieve healthy nutrition and reduce consumption of unhealthy foods and drinks (Mernagh *et al.*, 2011).

Obesity has also become a very acrimonious political issue in the USA (see US Department of Health and Human Services, 2001, 2005). In 2001, the US Surgeon General's Call to Action emphasized the need to create supportive environments which provide accessible and affordable healthy food choices and convenient opportunities for regular physical activity (US Department of Health and Human Services, 2001). In May 2002, a $4.1 million USDA Team Nutrition programme began to teach children healthy eating habits (Kersh and Morone, 2002) and in June of that year the White House implemented the Health and Fitness Initiative to highlight physical activity (US Department of Health and Human Services, 2004).

Unlike other countries, however, policies in the individualistic USA have been aimed more at ensuring that obese patients are not discriminated against by medical professionals and less at encouraging behavioural changes. In fact, there has been considerable emphasis on making allowances for obese patients so as not to make them feel inferior (see Box 7.7). For example, Medicare redefined obesity as a medical problem and approved payment for a wide array of surgical weight-loss procedures for obese elderly patients. For instance, the number of bariatric surgeries has quadrupled since 2000 and is forecast to proliferate in the future (American Society for Bariatric Surgery, 2006). Obesity-related hip and knee replacements are also predicted to grow by 600 per cent in the coming decade. Furthermore, the Social Security Administration allows obesity to qualify for disability income, and, in 2002, the Internal Revenue Service acknowledged the medical importance of treating obesity, making physician-prescribed weight-loss programmes deductible medical expenses (Shortt, 2004).

One issue that has been simmering in many countries is the extent to which the government should intervene in the food choices of their citizens. For instance, the consumption of sugar-sweetened beverages has been linked to risks for obesity, diabetes and heart disease and some argue that

---

Box 7.7 Preparing for large patients

As Americans keep getting bigger, hospitals are revamping themselves to accommodate an influx of obese patients. When these patients check into a hospital, they are likely to find themselves in a room with a wider doorway than the 42-inch standard, a bed that holds up to 1,000 pounds and a ceiling lift system to move them to the bathroom. Toilets in such a room are extra sturdy and mounted to the floor instead of a wall. The obese are more likely to suffer from chronic medical ailments like diabetes and severe joint problems, bringing them into the hospital. Thus, more hospitals are making capital investments to set up separate wings and whole floors for obese patients to keep up with demand (Reuters, 2006).

a compelling case can be made for policies to reduce consumption of these beverages. Short of outright bans as proposed in New York City (Allen, 2012), taxation has been proposed as a means of reducing the intake of these beverages and, thus, lowering health care costs, as well as a means of generating revenue that governments can use for health programmes. In the USA, 33 states currently have sales taxes on soft drinks (mean tax rate, 5.2 per cent), but the taxes are too small to affect consumption and the revenues tend not to be earmarked for programmes related to health (Brownell *et al.*, 2009). Although the impact of a tax cannot be known until it is implemented and studied, research to date suggests that a tax on sugar-sweetened beverages could reduce consumption if the rate was sufficient. In addition, like tobacco taxes, it has the potential to generate needed revenue to prevent obesity and address other costs resulting from the consumption of sugar-rich beverages should the political will exist.

Schools are often identified as a natural site for intervention to improve the diets of students and help prevent excess weight gain and obesity. However, in their New Zealand study, Walton and colleagues (2010) found frequent barriers to improving school food environments and promoting healthy nutrition, including the high proportion of food brought to school from home, the crowded curriculum and limited resources to implement changes. Barriers that varied across socio-economic contexts included the capacity of home and community settings to support healthy diets, the degree to which schools relied on fundraising and a lack of engagement of parents and families with the school food environment.

Although the national level remains the primary focus of public health policies on obesity, increasingly there are initiatives at the international level. In the context of Europe, the Regional Office of the World Health Organization has been particularly active since the late 1990s. Initial consultations among member states culminated in a commitment in 2000 to create Nutrition Action Plans (Lang and Rayner, 2005). Other initiatives followed, most recently the European Charter on Counteracting Obesity (WHO, Regional Office for Europe, 2006). In contrast, the EU has been less active, not least reflecting the marginal position of health policy in relation to other policy issues within the EU and demonstrating that any policy initiative on obesity must compete for attention with other public health issues such as food safety.

Tobacco policy

Tobacco kills nearly 6 million people each year, including more than 600,000 who are non-smokers exposed to second-hand smoke (WHO, 2015b). Smoking is a major risk factor for at least two of the leading causes of premature mortality – cardiovascular diseases and cancer, increasing the risk of heart attack, stroke, lung cancer, cancers of the larynx and mouth, and pancreatic cancer, among others, as well as a dominant contributing factor for respiratory diseases such as chronic obstructive pulmonary disease (US DHHS, 2014). For this reason, most countries have instituted public health measures designed to reduce the incidence of smoking. In January 2009, for instance, Taiwan became the second country in Asia to ban indoor smoking in all public facilities including hotels, restaurants, karaoke bars, internet cafes and transport stations (see Box 7.8), an approach that has been adopted in many of the other countries examined here. Other strategies include raising the price of tobacco products through taxes, banning certain types of advertising, requiring health warnings on tobacco products and enforcing the minimum purchasing age (for specific country regulations, see www5.who.int/tobacco/).

Other countries, like Singapore, have very restrictive and rigid policies where, as part of the Smoking Regulations 2003, cigarette packets sold in Singapore must carry graphic images of the harmful effects of smoking such as bleeding brains, toothless gums and blackened lungs aimed at making smokers face up to the serious health effects of smoking. Since the launch of the National Smoking Control Programme in 1986, smoking prevalence in Singapore declined from 20 to 14 per cent, one of the lowest in the world. More drastically, New Zealand plans to institute a multifaceted programme to become the first tobacco-free country (Box 7.9).

Box 7.8   Smoking policy in Taiwan

Smoking in Taiwan is regulated by the Tobacco Hazards Prevention Act promulgated in July 2007. Tobacco advertising is banned and smoking is prohibited in all indoor public places. Smoking is already prohibited in all educational facilities; libraries, museums, art galleries and other institutions for cultural or social education; medical centres, nursing institutions, other medical institutions and social welfare organizations; governmental agencies and state-owned enterprises; mass transportation vehicles, taxicabs, tour buses, the Taipei Metro system, stations and traveller waiting areas; financial institutions and post offices; physical training, sports, or body fitness facilities; opera houses, movie theatres, and other entertainment places; hotels, shopping malls, dining and drinking establishments; and indoor workplaces shared by more than three persons. It is also banned in all parks and on the pavements around schools and other public buildings. Fines have been issued to both individuals and businesses for violations ('Smoking in Taiwan', 2012). The government created a hotline and offers a monetary reward for citizens who submit photos of violators. Individuals found smoking in smoke-free facilities can be fined between NT$2,000 and NT$10,000 (US$67 to US$334).

Box 7.9   A smoke-free country?

There are smoke-free bars, smoke-free parks, even smoke-free college campuses. But a smoke-free country? In 2012, New Zealand's government squeezed smokers more than ever by announcing a 40 per cent hike in tobacco taxes over the next four years. New Zealand already charges more than 70 per cent tax on cigarettes, compared to 41 per cent on average for China and 45 per cent on average for the USA. Prices there are already among the highest in the world, and by 2016 they will top NZ$20 (US$15) a pack. Officials hope higher taxes and new restrictions will bring the nation closer to a recent pledge to snuff out the habit entirely by 2025. Other countries have lauded the idea of trying to wean their populace off tobacco, but few, if any, have been willing to put a date on it. Health officials are so serious they recently considered hiking the cost of a pack of cigarettes to NZ$100 (US$75). Although that idea was dismissed, another measure, which will force retailers to hide cigarettes below the counter rather than putting them on display, similar to a law in the UK, has been implemented (Perry, 2012).

The WHO Framework Convention on Tobacco Control (FCTC) is an international treaty in response to second-hand smoking. It specifies the measures that governments should implement (e.g. advertising bans, taxation, smoke-free policy, health promotion and cessation support). The FCTC came into force in 2005, after being the international treaty ratified by the largest number of countries at the fastest rate, but as of 2008 very few countries were implementing all its measures. In Europe, for instance, implementation is at best incomplete and in most developing countries it is minimal (Wipfli and Huang, 2011). Although Article 8 of FCTC mandates its signatory and accession countries to enforce smoke-free public places through legislative, executive or administrative measures, only 5 per cent of the world's population benefits from national legislation covering a wide range of public places. Moreover, over half of the world's population is not currently protected from second-hand smoking by any law, even though they live in countries where sub-national jurisdictions have the legal power to restrict smoking in public places (WHO, 2009b).

Many studies suggest that prominent health warnings with graphic pictures can reduce demand for cigarettes, with pictorial warnings on plain packaging producing the greatest decrease (Hammond *et al.*, 2009; Germain *et al.*, 2010; Thrasher *et al.*, 2011). After taxation, the other two regulatory changes that concern the tobacco industry the most are homogeneous packaging and below-the-counter sales. Mitchell (2010) argues that both would significantly restrict the industry's ability to promote their products, particularly in 'dark' markets, such as Australia, where

244 Comparative Health Policy

tobacco advertising is banned. As illustrated in Box 7.10, plain packaging allows manufacturers to print only the brand name in a mandated size, font and place (Freeman *et al.*, 2008).

In line with these WHO guidelines, ground-breaking legislation that all tobacco products sold in Australia must be in plain packaging went into effect on 1 December 2012. In advance of its implementation, tobacco companies launched High Court challenges against the law, arguing it infringes their trademark rights and violates minimum obligations for the protection of intellectual property rights under the TRIPS Agreement and the Paris Convention that require World Trade Organization (WTO) Member States to maintain a register of trademarks and establish minimum standards governing the registration of such marks. Trademarks are signs or combinations of signs capable of distinguishing goods or services from other goods or services which plain packaging negates.

In addition, three legal challenges were mounted at the WTO by the Dominican Republic, Ukraine and Honduras, charging that the Australian laws unfairly restrict trade. Trade diplomats expect the three complaints against Australia will be bundled together before moving to the adjudication stage, with little chance of a settlement before then. Mitchell

---

Box 7.10   WHO and plain packaging of tobacco products

Guidelines for the implementation of Article 11 of the FCTC, concerning the packaging and labelling of tobacco products, states that parties should consider adopting measures to restrict or prohibit the use of logos, colours, brand images or promotional information on packaging. This 'plain packaging' increases the noticeability and effectiveness of health warnings and messages, prevents the package from detracting attention from them and counters industry package design techniques that suggest that some products are less harmful than others. Article 13 of the FCTC requires each party, within constitutional limits, to 'undertake a comprehensive ban of all tobacco advertising, promotion and sponsorship'. Paragraphs 15 to 17 of the guidelines refer to the potential for plain packaging to eliminate the effect of advertising and promotion. Paragraph 16 defines plain packaging as packaging with:

> black and white or two other contrasting colours, as prescribed by national authorities; nothing other than a brand name, a product name and/or manufacturer's name, contact details and the quantity of product in the packaging, without any logos or other features apart from health warnings, tax stamps and other government-mandated information or markings; prescribed font style and size; and standardized shape, size and materials. (Conference of the Parties to the WHO FCTC, 2008: 16)

(2010), however, expects the claims to be dismissed and argues that plain packaging is WTO compliant. She argues that it does not violate any provisions of the TRIPS Agreement or the Paris Convention. It is implicit within the TRIPS Agreement itself, and especially Article 20, that a high degree of domestic regulatory autonomy shall be afforded to a Member State to enact measures to protect and promote public health. While details of the regulations have not yet been released, the general move towards plain packaging is consistent with the FCTC and should fall within the scope of permissible regulation under Article 20. 'No concern about plain packaging ... should prevent the Government from implementing what is an important initiative at the top of the global public health agenda.' (Mitchell, 2010: 422)

Ueda *et al.* (2011) note that although the Japanese government ratified the FCTC in 2004, there is yet to be effective national tobacco control. Until 1985, the tobacco industry was a government-run monopoly. Currently, the government is still involved in tobacco advertising and etiquette campaigns and the Ministry of Finance controls 50.2 per cent of Japan Tobacco, the world's third biggest tobacco company. Not surprisingly, unlike other countries included here, non-smoking areas are uncommon, although all trains either have non-smoking cars or are completely smoke-free. Cigarettes can be bought in tobacco stores or at an estimated 500,000 vending machines. Since 2008, a customer must have a Taspo smart card developed by the Tobacco Institute of Japan, the nationwide association of tobacco retailers, and the Japan Vending Machine Manufacturers Association to purchase cigarettes from vending machines. In 2003, the Ministry of Health, Labour and Welfare introduced a National Health Promotion Plan to improve national health, including the launch of the Healthy Japan 21 campaign for 2000–10 that was intended to enable people to take positive steps towards improving their health. Alongside these programmes, the Health Promotion Act went into effect in 2003 that establishes targets to prevent lifestyle-related diseases. Prevention of second-hand smoke exposure was one aim, and Article 25 in this law suggested that persons in charge of public places such as schools, gymnasiums, hospitals and theatres take measures to prohibit smoking.

Although systematic comparative estimates on the societal costs of smoking are unavailable, smoking causes a significant number of deaths and smokers generally consume more health care resources than non-smokers. In the USA, for example, it is estimated that 19 per cent of all premature deaths – an estimated 291,000 deaths among men and 229,000 among women – annually from 2002 through 2006 were smoking attributable (Rostron, 2011). Given that the USA has relatively low levels of smoking, death rates from smoking in other countries are assumed to be similar, if not higher.

Variation in smoking rates

Table 7.3 illustrates that smoking rates vary significantly across countries, especially among women. In Singapore, high prices and strict regulations have cut overall smoking rates, but the extremely low rate for women is obviously cultural since male smoking is near the average. Japan and, until recently, Taiwan have had relatively relaxed regulations and by far the highest rates of male smoking. Evidence suggests, however, that laws can make a difference and that public health and education programmes reduce smoking rates (see Box 7.11). Data from ten European countries where rigorous tobacco control policies have been implemented, including Sweden and the UK, show a decrease in the number of tobacco-related deaths in recent years (WHO, 2003). The most effective control measures include high prices on tobacco products, total bans on

Table 7.3   *Smoking rates, men and women (%), ranked by men, 2012*

	Women	Men
Taiwan	5.2	41.1
Japan	8.4	32.2
Netherlands	18.8	23.1
Germany	17.6	26.4
Singapore	3.0	26.3
UK	20.7	22.3
New Zealand	17.0	19.3
Sweden	15.1	12.8
USA	13.6	16.7
Australia	13.9	16.4

Source: Data from OECD (2013).

Box 7.11   English smoking ban

The number of people who quit smoking through NHS stop smoking services in England in mid-2007 when the ban on smoking in public places came into force was 28 per cent higher than the same period in the previous year before the ban. Nearly 165,000 smokers gave up the habit (National Health Service, 2008). In September 2012, NHS announced the Stoptober campaign to encourage the nation's 8 million smokers to give up smoking for 28 days from 1 October. People who stop smoking for 28 days are five times more likely to stay smoke-free, so smokers who signed up were given support and encouragement throughout the month.

advertising, support for cessation treatment and policies requiring the creation of smoke-free environments.

In their study of 15 countries, Borland *et al.* (2011) found wide variation in the availability of assistance to stop smoking but overall a higher use of medication than behavioural support. There is also disparity in the provision of advice to patients from health professionals to stop. WHO (2003) notes that most countries would benefit from clarifying and strengthening anti-tobacco controls. For example, less than 25 per cent of countries in the European Region earmark any tobacco tax revenues for control measures or health promotion, and of those only five allocate more than 1 per cent.

A European report on tobacco control policy shows that while smoking rates stabilized at 30 per cent for the region (38 per cent for men and 23 per cent for women) over the last five years, increases in population meant that the number of smokers rose (WHO, 2003). Most countries show a gap in smoking rates between the lowest and highest socio-economic groups. In some countries, the poorest smoke three times as much as the richest. This report further found that smoking rates among young people across Europe are converging, eliminating former differences of gender and geography, and that although several countries reported reductions in adult smoking, none showed significant reductions in smoking by young people. In addition, the gender gap has become less significant among teenagers: in 12 countries girls smoked as much as, or more than, boys (WHO, 2003).

E-Cigarettes

Virtually unheard of ten years ago, e-cigarettes (see Box 7.12) have skyrocketed in popularity. Since their introduction to the market in 2004, global usage has risen exponentially (Hagopian *et al.*, 2015). A significant increase in e-cigarette use has been spurred by marketing that promises a safe product, especially in comparison to other tobacco products. Perhaps due to this marketing, which includes product designs that appeal to youth, e-cigarette use tripled among high school students between 2012 and 2014 in the USA, and there is now evidence that e-cigarettes surpass conventional tobacco products in popularity among young people. Relative to combustible products, e-cigarettes appear to be less dangerous, but there is little data about their health effects and considerable variability between vaporizers and the quality of their liquid ingredients (Grana *et al.*, 2014).

A recent WHO report cautioned about potential risks of using e-cigarettes (WHO, 2016a). A 2014 systematic review, however, concluded that the risks of e-cigarettes have been exaggerated by health authorities and stated that while there may be some remaining risk, the risk of e-cigarette use is likely small compared to smoking tobacco

---

Box 7.12　E-cigarettes

Basically, an e-cigarette is a battery-powered vaporizer which simulates the feeling of smoking, but without burning tobacco. Instead of the traditional combustible cigarette, it uses a battery-operated heating element, called an atomizer, that vaporizes a liquid solution from a small cartridge of flavoured liquid into an aerosol mist that resembles smoke. The e-liquid, usually, but not always, contains nicotine. The user activates the e-cigarette by taking a puff or pressing a button. Instead of cigarette smoke, the user inhales an aerosol, commonly called vapour. The liquid typically contains 95 per cent propylene glycol and glycerine, and natural or artificial flavourings estimated to number about 8,000. First-generation e-cigarettes looked like tobacco cigarettes and were called cigalikes. Second generation devices are larger overall and look less like tobacco cigarettes while third generation devices include mechanical mods and variable voltage devices. The fourth generation includes Sub ohm tanks and temperature control devices (Farsalinos *et al.*, 2014). The power source, which is frequently a rechargeable lithium battery, is the biggest component of an e-cigarette (Rom *et al.*, 2014).

(Farsalinos and Polosa, 2014; Farsalinos *et al.*, 2014). However, e-cigarettes cannot be considered harmless and a recent review recommended that e-cigarettes at least should be regulated for consumer safety (Saitta *et al.*, 2014) especially given the aggressive marketing in the media and on brand websites that promote them as safe and beneficial (England *et al.*, 2015).

The assertion that e-cigarettes emit only water vapour is inaccurate because the evidence shows that the vapour consists of ultrafine particles that can contain harmful chemicals including nicotine, carbonyls, metals and organic volatile compounds (Fernandez *et al.*, 2015). However, e-cigarette vapour contains fewer toxic substances, has lower concentrations of potential toxic substances and is likely less harmful to users and bystanders than cigarette smoke (Grana *et al.*, 2014; Fernandez *et al.*, 2015). No serious adverse effects from e-cigarettes have been reported in trials, but the long-term effects of e-cigarette use are unknown (Drummond and Upson, 2014; Orellana-Barrios *et al.*, 2015).

Yet unanswered questions surrounding e-cigarettes include the efficacy of e-cigarettes as a smoking cessation device, whether vaping represents a 'gateway' to smoking among the young (Hagopian *et al.*, 2015) and the safety of the vapour itself for users and people around them. Although the US Food and Drug Administration (FDA) recently concluded that we currently do not have sufficient data to determine what effects e-cigarettes have on the public health, the evidence suggests that they can supply nicotine at concentrations able to substitute for traditional cigarettes.

A 2014 cross-sectional population survey of UK smokers who tried to stop without professional assistance found that those who used e-cigarettes were more likely to stop smoking than those who used nicotine replacement products (McNeill *et al.*, 2015). Similarly, a 2015 review found that e-cigarette users had 20 per cent higher cessation rates than users of conventional nicotine replacement products (Rahman, 2015).

With the rapid escalation of their use, public health officials have become concerned about the health implications of the use of e-cigarettes. Because of the limited evidence of effectiveness and safety, many health care groups have hesitated to recommend e-cigarettes for quitting smoking. For instance, a 2014 WHO report concluded that there was not enough evidence to determine if e-cigarettes could help people quit smoking (WHO, 2016b). In a recent joint statement of Public Health England and other UK medical bodies concluded 'e-cigarettes are significantly less harmful than smoking' (Public Health England, 2015; McNeill *et al.*, 2015;). The National Health Service followed with the statement that e-cigarettes have approximately 5 per cent of the risk of tobacco cigarettes (National Health Service, 2015; West et al., 2015). Green, Bayer and Fairchild (2016) suggest that the British studies will reframe the e-cigarette policy debate.

Governments have the power to prohibit the sale of such products, ban the sale of such products to minors, and dictate the conditions under which they can be marketed and sold as well as protect the public from false or misleading claims about any product. Additionally, governments could regulate them in ways such as banning their use in various public places, often under existing or new smoke-free laws, to minimize the use of products that pose unknown health risks, even in the absence of evidence that exhaled vapour produces exposure to contaminants that would warrant health concerns by the standards that are used to ensure safety of workplaces (Goniewicz *et al.* 2014). Saitta *et al.* argue that there is no justification for a blanket inclusion of e-cigarettes in existing 'clean air' regulations (2014: 57).

Regulating e-cigarettes

In response to critics of e-cigarettes, however, policy makers have begun developing rules for if and how they can be marketed and sold (Health Affairs, 2014). Among the existing tobacco control policies that can be applied to e-cigarettes are retail licensing, taxation, age restrictions, labelling and disclosure requirements, restrictions on product flavourings, limits on internet sales, regulation of marketing and prohibiting use in public and/or indoor places. E-liquids could be marketed as dietary supplements or as cosmetic products, while marketing and safety of e-cigarettes' electronics, batteries and spare parts are already regulated by the existing directives on electronic product design. Although Saitta *et al.* note that it should be relatively easy to implement a reasonable regulation of e-cigarettes, it might be politically difficult to implement because of their growing popularity and the threats they threat pose to the interests of the tobacco industry and the pharmaceutical industry as well as the dependence of national, state and local governments on the large revenues generated by tobacco excise (2014: 57).

Regulation of e-cigarettes varies across countries and states, ranging from no regulation to banning them entirely. Moreover, the legal status of e-cigarettes is fast-changing in many countries. As of 2015, approximately two-thirds of countries had regulated e-cigarettes in some way. Some countries such Argentina, Austria, Brazil, Columbia, Indonesia, Malaysia, Mexico, Panama, Singapore, Thailand, Turkey, Uruguay, and Venezuela had banned their sale and distribution completely (E-Cigarette Politics, 2016). Taiwan has a de facto ban in that all e-cigarette-related products require a licence and no licences have yet been issued.

In addition, many countries operate a two-tier system where they distinguish nicotine from non-nicotine products. The hardware which does not contain nicotine as well as refills without nicotine are permitted while units sold pre-filled with a nicotine-containing liquid or refills with nicotine require a medical licence. For practical reasons this is a de facto ban and frequently had led to a black market. Countries that have instituted such policies include Australia, Denmark, Finland, Hong Kong, Hungary, Ireland, Japan, New Zealand, Norway, South Africa, Sweden and Switzerland. For instance, in New Zealand e-cigarettes and nicotine-free cartridges may be sold, but nicotine-containing refills are prohibited. Nicotine-containing cartridges and liquid are classed as medicines and banned until the manufacturer or distributor of the product applies. The delivery device, without the nicotine cartridge, may be sold on its own so long as no therapeutic claims are made. Canada, too, is attempting to implement a two-tier system but appears not to have the legal foundation on which to act. Personal import of refills with nicotine is legal in Belgium if it is for personal use and sold by a vendor located in a EU country where sale of refills with nicotine is allowed.

Among the countries that generally permit e-cigarettes are the USA, China, Czech Republic, Estonia, Germany, Greece, Israel, Poland, Russia and Italy, which has imposed a new tax of 58.5 per cent (on top of the 21 per cent VAT) on all e-cigarette products mainly to replace taxes lost due to falling cigarette sales resulting from rising e-cigarette sales. South Korea considers e-cigarettes a tobacco product and subject to tobacco control legislation with high taxes. The Netherlands government attempted a blanket ban, but the Gravenhage court legalized the import and sale of electronic cigarettes and nicotine-containing e-liquids. Although the United Kingdom permits the import, sale, advertising and use of e-cigarettes, they are comprehensively and effectively regulated. All standard consumer protections are in force, meaning that 17 separate statutes apply to e-cigarettes, refills and ancillaries. The Department of Business oversees consumer product sales and has enforcement duties shared with the Trading Standards Institute, which provides the inspection, analysis and enforcement staff at local level. No therapeutic claims are permitted since this implies a medicinal function and would require a pharmaceutical licence.

In France e-cigarettes and nicotine liquid are considered consumer goods regulated by general product safety regulations, unless they meet the criteria for medical licensing. If a product claims to be for smoking cessation; or if the amount of nicotine in a cartridge is greater than or equal to 10 mg; or if the nicotine strength in a refill is more than or equal to 20mg/ml, then a medical application is required. As of 2015, no medical licences have been issued in any country for any e-cigarette or nicotine-containing liquid, thus where medical licences and prescriptions are required, a de facto ban exists (E-Cigarette Politics, 2016).

Import, sale, advertising and use are permitted in the USA, but as usual in the decentralized federal system, most action regarding e-cigarettes is at the state or even local levels, which have the power to introduce their own regulations. As of 2015, 48 states prohibit e-cigarette sales to minors. At least 15 states have restricted e-cigarette use in public places while two states and one city have levied taxes on them and several have attempted to regulate packaging and marketing of e-cigarettes. In California, many communities have adopted smoke-free multi-unit housing policies to shield their residents from breathing in second-hand smoke drifting from neighbouring units, balconies and outdoor areas. At least 29 cities and counties in California prohibit the use of e-cigarettes in multi-unit housing through special language in the definition of smoke and smoking in their smoke-free air laws (American Lung Association, 2015). In New Jersey e-cigarettes are included in the Smoke Free Air Act which prohibits smoking in indoor public places and workplaces, while in contrast, in Virginia, e-cigarettes are not covered by smoking ban legislation and cannot be considered as smoking devices.

The FDA has announced its intention to regulate e-cigarettes and refills as a tobacco product (FDA, 2014). This would allow it to form a legal framework to do so and then gradually tighten the regulations to remove e-cigarettes from the market. It attempted a ban in 2010 but this was rejected by a series of appeal courts that upheld the rejection of a pharmaceutical classification and ruled that if regulation was required, then as a tobacco product would be more appropriate. The FDA has announced that it intends to assert authority over products that meet the statutory definition of 'tobacco products' under the 2009 tobacco regulation law. This would include regulating e-cigarettes as a new tobacco product. This will require the FDA to issue a 'deeming' notice, to state that it deems e-cigarettes to be tobacco products and that it will proceed with regulation. In February 2014, the European Parliament passed regulations requiring standardization and quality control for liquids and vaporizers, disclosure of ingredients in liquids, and child-proofing and tamper-proofing for liquid packaging. Although e-cigarettes are permitted in the EU member countries that have their own regulations, the EU has been struggling with an attempt to implement a range of restrictions that could mean a ban on all current hardware, all refills over 20mg strength, all advertising, and international web sales (E-Cigarette Politics, 2016).

So far, this chapter has examined the structures and funding sources for public health and health promotion strategies and activities, particularly those surrounding obesity and tobacco use. It is evident that many of these efforts lead us far from health care as medicine into the realm of health education and social welfare policy. The next two sections extend these linkages even further afield into housing and environmental policy areas. Still other dimensions of public health that we are unable to discuss here due to space limitations are occupational health, food safety, crime/violence, transportation safety, drug and alcohol abuse and ageing, and failing infrastructures such as the Flint Michigan water system (Bellinger, 2016). Public health policy also increasingly pays attention to violence against women and its severe health effects (Amin *et al.*, 2015) and, most recently, to the new demands arising from civil wars and growing numbers of migrants and refugees (UNDESA, 2015; Langlois *et al.*, 2016). In combination, they all entail major health concerns that are largely neglected by the medical model.

Homelessness and inadequate housing

One health factor virtually ignored by the medical model, but which takes on importance in the more inclusive social model, is housing. A lack of adequate housing, especially when it involves homelessness, puts people, particularly children, at serious health risk (Hwang *et al.*, 2011). For Hayashi (2016), the 'connection between housing and health is coldly logical. The sick and vulnerable become homeless, and the homeless become sicker and more vulnerable'. While homeless people suffer from the same acute and chronic illnesses as those in the general population, they do so at much higher rates. Among other deficiencies, homeless people often have little or no access to adequate bathing and hygienic facilities, survive on the streets or in unsafe and generally unsanitary shelters and suffer from inadequate diets. Subsequently, upper respiratory tract infections, trauma and skin ailments are commonplace. High levels of alcohol and drug abuse and mental illness complicate the picture for many homeless people.

Although the health impact of living on the streets is most severe, inadequate housing can also lead to poor health. Poor housing is linked to a wide array of physical and mental health problems as described in Box 7.13. Sub-standard housing is related to house fires and increased accidents. Furthermore, damp, cold and often mouldy living conditions are associated with respiratory ailments, while improperly ventilated housing is linked to heat-related health problems. However, it is difficult to quantify the amount of ill health caused by poor housing because many health effects are qualitative in nature and reflect poor quality of life and social isolation. Housing-related health problems are particularly acute in inner city areas where the housing stock is comparatively old and often of poor quality and poorly maintained.

In combination with underlying poverty, unemployment, poor education, violence and crime, inadequate housing remains a significant health hazard for many citizens. These factors share an isolation from the medical model. Although medical care is beneficial for many individuals affected by these health-threatening factors, 'medical care cannot compensate for economic deprivation, social disorganization, personal alienation, and low levels of education and social integration' (Mechanic, 1994: 3). In the end, solutions to these problems lie fully outside the

---

Box 7.13   Homelessness creates new health problems and exacerbates existing ones

Living on the street or in crowded homeless shelters is stressful and made worse by being exposed to communicable diseases, violence, malnutrition and harmful weather exposure. Common conditions such as high blood pressure, diabetes and asthma worsen and behavioural health issues such as depression or alcoholism are aggravated. Minor issues such as cuts or common colds can develop into larger problems such as infections or pneumonia. Whether a primary or contributing factor to losing housing, or a condition acquired or made worse afterwards, individuals who are homeless have disproportionately high rates of acute and chronic health problems. Moreover, conditions among homeless people are frequently co-occurring, with a complex mix of severe physical, psychiatric, substance use and social problems. High stress, unhealthy and dangerous environments and an inability to control food intake often result in visits to emergency rooms and hospitalization which worsens overall health. Therefore, it is no surprise that those experiencing homelessness are three to four times more likely to die prematurely than their housed counterparts, and experience an average life expectancy as low as 41 years (National Health Care for the Homeless Council, 2011).

medical community. Unfortunately, health care reformers have focused so much on medical care that they have ignored those factors that ultimately make the biggest difference in people's health.

Environmental health

The environment has always been intimately related to public health. Likewise, any major environmental change ultimately is a matter of health concern. 'There is an intrinsic relationship between the health of ecological systems, health of communities and the health of people' (Strand *et al.*, 2010: 442). However, while the health effects of environmental change have received considerable public attention, comprehensive policy efforts have been more subdued, in part because they are highly complex and often viewed as transnational problems. Although local and national environmental health hazards are endemic (see Quah and Boon, 2003), concern has recently been raised over new global threats.

Climate change

For instance, global climate change resulting from the accumulation of greenhouse gases is likely to have a significant impact on the health of the populations most affected (WHO, 2010a; Huang *et al.*, 2011; Kang, 2011). After decades of debate, there is now a consensus that we are increasing the atmospheric concentration of energy-trapping gases, thus amplifying the natural 'greenhouse effect' that makes the Earth habitable. These greenhouse gases are comprised principally of carbon dioxide (mostly from fossil fuel combustion and forest burning) plus other heat-trapping gases such as methane (from irrigated agriculture, animal husbandry and oil extraction), nitrous oxide and various human-made halocarbons. In the last 100 years, the world has warmed by approximately $0.75°C$. Over the last 25 years, the rate of global warming has accelerated, at over $0.18°C$ per decade. Sea levels are rising, glaciers are melting and precipitation patterns are changing. Extreme weather events are becoming more intense and frequent (WHO, 2010a).

Although climate change may bring some localized benefits, such as fewer winter deaths in temperate climates and increased food production in certain areas, overall the effects of a changing climate are likely to have an overwhelmingly negative impact on the fundamental requirements for health, including clean air, safe drinking water, sufficient food and secure shelter (McMichael and Lindgren, 2011). Because of their complexity, measuring the health effects from climate change can only be very tentative. Nevertheless, a WHO (2010a) assessment, accounting for only a subset of the possible health impacts, concluded that by 2004 the modest warming since the 1970s was already causing over 140,000 excess deaths annually, of whom 88 per cent were children (Sheffield and Landrigan, 2011).

Extreme high air temperatures contribute directly to deaths from cardiovascular and respiratory disease, particularly among elderly people. During the heat wave of summer 2003 in Europe, for example, more than 70,000 excess deaths were recorded (Robine *et al.*, 2008). High temperatures also raise the levels of ozone and other pollutants in the air that exacerbate cardiovascular and respiratory disease. Excess morbidity and mortality related to extremely hot weather and poor air quality affect cities on six continents and will worsen (Ebi, 2011). The interaction of global climate change, urban heat islands and air pollution are predicted to place intensifying health burdens on large cities. Pollen and other aeroallergen levels are also higher in extreme heat and can trigger asthma, which affects around 300 million people. Ongoing temperature increases are expected to heighten this burden (WHO, 2010a).

Climate change is also manifested by reported weather-related natural disasters, which have more than tripled since the 1960s. On average, these catastrophes result in over 60,000 deaths each year, predominantly in the poorest countries (WHO, 2010a). Rising sea levels and increasingly dangerous weather events also destroy homes, medical facilities and other essential services. More than half of the world's population lives within 60 km of the sea. Moreover, progressively variable rainfall patterns are likely to affect the supply of fresh water. A lack of safe water can compromise hygiene and increase the risk of diarrhoeal disease, which kills 2.2 million people every year (WHO, 2010a). In extreme cases, water scarcity leads to drought and famine. Contrariwise, floods are also increasing in frequency and intensity; these contaminate freshwater supplies, heighten the risk of water-borne diseases and create breeding grounds for disease-carrying insects such as mosquitoes.

Rising temperatures and variable precipitation are also likely to decrease the production of staple foods in many of the poorest regions – by up to 50 per cent in some African countries. This will increase the prevalence of malnutrition and under-nutrition, which currently cause 3.5 million deaths every year. Areas with weak health infrastructure, chiefly in the poorest developing countries, will be the least able to cope without assistance to prepare and respond. Moreover, many perilous diseases, including common vector-borne diseases such as malaria and dengue and yellow fever are highly sensitive to changing temperatures and precipitation (US Environmental Protection Agency, 2009). Transmitted by Anopheles mosquitoes, malaria kills almost 1 million people each year, mainly African children under 5 years old. The Aedes mosquito vector of dengue is also highly sensitive to climate conditions. Studies suggest that climate change could expose an additional 2 billion people to dengue transmission by the latter half of the century (WHO, 2010a).

The Intergovernmental Panel on Climate Change (IPCC) Fourth Assessment Report found that 'warming of the climate system is unequivocal' and that 'most of the observed increase in globally averaged temperatures since the mid-20th century is very likely due to the observed increase in anthropogenic greenhouse gas concentrations' (IPCC, 2007: 22). If even more conservative climate change predictions are accurate, the increase in the number of days with temperatures over 100°F (38°C) will produce a sharp rise in heat-related mortality from heat strokes, heart attacks and cerebral strokes, especially among the very young, the elderly and those with chronic respiratory diseases.

Climate change is also expected to trigger substantial increases in the scale of human population movement in coming decades. Forecasts of the number of people who are forced to relocate by mid-century in response to the effects of climate change vary from tens of millions to 250 million people (McMichael *et al.*, 2012). Climate-change-related migration is likely to amplify adverse health outcomes, both for displaced and host populations. Current scientific assessments project that climate change will, to varying extents among different regions and communities, exacerbate morbidity and mortality, reduce income and decrease access to important forms of natural capital.

Climate change, therefore, endangers human health, affecting all sectors of society, both domestically and globally. The environmental consequences of climate change, both already observed and those that are anticipated, such as sea-level rise, changes in precipitation resulting in flooding and drought, heat waves, more intense hurricanes and storms and degraded air quality, will affect human health both directly and indirectly (Portier *et al.*, 2010). Although indeterminate, the future health costs associated with predicted climate change are projected to be enormous. Knowlton *et al.* (2011) estimate that the health costs associated with six climate change-related events that struck the USA between 2000 and 2009 – ozone pollution, heat waves, hurricanes, infectious disease outbreaks, river flooding and wildfires – exceeded $14 billion, with 95 per cent due to the value of lives lost prematurely. Actual health care costs were an estimated $740 million with more than 760,000 encounters with the health care system.

Hess *et al.* (2012) contend that public health capacity must be increased to deal with climate-health threats. They argue that public health adaptation is imperative, but contend that there has been little discussion of how to increase adaptive capacity and resilience in public health systems. In the USA, the Environmental Protection Agency's mission to protect human health and the environment has focused on the potential for future climate change to cause air quality degradation via climate-induced changes in meteorology and atmospheric chemistry, posing challenges to the US air quality management system and the effectiveness of its pollution mitigation strategies (Post *et al.*, 2012). The WHO, and similarly the United Nations Population Fund (UNFPA, 2009), have revealed that climate change often hits women the hardest, and argued the need for gender assessment of the health effects and public health responses (WHO Public Health and Environment Department, 2011).

Depletion of the ozone layer

In addition to climate change, the depletion of the ozone layer poses severe global health risks (Norval *et al.*, 2011). Higher levels of ultraviolet B radiation (UVB) reaching the surface of the earth can damage DNA and proteins and kill cells in all living organisms (see Box 7.14). The adverse effects of UV radiation are primarily on the eye and the skin. Overexposure to the sun is the major identified environmental risk factor in skin cancer (Ferguson, 2005). At highest risk are Australia and New Zealand, although the incidence of malignant melanomas, with mortality rates of 25 per cent, have increased faster than any other cancer – even in Scotland where the incidence of melanoma for men tripled between 1980 and 2000 (British United Provident Association, 2002). Worldwide, the WHO estimates there are 132,000 new cases of malignant melanoma (the most dangerous form of skin cancer) and 66,000 deaths from this and other skin cancers each year. One in three cancers worldwide is

---

Box 7.14   Depletion of the ozone layer

Stratospheric ozone absorbs much of the incoming solar ultraviolet radiation (UVR) especially the biologically more damaging shorter-wavelength. Various halogenated chemicals such as the chlorofluorocarbons (used in refrigeration, insulation and spray can propellants) and methyl bromide, while inert at ambient Earth-surface temperatures, react with ozone in the extremely cold polar stratosphere. During the 1980s and 1990s the average year-round ozone concentration declined by around 4 per cent per decade at northern mid-latitudes and 6 to 7 per cent over the southern regions including Australia and New Zealand. Although estimating the resultant changes in actual ground-level ultraviolet radiation remains technically complex, exposures at northern mid-latitudes are likely to peak around 2020, with an estimated 10 per cent increase in effective ultraviolet radiation relative to 1980s levels. In the mid-1980s, governments recognized the emerging hazard from ozone depletion. The Montreal Protocol of 1987 was adopted, widely ratified, and the phasing out of major ozone-destroying gases began. The protocol was tightened in the 1990s (WHO, 2009a).

skin-related and in the USA that figure is one in two. Moreover, suppression of some aspects of immunity follows exposure to UV radiation and the consequences of this action for the immune control of infectious diseases, for vaccination and for tumours, are added concerns (Norval *et al.*, 2011).

Because Australia has the highest rate of skin cancer in the world, with exposure to ultraviolet radiation emitted by the sun being the primary cause, it is a significant public health issue. Thus, it has become a world leader in efforts to protect the ozone layer, the main line of defence against the ultraviolet radiation emitted by the sun. State cancer councils have developed sun safety and awareness campaigns, such as 'Slip! Slop! Slap!' and 'SunSmart', to educate the population about sun exposure and encourage early detection of skin cancers.

In addition to promoting cancer, burns, loss of elasticity, wrinkling and freckling of the skin, excess UV exposure can also harm the eyes and may compromise immune function. In terms of numbers, cataracts represent an even wider health threat. Some 20 million people worldwide are blinded by cataracts, with 20 per cent the result of UV exposure (WHO, 2008b). Because UVB exposure can be reduced by 90 per cent through a combination of the use of plastic lens glasses and a hat, this is one area where relatively straightforward strategies could easily be integrated in health promotion programmes such as that of Singapore to avert considerable health problems and costs. Ironically, however, there are major health benefits from exposure to sunshine and it is also implicated in protection against a wide range of diseases. Norval *et al.* (2011) argue that it is difficult to provide easily understandable public health messages regarding 'safe' sun exposure, so that the positive effects of vitamin D production are balanced against the negative effects of excessive exposure.

Environmental health policy

Alongside the health threats of long-term environmental changes, more immediate and localized conditions can have considerable adverse health consequences for exposed populations. Despite efforts to reduce their impact, air and water pollution levels remain high in many locales and continue to put large numbers of persons at risk. Respiratory problems in urban areas caused or aggravated by air pollution are also likely to be exacerbated by global warming and population concentration (Epstein, 2000). Drinking water systems are not only threatened by industrial and waste disposal contamination but also by the methods used for disinfecting them due to the toxic effects of the disinfectants and their by-products. The imminent breakdown of old and deteriorating water and sewage systems in some of the larger urban centres of many countries represents a growing health concern that requires urgent attention. Unfortunately, infrastructure funding in many countries has decreased as medical care consumes larger shares of state and local budgets.

All this is not to say that there have been no efforts to deal with environmental health problems. At the international level, many initiatives have followed the 1984 WHO 'Health for All' strategy (see page 186). Its definition of health as physical, mental and social well-being directed attention to the importance of the environment for promoting health. In 1989, the member states of the WHO's European region agreed on a 'European Charter on Environment and Health', which recognized the right to an environment conducive to health and the right to relevant information. In 1994, this was followed by an 'Environmental Action Plan for Europe' prepared by the WHO. The Plan calls for management instruments in environmental protection where this is relevant to health. The participating member states committed themselves to implementing the Plan through 'National Action Plans on Environment and Health' (WHO, Regional Office for Europe, 2003c).

The WHO also established the European Environment and Health Committee to support the implementation of the Action Plan (WHO, Regional Office for Europe, 2003a). The member states of the WHO European Region reconfirmed their commitment to earlier policies as part of the Fourth Ministerial Conference on Environment and Health in 2004 (WHO, Regional Office for Europe, 2004). The work of the Committee is complemented by the WHO Programme on Global Change and Health, which is concerned with assessing and monitoring the health impact of global environmental changes (WHO, Regional Office for Europe, 2003b). In 2008, WHO member states passed a World Health Assembly resolution identifying five priority areas relating to health vulnerability; health protection; health impacts of mitigation and adaptation policies; decision support and other tools; and the costs of health protection from climate change (Hosking and Campbell-Lendrum, 2012).

In 2009, the World Health Assembly endorsed a new WHO work plan focused on climate change and health that includes: advocacy to raise awareness that climate change is a fundamental threat to human health; partnerships to coordinate with partner agencies within the UN system and ensure that health is properly represented in the climate change agenda; science and evidence to coordinate reviews of the scientific evidence on the links between climate change and health and develop a global research agenda; and health system strengthening to assist countries to assess their health vulnerabilities and build capacity to reduce health vulnerability to climate change (WHO, 2010a).

Sweden considers environmental health an important issue and has had a pioneering role in environmental policies (Glenngård *et al.*, 2005). In Sweden, the municipalities are responsible for a wide range of areas of environmental health, including disease prevention, food quality, water management and chemical control. Municipalities are also experimenting with new forms of auditing and accounting as well as with new tariffs to improve environmental protection and food security. They were also at the forefront of implementing the UN's Local Agenda 21, a participatory process that targeted sustainable development, which includes health issues (Eckerberg *et al.*, 1998).

Public health: putting the medical model in perspective

There are considerable comparative data that demonstrate that the amount spent on medical care has little correlation with health improvement of populations or that medical care reduces health disparities (McGinnis *et al.*, 2002; Unal *et al.*, 2005; Kabir *et al.*, 2007; Lewis and Leeder, 2009). Medical care has a limited health effect, estimated to account at best for 10 to 15 per cent among the determinants of a nation's health (Isaacs and Schroeder, 2004). '[A]t the population level, more intensive use of supply-sensitive care – more frequent physician visits, hospitalizations, and stays in intensive care among the chronically ill – does not result in better health outcomes' (Center for the Evaluative Clinical Sciences, 2008). Although about half the decline of deaths from coronary heart disease are attributable to reductions in major risk factors and half to evidence-based medicine (Ford *et al.*, 2007), the proportion spent on medicine is about 30 times that of promotion. Moreover, health inequalities are associated heavily with the fundamental causes of health determinants such as the distribution of income and access to health-promoting resources (Rainham, 2007: 128). 'All the international evidence is that a health system oriented toward primary care achieves better health outcomes, lower rates of mortality and greater equity than a health system centred on hospitals' (Dragon, 2008: 20).

If the goal of health care is to improve the health of populations, then the heavy dependence on the medical model must be reassessed. Four decades ago, Ivan Illich (1976) vehemently criticized modern medicine as a nemesis and a cause, not a cure, of illness. Although Illich's critique of medicine problematically oversimplifies complex issues and was unduly severe, he raised many legitimate questions and forced placement of medicine in a social context. There is convincing support, for instance, for his conclusion that major improvements in health derive from changes in the way in which people live, not medical care. In fact, too much medicine is not good for health! Not only does it divert resources from more beneficial endeavours, but it also produces ill health and disrupts traditional social and cultural institutions and values that are central to good health in a broader sense. Medical misadventure contributes to many deaths each year, over 100,000 in the USA alone (Starfield, 2000). Likewise, the prevalence of inappropriate drug use is alarming. From 1996 to 2005, an elderly individual had a 19 per cent chance of being prescribed an inappropriate medication (Costa-Font and Toyama, 2011).

Health, itself, must be put into perspective with a wide array of requisites of a good life including art, entertainment, music and work, as well as family and social interaction. To place health above everything else risks underestimating the contribution of myriad other factors that lead to the fulfilment of our goals and the enhancement of the human condition. For Lamm (2003), we cannot live by health alone, but must also invest in education, infrastructure and other essential components. Satisfying health needs is vital, but human life has other worthy goals as well (Sade, 2007). Thus, it makes no sense to devote disproportionate amounts of societal resources to medicine at the expense of those things that make life worth living. 'No nation can continue to allow health care to drain away resources that would be more socially productive in education, the environment, security, and other policy areas' (Fuchs, 2007: 1544). It appears that while Western nations accept the notion that health is but one aspect of well-being at the personal level, as societies we expect the health care systems to resolve many problems that at their core are social, not medical, ones. The point here is not to undermine medical care, but rather to restore a proper balance between patient-centred and population-centred health care.

For Schroeder (2007), the largest potential for further improvement in population health lies in reducing behavioural risk factors, especially smoking and obesity. We already have the tools at hand to make progress in tobacco control, and some of these are applicable to obesity. For McGinnis *et al.* (2002), the determinants of health and their contribution to premature death are: behavioural patterns (40 per cent); genetic predisposition (30 per cent); social circumstances (15 per cent); environmental exposures (5 per cent); and, finally, health care (10 per cent). Importantly, while lack of health care accounts for only 10 per cent of premature deaths, it receives by far the greatest share of resources and attention. Thus, if the public's health is to improve it is more likely to come from change in the social and environmental conditions of life and behavioural change than from technological innovation. Moreover, because all the actionable determinants of health – personal behaviour, social factors, health care and the environment – disproportionately affect the poor, strategies to improve national health rankings must focus on the least well-off.

Implicit in the conventional medical model is the assumption that improved health status is tied to increased spending on medical care, but, as noted above, beyond a minimal threshold there is little correlation between how much money is spent on doctors and hospitals and how healthy a society is. Countries that expend the highest amounts on health do not score higher on health outcomes and, in fact, often do considerably less well. Table 7.4 dramatically illustrates this when the high-spending USA is compared to other OECD countries. The impact of medical care is also restrained because many health conditions are self-limiting, some are incurable and for many others there is little or no effective treatment.

Moreover, in those cases where health gains have been presumed to be the result of medical intervention, data indicate that medical technology has, in fact, not played the principal role. For instance, it has been estimated that at least two-thirds of the reduction in mortality rates during the 1970s and 98 per cent of the modest mortality rate improvement in the 1980s was tied to the reduction in death from cardiovascular disease. Under the medical model, the reduction in deaths from cardiovascular

Table 7.4   *Comparison of USA and OECD on selected health statistics, 2014*

	USA	OECD	USA ranking
Life expectancy at birth (years)	78.7	80.2	27 out of 34
Life expectancy at birth, men (years)	76.3	77.5	26 out of 34
Life expectancy at birth, women (years)	81.1	82.8	29 out of 34
Mortality from cardiovascular diseases (per 100 000 pop.)	261.2	296.4	17 out of 34
Mortality from cancer (per 100 000 pop.)	198.7	213.1	25 out of 34
Health expenditure as a percentage of GDP	16.9	9.3	1 out of 34
Health expenditure per capita (US$ PPP)	8745	3484	1 out of 34
Pharmaceutical expenditure per capita (US$ PPP)	1010	498	1 out of 34
Public expenditure as percentage of total health expenditure	47.6	72.3	34 out of 34

Source: OECD (2015).

disease is assumed to be the result of impressive innovations in treatment, especially coronary bypass surgery and angioplasty. However, evidence suggests that most, if not all, of this drop is attributable to lifestyle changes reflected in the decline in smoking, increase in exercise and decrease in saturated fat consumption (Kabir *et al.*, 2007; Lewis and Leeder, 2009).

These findings regarding the inability to explain health status by medical care alone have significant implications for any efforts to restructure the health care system. If a country really wants to achieve the goal of maximizing the health of its population, resources would better be directed towards alleviating poverty, reducing crime, changing lifestyles and so forth. A healthy person does not need medical care! According to Oliver (2011), a new paradigm, 'health in all policies', has generated a variety of models for the production of population health that: 1) recognize a broad range of social determinants of health and well-being; 2) highlight the impact of health inequalities on overall levels of population health; and 3) claim that responsibility for population health improvement rests not only with governmental health agencies and providers of health services, but also with individuals and organizations across the spectrum of society.

An emphasis on lifestyle must be accompanied by the recognition that systemic factors in the form of social relations, economic conditions, environmental hazards and a variety of public policies play as large a role, or an even larger role, in health outcomes than medicine (Fielding *et al.*, 2010; Lantz *et al.*, 2010). Health is improved or harmed by activities in many sectors of society including schools, businesses, housing, food systems, community design, law enforcement, transportation and the like. Simply increasing the funding for acute medical care, therefore, is not the answer to many contemporary 'health' issues. Lewis and Leeder argue that no level of spending or rates of increase in spending can solve problems of access, quality or equity. The natural experiment to test whether we can spend our way to excellence has failed because we mistook a structural and cultural problem for a financial shortfall:

> The only option is to reinvent the delivery of care and invest more effectively in the production of health. For the near future, no country can continue to paper over the cracks in health care with hundred dollar bills. Abundance neither eliminated the fundamental problems in health care delivery nor reduced health disparities. Perhaps relative deprivation will create the urgency and courage to achieve both. (2009: 272)

For instance, in implementing the NHI in Taiwan many assumed, and the public expected, that the health of the population would be greatly improved and that health disparities would be reduced. However, recent studies indicate that it had only minor impact in these two areas. Wen *et al.* (2008) conclude that while the NHI has had high utilization and enjoyed strong support from the public, overall it demonstrates minimal impact on the health of the population. Moreover, while disparities did narrow, this was very limited and major gaps remain. Similarly, Chen *et al.* (2007) conclude that while the NHI greatly increased the utilization both of inpatient and outpatient services, this increased consumption did not reduce mortality or lead to better self-perceived health status for the elderly. 'Relying on universal insurance alone to eliminate health disparity does not seem realistic. To further reduce health disparity, we believe universal health insurance programs should incorporate primary prevention, focusing on lifestyle risk reductions' (Wen *et al.*, 2008: 258).

On these grounds, many recent efforts to reform health care systems appear misguided because no amount of restructuring health care along the lines proposed by the various reformers will have a decisive impact on the health of their populations. Reforms for universal access, improved quality of care and cost containment might improve the medical care system, but they cannot be expected to improve public health substantially if there is no radical turn – or, indeed, a paradigm shift – in health policy reform to take greater account of population needs.

This chapter unmistakably demonstrates that our countries vary significantly in the extent to which they are meeting the widespread challenges inherent in public health but that most still have an arduous path before them. It also demonstrates that public health is in fact a global issue that ultimately requires international cooperation transcending national boundaries. Chapter 8 brings these themes together.

Chapter 8

Understanding Health Policy Comparatively

In analysing health policy in a comparative context, the preceding chapters have covered a wide range of topics including the historical and cultural trajectories of health policy; systems of funding, providing and governing health care; policies of allocating health resources; issues in the health care workforce; primary care and long-term care; and the wide-ranging areas that constitute public health. As in any cross-country comparison, a tension emerges between similarities and difference, between common policy trends, such as the ubiquity of rationing, and policy divergence, such as welfare mix in the provision of hospital services. In their study of 11 high-income countries, Tenbensel *et al.* similarly found significant 'islands of difference' in an overall 'sea of similarity' among the health policy agendas of the selected countries (2012: 29).

This brings us back to the question of what contribution analysis of a range of countries can make to our understanding of health policy. Comparison is about juxtaposing health systems and health policies across different countries. This allows us to get a better idea about the scope of variation that exists and helps to avoid both false particularism ('everywhere is special') and false universalism ('everywhere is the same') (Saltman, 2012). Importantly, exploration often leads to deeper questions about *why* it is we find differences and similarities. As such, comparison offers an important groundwork for explanation. Finally, comparison can also offer a basis for evaluation as a way of assessing the relative success and failure of specific health policies and offer a facilitator of policy learning. This is a salient promise of comparison although, unfortunately, the actual performance of comparative policy studies considerably lags behind its full potential (Marmor *et al.*, 2005). The first rationale is central to the analysis presented in the preceding chapters and the next section critically discusses the extent to which the concept of the health system helps to explain health policies (see also Burau and Blank, 2006). The following section extends the discussion and assesses the potential for policy learning based on evaluating health policies across different countries. In short, given *what* we found in our comparative analysis, this final chapter returns to the other two fundamental questions in comparative health policy, *how* and *why* we compare (Tuohy, 2012a, b).

Health systems and explaining health policies

As introduced in Chapter 1, the notion of different health systems, as ordered in a typology of health systems, has been central to the comparative turn in health policy analysis. The notion has been used to conceptualize the (institutional) context which shapes the politics and policies of health care (see, for example, Ham, 1997b; Raffel, 1997; Freeman, 2000; Scott, 2001; for an overview see Wendt *et al.*, 2009; Marmor and Wendt, 2011a, 2012; Wendt, 2014). Cross-country comparison generates an abundance of information, and ordering this information by using a typology of health systems is crucial to using comparison to review, build and revise explanations about health policy emergence and health policy making. Against this background, the following analysis critically discusses two things: the importance of institutional embeddedness beyond the health system and the use of the concept of the health system in relation to non-medical health policies. The key issue here is whether the concept of the health system helps us to discover how countries vary (or are similar) in the health policies they adopt and whether we can gain insights into why these differences (or similarities) exist.

Health systems and institutional embeddedness

Table 8.1 maps out our countries using the typology of health systems introduced in Chapter 1 as a basis, but it also defines in more detail different aspects of government involvement in the funding and provision of health care emerging from the discussion in subsequent chapters. The institutions of governing the funding of health care are concerned with the mechanisms by which individual patients have access to services (such as social citizenship and earned insurance entitlements) and the mechanisms that decide on the total volume of resources allocated to the financing of health care (such as governing through public management and setting regulatory frameworks). In contrast, the institutions of governing the provision of health care include the mechanisms for regulating hospitals (such as the amount of public regulation and the mix of differently owned hospitals) and the regulation of doctors and broader healthcare workforce (especially different forms of private interest government). This reflects the centrality of hospitals and doctors for the provision of health care, but acknowledges that significant action occurs beyond hospitals and doctors.

Table 8.1   *Health systems and their policies*

	Governance of funding • *Extent of public access to health care* • *Extent of public control of total health care costs*	*Governance of provision* • *Extent of public control of hospitals*[1] • *Extent of constraints on private inter- est government of doctors*[2]
National health service • Extensive public access, high public control of costs • High public control of hospitals, highly constrained private interest government of doctors	Britain, Sweden Australia (access/ control) Japan (cost control) New Zealand (access) Netherlands (cost control) Singapore (cost control)	Britain, Sweden New Zealand
Social insurance systems • De facto public access, moderate public control of costs • Moderate public control of hospitals, some constraints on private interest government of doctors	Germany, Taiwan Japan (access) Netherlands (access) New Zealand (cost control)	Germany, Taiwan Australia Japan Netherlands Singapore
Private insurance system • Limited public access, low public control of costs • Little public control of hospitals, few constraints on private interest government of doctors	**USA** Singapore (access)	**USA**

[1] Share of hospitals in public ownership with degree of public regulation used as a proxy for extent of public control of hospitals.

[2] Share of publicly employed (hospital) doctors together with degree of professional self-regulation used as a proxy for extent of constraints on self-government of doctors.

Looking at the health systems in these countries across the differ-ent types and respective dimensions of governing health care, several findings stand out. Only five out of the ten countries included in the study fully fit one of the three types of health system (Britain, Sweden, Germany, Taiwan and the USA). In contrast, the remaining countries are only approximations of the individual ideal types. This highlights the fact that the institutional contexts of the governing of health care are more complex than suggested by the definition of the health system. Instead, institutional contexts are often highly specific in terms of how individual aspects combine themselves in individual countries. Such specificities also point to additional aspects of institutional context. Consequently, within a country the two sets of institutions associated with the governance of funding may fit different types of health systems thus making categorization problematic. The same problem might also apply to the comparison of the governance of funding and provision. Moreover, the inclusion of low- and middle-income countries to the mix confuses things even further, and this is also true for the inclusion of the human resources for health as an increasingly relevant field of health policy and governance.

Under the typology, public control of the total resources allocated to health care can be expected to be highest in national health services with access to health care based on social citizenship and lowest in private insurance systems where access to health care is based on private insurance, with public control in social insurance health systems lying in between. This is true for four of our countries, but the picture is more complex in the remaining six countries, again pointing to the importance of country-specific institutional contexts. In Australia, for example, federalism combined with the legacy of the private insurance systems weakens government authority over funding (Palmer and Short, 2000). In contrast, the unitary political system in Japan helps to concentrate authority in the hands of central government (Campbell and Ikegami, 2008). Despite significant decentralization of health services and insurance plans, for example, all billing and payment in Japan is centralized through the payment fund of National Health Insurance.

The Netherlands and Singapore are particularly interesting examples of how country-specific institutional contexts shape the public control of health care costs, thus making differences among countries particularly pertinent. In the Netherlands, the high public control of funding reflects the unusual combination of social insurance with strong universalist elements (for an overview, see Maarse, 1997; Exter *et al.*, 2004; Kroeneman *et al.*, 2016). Health funding combines a considerable diversity of sources, including private insurance for acute medical risks, and compulsory social insurance contributions to cover exceptional medical risks. This reflects the historical legacy of a society segmented into different groupings and the gradual weakening of this legacy in the Netherlands. The semi-federal political system also helps to concentrate authority in the hands of the central government, and, in contrast to Germany, corporatism is confined to the national level.

In Singapore, country-specific institutional contexts are such that public control is strong not only in relation to health care costs but also to other key aspects of health care (for an overview, see Barr, 2001; Ham, 2010; Mossialos *et al.*, 2016). Tight government control of funding coexists with a strong focus on individual responsibility and limited familial risk pooling. Health care is funded in part by individual savings accounts that are compulsory. The government also caps contribution rates, while out-of-pocket payments are high. As such, Singapore defies the dictum that private funding is unlikely to make for public control. The strength of government control reflects not only the spatial concentration of political power typical of city-states, but also a strongly centralized approach to health policy. Government education programmes are aimed at lowering the demand for health care and emphasize the importance of primary health care and prevention over hospital care. Not surprisingly, public health policies are strong, and the government heavily subsidizes health promotion and disease prevention programmes that emphasize the responsibility of the individual to look after his or her own health.

The importance of country-specific institutional contexts also applies, though to a lesser extent, when comparing the governance of funding and provision. Singapore, as mentioned above, has a centrally controlled health system but one based on individual savings accounts that give the impression of minimal government control over funding. Thus, it crosses the line between a social insurance and a private insurance health system. Furthermore, Singapore gives those persons with sufficient Medisave account balances considerable freedom of choice as to public and private doctors and hospitals as well as allowing them to purchase private insurance with their account should they so desire. While provision best fits a private insurance health system, a large proportion of health care is provided in publicly owned hospitals by government-set salaried doctors. Despite this, there are few controls on medical intervention in Singapore because in the end individuals have the choice of what services to use with their compulsory but private accounts.

The analysis suggests two things. First, the ideal type of the health system holds as an approximation of 'real' health systems. It is, therefore, a classical ideal type that is useful as a heuristic device that simplifies the complex real world of governing health care (following Weber, 1949). Thereby, the concept of the health system helps to move the analysis beyond the specificity of individual cases and towards more generalized observations, overcoming a salient tension inherent in comparative enquiry (Goodin and Smitsman, 2000). The health system as an ideal type, therefore, does not need to fit the real types completely to be useful.

Second, it is important to remember that it is primarily through the comparison and contrast with real types that explanations can be advanced (see Arts and Glissen, 2002). The central question, then, is how to explain the extent to which 'real' health systems do or do not fit the ideal types. The different degrees of 'misfits' among these countries and the types of health systems presented in the analysis raise many such 'why' questions. In turn, this underlines the fact that the concept of the health system indeed only provides a starting point for a comparative analysis and must be complemented by additional, more specific, institutional explanations. The importance of a detailed study of institutional contexts is well recognized in the comparative study of health policy (see, for example, Döhler, 1991; Immergut, 1992; Wilsford, 1994; Burau *et al.*, 2015).

Significantly, then, there is institutional embeddedness beyond the health system (more generally on this point see Burau, 2012). As the analysis of our countries suggests, governing health care is embedded in institutional contexts that are broader than those institutions making up the health system, and institutional contexts that are often also highly specific to individual countries. Our analysis, for example, points to the importance of the specific characteristics of political systems (such as federalism in Australia), social structures (such as the legacy of societal pillars in the Netherlands) and social values (such as the high degree of individual self-reliance in Singapore). The governing of health care reflects specific configurations of these different aspects of institutional context, all of which are changeable over time. Therefore, more often than not, health policies follow trajectories that are highly complex and specific.

Similarly, in her comparative analysis of health reform Tuohy (2012b; also Schmid *et al.*, 2010) points to the emergence of distinct national hybrids in Britain and the Netherlands, reflecting politics of redesign driven by institutional entrepreneurs. In a similar vein, Saltman (2012) highlights the softening of boundaries of health systems, especially between public and private provision, between social insurance and tax funding and between individual and collective responsibility. In contrast, Freeman and Frisina (2012), in their review of the use of typologies of comparative health policy, stress that classification, although highly problematic, remains integral to comparison. Instead, the authors call for a better understanding of how health systems work, using typologies as a first step (also see Denis and Forest, 2012).

Generally, the 'blind spots' of the available typologies and classification schemes are most obvious when looking at new emergent areas of health care provision and health care governance that have previously been at the margins of health systems. Examples of these are the establishment of a long-term care sector as observed in resource-rich countries (Campbell *et al.*, 2016) which questions the boundaries between health and social care, and between formal and informal care. Similarly, as the human resources for health gained momentum in health policy and brought the importance of middle-level professions and new role of nurses into perspective, the focus on the medical profession is no longer sustainable (Campbell *et al.*, 2013; WHO, 2015b). These developments clearly challenge the classic typologies but at the same time they embody new opportunities for a more fine-grained analysis of institutional contexts and for the development of more inclusive frameworks for comparative analysis.

Health systems and non-medical health policies

The analysis above suggests that the institutional context of governing health care itself is highly complex. This echoes Freeman's (2000) observation that the organization of health care is not very systematic. The complex historical emergence of policies of health care often defies the order implied by the notion of a *system*. Consequently, the health system perspective may be looking for order where there is little. Instead, the institutional context of governing health care is highly differentiated, to the extent that such contexts are often somewhat specific to individual countries. Importantly, there is also specificity in relation to sub-sectors of health care and policy. This is particularly apparent in relation to those sub-sectors that have traditionally been at the margins of the 'health system', such as long-term care, but that are increasingly relevant to health policy. Focusing on home and community-based health care as an example, this section assesses the use of the notion of the health system for capturing the institutions central to non-medical health care and for explaining such 'new' health policies across countries.

Debates about ageing populations and their implications for health care costs and services have put long-term community-based and home health care on the health policy agenda. At the international level it is indicative, for example, that long-term care for elderly people was one of the components of a major OECD Health Project (OECD, 2005a). The OECD Health Project echoes developments across the countries included in our study in which there are many examples of major policy initiatives relating to home and community-based health care (see, for example, Jenson and Jacobzone, 2000; Burau *et al.*, 2007). Such policies often aim at the expansion of existing services to support informal care givers by integrating home and community-based health care into the regular organization of health care. The expansion of social insurance in Germany and Japan are indicative examples. Starting in the late 1980s, the government in Japan introduced a publicly funded scheme, the so-called Gold Plan, to expand care services for older people. The scheme was extended in the late 1990s and in effect became a separate branch of social insurance, funded by a mixture of social insurance premiums and taxes. Considering the traditional strength of family responsibility for care of the elderly, this is a significant policy development (Furuse, 1996).

This emergence of non-medical-based health care raises the question of how policies related to long-term care fit into the concept of the health system. The concept focuses on institutions and policies related to medical care. In contrast, home and community-based health care is located on two sets of interfaces: between formal and informal care, and between health and social care. In relation to the first aspect, it is indicative that few older people receive home nursing care and even when they do it only accounts for a small share of their care. Instead, home care predominantly means unpaid (informal) care by women and often also includes social care, such as help with domestic tasks. This reflects not only the inadequacy of existing home nursing services, but also the fact that many of the health care needs of older people are often not principally medically related.

This also places many limitations on using the concept of the health system for capturing the institutions governing home and community-based health care and for explaining corresponding health policies. The institutions related to the governance of funding are relevant to the extent that home and community-based health care is part of the organization of medical health care. Traditionally, parts of long-term care have by default been funded by the same scheme as medical health care. At the same time, parallel funding schemes relating to social care have existed. In Germany, for example, before the introduction of long-term care insurance, funding for home and community-based health care came from both health insurance and locally funded social assistance schemes. In many cases this organizational division continues and applies to the newly established schemes. This also applies to Japan, whereas in Australia, New Zealand, the Netherlands and Sweden funding of home and community-based long-term care is integrated. Furthermore, there tends to be formal or de facto limits to the scope of collective consumption. Instead private consumption in the form of private payments for formal services and informal care paid by lost income are important complementary aspects of consumption. The last aspect even applies to countries like Sweden, where the level of publicly funded services is relatively high.

There are even more extensive limitations in relation to applying the definitions of the governance of provision. Hospitals as settings of care provision and doctors as providers of care are of little importance. Instead, care workers such as community nurses, care assistants and social workers together with informal carers, all working in home and community settings, are central for the provision of this type of health care. Taken together this suggests that shared values and beliefs (and corresponding practices) are important for understanding non-medical health policies. Freeman and Ruskin (1999) refer to this as 'cultural embeddedness' and thereby point to diversity beyond the macro level and, notably, a type of diversity that is shaped by organizational bases that are ethnic, gendered, local and personal, rather than national and public.

Where does this leave capturing institutional arrangements as they apply to long-term health care and explaining corresponding non-medical health policies across our countries? The concept of the health system is of some use, notably to the extent to which long-term care is part the organization of medical health care. However, beyond that, using the concept of the health system has clear limits, as some institutions do not have the same importance, whereas others not included in the definition are central for understanding non-medical health policies. Instead, different aspects of institutional context need to be taken into consideration. This requires two things: first, redefining the institutions related to the governing of funding and provision to reflect the specific characteristics of long-term care (and, where applicable, across the health and social care divide); and second, to include gender as a set of social and cultural institutions. In this respect Pfau-Effinger's (2004) concept of 'gender arrangements' is particularly useful. The concept consists of two components. Gender order describes existing structures of gender relations not least as reflected in gendered divisions of labour. Gender culture for its part refers to deeply embedded beliefs and ideas about the relations between the generations in the family and the obligations associated with such relations.

Against this background one way forward would be to combine the different, yet complementary, aspects of institutional context discussed above as part of an 'organizing framework'. In the context of their study of multilevel governance Bache and Flinders (2004) define this as an analytical framework that provides a map of how things relate and that leads to a set of research questions. The value of such an approach is that it helps to explore complex issues and identifies interesting areas for further research.

Possibilities and limitations for cross-national learning

The discussion above concerning the extent to which the typology of health systems helps to explain health policy suggests three things. First, modelled on paradigmatic cases the concept of the health system holds as an ideal type. Second, as such the health system provides a useful springboard for the analysis of health policy, but one that needs to be complemented by more specific institutional explanations. Third, the concept of the health system is less applicable to increasingly important, non-medical areas of health policy. Instead, different aspects of institutional context come into play and they can be combined as part of a looser 'organizing framework'.

Nevertheless, cross-country comparison remains an attractive strategy for social enquiry, not least as it can also provide a basis for identifying the variety of policy options that exist in health policy. As such, comparison holds the implicit promise of learning from other countries and their policy successes and failures. Health policy learning occurs naturally as information about other countries has become more readily available as part of the process of globalization. Policy learning is also explicitly encouraged by international organizations, such as the OECD and the WHO, when they disseminate information about health systems and reforms in different countries. Policy learning, therefore, is becoming more explicitly transnational and global agendas for health reform increasingly are setting the scene for 'local' health policies. For example, this is what the development in primary health care as described in Chapter 6 suggests. Here, a strong transnational model of reform has created a variety of national models with highly diverse institutional characteristics ranging from differences in funding schemes to providers and staffing levels and skill mixes (Gauld, 2015; Groenewegen *et al.*, 2015; Maier, 2015). Similarly, in relation to tobacco control, Farquharson (2003) highlights the existence of global advocacy networks that either promote or oppose tobacco, and their importance for shaping domestic policies.

To policy makers, cross-country comparison and the opportunity to identify which health policy/system works 'best' is attractive for several reasons. Looking at other countries offers a virtual 'test' of different policy options and as such promises 'evidence-based' policy making, policy innovation and, above all, policy success (Stone, 1999; Klein, 2009). This is particularly attractive in times of crisis, which are often rooted in a sense of converging policy problems and possible solutions, as it triggers a search for new policy ideas (Marmor *et al.*, 2005; Cortez, 2008a)

However, there are various models of policy learning as Freeman (2005, 2006) argues, two of which are particularly relevant in the present context. First, policy learning as transfer is based on a rationalist conception that policy input and policy output relate to each other as cause and effect. Policy learning emerges as an instrumental process that is based on evidence. In other words, policy makers learn in order to address specific problems and policies easily transfer from one country to another. In contrast and second, policy learning as transplant is based on an institutionalist perspective and governments are seen to show different capacities for learning. The process of learning itself is related to experience and experiment. In other words, policy makers learn in an iterative way through trial and error, and the travel of policies from one country to the next is contingent upon there being a special institutional context.

The work of the OECD and its OECD Health Project powerfully represents a model of policy learning that is based on transfer. Indeed, this view is widespread among policy practitioners and analysts (Russell *et al.*, 2008). For example, in the foreword to the final report, the

Director-General of the OECD stresses that the Project offers a means for member countries to learn from each other, drawing on 'the best expertise' that exists (OECD, 2005a: 3). Consequently, the report lists goals of health systems as generic to health policy and which, as such, are applicable across different countries. Similarly, the report presents policy initiatives in individual countries as equally possible policy options. In short, this is about evaluating health reforms to identify best practice for transfer, where the capacity of governments to learn is assumed.

Health System Performance Assessment (HSPA)

HSPA is the process of monitoring, evaluating and communicating to what extent various aspects of a health system meet key objectives. The central purpose of HSPA is to assess whether progress is being made towards desired goals and whether appropriate activities are undertaken to promote achievement of those goals. HSPA, therefore, can help states monitor and evaluate their own performance and build the evidence base on the relationship among the structure, organization and content of health systems and performance. Health system performance acknowledges the broad range of determinants of population health that are not directly related to health care service delivery. As emphasized here, it recognizes that the health status of a population is only partly influenced by the availability of health care services, and that there are many other social, cultural, political, economic, environmental, educational and demographic factors influencing population health.

In the late 1990s, the WHO launched a major effort to establish a common conceptual framework for HSPA to foster the development of tools to measure its components and work with countries in applying these tools to measure and then improve their health system's performance. The first milestone in this project was the publication of *The World Health Report 2000* (WHO, 2000) which established an outcome-focused framework to use regularly over time and across member states. The WHO committed to measuring and reporting HSPA for all 191 Member States and to compile a report on the performance of each health system every two years. The WHO framework focuses attention on outcomes, particularly inequalities in health, responsiveness and financial contributions. It also has the potential to help policy makers identify opportunities for improving health systems performance by increasing coverage of effective interventions through moderating financing, resource generation, service provision and stewardship (Murray and Evans, 2003). However, comprehensive, recurring application of the framework at the national and subnational levels is needed to expand the evidence base that can be used to share knowledge and experience on what works and what does not (Box 8.1).

Box 8.1 Key characteristics of HSPA

There are five key characteristics for adequately applying the concept of HSPA. HSPA should be:

Regular: Assessing the performance of a health system is a continuous and iterative process.

Systematic: The approach should be structured and consistent.

Transparent: The assessment must be clear, unambiguous and understandable for others.

Comprehensive: The whole system should be covered. Moreover, the performance of a system does not simply equal the sum of the performance of its various components.

Analytical: Complementary sources of information should be consulted to obtain a comprehensive and well-founded overview of the health system's performance. Quantitative indicators must be supported by qualitative insights, and performance indicators by a policy analysis. HSPA is a comparative evaluation, and the reference points for comparison must be chosen wisely. Some relevant reference points for comparison could be: developments over time; local, regional, national, or international differences; differences among population groups (e.g. based on age, gender, income, SES etc.); and comparisons to certain targets or benchmarks (European Public Health, 2016).

The WHO report generated enormous interest but also triggered a political debate related to the estimates of country-level performance and, especially, the associated league tables. Since then, the WHO European and Eastern Mediterranean Regional Offices have maintained health system observatories, with detailed descriptions of their country systems. In developed countries, primary concerns include costs, quality of care, ageing and chronic diseases. However, in developing countries, health system constraints have restricted progress towards the UN Millennium Development Goals (Boerma *et al.*, 2009). Moreover, while the methods and measures needed to assess progress and performance of specific health programmes are firmly grounded, assessment of the extent to which health systems achieve their goals remains less developed. An increasing number of countries conduct self-assessments of their performance, mostly performed by government-funded research institutes in partnership with academic institutions. For instance, the Netherlands publishes a Dutch health care performance report every four years, focusing on quality, access and costs using more than 100 indicators (Van den Berg *et al.*, 2014).

In addition to the challenges of developing indicators and analytical methods, the availability and quality of core data on basic health system building blocks remains a challenge especially in low-income countries. The key issues in health systems of high-income countries tend to revolve around containing costs while maintaining high-quality services, in an environment of advancing technology and high expectations from the society. In low- and some middle-income countries, however, the priority is increasing geographical and package coverage of basic services within the context of marked needs and minimal funding. According to Tashobya *et al.* (2014), however, low-income countries seeking to develop/adjust HSPA frameworks need not reinvent the wheel: it is possible for them to learn from literature and the experience of HSPA in other contexts, including high-income countries.

Determining the 'best' health system

The analysis presented in the preceding chapters, however, challenges the model of policy learning which assumes that identifying what is 'best' and transferring what is 'best' from one country to another is straight-forward. The complexity of health systems and policies in different countries emerging from our analysis suggests otherwise. Health policy making is not necessarily rationalist, driven by knowledge and evidence, but instead constitutes a struggle over ideas and values (Russell *et al.*, 2008). There are many definitions of what are 'best' health policies/systems, and transferring 'best practice' across countries is difficult because health policies are deeply embedded in country-specific contexts. For instance, in their study of Taiwan, Korea, Japan and Singapore, Blank and Cheng (2015) suggest that, even when seeking to emulate seemingly successful policies of these health systems, policy makers must be cautious, because what works in one cultural environment might not work in another. They conclude, however, that low- and middle-income countries in Asia, especially, might gain valuable lessons from these four health care systems.

Health policy making is a complex process. Chapter 4 identifies equity/access, quality and cost containment/efficiency as the central goals of health policy. These three goals represent different and potentially competing ideas about what is the 'best' health policy/system. This makes learning from other countries a value-laden exercise, further complicated by the fact that different actors in health care have different ideas of what is 'best'. Thus, what is the 'best' health policy/system also depends on whom you ask. Importantly, the institutional set-up of different health systems means that actors enjoy different degrees of power. For example, providers are often particularly influential in private insurance systems, as the example of the USA demonstrates, whereas their power is more limited in national health services, as the example of the UK suggests. The same applies to patients whose power varies widely across systems.

As Figure 8.1 suggests, there are four sets of actors in health care: users, payers (including both third-party payers and the public), providers and the state. As noted above, the different actors in health care often support different goals of health policy and as such have conflicting ideas about what the 'best' health system or policy is. Payers are primarily concerned with cost containment and efficiency, whereas for providers the quality of health care is the key. In contrast, the goal orientation of the public is ambivalent; as patients, the public put quality and access/equality first, whereas as payers the public has a predominant interest in cost containment/efficiency. Importantly, the different actors in health care may also have different ideas about the same goal. For users of health care, quality means a well-funded health system that allows for patient choice and fast access to medical technology. This definition of quality is shared by providers of health care, who also emphasize the importance of autonomy in the provision of health care services. In contrast, states are more likely to highlight the population health aspects of quality.

The discussion above suggests that health policies/systems are 'best' in relation to specific goals, and that the importance attached to the individual goals (and ideas about what is 'best') varies widely among different actors in health care. Figure 8.2 offers an overview of the 'best' health systems in relation to the goals of quality, equity/access and cost containment/efficiency for our countries. It also includes several definitions (or indicators) of each health policy goal. Considering the complexity of health care this overview uses selected indicators and examples and does not claim to be comprehensive (some HSPAs include over 100 indicators).

| | | **Actors in Health Care** | | | |
		Users	*Payers*	*Providers*	*The State*
Goals of Health Policy	Quality	X		X	X
	Equity/Access	X		X	
	Cost Containment/ Efficiency		X		X

Figure 8.1   *The goal orientation of actors in health care*

Quality
Defined as ...

Level of health care spending (percentage of GDP)	*High*: USA, Sweden, Japan, Germany *Medium*: Netherlands, Britain, New Zealand, Australia *Low*: Singapore, Taiwan
Speed of access to medical technology	*Fast*: USA, Germany, Taiwan *Medium*: Singapore, Sweden, Japan, New Zealand *Slow*: Britain, Netherlands
Doctors and nurses per 1,000 population	*High:* Germany, Sweden, Australia *Medium:* Netherlands, New Zealand, Japan *Low*: Britain, Taiwan, Singapore, USA
Extent of patient choice	*High*: Taiwan, Singapore, USA *Medium*: Germany, Sweden, Australia, Japan *Low*: Britain, Netherlands, New Zealand
Commitment to public health	*High*: Singapore, Sweden, New Zealand *Medium:* Australia, Netherlands, Japan *Low*: Britain, Germany, Taiwan, USA

Access/equity
Defined as ...

Public funding of health care (percentage of total expenditure)	*High*: Germany, Japan, Sweden, Netherlands *Medium*: Britain, New Zealand *Low*: Australia, Taiwan, Singapore, USA
Coverage of population	*High*: Britain, Sweden, Japan, Taiwan, New Zealand *Medium:* Australia, Germany, Netherlands, Singapore *Low*: USA

Cost containment/efficiency
Defined as ...

Control of costs	*High (direct budget control)*: Britain, Japan, New Zealand, Sweden, Taiwan *Medium (contractual control)*: Germany, Netherlands, Australia *Low (decentralized, market-oriented systems)*: USA
Supply-side rationing	*High (national health services)*: Britain, New Zealand, Sweden *Medium*: Germany, Japan, Netherlands, Australia *Low (market-based health systems)*: Singapore, Taiwan, USA

Figure 8.2 *Identifying 'best' health systems*

Quality of health care is often measured in terms of the financial resources spent on health care. Based on the measure of the percentage of GDP spent on health care, the USA and the Netherlands are the 'best' health systems. Other measures of quality relate to the technical and human resources of health systems such as the speed of access to medical technology and the number of doctors, respectively. Subsidiary policy goals are patient choice and commitment to public health. The assumption is that the more money spent, the better the technical and human resources of health systems. Countries such as Germany and Britain support this assumption, although the relationship among different indicators of quality is far more complex than this. For example, while the health system in Singapore ranks very low in terms of the level of health care spending and the number of doctors, quality in terms of the extent of patient choice and commitment to public health is high. Similarly, Taiwan ranks low in both the number of doctors and the commitment to public health but high in patient choice and access to new technologies. Other cases highlight the trade-offs among various indicators of quality. Germany, for example, does very well on all indicators except commitment to public health, suggesting that quality is primarily defined as high-tech medical care.

The share of health care expenditure coming from public sources is an important indicator of equity/access in health systems. Public funding in the form of taxes or social insurance contributions is founded on the principles of universality and social solidarity, respectively, and as such makes for universal or near universal (and in principle equitable) access to health care. On this count, Sweden, Germany, the Netherlands and Japan are the three 'best' health systems, whereas Singapore and the USA are among the 'worst'. Here, low coverage means that a significant proportion of the population is excluded from what is otherwise a very 'high quality' health system.

Such trade-offs also exist between the policy goals of cost containment/efficiency and quality. The extent of control of costs is an important indicator of cost containment and here the 'best' health systems are those characterized by tight control over costs. Direct budget control, such as in Britain, Japan, New Zealand, Sweden, and Taiwan, allows for greatest cost control, followed by contractual control as it exists in Germany and the Netherlands. Cost control is weakest in decentralized, market-oriented systems such as Australia (until recently) and the USA. Health systems with extensive cost controls also make greater use of supply-side rationing. However, this comes at the price of quality in terms of the level of health care spending (such as in Japan), speed of access to medical technology (such as in Britain) and the extent of patient choice (such as in New Zealand). The inverse is also true. In the USA and Germany, high quality in terms of level of health care spending and fast access to medical technology come at the price of low to medium control of costs.

Identifying the 'best' health system/policy is a highly complex process that depends on what is defined as 'best': that is, which policy goal is considered most important. In an ideal world, all three goals would be equally important. However, because health care resources are ultimately limited, the different policy goals, in effect, compete against each other. The emphasis put on individual goals and definitions of what is the 'best' health policy/system varies over time as well as among countries. This reflects historical trajectories and the health systems in individual countries together with the balance of power among the different actors in the health care arena.

As such, and as suggested by the institutionally based, transplant approach to policy learning, the lessons policy makers want to learn from other countries also vary among individual health systems, not the least because health systems have different policy agendas (Tenbensel *et al.*, 2012). Lesson learning is not necessarily a politically neutral process, but the value of policy lessons lies precisely in their power to bias policy choice (Stone, 1999; Marmor *et al.*, 2005). For instance, while HSPAs can be an important potential driver of health system improvement, even the blunt presentation of league tables is not likely to routinely lead to appropriate changes by policy makers (Papanicolas and Cylus, 2015). Lesson learning is politically motivated and selective and is often used to substantiate already made policy choices.

Here, Britain is an indicative example. In response to the perceived funding crisis of the British NHS in the late 1980s, the government looked towards the USA and its models of managed care. The strong market orientation of the US health system resonated with the neo-liberal outlook of the Conservative government of the time. The focus on the organization of health services also helped to avoid the politically sensitive issue of making changes to the way in which the NHS was funded. Similarly, in their analysis of the introduction of DRGs across countries, Gilardi *et al.* (2009) observe that introduction is most likely where existing policy is considered ineffective and where experiences from other countries suggest the achievement of desired results. In their study of how quasi-market mechanisms become incorporated into national contexts, Hassenteufel *et al.* (2010) also underscore the importance of actors, notably small groups of 'programmatic actors' like politicians, civil servants and medical doctors.

Moreover, there are only certain lessons policy makers in individual countries can learn, and this points to the limits of transferring 'best practice'. As Chapter 2 emphasizes, health policies are embedded in highly specific historical, cultural and political contexts, and any policy success is ultimately tied to a specific place and point in time. Irrespective of political will, not all policies work everywhere. Successful lesson learning is both about the substance of policies and about the circumstances in which policies succeed (Klein, 1997; Marmor *et al.*, 2009a). For instance, the New Zealand government's attempts to introduce partial charges for users for hospital care in the early 1990s were inspired by a series of reports by US-based health care consultants; but they failed. The policy engendered strong opposition not only from the public but also from the health care professions, which forced the government to withdraw the policy. A possible explanation is that the success of this policy was predicated on a health system that puts great emphasis on individual responsibility (as in the USA) rather than public responsibility (as in New Zealand). The relative match with institutional contexts is even less likely in relation to developing countries and as McPake (2002) demonstrates in relation to hospital reform and the introduction of co-payments, inadequate contextualization of policies can impose serious costs and be even worse than the absence of change.

The complexity and contingency of identifying 'best practice' and cross-country learning in health policy does not mean that it cannot or should not be done. Instead, cross-country learning requires sensitivity, notably in two respects. Cross-country learning requires sensitivity towards different and potentially competing ideas about what are the 'best' health policies/systems. There is no single, universally applicable definition of what is 'best', but rather there are as many definitions as there are goals of health policy. Some health systems are particularly successful in relation to cost containment/efficiency, whereas others score highly on quality as measured in terms of levels of spending and access to medical technology. Importantly, there are trade-offs between different goals of health policy, and health systems are unlikely to be 'best' in respect of all policy goals. Which health policies are considered 'best' and worthy of lesson learning is ultimately a political decision.

Nevertheless, cross-country learning also requires sensitivity towards the specific contexts under which policies succeed (Klein, 2009). Indeed, this is one of the major conclusions from the experiences with an on-call facility for health care policy that the UK government created to facilitate learning from other countries (Nolte *et al.*, 2008). Okma (2008; also see Rovere and Barua, 2012) makes a similar observation in her commentary on the US interest in recent Dutch health reforms, while Or and colleagues (2010) argue that the heterogeneity in organizational design and governance within and across health systems makes it highly unlikely that a 'copy and paste' approach to health reform is effective. Rather, as Kirkpatrick and colleagues (2011, 2016) show in relation to the adoption of medical manager roles in European health systems, this involves extensive translation not least at the level of the organization. Such a process is shaped by a range of aspects surrounding institutional context, including the characteristics of hospital governance regimes and the position of the medical profession, as well as the timing/process of health management reform.

Contribution to the comparative study of health policy

In many respects the analysis presented in this book has covered familiar ground. Analyses of health systems, doctors and health reform are central topics in the comparative study of health policy. What, then, does this book contribute to the debate? The contribution of the present analysis lies in the range of countries and policy issues covered. The breadth of the analysis results in a relatively comprehensive map within which specific health policies in individual countries can be located. As such, the analysis offers a basis for more in-depth analyses of a wide range of more specific cases that vary in terms both of countries and policy issues.

The map is based on an analysis that covers a diverse range of countries from the pioneers of publicly funded health systems (such as Germany and Sweden) to health systems that put individual responsibility first (such as Singapore and the USA) and hybrids (such as Australia and Taiwan); from health systems embedded in Western capitalist democracies to health systems embedded in Asian political systems; and from large health systems such as America's which covers 330 million people to small health systems such as New Zealand's which covers only 4.5 million people. The map is also based on an analysis that includes a diverse range of health policy issues including basic ones such as the funding and provision of health care, health policy issues that are high on the political agenda such as those relating to the allocation of health care resources increasingly also including the health workforce as the human capital, and health policy issues that are located on the margins of the health systems such as home care and public health. However, no matter how inclusive, such a loose framework has its own limitations. As Mabbett and Bolderson (1999) argue, the deconstruction of broad-brush categorizations and typologies makes all-encompassing, cross-country comparison and contrast more difficult.

Nevertheless, by offering a comprehensive map in which specific health policies in individual countries can be located, the analysis presented in this book contributes to the comparative study of health policy in another way. The map offers one way of moving away from the notion that health policies across countries are either different or similar and that they will either continue to be embedded in country-specific contexts or will be submerged by convergence. Over time, health policies across countries will be both different and similar in differing degrees and in different respects. Adopting a map also means embracing complexity, exploring differences in health policy within the same country, and analysing the interfaces with other, related policies. In short, using a map acknowledges the existence of similarities within differences and differences within similarities, and acknowledges that health policy includes more than just health systems. Although this more complex and dynamic view of health policy might lack the comfort that comes with the typology of health systems, the analysis in the earlier chapters demonstrates that it better reflects the real world of health care and its diverse actors.

Glossary

Acute care: Medical treatment rendered to people whose illnesses or medical problems are short term or don't require long-term continuing care. Acute care facilities are hospitals that mainly treat people with short-term health problems.

Ambulatory care: All health services delivered outside hospitals (that is, in primary care settings).

Capitation fee: A payment system based on a fixed pre-payment, per patient, paid to a health care provider to deliver medical services to a specific group of patients. The payment is the same no matter how many services or what type of services each patient receives.

Chronic illnesses: Health problems that are long term and continuing. Nursing homes, mental hospitals and rehabilitation facilities are examples of chronic care facilities.

Clinical guidelines: Carefully developed information on diagnosing and treating specific medical conditions. Guidelines are usually based on clinical literature and expert consensus, are designed to help physicians make decisions and to help funding organizations evaluate appropriateness and medical necessity of care.

Coordinated and integrated services: Delivery of systematic, responsive and supportive care to people with complex needs, for example chronic illness. Coordinated care typically spans across different sectors of health care delivery and involves different health professions.

Co-payments: Flat fees or payments that a patient pays for each doctor visit or prescription or other health care service.

Core services: A package of health care services deemed basic for all citizens.

Cost containment: The method of constraining health care costs from increasing beyond a set level by controlling or reducing inefficiency and waste in the health care system.

Cost sharing: The requirement that the patient pay a portion of the costs of covered services. Deductibles, co-insurance and co-payments are cost-sharing techniques.

Cost shifting: When one group of patients does not pay the full cost for a service, health care providers pass on the costs for these services to other groups of patients.

Covered services: Treatments or other services for which a health plan pays at least part of the charge.

Deductible: The amount of money, or value of certain services (such as one physician visit) a patient or family must pay before costs (or percentages of costs) are covered by the health plan or insurance company, usually per year.

Diagnosis-related groups (DRGs): A system for classifying hospital stays based on the diagnosis of the medical problem being treated for the purposes of payment.

Disease management: Programmes for persons who have chronic illnesses such as asthma or diabetes that encourage them to live a healthy lifestyle and take medications as prescribed.

Effectiveness: A measure of the extent to which a specific intervention, procedure, regimen or service, when deployed in the field in routine circumstances, does what it is intended to do for a specified population.

Elective: A health care procedure that is not an emergency and that the patient and doctor plan in advance.

Electronic health record (EHR): Also, electronic medical record (EMR). An evolving concept defined as a systematic collection of electronic health information about individual patients or populations. It is a record in digital format that is theoretically capable of being shared across many health care settings.

Fee-for-service: The traditional payment method where the insurer (patient, insurance plan or government) pays providers per services rendered. The doctor charges a fee for each service provided.

Gatekeeper: A primary care physician responsible for overseeing and coordinating all aspects of a patient's medical care. The gatekeeper usually must pre-authorize other speciality care, diagnostic tests or hospital admission.

General practitioners (GPs): Physicians with no speciality training who provide a wide range of primary health care services to patients.

Global budgets: Budgets set to contain health care costs. Common in national health systems that annually set the maximum amount of money that will be spent on health care.

Halfway technology: Focuses on alleviating problematic symptoms instead of the root causes of poor health.

Health indicator: An indicator applicable to a health or health-related situation.

Health inequalities: Differences in health among people and groups within and between countries that are the consequence of social injustice.

Health inequities or disparities: Systematic and potentially remediable differences in one or more aspects of health across population groups defined socially, economically, demographically or geographically.

Health information technology (HIT): The umbrella term to describe the comprehensive management of health information across computerized systems and its secure exchange between consumers, providers, government and quality entities and insurers.

Health insurance: Financial protection against the health care costs caused by treating disease or accidental injury. A system of risk sharing through pooled resources.

Health Maintenance Organization (HMO): A health plan providing comprehensive medical services to its members for a fixed, prepaid premium. Members must use participating providers and are enrolled for a fixed period. HMOs can be either for-profit or not-for-profit. Most HMOs provide care through a network of doctors, hospitals and other medical professionals that their members must use to be covered for that care.

Health outcomes: Measures of the effectiveness of specific kinds of medical treatment. This refers to research-based information that asks what difference a drug, procedure or other health care intervention really makes to a patient's health.

Health sector: Part of the economy dealing with health-related issues in society.

Health system: The people, institutions and resources, arranged together in accordance with established policies to improve the health of the population they serve, while responding to people's legitimate expectations and protecting them against the cost of ill health through a variety of activities whose primary intent is to improve health. The set of elements and their relations in a complex whole, designed to serve the health needs of the population.

Health system performance assessment (HSPA): The process of monitoring, evaluating and communicating to what extent various aspects of a health system meet key objectives. The central purpose of HSPA is to assess whether progress is being made towards desired goals and whether appropriate activities are undertaken to promote achievement of those goals.

Home health care: Skilled nurses and trained aides who provide nursing services and related care to someone in his or her home.

Inpatient care: Care for a person who has been admitted to a hospital or other health facility for a period of at least 24 hours.

Long-term care (LTC): Health care, personal care and social services provided to people who have a chronic illness or disability and do not have full functional capacity. This care can take place in an institution or at home on a long-term basis.

Malpractice insurance: Coverage for medical professionals which pays the costs of legal fees and/or any damages assessed by a court in a lawsuit brought against a professional who has been charged with negligence. Endemic in the USA.

Managed care organization: An umbrella term for HMOs and all health plans that provide health care in return for pre-set monthly payments and coordinate care through a defined network of primary care physicians and hospitals. Prepaid medical plans that attempt to control health care costs through a preventative health care approach.

Means test: An assessment of a person's or family's income or assets so that it can be determined if they are eligible to receive public support.

Medical home model: An organizational and financing system that is meant to enhance primary care services through a financial mechanism (care management payments) and communications (information technology). It emphasizes continuity and coordination among specialists and first-contact practitioners without specifying who would coordinate the care.

Medical tourism: Patient movement generally from highly developed nations to less developed ones to obtain medical treatment that is less expensive or unavailable in their home country. Medical tourism differs from the traditional model of international health travel where patients go from less developed countries to major medical centres in highly developed countries for medical treatment that is unavailable in their own communities.

Out-of-pocket payments: The amount of money that a person must pay directly for his or her health care, including: deductibles, co-payments, payments for services that are not covered, and/or in the US health insurance premiums that are not paid by his or her employer.

Outpatient care: Health care services that do not require a patient to receive overnight care in a hospital (such as day surgery).

Premature mortality: A premature death from causes that should not occur in the presence of timely and effective health care.

Preventive health care: An approach to medicine that attempts to promote and maintain the health of people by preventing disease or its consequences. It includes primary prevention to keep people from getting sick (such as immunizations), secondary prevention to detect early disease (such as Pap smears) and tertiary prevention to keep ill people or those at high risk of disease from getting sicker (such as helping someone with lung disease to quit smoking).

Primary care: Preventive health care and routine medical care that is typically provided by a doctor trained in internal medicine, paediatrics or family practice, or by a nurse, nurse practitioner or physician's assistant.

Primary care provider: The health professional who provides basic health care services and may control patients' access to the rest of the health care system through referrals.

Private insurance: Health insurance that is provided by commercial insurance companies and where insurance premiums are risk-based.

Quality assurance: A systematic process to improve the quality of health care by monitoring quality, finding out what is not working and fixing the problems of health care delivery.

Rationing: The denial of a treatment to a patient who would benefit from it.

Referral system: The process through which a primary care provider authorizes a patient to see a specialist to receive additional care.

Single payer system: A health care system where costs are paid by taxes or compulsory contributions to sickness funds or social insurance plans rather than by the employer and employee.

Social determinants of health: The broad and complex array of social, political, economic, environmental and cultural factors that strongly impact on health status and equity between and within countries.

Third-party payer: An organization other than the patient or health care provider involved in the financing of personal health services.

Universal coverage: This refers to health systems that guarantee health care to all people regardless of the way that the system is financed.

Guide to Further Reading

1 Comparative Health Policy: An Introduction

There are many useful works on comparative health systems and health policy for readers to explore for more information. The OECD (2011) *Health at a Glance* presents the most current comparable data on key indicators of health and health systems across OECD countries. Kuhlmann *et al.* (2015b) *The Palgrave International Handbook of Healthcare Policy and Governance* includes extensive coverage of numerous countries. Thomson *et al.* (2013) *International Profiles of Health Care Systems* includes coverage of 13 countries, including some of ours. Matcha (2003) provides an analysis of health care systems in Canada, Germany, Sweden, Japan, the UK and the USA, including the history, financing and delivery of services. Masis and Smith (2010) detail health policies and systems from diverse countries such as Argentina, Bangladesh, Cambodia, Cameroon, Chile, Mexico, Nigeria, Peru, Sri Lanka and Taiwan. Similarly, Smith and Hanson (2012) examine health systems in low- and middle-income countries. Raffel (1997), DeVoe (2001), Okma and Crivelli (2009), Marmor and Wendt (2011b) and Hwang (2008) specifically look at health reform in an international context. Freeman (2000) offers a good overview of the politics of health in Europe, as does Moran (1999). Coulter and Ham (2000) specifically discuss the global challenge of rationing, and Ham and Robert (2003) place it in the international context. Gauld *et al.* (2006) and Wagstaff (2007) present excellent comparisons of Asian health systems, including Japan, Singapore, South Korea and Taiwan, while Blank and Merrick (2005) specifically examine end-of-life policies in 12 countries. Ranade (1998), Callahan and Wasunna (2006) and Harrison (2004) offer valuable comparative analyses of the role of markets. Scott (2001) compares private and public roles in health systems, while Thomson *et al.* (2009) focus on the international experience with private insurance and medical savings accounts across 20 countries. Lewis (2005) analyses health policy and politics in Australia, the Netherlands and the UK. Behan (2006) explores American health care policy failure by looking at the policies of Canada and Australia and provides a systematic comparison of these three countries while Lee *et al.* (2002) explore the global dimensions of health policy. For a look at how health care in developing countries differs from the countries analysed here, see Green (2007) and Mills *et al.* (2001). Green *et al.* (2009) offer a valuable overview of ethical issues raised by the globalization of health care.

2   The Context of Health Care

There are many valuable resources on the context of health care for our countries. The Guide to Websites contains the most useful current data as well as contextual information. For Australia, the key books are Duckett (2004a), Dugdale (2008) and Palmer and Short (2000). A very useful contextual book on New Zealand health care is Davis and Dew (2000), while Blank (1994), Davis and Ashton (2001) and Gauld (2001) provide good overviews of the New Zealand health care system. There are numerous books on US society as it relates to health policy including an excellent historical perspective in Weissert and Weissert (2002). For a good analysis of the US legal context see Sage and Kersh (2006) and for one of the best of many books on recent reforms in the USA see Jacobs and Skocpol (2010). Also, valuable insights into the unique US value context are found in Musgrave (2006), Kleinke (2001) and Lamm and Blank (2007). Still an excellent source on Japanese culture and health care is Ohnuki-Tiernev (1984). Other books on Japanese health policy and society include Campbell and Ikegami (2008), Powell and Anesaki (2011) and Feldman (2000), while Tatara and Okamoto (2009) provide a very comprehensive and current overview of Japan's health care system. Ham (2010) provides a useful article on values and health policy in Singapore, and the work of Haseltine (2012) and Lim (2004) are most helpful in understanding the Singapore system. Some of the essays in Shih *et al.* (2009) are useful for understanding the transformation of Taiwan culture as a context for health policy. Klein (2001) provides a detailed analysis of the politics of the British NHS since it was established, while Ham (2009) offers excellent analysis of more recent health policy in the UK. Twaddle (1999) focuses on policies of health reform in Sweden. Marmot and Wilkinson (1999) offer a valuable review of the social determinants of health across countries and Kawachi *et al.* (1999) delve more deeply into the relationship between inequality and poor health.

3   Funding, Provision and Governance

Suggestions for further reading on the funding, provision and governance of health care must necessarily be highly selective. Scott (2001) examines public and private sector roles in health care funding, provision and regulation, drawing on the experiences of Australia, Canada, Germany, the Netherlands, New Zealand, the UK and the USA. Thomson *et al.* (2013) offer an excellent summary of health care systems of a variety of countries, including many of those in this book. The Marmor *et al.* (2009b) edited book includes chapters on health care regulation, financing and delivery across countries, while Okma *et al.* (2010) analyse the health reform experiences of Chile, Israel, Singapore, Switzerland, Taiwan and the Netherlands and describe current provisions for funding, contracting and payment, ownership, and governance of these health care systems. Verspohl (2012) specifically focuses on the introduction of market mechanisms in Germany, the Netherlands and Sweden, whereas Rothgang *et al.* (2010) examine the changing role of the state. Henderson and Peterson (2002) explore the diverse meanings and applications of the term 'consumer' in the health systems of Australia, the UK and Canada. The edited volumes by Altenstetter and Björkman (1997), Ham (1997a), Mossialos and Le Grand (1999) and Ranade (1998), together with the special issues of the *Journal of Health Politics, Policy and Law* (2005) 20 (1–2) and *Health Economics, Policy and Law* (2012) 7 (1), contain chapters on European countries, focusing on health policy from the perspective of reform, while Mladovsky *et al.* (2012) are specifically concerned with health policy responses to the financial crisis. As a complement, the reports by the European Observatory offer detailed overviews of health systems in Britain (Boyle, 2011), Germany (Busse and Riesberg, 2004), the Netherlands (Schäfer *et al.*, 2010) and Sweden (Anell *et al.*, 2012). For the Netherlands see Okma (2001) and for health reform in the UK see Harrison and McDonald (2008) and Hunter (2008). Davis and Ashton (2001) provide a detailed account of New Zealand health reforms while Ashton (2005) provides a useful summary of recent changes in funding. A good general work on Australia is Palmer and Short (2000), while Dugdale (2008) provides a comprehensive introduction to health policy in that country. Among the countless books on US health policy are Barr (2011), Porter and Teisberg (2006), Musgrave (2006) and Starr (2011). The publication on affordable health care published by the Singapore Ministry of Health (1995) is invaluable in explaining its unique system. For good summaries of the Japanese health care system, see Campbell and Ikegami (2008), Imai and Fushimi (2012) and especially the Japan Ministry of Health, Labour and Welfare (2004). For those with a special interest in Asia, Kwon (2011) examines the major elements of health care financing of 26 South Pacific and Asian countries.

4   Setting Priorities and Allocating Resources

Twaddle (2002) looks at market-oriented health care reforms in numerous countries and analyses the recent concern with the efficiency of medical care while Jacobs *et al.* (2006) examine the pursuit of efficiency across health systems and the techniques available to measure it. General books on rationing medicine include Wütscher *et al.* (2010), Syrett (2008) and Ubel (2001), while Sauerland (2009) specifically focuses on issues of quality assurance in Germany. Locock (2000) deals with rationing in Britain and Lamm and Blank (2007) in the USA. Coulter and Ham (2000) and Ham and Robert (2003) provide very useful comparative analyses of rationing and argue it is a global issue, whereas Williams *et al.* (2011) and Thomson and Dixon (2006) specifically focus on priority setting and choice in health care respectively. Sabik and Lie (2008) offer a good overview of priority setting in eight countries, whereas the volumes by Garrido *et al.* (2008) and Schlander (2010) specifically look at health technology assessment. Ranade's (1998) and Harrison's (2004) comparative analyses of health care markets are a good introduction to this topic. Ikegami and Campbell (1999) provide an important analysis of cost containment in Japan, and Campbell and Ikegami (2008) extend this analysis to priority setting. More technical books on health allocation techniques include Drummond *et al.* (2005) and McKie *et al.* (1998). McIntosh *et al.* (2010) offer a good introduction to cost–benefit analysis in health care and Morris *et al.* (2012) to economic analyses. WHO (2000) *Health Systems: Improving Performance* remains a valuable reference work for assessing health systems. This work was followed by Murray and Evans (eds) (2003) *Health Systems Performance Assessment: Debates, Methods, and Empiricism.*

5   The Health Workforce

Johnson (1995) and Light (1995) provide useful introductions to the conceptual issues surrounding doctors and health policy, as do Moran and Wood (1993) and Moran (1999) in their comparative analyses of Britain, Germany and the USA. Bodenheimer and Bauer (2016) show the growing importance of physicians' assistants and nurse practitioners, as well as nurses, in providing health care in the 21st century. Attention recently has shifted to the human resources of health systems (OECD, 2008a; WHO, 2008a; Vujicic et al., 2012; Dussault, 2015) reminding us 'that there is 'no health without a workforce' (Campbell et al., 2013). Health workers build the backbone of every health care system, thus shortages, maldistribution and mismanagement challenge equity and quality of care in the global North and threaten the implementation of universal health care coverage in low- and middle-income countries (Bowser *et al.*, 2014; Glinos *et al.*, 2015). The edited collection by Bovens *et al.* (2001) contains chapters on recent medical reform in European countries, whereas the special issue edited by Burau (2009b) focuses on reforms of the governance of medical performance. Harrison (2001) and Harrison *et al.* (2002) have written widely about doctors in Britain, whereas Garpenby (2001) has focused on Sweden. Allsop and Saks (2002) offer a critical perspective on regulation of the medical profession in the UK. Yoshikawa *et al.* (1996) provide good coverage of the medical profession in Japan.

A good introduction to the medical profession in the USA is provided by Badasch (1993), while Judson and Harrison (2012) analyse the legal and ethical issues that all health care professionals face.

6 Health Care Beyond the Hospital

A variety of recent works examine funding schemes for LTC (Carrera *et al.*, 2013; Campbell *et al.*, 2016; Fernández and Nadash, 2016; Mossialos *et al.*, 2016) while Rummery and Fine (2012) outline the diversity of care necessary to meet needs of people who require long-term care. Other health policy works that focus on care for older people include Gori *et al.* (2016), Pavolini and Theobald (2015) and Campbell *et al.* (2016). Among the few comparative works that focus specifically on home care are Burau *et al.* (2007) and Doyle and Timonen (2007). In addition, Alber and Kohler (2006) and Anttonen *et al.* (2003) offer more general introductions to key issues and concepts for comparing home care. Ranci and Pavolini (2013) analyse current reforms and Lundsgaard (2004) focuses on payments of informal carers. More specific country perspectives include works by Campbell and Morgan (2005) on Germany and the USA, Theobald (2012) and Rothgang (2010) on Germany, Schut and Berg (2010) on the Netherlands, Ashton (2000) and Davey and Keeling (2004) on New Zealand, Comas-Herrera *et al.* (2010) and Glendinning (2013) on Britain and Meagher and Szebehely (2013) and Anell *et al.* (2012) on Sweden. Campbell and Ikegami (2003), Izuhara (2003), Fukuda *et al.* (2008) and Noguchi and Shimizutani (2005) provide a useful range of perspectives on home care policy in Japan, while Reisman (2009) analyses the challenges of the ageing Singapore population. Watson and Mears' (1999) book on women and care of the elderly is a good overview of the social issues surrounding home care in Australia. Kitchener *et al.* (2007) and Centers for Medicare and Medicaid Services (2008, 2009a) review home and community-based services in the USA while Marrelli (2011) is a useful handbook of home health standards and documentation guidelines.

7 Public Health

Since public health comprises such a broad range of areas, many of which fall outside the scope of health care, the resources here are expansive. Among the most helpful recent general works on public health per se are Schneider (2016), Merson *et al.* (2011), Henderson *et al.* (2001) and Wallace (2007). For public health nursing, see Stanhope and Lancaster (2011). Dawson and Verweij (2007) offer constructive insights on the ethical aspects of prevention and public health, while Levy and Sidel (2009) look at social justice and public health. Bennett *et al.* (2010) look at the problems of communicating risk to the public. One of the best general books on health promotion is DiClemente *et al.* (2002). For a comprehensive guide to the frameworks, theories and methods used to evaluate health promotion programmes see Valente (2002). For a good analysis of occupational health and safety see Tompa *et al.* (2008). More specific country perspectives on public health include books on Europe by Greer and Kurzer (2012), the USA by Milio (2000) and Turnock (2011), Australia by Leeder (1999), Britain by Baggott (2010) and Japan by Okamoto (2001). Reynolds (2011) looks at health and environmental law in Australia and New Zealand. Other books on environmental and global health include Ball (2006), Skolnick (2011), Moeller (2011) and the huge edited collections of Merson *et al.* (2011) and Koop *et al.* (2002). For global health care governance, see Keefe and Zacher (2011), Davies (2010), Harman (2012a) and Crisp (2010). Moreover, Ferri *et al.* (2012) examine mortality among older people as a neglected topic in global health with a focus on Latin America, India and China. Taylor (2009) analyses the relationship between economic growth and equitable health within globalization, while Talbot and Verrinder (2010) address public health challenges emerging from the social and environmental consequences of globalization. Finally, Levy and Sidel (2007) document the public health consequences of war. Holtz (2012) offers a comprehensive set of articles on a variety of global health topics and perspectives, and Birn and Pillay (2009) synthesize historical, cultural, environmental, economic and political considerations to provide a comprehensive global overview of the many factors that determine the health of individuals and populations.

Guide to Websites

In the light of the growing importance of the internet for transferring health policy information, here is a selection of health-related websites for our countries and for key international health organizations. Where possible, we have included English language sites; otherwise an English option is often available. This list of websites is also available online at www.palgrave.com/politics/blank, where it will be updated periodically.

Australia

Bureau of Statistics: www.abs.gov.au
Commonwealth Government: www.australia.gov.au
Department of Health: www.health.gov.au
Department of Health, Australian Capital Territory: www.health.act.gov.au
Institute of Health and Welfare: www.aihw.gov.au
Public Health Association of Australia: www.phaa.net.au

Germany

Federal Association of Insurance Funds (*Spitzenverband Bund der Krankenkassen*): www.gkv-spitzenverband.de/Home.gkvnet
Federal Association of Insurance Fund Doctors (*Kassenärztliche Bundesvereinigung*): www.kbv.de
Federal Association of Welfare Organizations (*Bundesarbeitsgemeinschaft der Freien Wohlfahrtspflege*): www.bagfw.de
Federal Centre for Health Education (*Bundeszentrale für Gesundheitliche Aufklärung*): www.bzga.de
Federal Chamber of Doctors (*Bundesärztekammer*): www.bundesaerztekammer.de
Federal Ministry of Labour and Social Affairs (*Bundesministerium für Arbeit und Soziales*): www.bmas.bund.de
German Hospital Association (*Deutsche Krankenhaus Gesellschaft*): www.dkgev.de

Japan

Ministry of Health, Labour and Welfare: www.mhlw.go.jp/english

The Netherlands

Association of Health Insurance Providers (*Zorgverzekeraars Nederland*): www.zn.nl
Ministry for Health, Welfare and Sport (*Ministerie van Volksgezondheid, Welzijn en Sport*): www.minvws.nl/en/
Statistics Netherlands (*Centraal Bureau voor de Statistiek*): www.cbs.nl/en-gb

New Zealand

Health Quality & Safety Commission: www.hqsc.govt.nz
Ministry of Health: www.moh.govt.nz
New Zealand Guidelines Group: www.health.govt.nz/about-ministry/ministry-health-websites/new-zealand-guidelines-group
New Zealand Health Information Service: www.nzhis.govt.nz
New Zealand Health Network: www.nzhealth.net.nz
New Zealand National Health Committee, www.inahta.org/members/nhc/.

Singapore

Health Sciences Authority: www.hsa.gov.sg
Ministry of Health: www.moh.gov.sg
National Center for Policy Analysis: www.ncpa.org

Sweden

Medical Responsibility Board (*Hälso-och sjukvårdens ansvarsnämnd*): www.hsan.se/eng/start.asp
Ministry for Health and Social Affairs (*Socialdepartementet*): www.sweden.gov.se/sb/d/2061
National Board of Health and Welfare (*Socialstyrelsen*): www.socialstyrelsen.se/english
Swedish Medical Association (*Sveriges läkarförbund*): www.slf.se/info-in-English/Swedish-Medical-Association/

Taiwan

Ministry of Health and Welfare: www.mohw.gov.tw/EN/Ministry/Index.aspx

NationalHealthInsuranceAdministration(NHIA):www.nhi.gov.tw/english/
   index.aspx?menu=8&menu_id=30&webdata_id=0&WD_ID=30
National Health Research Institutes: http://english.nhri.org.tw/

UK

British Medical Association (BMA): www.bma.org.uk
Care Quality Commission: www.cqc.org.uk
Department of Health: www.doh.gov.uk
General Medical Council (GMC): www.gmc-uk.org
The King's Fund: www.kingsfund.org.uk
National Institute for Health and Care Excellence: www.nice.org.uk
NHS Confederation: www.nhsconfed.org
Office of Public Sector Information: www.opsi.gov.uk

USA

Agency for Healthcare Research and Quality: www.ahcpr.gov
American Hospital Association: www.aha.org
Centers for Disease Control and Prevention (CDC): www.cdc.gov
Center for Medicare and Medicaid Services: www.medicare.gov
Department of Health and Human Services: www.hhs.gov
Department of Veterans Affairs: www.va.gov
Health Resources & Services Administration: www.hrsa.gov
Institute of Medicine: www.nationalacademies.org/hmd
National Center for Health Statistics: www.cdc.gov/nchs
National Institutes of Health: www.nih.gov
National Library of Medicine/National Institutes of Health: www.nlm.
   nih.gov

International organizations

European Observatory on Health Systems and Policies: www.euro.who.
   int/observatory
Organisation for Economic Co-operation and Development (OECD):
   www.oecd.org
World Health Organization (WHO): www.who.org
World Health Organization, Regional Office for Europe: www.who.dk

Bibliography

Aaron, H.J. (2003) 'Should Public Policy Seek to Control the Growth of Health Care Spending?', *Health Affairs*, 8 January.

Abrams, J. (2002) 'Divided Congress Puts off Many Issues Until after the Election', *Associated Press*, 17 October.

Adams, P.J., J. Raeburn and K.A. de Silva (2009) 'Question of Balance: Prioritizing Public Health Responses to Harm from Gambling', *Addiction* 104: 688–91.

Advisory Council for the Concerted Action in Health Care (2009) *Coordination and Integration – Health Care in an Ageing Society,* Report, English version, http://www.svr-gesundheit.de/fileadmin/user_upload/Gutachten/2009/KF_engl_final.pdf.

Advisory Council on the Assessment of Developments in the Health Care System (2014) 'Needs-based Health Care: Opportunities for Rural Regions and Selected Health Care Sectors', Report, English, abridged version, www.svr-gesundheit.de/fileadmin/user_upload/Gutachten/2014/SVR-Gutachten_2014_Kurzfassung_engl.pdf.

Afzal, M., G. Cometto, E. Rosskam and M. Sheikh (2011) 'Global Health Workforce Alliance: Increasing the Momentum for Health Workforce Development', *Revista Peruana de Medicina Experimental y Salud Publica* 28 (2): www.scielosp.org/scielo.php?pid=S1726-46342011000200018&script=sci_arttext&tlng=en.

Agartan, T.I. (2015) 'Health Workforce Policy and Turkey's Health Care Reform', *Health Policy* 119 (12): 1621–6.

Aiken, L.H., D.M. Sloane, L. Bryneel, K. van den Heede and W. Sermeus – for the RN4CAST Consortium (2013) 'Nurses Reports of Working Conditions and Hospital Quality of Care in 12 Countries in Europe', *International Journal of Nursing Studies* 50: 143–53.

Aiken, L.H., D.M. Sloane L Bruyneel, K. van den Heede, P. Griffiths, R. Busse *et al.* (2014) 'Nurse Staffing and Education and Hospital Mortality in Nine European Countries: A Retrospective Observational Study', *The Lancet* 383 (9931): 1824–30.

Alber, J. (1995) 'A Framework for the Comparative Study of Social Services', *Journal of European Social Policy* 5 (2): 131–49.

Alber, J. and U. Kohler (2006) *Health and Care in an Enlarged Europe,* Luxembourg, Official Publications of the European Communities, European Foundation for the Improvement Working Conditions.

Allen, J. (2012) 'New York OKs Nation's First Ban on Supersized Sugary Drinks', Reuters, 13 September.

Allsop, J. and M. Saks, eds., (2002) Regulating the Health Professions. London: Sage.

Altenstetter, C. and J.W. Björkman (eds) (1997) *Health Policy Reform, National Variations and Globalization.* London: Macmillan.

Altman, S.H., C.P. Tompkins, E. Eilat and M.P.V. Glavin (2003) 'Escalating Health Care Spending: Is It Desirable or Inevitable?' *Health Affairs*, 8 January.

AMA – American Medical Association (2016). *Health Policy*, www.ama-assn.org/ama/pub/advocacy/health-policy.page.

American College of Physicians (2008) 'Achieving a High-Performance Health Care System with Universal Access: What the United States Can Learn from Other Countries', *Annals of Internal Medicine* 148: 55–75.

American Hospital Association (2009) 'Fast Facts on US Hospitals', www.aha.org.

American Lung Association (2015) 'Myths and Facts about E-Cigarettes', www.lung.org/stop-smoking/smoking-facts/myths-and-facts-about-e-cigs.html.

American Society for Bariatric Surgery (2006) 'Rationale for the Surgical Treatment of Morbid Obesity', http://asmbs.org/wp/uploads/2005/10/GrantingPrivileges-Jan2006.pdf.

Amin, A., E. Kismödi and C. García-Moreno (2015) 'Addressing Violence against Women in Health Policies', in E. Kuhlmann, R.H. Blank, I.L. Bourgeault and C. Wendt (eds) *The Palgrave International Handbook on Health Policy and Governance*. Basingstoke: Palgrave.

Anderson, G.F., B.K. Frogner, R.A. Johns and U.E. Reinhardt (2006) 'Health Care Spending and Use of Information Technology in OECD Countries', *Health Affairs* 25 (3): 819–31.

Andersson Bäck, M. (2016) 'Risks and Opportunities of Reforms Putting Primary Care in the Driver's Seat: Comment on "Governance, Government, and the Search for New Provider Models"', *International Journal of Health Policy and Management* 5 (8): 511–13.

Anell, A. (2010) 'Choice and Privatisation in Swedish Primary Care', *Health Economics, Policy and Law* 6 (4): 549–69.

Anell, A., A.H. Glengård and S. Merkur (2012) 'Sweden: Health System Review', *Health Systems in Transition* 14 (5): 1–144.

Anttonen, A., J. Baldock and J. Sipila (eds) (2003) *The Young, the Old and the State. Social Care Systems in Five Industrial Nations*. Cheltenham: Edward Elgar.

Arts, W. and J. Glissen (2002) 'Three Worlds of Welfare Capitalism or More? A State-of-the-Art Report', *Journal of European Social Policy* 12: 137–48.

Asher, M., M. Ramesh and A. Maresso (2008) 'Medical Savings Accounts: Can They Improve Health System Performance in Europe?' *EuroObserver* 10 (4): 9–11.

Ashton, T. (2000) 'New Zealand: Long-Term Care in a Decade of Change', *Health Affairs* 19 (3): 72–81.

Ashton, T. (2005) 'Recent Developments in the Funding and Organisation of the New Zealand Health System', *Australia and New Zealand Health Policy* 2 (9), www.anzhealthpolicy.com/content/2/1/9.

Aslan, A. (2009) 'Convergence of Per Capita Health Care Expenditures in OECD Countries', *International Research Journal of Finance and Economics* 24: 48–53.

Associated Press (2006) 'Singapore Takes Strict Steps against Obesity', www.msnbc.msn.com/id/6124732, 12 October.

Association of American Medical Colleges (2008) 'Residences Revolve around Rural Care', *AAMC Reporter*, July.

Astolfi, R., L. Lorenzoni and J. Oderkirk (2012) 'Informing Policy Makers about Future Health Spending: A Comparative Analysis of Forecasting Methods in OECD Countries', *Health Policy* 107: 1–10.

Attia, N. and V. Bérenger (2009) 'European Integration and Social Convergence: A Qualitative Appraisal', *Panoeconomicus* 364 (4): 3–19.

Australian Department of Health and Ageing (2006) 'Home and Community Care Programme', http://ww2.health.wa.gov.au/Articles/F_I/HACC-Home-and-Community-Care-Program.

Axon, R. (2016) '150 Health Professionals Call for Olympics in Rio to be Postponed due to Zika', *USA Today Sports*, www.smh.com.au/sport/olympics/rio-2016/150-health-professionals-call-for-olympics-in-rio-to-be-postponed-due-to-zika-20160527-gp629o.html.

Bache, I. and M. Flinders (2004) 'Multi-level Governance and British Politics', in I. Bache and M. Flinders (eds) *Multi-level Governance*. Oxford: Oxford University Press.

Badasch, S.A. (1993) *Introduction to Health Occupations*. New York: Regents/Prentice Hall.

Baggott, R. (2010) *Public Health: Policy and Politics*, 2nd edn. Basingstoke: Palgrave Macmillan.

Baker, L., H. Birnbaum, J. Geppert, D. Mishol and E. Moyneur (2003) 'The Relationship between Technology Availability and Health Care Spending', *Health Affairs 5*, November.

Baldock, J. (2003) 'Social Care in the United Kingdom: A Pattern of Discretionary Social Administration', in A. Anttonnen, J. Baldock and J. Sipilä (eds) *The Young, the Old and the State. Social Care Systems in Five Industrial Nations*. Cheltenham: Edward Elgar.

Ball, D. (2006) *Environmental Health Policy*. Buckingham: Open University Press.

Bandelow, N.C. (2007) 'Health Policy: Obstacles to Policy Convergence in Britain and Germany', *German Politics* 16 (1): 150–63.

Banks, J., M. Marmot, Z. Oldfield and J.P. Smith (2006) 'Disease and Disadvantage in the United States and in England', *Journal of the American Medical Association* 295: 2037–45.

Banta, D. (2002) 'The Development of Health Technology Assessment', *Health Policy* 63 (2): 121–32.

Bäringhausen, T. and R. Sauerborn (2003) 'One Hundred and Eighteen Years of the German Health Insurance System: Are there any Lessons for Middle- and Low-Income Countries?', *Social Science and Medicine* 54: 1559–87.

Barr, D.A. (2011) *Introduction to U.S. Health Policy: The Organization, Financing, and Delivery of Health Care in America*, 3rd edn. Baltimore: Johns Hopkins University Press.

Barr, M.D. (2001) 'Medical Savings Accounts in Singapore: A Critical Inquiry', *Journal of Health Politics, Policy and Law* 26 (4): 709–26.

Bartholomée, Y. and H. Maarse (2006) 'Health Insurance Reform in the Netherlands', *Eurohealth* 12 (2): 7–9.

Batenburg, R. (2015) 'Comparing Health Workforce Planning in the European Union', *Health Policy* 119 (12): 1537–44.

Begley, S. (2012) 'Fat and Getting Fatter: U.S. Obesity Rates to Soar by 2030', http://www.reuters.com/article/us-obesity-us-idUSBRE88H0RA20120918.

Behan, P. (2006) *Solving the Health Care Problem: How Other Countries Have Succeeded and Why the United States Has Failed*. Albany: State University of New York Press.

Bejerot, E. and H. Hasselbladh (2011) 'Professional Autonomy and Pastoral Power: The Transformation of Quality Registers in Swedish Health Care', *Public Administration* 89 (4): 1604–21.

Bellinger, D.C. (2016) 'Lead Contamination in Flint: An Abject Failure to Protect Public Health', *The New England Journal of Medicine* 374 (12): 1101–3.

Belsky, L., R. Lie, A. Mattoo, E.J. Emanuel and G. Sreenivasan (2004) 'The General Agreements on Trade in Services: Implications for Health Policymakers', *Health Affairs* 23 (3): 137–45.

Bennett, B. and T. Carney (2010) 'Law, Ethics and Pandemic Preparedness: The Importance of Cross-Jurisdictional and Cross-Cultural Perspectives', *Australian and New Zealand Journal of Public Health* 34 (2): 106–17.

Bennett, C.J. (1991) 'What is Policy Convergence and What Causes It?', *British Journal of Political Science* 21 (2): 215–33.

Bennett, P., K. Calman, S. Curtis and D. Smith (2010) *Risk Communication and Public Health*. New York: Oxford University Press.

Benoit, C., E. Declercq, S.F. Murray, J. Sandall, E. van Teijlingen, and S. Wrede (2015) 'Maternity Care as a Global Health Policy Issue', in E. Kuhlmann, R.H. Blank, I.L. Bourgeault and C. Wendt (eds) *The Palgrave International Handbook of Healthcare Policy and Governance*. Basingstoke: Palgrave.

Bergh, A. and T. Nilsson (2010) 'Good for Living? On the Relationship between Globalization and Life Expectancy', *World Development* 38 (9): 1191–1203.

Berk, M.L. and A.C. Monheit (2001) 'The Concentration of Health Care Expenditures Revisited', *Health Affairs* 20 (2): 9–18.

Birn, A.-E. and Y. Pillay (2009) *Textbook of International Health: Global Health in a Dynamic World*. New York: Oxford University Press.

Björkman, J.W. and K.G.H. Okma (1997) 'Restructuring Health Care Systems in the Netherlands: The Institutional Heritage of Dutch Health Policy Reforms', in C. Altenstetter and J.W. Björkman (eds) *Health Policy Reform, National Variations and Globalization*. London: Macmillan.

Blank, R.H. (1994) *New Zealand Health Policy: A Comparative Study*. Auckland: Oxford University Press.

Blank, R.H. (1997) *The Price of Life: The Future of American Health Care*. New York: Columbia University Press.

Blank, R.H. (2012). 'Transformations of the US Healthcare System: Why is Change So Difficult?', *Current Sociology* 60 (4): 415–26.

Blank, R.H. and S-H Cheng (2015). 'Mixed Healthcare Finance in East Asian Healthcare Systems', in E. Kuhlmann, R.H. Blank, I.L. Bourgeault and C. Wendt (eds) *The Palgrave International Handbook of Healthcare Policy and Governance*. Basingstoke: Palgrave, 359–75.

Blank, R.H. and V. Burau (2006) 'Setting Health Priorities across Nations: More Convergence than Divergence?', *Journal of Public Health Policy* 27 (3): 265–81.

Blank, R.H. and J.C. Merrick (eds) (2005) *End-of-Life Decision Making: A Cross-National Study*. Cambridge, MA: MIT Press.

Blendon, R.J., M. Kim and J.M. Benson (2001) 'The Public versus the World Health Organization on Health System Performance', *Health Affairs* 20 (3): 10–20.

Blondel, Jean (1990) *Comparative Government: An Introduction*. Hemel Hempstead: Philip Allan.

Blumenthal, D., B. Chernof, T. Fulmer, J. Lumpkin and J. Selberg (2016). Caring for High-Need, High-Cost Patients: An Urgent Priority. *The New England Journal of Medicine*, doi: 10.1056/NEJMp1608511.

Bodenheimer, T. (2005) 'High and Rising Health Care Costs. Part 2: Technologic Innovation', *Annals of Internal Medicine* 142 (11): 932–7.

Bodenheimer, T. and L. Bauer (2016). 'Rethinking the Primary Care Workforce: An Expanded Role for Nurses', *New England Journal of Medicine* 375 (11): 1015–17.

Bodenheimer, T. and A. Fernandez (2005) 'High and Rising Health Care Costs. Part 4: Can Costs Be Controlled While Preserving Quality?', *Annals of Internal Medicine* 143 (1): 26–31.

Boerma, T., M. Chopra and D. Evans (2009) 'Health Systems Performance Assessment in the Bulletin', *Bulletin of the World Health Organization* 87: 2, doi:10.2471/BLT.08.061945.

Böhm. K., A. Schmid, R. Götze, C. Landwehra and H. Rothgang (2013) 'Five Types of OECD Healthcare Systems: Empirical Results of a Deductive Classification', *Health Policy*, http://dx.doi.org/10.1016/j.healthpol.2013.09.003.

Borland, R., L. Li, P. Driezen, N. Wilson, D. Hammond, M.E. Thompson, G.T. Fong, U. Mons, M.C. Willemsen, A. McNeill, J.F. Thrasher and K.M. Cummings (2011) 'Cessation Assistance Reported by Smokers in 15 Countries Participating in the International Tobacco Control (ITC) Policy Evaluation Surveys', *Addiction* 107 (1): 197–205.

Bourgeault, I.L. and K. Merritt (2015) 'Deploying and Managing Health Human Resources', in E. Kuhlmann, R.H. Blank, I.L. Bourgeault and C. Wendt (eds) *The Palgrave International Handbook of Healthcare Policy and Governance*. Basingstoke: Palgrave.

Bourgeault I.L., S. Wrede, C. Benoit and E. Neiterman (2016) 'Professions and the Migration of Expert Labour: Towards an Intersectional Analysis of Transnational Mobility Patterns and Integration Pathways of Health Professionals', in M. Dent, I. Bourgeault, J-L. Denis and E. Kuhlmann (eds) *The Routledge Companion to the Professions and Professionalism*. London: Routledge.

Bovens, M., P. t'Hart and B.G. Peters (eds) (2001) *Success and Failure in Public Governance. A Comparative Analysis*. Cheltenham: Edward Elgar.

Bowser, D., S.P. Sparkes, A. Mitchell, T.J. Bossert, T. Bärninghausen, G. Gedik and R. Atun (2014) 'Global Funds Investment in Human Resources for Health: Innovation and Missed Opportunities for Health Systems Strengthening', *Health Policy and Planning* 29: 986–97.

Boxall, A.-M. and S.D. Short (2006) 'Political Economy and Population Health: Is Australia Exceptional?', *Australia and New Zealand Health Policy* 3 (6), doi:10.1186/1743-8462-3-6.

Boyle, S. (2011) *United Kingdom (England). Health System Review, Health Systems in Transition, 13/1*, Copenhagen: European Observatory on Health Systems and Policies.

Brenner, M.H. (2001) 'Unemployment, Employment Policy and the Public Health', paper presented at European Commission Expert Meeting on Unemployment and Health in Europe, Berlin, 6–7 July.

British Medical Association (2016) 'BMA Launches Judicial Review as Government Publishes Junior Doctor Contract', http://oneprofession.bma.org.uk/.

British United Provident Association (2002) 'Skin Cancer on the Rise', https://www.sciencedaily.com/releases/2017/05/170515141000.htm.

Brodsky, J., J. Habib and M. Hirschfeld (2003) *Long-term Care in Developing Countries: Ten Case-studies*. Geneva: World Health Organization.

Broutet, N., F. Krauer, M. Riesen, A. Khalakdina, M. Almiron, S. Aldighieri, M. Espinal, N. Low and C. Dye (2016) 'Zika Virus as a Cause of Neurologic Disorders', *The New England Journal of Medicine*, doi:10.1056/NEJMp1602708.

Brown, D. and H. Harrison (2013). *Governance for Health Equity in the WHO European Region*. Copenhagen: WHO.

Brownell, K.D., T. Farley, W.C. Willett, B.M. Popkin, F.J. Chaloupka, J.W. Thompson and D.S. Ludwig (2009) 'The Public Health and Economic Benefits of Taxing Sugar-Sweetened Beverages', *New England Journal of Medicine* 361: 1599–1605.

Bruyneel, L., L. Baoyue, L. Aiken, E. Lesaffre, K. Van den Heede and W. Sermeus (2014) 'A Multi-County Perspective on Nurses' Tasks Below their Skill Level: Reports from Domestically Trained and Foreign-trained Nurses from Developing Countries', in J. Buchan, M. Wismar, I.A. Glinos and J. Bremner (eds) *Health Professional Mobility in a Changing Europe: New Dynamics, Mobile Individuals and Diverse Responses*. Observatory Studies Series 32. Copenhagen: WHO.

Buchan, J. (2015) 'Health Worker Migration in Context', in E. Kuhlmann, R.H. Blank, I.L. Bourgeault and C. Wendt (eds) *The Palgrave International Handbook of Healthcare Policy and Governance*. Basingstoke: Palgrave.

Buchan, J., I.A. Glinos and M. Wismar (2014) 'Introduction to Health Professional Mobility in a Changing Europe', in J. Buchan, M. Wismar, I.A. Glinos and J. Bremner (eds) *Health Professional Mobility in a Changing Europe: New Dynamics, Mobile Individuals and Diverse Responses*. Observatory Studies Series 32. Copenhagen: WHO.

Burau, V. (2001) 'Medical Reform in Germany: The 1993 Health Care Legislation as an Impromptu Success', in M. Bovens, P. t'Hart and B.G. Peters (eds) *Success and Failure in Public Governance: A Comparative Analysis*. Cheltenham: Edward Elgar.

Burau, V. (2007a) 'Comparative Health Research', in M. Saks and J. Allsop (eds) *Researching Health*. London: Sage.

Burau, V. (2007b) 'The Complexity of Governance Change: Reforming the Governance of Medical Performance in Germany', *Health Economics, Policy and Law* 2 (4): 391–407.

Burau, V. (2009a) 'Negotiating Reform at an Arm's Length from the State: Disease Management Programmes and the Introduction of Clinical Standards in Germany', *Health Economics, Policy and Law* 4 (4): 347–465.

Burau, V. (ed.) (2009b) 'Governing Medical Performance: A Comparative Analysis of Pathways of Change', *Health Economics, Policy and Law* 4 (3): 265–382.

Burau, V. (2012) 'Transforming Health Policy and Services: Challenges for Comparative Research', *Current Sociology* 60 (4): 569–78.

Burau, V. (2016) 'Governing through Professional Experts', in M. Dent, I. Bourgeault, J-L. Denis and E. Kuhlmann (eds) *The Routledge Companion to the Professions and Professionalism*. London: Routledge.

Burau, V. and R.H. Blank (2006) 'Comparing Health Policy – An Assessment of Typologies of Health Systems', *Journal of Comparative Policy Analysis* 8 (1): 63–76.

Burau, V. and L. Fenton (2009) 'How Health Care States Matter: Introducing Clinical Standards in Britain and Germany', *Journal of Health Organization and Management* 23 (3): 289–303.

Burau, V. and T. Kröger (2004) 'Towards Local Comparisons of Community Care Governance: Exploring the Relationship between Policy and Politics', *Social Policy & Administration* 38 (7): 793–810.

Burau, V., R.H. Blank and E. Pavolini (2015) 'Typologies of Healthcare Systems and Policies', in E. Kuhlmann, R.H. Blank, I.L. Bourgeault and C. Wendt (eds) *The Palgrave International Handbook of Healthcare Policy and Governance.* Basingstoke: Palgrave.

Burau, V., H. Theobald and R.H. Blank (2007) *Governing Home Care: A Cross-National Comparison.* Cheltenham: Edward Elgar.

Burau, V., D. Wilsford and G. France (2009) 'Reforming Medical Governance in Europe. What is it about Institutions?', *Health Economic, Policy & Law* 4 (3): 265–82.

Bureau of National Health Insurance (BNHI) (2008) *National Health Insurance Statistics,* http://www.nhi.gov.tw/English/webdata/webdata.aspx?menu=11&menu_id=296&webdata_id=1942&WD_ID=296.

Bureau of National Health Insurance (BNHI) (2012) 'Statistics', www.nhi.gov.tw/English/webdata/webdata.aspx?menu=11&menu_id=296&WD_ID=296&webdata_id=4229.

Burstrom, B. (2004) 'User Charges in Sweden', *Euro Observer* 6 (3): 5–6.

Busse, R. and M. Blümel (2014) 'Germany, Health System Review', *Health Systems in Transition* 16 (2): 1–61.

Busse, R. and A. Riesberg (2004) *Health Systems in Transition: Germany.* Copenhagen: WHO Regional Office for Europe on Behalf of the European Observatory on Health Care Systems.

Cailhol, J., I. Craveiro, T. Madede, E. Makoa, T. Mathole, A.N. Parsons, L. Van Leemput, R. Biesma, R. Brugha, B. Chilundo, U. Lehmann, G. Dussault, W. Van Damme and D. Sanders (2013) 'Analysis of Human Resources for Health Strategies and Policies in 5 Countries in Sub-Saharan Africa, in Response to GFATM and PEPFAR-funded HIV-activities', *Globalization and Health* 9: 52–65.

Callahan, D. (1990) *What Kind of Life? The Limits of Medical Progress.* New York: Simon & Schuster.

Callahan, D. and A.A. Wasunna (2006) *Medicine and the Market: Equity v. Choice.* Baltimore: The Johns Hopkins University Press.

Campbell, A.L. and K.J. Morgan (2005) 'Federalism and the Politics of Old-Age Care in Germany and the United States', *Comparative Political Studies* 38 (8): 1–28.

Campbell, J., G. Dussault, J. Buchan, F. Pozo-Martin, M. Guerra Arias, C. Leone, A. Siyam and G. Cometto (2013). *A Universal Truth: No Health without a Workforce,* Forum Report. Geneva: Global Health Workforce Alliance and WHO.

Campbell, J., N. Ikegami, C. Gori, F. Barbabella, R. Chomik, F. D'Amico, H. Holder, T. Ishibashi, L. Johansson, M. Ring and H. Theobald (2016) 'How Different Countries Allocate Long-term Care Resources to Older Users: A Comparative Snapshot', in C. Gori, J-L. Fernández and R. Wittenberg (eds) *Long-term Care Reforms in OECD Countries: Successes and Failures.* Bristol: Policy Press.

Campbell, J.C. and N. Ikegami (2003) 'Japan's Radical Reform of Long-Term Care', *Social Policy and Administration* 37 (1): 21–34.

Campbell, J.C. and N. Ikegami (2008) *The Art of Balance in Health Policy: Maintaining Japan's Low-Cost, Egalitarian System.* Cambridge: Cambridge University Press.

Campillo-Artero, C. (2011) 'When Health Technologies Do Not Reach Their Effectiveness Potential: A Health Service Research Perspective', *Health Policy* 104 (1): 92–8.

Carrera, F., E. Pavolini, C. Ranci and A. Sabbatini (2013) 'Long-term Care Systems in Comparative Perspective', in C. Ranci and E. Pavolini (eds) *Reforms in Long-term Care Policies in Europe.* Basingstoke: Palgrave.

Carrera, P.M., K.K. Siemens and J. Bridges (2008) 'Health Care Financing in Germany: The Case for Rethinking the Evolutionary Approach to Reforms', *Journal of Health Politics, Policy and Law* 33 (5): 979–1005.

Carson, D., A. Schoo and P. Berggren (2015) 'The 'Rural Pipeline' and Retention of Health Professionals in Europe's Northern Periphery', *Health Policy* 119 (12): 1550–6.

Castles, F.G. (1999) *Comparative Public Policy. Patterns of Post-war Transformation.* Cheltenham: Edward Elgar.

Cawley, J. (2007) 'The Cost-Effectiveness of Programs to Prevent or Reduce Obesity: The State of the Literature and a Future Research Agenda', *Archives of Pediatrics and Adolescent Medicine* 161: 611–14.

CBS News (2009) 'Nations Urge Caution over Flu Response', www.cbsnews.com/news/nations-urge-caution-over-flu-response.

Center for the Evaluative Clinical Sciences (2008) *The Care of Patients with Severe Chronic Illness: An Online Report on the Medicare Program. The Dartmouth Atlas of Health Care*, www.dartmouthatlas.org.

Centers for Medicare and Medicaid Services (2008) 'Home Health PPS', www.cms.hhs.gov/HomeHealthPPS/.

Centers for Disease Control and Prevention (CDC) (2007) *The State of Aging and Health in America.* Atlanta, GA: Centers for Disease Control and Prevention

Centers for Medicare and Medicaid Services (2009a) 'Program of All-Inclusive Care for the Elderly (PACE)', www.medicare.gov/Pubs/pdf/11341.pdf.

Centers for Medicare and Medicaid Services (2009b) 'Regulations and Guidance', www.cms.gov/Regulations-and-Guidance/Regulations-and-Guidance.html.

Centers for Medicare and Medicaid Services (2010) 'Consumer Information and Insurance Oversight', http://cciio.cms.gov/programs/marketreforms/prevention/index.html.

Chang, L. and J.-H. Hung (2008) 'The Effects of the Global Budget System on Cost Containment and the Quality of Care: Experience in Taiwan', *Health Services Management Research* 21: 106–16.

Charlie Rose–Peter Orszag Interview – November 3 (2009), http://seekingalpha.com/article/171551-charlie-rose-interviews-the-white-houses-peter-orszag.

Chaudhry, B., J. Wang, S. Wu, M. Maglione, W. Mojica, E. Roth, S.C. Morton and P.G. Shekelle (2006) 'Systematic Review: Impact of Health Information Technology on Quality, Efficiency, and Costs of Medical Care', *Annals of Internal Medicine* 144 (10): 742–52.

Chen, L.K., W. Yip, M-C. Chang, H-S. Lin, S-D. Lee, Y-L. Chiu and Y-H. Lin (2007) 'The Effects of Taiwan's National Health Insurance on Access and Health Status of the Elderly', *Health Economics* 16 (3): 223–42.

Chen, Y.T., C.M. Huang, P.P. Huang and W.C. Chu (2008) 'Design a Wireless Radio Frequency Identification Based Intelligent Drug Preparation System', *Technology and Applications in Biomedicine* 30–1: 549–51.

Cheng, L-F., E. Kuhlmann and E. Annandale (2012) 'Gender Mainstreaming at the Crossroads of Eastern-western Healthcare', in E. Kuhlmann and E. Annandale (eds) *The Palgrave Handbook of Gender and Healthcare*, 2nd edn. Basingstoke: Palgrave.

Cheng, S-H. and W-L. Chang (2007) 'Hospital Response to the Global Budget Program Implemented by Taiwan's National Health Insurance', IHEA 2007 6th World Congress: Explorations in Health Economics Paper, http://ssrn.com/abstract=992643.

Cheng, S-H., Y-J. Wei and H-J. Chang (2006) 'Quality Competition among Hospitals: The Effects of Perceived Quality and Perceived Expensiveness on Health Care Consumers', *American Journal of Medical Quality* 21 (1): 68–76.

Cheng, S-H. C-M. Chang, C-C. Chen, C-Y. Shih and S-L. Tsai (2015). 'Half-Managed Care: A Preliminary Assessment of a Capitation Program in a Health Care System Without Gatekeepers', *International Journal of Health Services*, doi: 10.1177/0020731415615310.

Cheng, T-M. (2015) 'Taiwan's Health Care System: The Next 20 Years', *Taiwan-U.S. Quarterly Analysis* 17, www.brookings.edu/research/opinions/2015/05/14-taiwan-national-healthcare-cheng.

Chernichovsky, D. (1995) 'Health System Reforms in Industrialized Democracies: An Emerging Paradigm', *The Milbank Quarterly* 73 (3): 339–56.

Chi, C., J.L. Lee and R. Schoon (2012) 'Assessing Health Information Technology in a National Health Care System: An Example from Taiwan', *Advances in Health Care Management* 12: 75–109.

Chiu, Y-C., K.C. Smith and L. Morlock (2007) 'Gifts, Bribes and Solicitations: Print Media and the Social Construction of Informal Payments to Doctors in Taiwan', *Social Science & Medicine* 64 (3): 521–30.

Churchill, L.R. (2005) 'Age-Rationing in Health Care: Flawed Policy, Personal Virtue', *Health Care Analysis* 13 (2): 137–46.

Ciarini, A. (2008) 'Family, Market and Voluntary Action in the Regulation of the "Care System": A Comparison between Italy and Sweden', *World Political Science Review* 4 (1), doi: 10.2202/1935-6226.1043.

Clasen, J. (ed.) (1999) *Comparative Social Policy.* Oxford: Blackwell.

Clinical Advisory Board (2001) *Elevating the Standard of Critical Care.* Washington, DC: The Advisory Board Company.

Cohen, J.T., P.J. Neumann and M.C. Weinstein (2008) 'Does Preventive Care Save Money? Health Economics and the Presidential Candidates', *New England Journal of Medicine* 358 (7): 661–13.

Cohen, S. (2015) 'The Concentration and Persistence in the Level of Health Expenditures over Time: Estimates for the U.S. Population, 2012–2013'. Statistical Brief #481. September 2015. Agency for Healthcare Research and Quality, Rockville, MD, www.meps.ahrq.gov/mepsweb/data_files/publications/st481/stat481.pdf.

Collier, D. and S. Levitsky (1997) 'Democracy with Adjectives: Conceptual Innovation in Comparative Research', *World Politics* 49: 430–51.

Comas-Herrera, A., R. Wittenberg and L. Pickard (2010) 'The Long Road to Universalism? Recent Developments in the Financing of Long-term Care in England', *Social Policy & Administration* 44 (4): 375–91.

Commonwealth Fund Commission on a High Performance Health System (2009) *The Path to a High Performance U.S. Health System: A 2020 Vision and the Policies to Pave the Way*. New York: The Commonwealth Fund.

Conceição, C. and M. McCarthy (2011) 'Public Health Research Systems in the European Union', *Health Research Policy and Systems* 9: 38–53.

Conference of the Parties to the WHO FCTC (2008) *Guidelines for Implementation of Article 11 of the WHO Framework Convention on Tobacco Control on Packaging and Labelling of Tobacco Products,* Decision FCTC/COP3 (10) (November).

Contandriopoulos, D, A. Brousselle, M. Breton, E. Sangster-Gormley, K. Kilpatrick, A. Dubois, I. Brault and M. Perroux (2016) 'Nurse Practitioners, Canaries in the Mine of Primary Care Reform', *Health Policy* 120: 682–9.

Cooper, Z., F.P. Rivara, J. Wang and E.J. MacKenzie (2012) 'Racial Disparities in Intensity of Care at the End-of-Life: Are Trauma Patients the Same as the Rest?', *Journal of Health Care for the Poor and Underserved* 23 (2): 857–74.

Correia, T. and J-L. Denis (2016) 'Hybrid Management, Organizational Configuration, and Medical Professionalism: Evidence from the Establishment of a Clinical Directorate in Portugal', *BMC Health Services Research* 16 (Suppl. 2): 161.

Correia, T., G. Dussault and C. Pontes (2015) 'The Impact of the Financial Crisis on Human Resources for Health Policies in Three Southern-Europe Countries', *Health Policy* 119 (12): 1600–5.

Cortez, N. (2008a) 'International Health Care Convergence: The Benefits and Burdens of Market-driven Standardization', *Wisconsin International Law Journal* 26 (3): 646–704.

Cortez, N. (2008b) 'Patients without Borders: The Emerging Global Market for Patients and the Evolution of Modern Health Care', *Indiana Law Journal* 83: 71–132.

Costa-Font, J. and C. Hernández Quevedo (2012) 'Measuring Inequalities in Health: What do We Know? What do We Need to Know?', *Health Policy* 106: 195–206.

Costa-Font, J. and M.G. Toyama (2011) 'Does Cost Sharing Really Reduce Inappropriate Prescriptions among the Elderly?', *Health Policy* 101 (2): 195–208.

Coulter, A. and C. Ham (eds) (2000) *The Global Challenge of Health Care Rationing*. Buckingham: Open University Press.

Craddock, S. and S. Hinchliffe (2015) 'One World, One Health? Social Science Engages with the One Health Agenda', *Social Science & Medicine* 129: 1–4.

Creagh, H. (2008) 'Strategy to Stem the Rise of Obesity Criticised as "Feeble Fantasy"', *British Medical Journal* 336: 240–1.

Crisp, A. (2010) *Turning the World Upside Down: The Search for Global Health in the 21st Century*. London: CRC Press.

Cubit, K.A. and C. Meyer (2011) 'Aging in Australia', *Gerontologist* 51 (5): 583–9.

Cylus, J., E. Richardson, L. Findley, M. Longley, C. O'Neill and D. Steele (2015) 'United Kingdom: Health System Review', *Health Systems in Transition* 17 (5): 1–155.

Cylus, J. (2016) Realigning Financing to Better Meet Individual Health Care Needs', in *OECD Reviews of Health Systems*. Paris: OECD.

Davey, J.A. and S. Keeling (2004) 'Combining Work and Eldercare: A Neglected Work-Life Balance Issue', *Labour, Employment and Work in New Zealand*. Wellington: Victoria University Institute for Research on Ageing.

Davies, G.P., W. Hu, J. McDonald, J. Furier, E. Harris and M. Harris (2006) 'Developments in Australian General Practice 2000–2002: What Did These Contribute to a Well-Functioning and Comprehensive Primary Health Care System?', *Australia and New Zealand Health Policy* 3 (1), www.anzhealth-policy.com/content/3/1/1.

Davies, S.E. (2010) *Global Politics of Health*. Cambridge. UK: Polity Press.

Davis, C. and J.C. Carter (2009) 'Compulsive Overeating as an Addiction Disorder: A Review of Theory and Evidence', *Appetite* 53: 1–8.

Davis, E. (2016) 'How Health Care Providers Prevent Adverse Selection', www.verywell.com/adverse-selection-what-it-is-how-health-plans-avoid-it-1738416.

Davis, K., M.M. Doty, K. Shea and K. Stremikis (2009) 'Health Information Technology and Physician Perceptions of Quality of Care and Satisfaction', *Health Policy* 90 (2–3): 239–46.

Davis, P. and T. Ashton (eds) (2001) *Health and Public Policy in New Zealand*. Auckland: Oxford University Press.

Davis, P. and K. Dew (eds) (2000) *Health and Society in Aotearoa New Zealand*. Auckland: Oxford University Press.

Dawson, A. and M. Verweij (eds) (2007) *Ethics, Prevention, and Public Health*. New York: Oxford University Press.

De Ferranti, D. (1985) 'Paying for Health Services in Developing Countries: An Overview', *World Bank Staff Working Paper 721*. Washington, DC: The World Bank.

De Raeve, P., A.M. Rafferty and L. Barriball (2016) 'EU Accession: A Policy Window for Nursing?', *EuroHealth* 22 (1): 10–13.

de Silva-Sanigorski, A., L. Prosser, L. Carpenter, S. Honisett, L. Gibbs, M. Moodie, L. Sheppard, B. Swinburn and E. Waters (2010) 'Evaluation of the Childhood Obesity Prevention Program Kids – "Go for your life"', *BMC Public Health* 10: 288, doi:10.1186/1471-2458-10-288.

Deleon, P. and P. Resnick-Terry (1999) 'Comparative Policy Analysis: Déjà vu all over Again?', *Comparative Policy Analysis* 1: 9–22.

Denis, J.-L. and P.-G. Forest (2012) 'Real Reform Begins Within: An Organizational Approach to Health Care Reform', *Journal of Health Politics, Policy and Law* 37 (4): 633–45.

Denis, J-L., N. van Gestel and A. Lepage (2016) 'Professional Agency, Leadership and Organizational Change', in M. Dent, I. Bourgeault, J-L. Denis and E. Kuhlmann (eds) *The Routledge Companion to the Professions and Professionalism*. London: Routledge.

Dent, M., I. Kirkpatrick and I. Neogy (2012) 'Medical Leadership and Management Reforms in Hospital: A Comparative Study', in C. Teelken, E. Ferlie and M. Dent (eds) *Leadership in the Public Sector: Promises and Pitfalls*. London: Routledge.

Dent, M., I. Bourgeault, J-L. Denis and E. Kuhlmann (2016) 'Introduction: The Changing World of Professions and Professionalism', in M. Dent, I. Bourgeault, J.L. Denis and E. Kuhlmann (eds) *The Routledge Companion to the Professions and Professionalism*. London: Routledge.

Department of Health (2012a) *Clinically-led Commissioning: The Health and Social Care Act 2012*. Factsheet B1. London: Department of Health, www.gov.uk/government/uploads/system/uploads/attachment_data/file/138260/B1.-Factsheet-Clinically-led-commissioning-2404121.pdf (18 December 2012).

Department of Health (2012b) *Greater Accountability Locally and Nationally – The Health and Social Care Act 2012. Factsheet B5*. London: Department of Health, www.dh.gov.uk/healthandsocialcarebill (18 December 2012).

Department of Health (2012c) *Overview of Health and Care Structures – The Health and Social Care Act 2012. Factsheet A3*. London: Department of Health, www.dh.gov.uk/healthandsocialcarebill (18 December 2012).

Department of Health (2012d) *The Health and Social Care Act 2012*. Factsheet A1. London: Department of Health, www.dh.gov.uk/healthandsocialcarebill (18 December 2012).

Derrett, S., T.H. Bevin, P. Herbison and C. Paul (2009) 'Access to Elective Surgery in New Zealand: Considering Equity and the Private and Public Mix', *International Journal of Health Planning and Management* 24: 147–60.

DeVoe, J.E. (2001) *The Politics of Health Care Reform: A Comparative Study of National Health Insurance in Britain and Australia*. Kensington, NSW: School of Health Services Management.

DiClemente, R.J., R.A. Crosby and M.C. Kegler (2002) *Emerging Theories in Health Promotion Practice and Research: Strategies for Improving Public Health*. San Francisco: Jossey-Bass.

Dieleman, J.L., T. Templin, N. Sadat, P. Reidy, A. Chapin, K. Foreman, A. Haakenstad, T. Evans, C.J.L. Murray and C. Kurowski, (2016) 'National Spending on Health by Source for 184 Countries between 2013 and 2040', *The Lancet* 387: 2521–35.

Directive 2013/55/EU of the European Parliament and the Council of 20 November 2013 amending Directive 2005/36/EC on the recognition of professional qualifications and Regulation (EU) No 1024/2012 on administrative cooperation through the Internal Market Information System ('the IMI Regulation'), http://eur-lex.europa.eu/legal-content/EN/TXT/PDF/?uri=CELEX:32013L0055&from=EN.>.

Dobbin, F., B.A. Simmons and G. Garrett (2007) 'The Global Diffusion of Public Policies: Social Construction, Coercion, Competition, or Learning', *Annual Review of Sociology* 33: 449–72.

Docteur, E., H. Suppanz and J. Woo (2003) 'The US Health System: An Assessment and Prospective Directions for Reform', *Economics Department Working Papers No. 350*, www.oecd.org/eco.

Döhler, M. (1991) 'Policy Networks, Opportunity Structures and Neo-Conservative Reform Strategies in Health Policy', in B. Marin and

R. Mayntz (eds) *Policy Networks: Empirical Evidence and Theoretical Considerations*. Boulder, CO: Westview Press.

Donato, R. and L. Segal (2010) 'The Economics of Primary Healthcare Reform in Australia – Towards Single Fundholding through Development of Primary Care Organisations', *Australia and New Zealand Journal of Public Health* 34 (6): 613–19.

Doniec, K., R. Dall'Alba and L. King (2016) 'Austerity Threatens Universal Health Coverage in Brazil', *The Lancet* 388 (10047): 867–8.

Donnelly, H. (2013) '"Jaw-Dropping" Rise in NHS Claims after Scandals', www.telegraph.co.uk/news/health/news/10189204/Jaw-dropping-rise-in-NHS-claims-after-scandals.html.

Doorslaer, E.V., P. Clarke, E. Savage and J. Hall (2008) 'Horizontal Inequities in Australia's Mixed Public/Private Health Care System', *Health Policy* 86: 97–108.

Dosso, Z. (2016) 'WHO Declares Ebola Outbreak Over', www.yahoo.com/news/declares-worst-ever-ebola-outbreak-over-092344314.html?ref=gs.

Dovey, S., M. Tilyard, W. Cunningham and M. Williamson (2011) 'Public and Private Funding of General Practice Services for Children and Adolescents in New Zealand', *Health Policy* 103 (1): 24–30.

Doyle, M. and V. Timonen (2007) *Home Care for Ageing Populations: A Comparative Analysis of Domiciliary Care in Denmark, the United States and Germany*. Cheltenham: Edward Elgar.

Dragon, N. (2008) 'Health Reform: Finding the Way', *Australian Nursing Journal* 15 (7): 20–3.

Drummond, M.B. and D. Upson (2014). 'Electronic Cigarettes: Potential Harms and Benefits'. *Annals of the American Thoracic Society* 11 (2): 236–42.

Drummond, M.F., M.J. Sculpher, G.W. Torrance and B.J. O'Brien (2005) *Methods for the Economic Evaluation of Health Care Programmes*. New York: Oxford University Press.

Duckett, S.J. (2004a) *The Australian Health Care System*, 2nd edn. Melbourne: Oxford University Press.

Duckett, S.J. (2004b) 'The Australian Health Care Agreements, 2003–2008', *Australia and New Zealand Health Policy* 1 (5), www.anzhealth policy.com/content/1/1/5.

Duff, J. (2001) 'Financing to Foster Community Health Care: A Comparative Analysis of Singapore, Europe, North America, and Australia', *Current Sociology* 49 (3): 135–54.

Dugdale, P. (2008) *Doing Health Policy in Australia*. Sydney: Allen and Unwin.

Dussault, G. (2015) 'Bringing the Health Workforce Challenges on the Policy Agenda', in E. Kuhlmann, R.H. Blank, I.L. Bourgeault and C. Wendt (eds) *The Palgrave International Handbook of Healthcare Policy and Governance*. Basingstoke: Palgrave.

Dussault, G. and J. Buchan (2014) 'The Economic Crisis in the EU: Impact on Health Workforce Mobility', in J. Buchan, M. Wismar, I.A. Glinos and J. Bremner (eds) *Health Professional Mobility in a Changing Europe: New Dynamics, Mobile Individuals and Diverse Responses*. Observatory Studies Series 32. Copenhagen: WHO.

Dwyer, J.M. (2004) 'Australian Health System Restructuring: What Problem Is Being Solved?', *Australia and New Zealand Health Policy*, 19 November: 1–6.

Ebi, K. (2011) 'Climate Change and Health Risks: Assessing and Responding to Them through "Adaptive Management"', *Health Affairs* 30 (5): 924–30.

E-Cigarette Politics (2016) 'E-Cigarette Laws Worldwide', www.ecigarette-politics.com/electronic-cigarettes-global-legal-status.html.

Eckerberg, K., B. Fordberg and P. Wickenberg (1998) 'Sweden: Setting the Pace with Pioneers, Municipalities and Schools', in W.M. Lafferty and K. Eckerberg (eds) *From the Earth Summit to Local Agenda 21*. London: Earthscan.

Ehrlich, C., E. Kendall, H. Muenchberger and K. Armstrong (2009) 'Coordinated Care: What Does That Really Mean?', *Health and Social Care in the Community* 44 (2): 147–52.

Elston, M.A. (1991) 'The Politics of Professional Power: Medicine in a Changing Health Service', in J. Gabe, M. Calnan and M. Bury (eds) *The Sociology of the Health Service*. London: Routledge.

Emanuel, E.J. and S.D. Pearson (2012) 'It Costs More, But Is It Worth More?' *New York Times*. 1 January. Sect. Opinionator online.

England, L.J., R.E. Bunnell, T.F. Pechacek, V.T. Tong and T.A. McAfee (2015) 'Nicotine and the Developing Human', *American Journal of Preventive Medicine*. doi:10.1016/j.amepre.2015.01.015.

Epstein, P.R. (2000) 'Is Global Warming Harmful to Health?', *Scientific American*, 20 August.

Esping-Andersen, G. (1990) *The Three Worlds of Welfare Capitalism*. Oxford: Polity Press.

Ettelt, S., M. Fazekas, N. Mays and E. Nolte (2012) 'Assessing Health Care Planning: A Framework-led Comparison of Germany and New Zealand', *Health Policy* 106: 50–9.

European Commission (2008). *Green Paper on the European Workforce for Health*, 10.12.2008, COM (2008) 725 final. Brussels: European Commission.

European Observatory on Health Care Systems (1999) *Health Care Systems in Transition: United Kingdom*. Copenhagen: European Observatory on Health Care Systems.

European Public Health (2016) 'Health System Performance Assessment', www.europeanpublichealth.com/health-systems/health-system-performance-assessment.

Evans, T. and A. Pablos-Méndez (2016) 'Shaping of a New Era for Health Funding', *The Lancet* 387 (10037): 2482–84.

Evers, A. and I. Svetlik (eds) (1993) *Balancing Pluralism. New Welfare Mixes in Care for the Elderly*. Aldershot: Avebury.

Executive Office of the President (2010) *Report to the President: Realizing the Full Potential of Information Technology to Improve Healthcare for Americans: The Path Forward*. Washington, DC: President's Council of Advisors on Science and Technology.

Exter, A. den, H. Hermans, M. Dosljak and R. Busse (2004) *Health Care Systems in Transition: Netherlands*. Copenhagen: WHO Regional Office for Europe on Behalf of the European Observatory on Health Care Systems.

FarmOnline (2009) '$120,000 Lure for Doctors to go Bush'. Canberra: National News Bureau.

Farquharson, K. (2003) 'Influencing Policy Transnationally: Pro- and Anti-Tobacco Global Advocacy Networks', *Australian Journal of Public Administration* 62 (4): 80–92.

Farsalinos, K.E. and R. Polosa (2014) 'Safety Evaluation and Risk Assessment of Electronic Cigarettes as Tobacco Cigarette Substitutes: A Systematic Review', *Therapeutic Advances in Drug Safety* 5 (2): 67–86.

Farsalinos, K.E., A. Spyrou, K. Tsimopoulou, C. Stefopoulos, G. Romagna and V. Voudris (2014) 'Nicotine Absorption from Electronic Cigarette Use: Comparison between First and New-Generation Devices', *Scientific Reports* 4: 4133. doi:10.1038/srep04133.

Fauci, A.S. and D.M. Morens (2016). 'Zika Virus in the Americas – Yet Another Arbovirus Threat', *The New England Journal of Medicine* 374 (7): 601–4.

FDA (2014) 'Vaporizers, E-Cigarettes, and other Electronic Nicotine Delivery Systems', www.fda.gov/TobaccoProducts/Labeling/ProductsIngredients Components/ucm456610.htm.

Feldman, E.A. (2000) *The Ritual of Rights in Japan: Law, Society, and Health Policy*. Cambridge: Cambridge University Press.

Fenton, L. and B. Salter (2009) 'Competition and Compromise in Negotiating the New Governance of Medical Performance: The Clinical Governance and Revalidation Policies in the UK', *Health Economics, Policy and Law* 4 (3): 283–304.

Ferguson, J. (2005) 'WHO Says Skin Cancer Incidence Is Rising', *Journal Watch*, http://dermatology.jwatch.org/cgi/content/full/2005/426/1#primary content.

Fernández, E., M. Ballbè, X. Sureda, M. Fu, E. Saltó and J.M. Martínez-Sánchez (2015) 'Particulate Matter from Electronic Cigarettes and Conventional Cigarettes: A Systematic Review and Observational Study', *Current Environmental Health Reports*. doi:10.1007/s40572-015-0072-x.

Fernández, J.-L. and P. Nadash (2016) 'The Long-term Care Financing Problem', in C. Gori, J-L. Fernández and E. Wittenberg (eds) *Long-term Care Reforms in OECD Countries: Successes and Failures*. Bristol: Policy Press.

Ferri, C.P., D. Acosta, M. Guerra, Y. Huang, J.J. Llibre-Rodriguez, A. Salas, A.L. Sosa, J.D. Williams, C. Gaona, Z. Liu, L. Noriega-Fernandez and M.J. Prince (2012) 'Socioeconomic Factors and All Cause and Cause-Specific Mortality among Older People in Latin America, India, and China: A Population-Based Cohort Study', *PLoS Med* (2):e1001179. doi:10.1371/journal.pmed.1001179.

Field, M.G. (1999) 'Comparative Health Systems and the Convergence Hypothesis: The Dialectics of Universalism and Particularism', in F.D. Powell and A.F. Wessen (eds) *Health Care Systems in Transition: An International Perspective*. Thousand Oaks, CA: Sage.

Fielding, J.E., S. Teutsch and L. Breslow (2010) 'A Framework for Public Health in the United States', *Public Health Reviews* 32 (1): 174–89.

Fielding, J.E., S. Teutsch and H. Koh (2012) 'Health Reform and Healthy People Initiative', *American Journal of Public Health* 102 (1): 30–3.

Finkelstein, E.A., J.G. Trogdon, J.W. Cohen and W. Dietz (2009) 'Annual Medical Spending Attributable to Obesity: Payer- and Service-Specific Estimates', *Health Affairs* 28 (5): w822–w831.

Fleck, L.M. (2002) 'Rationing: Don't Give Up: It's Not Only Necessary, but Possible, if the Public Can Be Educated', *The Hastings Center Report* 32 (2): 35–8.

Ford, E.S., U.A. Ajani, J.B. Croft, J. Critchley, D.R. Labarthe, T.E. Kottle, W.H. Giles and S. Capewell (2007) 'Explaining the Decrease in U.S. Deaths from Coronary Disease, 1980–2000', *New England Journal of Medicine* 356: 2388–98.

Foster, D. (2001) 'Frequent Flyer Racks Up Big Bill', *Detroit News*, 10 October.

Foundation for AIDS Research (2016) 'Statistics: Worldwide', www.amfar.org/worldwide-aids-stats.

Franck, M.J. (1996) *Against the Imperial Judiciary. The Supreme Court vs. the Sovereignty of the People.* Lawrence: University of Kansas Press.

Fredriksson, M. and U. Winblad (2008) 'Consequences of a Decentralized Healthcare Governance Model: Measuring Regional Authority Support for Patient Choice in Sweden', *Social Science and Medicine* 67 (2): 271–9.

Fredriksson, M., P. Blomqvist and U. Winblad (2012) 'Conflict and Compliance in Swedish Health Care Governance: Soft Law in the "Shadow of Hierarchy"', *Scandinavian Political Studies* 35 (1): 48–70.

Freeman, B., S. Chapman and M. Rimmer (2008) 'The Case for Plain Packaging of Tobacco Products', *Addiction* 103: 580–90.

Freeman, R. (1998) 'Competition in Context: The Politics of Health Care Reform in Europe', *International Journal of Quality in Health Care* 10 (5): 395–401.

Freeman, R. (2000) *The Politics of Health in Europe.* Manchester: Manchester University Press.

Freeman, R. (2005) 'Learning in Health Policy', Text of a Presentation to the Social Policy Forum, Bogazici University, Istanbul, 17–18 June, unpublished manuscript, University of Edinburgh, http://www.tandfonline.com/doi/abs/10.1080/13876980500319253.

Freeman, R. (2006) 'Of Transfers, Transplants and Translations: How Health Policy Makers Learn from Abroad', Presentation at the Dansk Forum for Sundhedstjenesteforskning (Danish Forum for Health Services Research), Aarhus University, Denmark, 28 November.

Freeman, R. and L. Frisina (2012) 'Health Care Systems and the Problem of Classification', *Journal of Comparative Policy Analysis: Research and Practice* 12 (1–2): 163–78.

Freeman, R. and M. Ruskin (1999) 'Introduction: Welfare, Culture and Europe', in P. Chamberlayne *et al.* (eds) *Welfare and Culture in Europe: Towards a New Paradigm in Social Policy.* London: Jessica Kingsley.

Freidson, E. (1994) *Professionalism Reborn: Theory, Prophecy and Policy.* Cambridge: Polity.

Frenk, J. and S. Moon (2013) 'Governance Challenges in Global Health', *New England Journal of Medicine* 368: 936–42.

Fry, C.L. (2010) 'Critical Questions We Should Ask in a Changing Australian Preventative Health Landscape: Competing Interests, Intervention Limits and

Permissible Health Identities', *Health Promotion Journal of Australia* 21 (3): 170–5.

Fuchs, V.R. (2004) 'Reflections on the Socio-economic Correlates of Health', *Journal of Health Economics* 23 (4): 653–61.

Fuchs, V.R. (2005) 'Health Care Expenditures Reexamined', *Annals of Internal Medicine* 143 (1): 76–8.

Fuchs, V.R. (2007) 'What are the Prospects for Enduring Comprehensive Health Reform?', *Health Affairs* 26 (6): 1542–4.

Fujisawa, R. and G. Lafortune (2008) 'The Remuneration of General Practitioners and Specialists in 14 OECD Countries. What are the Factors Influencing Variations across Countries?', *OECD Health Working Papers no. 41*. Paris: OECD.

Fukuda, Y., K. Nakamura and T. Takano (2004) 'Wide Range of Socioeconomic Factors Associated with Mortality Among Cities in Japan', *Health Promotion International* 19 (2): 177–87.

Fukuda, Y., H. Nakao, Y. Yahata and H. Imai (2008) 'In-depth Descriptive Analysis of Trends in Prevalence of Long-term Care in Japan', *Geriatrics and Gerontology International* 2008 (8): 166–71.

Fulton, B.D., R.M. Scheffler, S.P. Sparkes, E. Yoonkyung Auh, M. Vujicic and A. Soucat (2011) 'Health Workforce Skill Mix and Task Shifting in Low Income Countries: A Review of Recent Evidence', *Human Resources for Health* 9: 1–18.

Furuse, T. (1996) 'Changing the Balance of Care: Japan', in OECD (ed.) *Caring for Frail Elderly People*. Paris: OECD.

Garpenby, P. (1999) 'Resource Dependency, Doctors and the State: Quality Control in Sweden', *Social Science and Medicine* 49: 405–24.

Garpenby, P. (2001) 'Making Health Policy in Sweden: The Rise and Fall of the 1994 Family Doctor Scheme', in M. Bovens, P. t'Hart and B.G. Peters (eds) *Success and Failure in Public Governance. A Comparative Analysis*. Cheltenham: Edward Elgar.

Garrido, M.V., F.B. Kristensen, C.P. Nielsen and R. Busse (eds) (2008) *Health Technology Assessment and Health-policy Making in Europe. Current Status, Challenges and Potential*. Copenhagen: European Observatory on Health Systems and Policy.

Gauld, R. (2001) *Revolving Doors: New Zealand's Health Reforms*. Wellington: Institute of Policy Studies and Health Services Research Centre.

Gauld, R. (2008) The Unintended Consequences of New Zealand's Primary Health Care Reforms. *Journal of Health Politics, Policy and Law* 33: 93–115.

Gauld, R. (2013) 'The New Zealand Health Care System, 2013', in S. Thomson, R. Osborn, D. Squires and M. Jun (eds) *International Profiles of Health Care Systems, 2013*. New York: The Commonwealth Fund.

Gauld, R. (2015) 'Primary Healthcare as a Global Healthcare Concept', in E. Kuhlmann, R.H. Blank, I.L. Bourgeault and C. Wendt (eds) *The Palgrave International Handbook of Healthcare Policy and Governance*. Basingstoke: Palgrave.

Gauld, R., R.H. Blank, J. Burgers, A.B. Cohen, M. Dobrow, N. Ikegami, S. Kwon, K. Luxford, C. Millett and C. Wendt (2012) 'The World Health Report 2008: Primary Health Care: How Wide is the Gap between its Agenda and Implementation in 12 High-income Health Systems?', *Healthcare Policy* 7 (3): 38–58.

Gauld, R., J. Burgers, M.J. Dobrow, K. Luxford, R. Minhas, C. Wendt and A.B. Cohen (2014) 'Healthcare System Performance Improvement: A Comparison of Key Policies in Seven High-income Countries', *Journal of Health Organization and Management* 28 (1): 2–20.

Gauld, R., N. Ikegami, M.D. Barr, T.-L. Chiang, D. Gould and S. Kwon (2006) 'Advanced Asia's Health Systems in Comparison', *Health Policy* 79: 325–36.

Gerdtham, U-G., B. Jönsson, M. MacFarlan and H. Oxley (1998) 'The Determinants of Health Care Expenditure in OECD Countries: A Pooled Data Analysis', *Developments in Health Economics and Public Policy* 6: 113–34.

Gerhardus, A., H. Becher, P. Groenewegen, U. Mansmann, T. Meyer, H. Pfaff, M. Puhan *et al.* (2016) 'Applying for, Reviewing and Funding Public Health Research in Germany and Beyond', *Health Research Policy and Systems* 14: 43–53.

Gerlach, F.M. and J. Szecsenyi (2013) 'Hausarztzentrierte Versorgung in Baden-Württemberg – Konzept und Ergebnisse der kontrollierten Begleitevaluation, Zeitschrift für Evidenz', *Fortbildung und Qualität im Gesundheitswesen* 107 (6): 365–71.

Gerlinger, T. (2010) 'Health Care Reform in Germany', *German Policy Studies* 6 (1): 107–42.

Germain, D., M.A. Wakefield and S.J. Durkin (2010) 'Adolescents' Perceptions of Cigarette Brand Image: Does Plain Packaging Make a Difference?', *Journal of Adolescent Health* 46 (4): 385–92.

Get America Fit (2012) 'Obesity in America', http://getamericafit.org/american-health-facts/.

Giamo, S. (2002) *Markets and Medicine: The Politics of Health Care Reform in Britain, Germany and the United States.* Ann Arbor, MI: The University of Michigan Press.

Gibson, D. and R. Means (2000) 'Policy Convergence: Restructuring Long-term Care in Australia and the UK', *Policy and Politics* 29 (1): 43–58.

Gilardi, F., K. Füglister and S. Luyet (2009) 'Learning from Others: Diffusion of Hospital Financing Reforms in OECD Countries', *Comparative Political Studies* 42 (4): 549–73.

Giovanella, L. and M. Faria (2015) 'Health Policy Reform in South America', in E. Kuhlmann, R.H. Blank, I.L. Bourgeault and C. Wendt (eds) *The Palgrave International Handbook of Healthcare Policy and Governance.* Basingstoke: Palgrave.

Glendinning, C. (2008) 'Increasing Choice and Control for Older and Disabled People: A Critical Review of New Developments in England', *Social Policy & Administration* 42 (5): 451–69.

Glendinning, C. (2013) 'Long Term Care Reform in England: A Long and Unfinished Story', in C. Ranci and E. Pavolini (eds) *Reforms in Long-Term Care Policies in Europe.* New York: Springer Science & Business Media.

Glennerster, H. and R.C. Lieberman (2011) 'Hidden Convergence: Toward a Historical Comparison of U.S. and U.K. Health Policy', *Journal of Health Politics, Policy and Law* 36 (1): 5–31.

Glenngård, A.H., F. Hjalte, M. Svensson, A. Anell and V. Bankauskaite (2005) *Health Systems in Transition: Sweden*. Copenhagen: WHO Regional Office for Europe on behalf of the European Observatory on Health Care Systems.

Glied, S. (2008) 'Medical Savings Accounts: Can They Improve Health System Performance in Europe?', *EuroObserver* 10 (4): 5–6.

Glinos, I.A., M. Wismar, J. Buchan and I. Rakovak (2015) 'How Can Countries Address the Efficiency and Equity Implications of Health Professional Mobility in Europe?' *Adapting Policies in the Context of the WHO Code and EU Freedom of Movement*. Policy Brief. Copenhagen: WHO.

Global Health Workforce Alliance (2010) *Mid-level Health Providers a Promising Resource to Achieve the Health Millennium Development Goals*. Geneva: WHO.

Global Health Workforce Alliance (2016) 'GHWA Completes its Ten Year Mandate', www.who.int/workforcealliance/en/.

Globerman, S. and A. Vining (1998) 'A Policy Perspective on "Mixed" Health Care Financial Systems of Business and Economics', *Journal of Risk Insurance* 65: 57–80.

Glover, J.D., D.M.S. Hetzel and S.K. Tennant (2004) 'The Socioeconomic Gradient and Chronic Illness and Associated Risk Factors in Australia', *Australia and New Zealand Health Policy* 1 (8).

Goetzel, R.Z. (2009) 'Do Prevention or Treatment Services Save Money? The Wrong Debate', *Health Affairs* 28(1): 37–41.

Goetzel, R.Z., D. Shechter, R.J. Ozminkowski, P.F. Marmet, M.J. Tabrizi and E.C. Roemer (2007) 'Can Health Promotion Programs Save Medicare Money?', *Clinical Interventions in Aging* 2 (1): 117–22.

Goldberg, R. (2012) 'Medical Malpractice and Compensation in the UK', *Chicago-Kent Law Review* 87 (7): 131–61.

Goniewicz, M.L. P. Hajek and H. McRobbie (2014) 'Nicotine Content of Electronic Cigarettes, its Release in Vapour and its Consistency across Batches: Regulatory Implications', *Addiction* 109 (3): 500–507.

Goodin, R.E. and A. Smitsman (2000) 'Placing Welfare States: The Netherlands as a Crucial Test', *Journal of Comparative Public Policy* 2: 39–64.

Göpffarth, D. and S. Bauhoff (2015) 'The Public Health Dimension of Germany's Refugee Crisis', HealthAffairs Blog, http://healthaffairs.org/blog/2015/10/22/the-public-health-dimension-of-germanys-refugee-crisis/.

Gori, C., J-L. Fernández and R. Wittenberg (eds) (2016) *Long-term Care Reforms in OECD Countries: Successes and Failures*. Bristol: Policy Press.

Gostin, L.O., P.D. Jacobson, K.L. Record and L.E. Hardcastle (2011) 'Restoring Health to Health Reform: Integrating Medicine and Public Health to Advance the Population's Well-Being', *University of Pennsylvania Law Review* 159: 1777–1824.

Gough, R. (1994) 'Från Hembiträden till Social Hemtjänst', in A. Baude and C. Rundström (eds) *Kvinnans plats i det tidiga välfardssamhället*. Stockholm: Carlsson.

Grana, R. A., L. Popova and P. M. Ling (2014). 'A Longitudinal Analysis of E-cigarette Use and Smoking Cessation', *JAMA Internal Medicine* 174 (5): 812–83.

Green, A. (2007) *An Introduction to Health Planning for Developing Health Systems*. New York: Oxford University Press.

Green, A., D. Ross and T. Mirzoe (2007) 'Primary Health Care and England: The Coming of Age of Alma Ata?', *Health Policy* 80: 11–31.

Green, R. (2011) 'The Ethics of Sin Taxes', *Public Health Nursing* 28: 68–77, doi: 10.1111/j.1525-1446.2010.00907x.

Green, R.M., A. Donovan and S.A. Jauss (eds) (2009) *Global Bioethics: Issues of Conscience for the Twenty-First Century*. New York: Oxford University Press.

Green, S.H., R. Bayer and A.L. Fairchild (2016) 'Evidence, Policy, and E-cigarettes: Will England Reframe the Debate?' *New England Journal of Medicine* 374 (14): 1301–3.

Greenlee, G. (2003) 'Singapore is Right to Get Tough', www.ctnow.com/news/opinion/oped.

Greer, S.L. (2012) 'The European Centre for Disease Prevention and Control: Hub or Hollow Core?', *Journal of Health Politics, Policy and Law*, doi: 10.1215/03616878-1813817.

Greer, S.L. and P. Kurzer (2012) *European Union Public Health Policy: Regional and Global Trends*. London: Routledge.

Greer, S.L. and E. Massard de Fonseca (2015) 'Decentralization and Health System Governance', in E. Kuhlmann, R.H. Blank, I.L. Bourgeault and C. Wendt (eds) *The Palgrave International Handbook of Healthcare Policy and Governance*. Basingstoke: Palgrave.

Greer, S.L. and M. Mätzke (2012) 'Bacteria without Borders: Communicable Disease Politics in Europe', *Journal of Health Politics, Policy and Law*, doi: 10.1215/03616878-1813763.

Greer, S.L. and M. Mätzke (2015) 'Health Policy in the European Union', in E. Kuhlmann, R.H. Blank, I.L. Bourgeault and C. Wendt (eds) *The Palgrave International Handbook of Healthcare Policy and Governance*. Basingstoke: Palgrave.

Greer, S.L., M. Wismar and J. Figueras (eds) (2016) *Strengthening Health System Governance: Better Policies, Stronger Performance*. Maidenhead: Open University Press. European Observatory on Health Systems and Policies Series.

Greer, S.L., M. Wismar and M. Kosinska (2015) 'Towards Intersectoral Governance: Lessons Learned from Health System Governance', *Public Health Panorama* 1 (2): 128–32, http://www.euro.who.int/__data/assets/pdf_file/0003/287139/Towards-intersectoral-governance-lessons-learned-Eng.pdf?ua=1.

Greer, S.L., M. Wismar, J. Figueras and N. Vasev (2016) 'Policy Lessons for Health Governance', in S.L. Greer, M. Wismar and J. Figueras (eds) *Strengthening Health System Governance: Better Policies, Stronger Performance*. Maidenhead: Open University Press.

Greß, S., P. Groenewegen, J. Kerssens, B. Braun and J. Wasem (2002) 'Free Choice of Sickness Funds in Regulated Competition: Evidence from Germany and the Netherlands', *Health Policy* 60: 235–54.

Grieshaber-Otto, J. and S. Sinclair (2004) *Bad Medicine: Trade Treaties, Privatization and Health Care Reform in Canada*. Ottawa: Canadian Centre for Policy Alternatives.

Grignon, M. (2012) 'A Democratic Responsiveness Approach to Real Reform: An Exploration of Health Care Systems' Resilience', *Journal of Health Politics, Policy and Law* 37 (4): 665–76.

Groene, O., H. Hildebrandt, L. Ferrer and V. Stein (2016) 'People-Centred Population Health Management in Germany', *Eurohealth* 22 (2): 7–10.

Groenewegen, P.P. (2008) 'Nursing as Grease in the Primary Care Machinery', *Quality in Primary Care* 16: 313–14.

Groenewegen, P.P, S. Heinemann, S. Greß and W. Schäfer (2015) 'Primary Health Care in 34 Countries', *Health Policy* 119 (12): 1576–83.

Hacker, J.S. (2011) 'Why Reform Happened', *Journal of Health Politics, Policy and Law* 36 (3): 437–41.

Haddon, K. (2006) 'Britain is Fattest Country in Europe', *Agence France Presse*, 10 October.

Hagopian, A., A. Halperin, P. Atwater, N. Fradkin, J.H. Gilroy and E. Medeiros (2015) *E-Cigarettes: Evidence and Policy Options for Washington State.* Seattle: University of Washington School of Public Health Department of Health Services.

Håkansson, S. and S. Nordling (1997) 'Sweden', in M.W. Raffel (ed.) *Health Care and Reform in Industrialized Countries.* University Park, PA: Pennsylvania State University Press.

Ham, C. (ed.) (1997a) *Health Care Reform: Learning from International Experience.* Buckingham: Open University Press.

Ham, C. (1997b) 'Priority Setting in Health Care: Learning from International Experience', *Health Policy* 42 (1): 49–66.

Ham, C. (2009) *Health Policy in Britain,* 6th edn. Basingstoke: Palgrave Macmillan.

Ham, C. (2010) 'The Ten Characteristics of the High-performing Chronic Care System', *Health Economics, Policy and Law* 5 (1): 71–90.

Ham, C. and G. Robert (eds) (2003) *Reasonable Rationing: International Experience of Priority Setting in Health Care.* Buckingham: Open University Press.

Hammond, D., D. Arnott, M. Dockrell, A. Lee and A.C. McNeill (2009) 'Cigarette Pack Design and Perceptions of Risk among UK Adult and Youth: Evidence in Support of Plain Packaging', *European Journal of Public Health* 19 (6): 631–7.

Hanibuchi, T., T. Nakaya and C. Murata (2010) 'Socio-economic Status and Self-Rated Health in East Asia: A Comparison of China, Japan, South Korea and Taiwan', *European Journal of Public Health* 22 (1): 47–52.

Hantrais, L. and S. Mangen (eds) (1996) *Cross-national Research Methods in the Social Sciences.* London: Pinter.

Harman, S. (2012a) *Global Health Governance* (Global Institutions). London: Routledge.

Harman, S. (2012b) *The World Bank and HIV/AIDS: Setting a Global Agenda.* London: Routledge.

Harris, M.F., N.A. Zwar, C.F. Walker and S.M. Knight (2011) 'Strategic Approaches to the Development of Australia's Future Primary Care Workforce', *Medical Journal of Australia* 194 (11): s88–s91.

Harrison, M.I. (2004) *Implementing Change in Health Systems. Market Reforms in the United Kingdom, Sweden and the Netherlands.* London: Sage.

Harrison, S. (2001) 'Reforming the Medical Profession in the United Kingdom, 1989–97: Structural Interests in Health Care', in M. Bovens, P. t'Hart and B.G. Peters (eds) *Success and Failure in Public Governance. A Comparative Analysis*. Cheltenham: Edward Elgar.

Harrison, S. and R. McDonald (2007) 'Fixing Legitimacy? The Case of NICE and the National Health Service', in A. Hann (ed.) *Health Policy and Politics*. Aldershot: Ashgate.

Harrison, S. and R. McDonald (2008) *The Politics of Healthcare in Britain*. London: Sage.

Harrison, S., M. Moran and B. Wood (2002) 'Policy Emergence and Policy Convergence: The Case of "Scientific-bureaucratic Medicine" in the United States and United Kingdom', *British Journal of Politics and International Relations* 4 (1): 1–24.

Haseltine, W.A. (2012) *Affordable Excellence: The Singapore Health System*. Singapore: National University of Singapore Press.

Hassenteufel, P., M. Smyrl, W. Genieys and F.J. Moreno-Fuentes (2010) 'Programmatic Actors and the Transformation of European Health Care States', *Journal of Health Politics, Policy and Law* 35 (4): 517–38.

Hayashi, S. (2016) 'How Health and Homelessness are Connected—Medically', *The Atlantic*, http://www.theatlantic.com/politics/archive/2016/01/how-health-and-homelessness-are-connectedmedically/458871/.

Healy, J. and P. Dugdale (2013) 'The Australian Health Care System, 2013', in S. Thomson, R. Osborn, D. Squires and M. Jun (eds) *International Profiles of Health Care Systems, 2013*. New York: The Commonwealth Fund.

Health Affairs (2014) 'Health Policy Brief: E-Cigarettes and Federal Regulation,' http://www.healthaffairs.org/healthpolicybriefs/brief.php?brief_id=120.

Health and Human Services (2013) *Projecting the Supply and Demand for Primary Care Practitioners through 2020*. Rockville, MD: US Department of Health and Human Resources.

Henderson, J.N., J. Coreil and C. Bryant (2001) *Social and Behavioural Foundations of Public Health*. London: Sage.

Henderson, S. and A. Peterson (2002) *Consuming Health: The Commodification of Health Care*. London: Routledge.

Henning, M., A. Goto, C. Chi and M.R. Reich (2015) 'Leveraging the Voice of Community Workers in Health Governance: A Two-case Study from Zambia and Japan', in M.R. Reich and K. Takemi (eds) *Governing Health Systems: For Nations and Communities around the World*. Boston MA: Lamprey & Lee.

Hernández Quevedo, C., A.M. Jones and N. Rice (2008) 'Persistence in Health Limitations: A European Comparative Analysis', *Journal of Health Economics* 27 (6): 1472–88.

Herper, M. (2004) 'Cancer's Cost Crisis', *Forbes*, 8 June.

Hervey, T.K. and J. McHale (2015) *European Union Health Law: Themes and Implications*. Cambridge: Cambridge University Press.

Herwartz, H. and B. Theilen (2010) 'The Determinants of Health-Care Expenditure: New Results from Semiparametric Estimation', *Health Economics* 19: 964–78.

Hess, J.J., J.Z. McDowell and G. Luber (2012) 'Integrating Climate Change Adaptation into Public Health Practice: Using Adaptive Management to

Increase Adaptive Capacity and Build Resilience', *Environmental Health Perspectives* 120: 171–9.

Heywood, A. (2002) *Politics*. Basingstoke: Palgrave.

Hill, M. (2009) *The Public Policy Process*, 5th edn. New York: Longman.

Hillestad, R., J. Bigelow, A. Bower, F. Girosi, R. Meili, R. Scoville and R. Taylor (2005) 'Can Electronic Medical Record Systems Transform Healthcare? An Assessment of Potential Health Benefits, Savings, and Costs', *Health Affairs* 24 (5): 1103–17.

Hitiris, T. and J. Nixon. (2001) 'Convergence of Health Care Expenditure in the EU Countries', *Applied Economic Letters* 8: 223–8.

Hoffman, A.K. (2010) 'Oil and Water: Mixing Individual Mandates, Fragmented Markets, and Health Reform', *American Journal of Law and Medicine* 36 (1): 7–77.

Hofler, R.A. and J. Ortiz (2016) 'Costs of Accountable Care Organization Participation for Primary Care Providers: Early Stage Results', *BMC Health Services Research* 16: 315.

Holtz, C. (2012) *Global Health Care*, 2nd edn. Burlington, MA: Jones and Bartlett Publishers.

Holzinger, K. and C. Knill (2005) 'Causes and Conditions of Cross-national Policy Convergence', *Journal of European Public Policy* 12 (5): 775–96.

Hosking, J. and D. Campbell-Lendrum (2012) 'How Well Does Climate Change and Human Health Research Match the Demands of Policymakers? A Scoping Review', *Environmental Health Perspectives*, http://dx.doi.org/10.1289/ehp.1104093.

House of Commons, Health Committee (2016) 'Primary Healthcare UK' (April 2016) Report, http://www.publications.parliament.uk/pa/cm201516/cmselect/cmhealth/408/40802.htm.

Howe, R.K. (2005) 'Moral Hazard Health Spending', *Health Affairs* 24 (2): 567–8.

Howell, B. (2005) 'Restructuring Primary Health Care Markets in New Zealand: From Welfare Benefits to Insurance Markets', *Australia and New Zealand Health Policy* 2 (2), www.anzhealthpolicy.com/content/2/1/20.

Howlett, M. and M. Ramesh (2009) *Studying Public Policy: Policy Cycles and Policy Subsystems*, 3rd edn. Oxford: Oxford University Press.

Howse, G. (2004) 'Managing Emerging Infectious Diseases: Is a Federal System an Impediment to Effective Laws?', *Australia and New Zealand Health Policy* 1 (7), www.anzhealthpolicy.com/content/1/1/7.

Hsiao, C.-T. and H.-H. Huang (2012) 'A Causal Model for the Development of Long-term Facilities: A Case in Taiwan', *Quality and Quantity Journal* 46: 471–81.

Hu, R., Y. Liao, Z. Du, Y. Hao, H. Liang and I. Shi (2016) 'Types of Health Care Facilities and the Quality of Primary Care: A Study of Characteristics and Experiences of Chinese Patients in Guangdong Province, China', *BMC Health Services Research* 16: 335.

Huang, C., P. Vaneckova, X. Wang, G. FitzGerald, Y. Guo and S. Tong (2011) 'Constraints and Barriers to Public Health Adaptation to Climate Change: A Review of the Literature', *American Journal of Preventive Medicine* 40 (2): 183–90.

Huang, J.-H. and C.-M. Tung (2008) 'The Effects of Outpatient Co-Payment Policy on Healthcare Usage by the Elderly in Taiwan', *Archives of Gerontology and Geriatrics* 43: 101–16.

Huggins, C.E. (2002) 'Poor Face Multitude of Environmental Health Threats', *Reuters*, 17 October.

Hunter, D.J. (2008) *The Health Debate*. Bristol: Policy Press.

Hunter, P. (2016) 'The Refugee Crisis Challenges National Health Care Systems', *EMBO Reports* 17 (4): 492–5.

Hurst, J. and J.-P. Poullier (1993) 'Paths to Health Reform', OECD *Observer* 179: 4–7.

Hwang, G.-J. (2008) 'Going Separate Ways? The Reform of Health Insurance Funds in Germany, Japan and South Korea', *Policy Studies* 29 (4): 421–35.

Hwang, S.W., C.C. Gososis, J.R. Dunn et al. (2011) 'Health Status, Quality of Life, Residential Stability, Substance Use, and Health Care Utilization among Adults Applying to a Supportive Housing Program', *Journal of Urban Health* (Epub 03 Jun 2011).

Iha, A., I. Kickbusch, P. Taylor and K. Abbassi on behalf of the SDG working group (2016) 'Accelerating Achievement of the Sustainable Development Goals', *British Medical Journal* 352: i409.

Ikegami, N. (2007) 'Rationale, Design and Sustainability of Long-Term Care Insurance in Japan: In Retrospect', *Social Policy & Society* 6 (3): 423–34.

Ikegami, N. (2016) 'Achieving Universal Health Coverage by Focusing on Primary Care in Japan: Lessons for Low- and Middle-Income Countries', *International Journal of Health Policy and Management* 5 (5): 291–3.

Ikegami, N. and J.C. Campbell (1999) 'Health Care Reform in Japan: The Virtues of Muddling Through', *Health Affairs* 18 (3): 56–75.

Iliffe, S. and J. Munro (2000) 'New Labour and Britain's National Health Service: An Overview of Current Reforms', *International Journal of Health Services* 30 (2): 309–34.

Illich, I. (1976) *Limits to Medicine: Medical Nemesis: The Expropriation of Health*. Harmondsworth: Penguin Books.

Imai, H. and K. Fushimi (2012) 'Factors Associated with the Use of Institutional Long-term Care in Japan', *Geriatrics and Gerontology International* 12: 72–9.

Immergut, E.M. (1992) *Health Politics: Interests and Institutions in Western Europe*. Cambridge: Cambridge University Press.

Inagaki, K. (2006) 'Japan Battles Rising Obesity: Frets Disease May Cut World-Class Longevity', www.ABCNews.go.com.

Institute of Medicine (2008) *Knowing What Works in Health Care: A Roadmap for the Nation*. Washington, DC: National Academy Press.

Intergovernmental Panel on Climate Change (2007) *Climate Change 2007: Impacts, Adaptation, and Vulnerability*. Cambridge: Cambridge University Press.

Isaacs, S.L. and S.A. Schroeder (2004) 'Class: the Ignored Determinant of the Nation's Health', *New England Journal of Medicine* 351: 1137–42.

ISAGS (2012) *Health Systems in South America: Challenges to the Universality, Integrality and Equity*. Rio de Janeiro: ISAGS.

Isaksson, D., P. Blomqvist and U. Winblad (2016) Free Establishment of Primary Health Care Providers: Effects on Geographical Equity', *BMC Health Services Research* 16.

Izuhara, M. (2003) 'Social Inequality under a New Social Contract: Long-Term Care in Japan', *Social Policy & Administration* 37 (4): 395–410.

Jacobs, L.R. (2011) 'America's Critical Juncture: The Affordable Care Act and Its Reverberations', *Journal of Health Politics, Policy and Law* 36 (3): 625–31.

Jacobs, L.R. and T. Skocpol (2010) *Health Care Reform and American Politics: What Everyone Needs to Know.* New York: Oxford University Press.

Jacobs, R., P.C. Smith and A. Street (2006) *Measuring Efficiency in Health Care: Analytic Techniques and Health Policy.* Cambridge: Cambridge University Press.

Jacobson, P.D. (2012) 'The Role of Networks in the European Union Public Health Experience', *Journal of Health Politics, Policy and Law,* doi: 10.1215/03616878-1813836.

Jacobson, P.D., L.M. Napiewocki and L.A. Voigt (2011) 'Regulating the U.S. Health Care System: Failure in Motion', *Journal of Health Politics, Policy and Law* 36 (3): 583–9.

Japan Ministry of Health, Labour and Welfare (2004) *Direction of Health and Welfare Policies for the Elderly over the Next 5 Years.* Tokyo: Ministry of Health, Labour and Welfare.

Jatrana, S. and P. Crampton (2009) 'Affiliation with a Primary Care Provider in New Zealand: Who Is and Who Isn't', *Health Policy* 91: 286–96.

Jenkin, G.L., L. Signal and G. Thomson (2011) 'Framing Obesity: The Framing Contest between Industry and Public Health at the New Zealand Inquiry into Obesity', *Obesity Review* 12: 1022–30.

Jenson, J. and S. Jacobzone (2000) 'Care Allowances for the Frail Elderly and Their Impact on Women Care-givers', *Labour Market and Social Policy Occasional Papers no. 41.* Paris: OECD.

Jha, A.K., D. Doolan, D. Grandt, T. Scott and D.W. Bates (2008) 'The Use of Health Information Technology in Seven Nations', *International Journal of Medical Informatics* 77 (12): 848–54.

Johnson, M. and L. Cullen (2000) 'Solidarity Put to the Test. Health and Social Care in the UK', *International Journal of Social Welfare* 9 (4): 228–37.

Johnson, T. (1995) 'Governmentality and the Institutionalization of Expertise', in T. Johnson, G. Larkin and M. Saks (eds) *Health Professions and the State in Europe.* London: Routledge.

Joint Action on Health Workforce Planning and Forecasting (2015). *Handbook on Health Workforce Planning across EU Countries.* Brussels: European Commission.

Jost, T.S. (2011) 'The Real Constitutional Problem with the Affordable Care Act', *Journal of Health Politics, Policy and Law* 36 (3): 501–6.

Judson, K. and C. Harrison (2012) *Law & Ethics for the Health Professions.* New York: McGraw Hill.

Kabir, Z., K. Bennett, E. Shelley, B. Unal, J.A. Critchley and S. Capewell (2007) 'Life-Years-Gained from Population Risk Factor Changes and Modern

Cardiology Treatments in Ireland', *European Journal of Public Health* 17: 193–8.

Kam, Y.W. (2012) 'The Contributions of the Health Decommodification Typologies to the Study of the East Asian Welfare Regime', *Social Policy and Administration* 46 (1): 108–28.

Kang, J. X. (2011). 'Omega-3: A Link between Global Climate Change and Human Health', *Biotechnology Advances* 29 (4): 388–90, http://doi.org/10.1016/j.biotechadv.2011.02.003.

Kassler, J. (1994) *Bitter Medicine: Greed and Chaos in American Health Care*. New York: Birch Lane Press.

Kawachi, I., B.P. Kennedy and R.G. Wilkinson (eds) (1999) *The Society and Population Health Reader: Income Inequality and Health*. New York: New Press.

Kay, A. (2001) 'Beyond Policy Community. The Case of the GP Fundholding Scheme', *Public Administration* 79 (3): 561–77.

Keefe, T.J. and M.W. Zacher (2011) *The Politics of Global Health Governance: United by Contagion*. Basingstoke, UK: Palgrave Macmillan.

Kelly, E. and J. Hurst (2006) *Health Care Quality Indicators Project: Initial Indicators Report*. Paris: OECD.

Kenner, D. (2001) 'The Role of Traditional Herbal Medicine in Modern Japan', *Acupuncture Today*, August.

Kersh, R. and J. Morone (2002) 'The Politics of Obesity: Seven Steps to Government Action', *Health Affairs* 21 (November/December): 142–53.

Kim, I.-H., C. Muntaner, F.V. Shahidie, A. Vivesd, C. Vanroelen and J. Benach (2012) 'Welfare States, Flexible Employment, and Health: A Critical Review', *Health Policy* 104: 99–127.

Kirkpatrick, I., B. Bullinger, M. Dent and F. Lega (2011) 'The Translation of Medical Manager Roles in European Health Systems: A Framework for Comparison'. Paper presented at the 27th EGOS Colloquium, Gothenberg, Sweden.

Kirkpatrick, I., E. Kuhlmann, K. Hartley, M. Dent and F. Lega (2016) 'Medicine and Management in European Hospitals: A Comparative Overview', *BMC Health Services Research* 16 (Suppl 2): 171, https://bmchealthservres.biomedcentral.com/articles/10.1186/s12913-016-1388-4.

Kitchener, M., T. Ng and C. Harrington (2007) 'Medicaid State Plan Personal Care Services: Trends in Programs and Policies', *Journal of Aging and Social Policy* 19 (3): 9–26.

Klein, R. (1997) 'Learning from Others: Shall the Last Be the First?', *Journal of Health Politics, Policy and Law* 22 (5): 1267–78.

Klein, R. (2001) *The New Politics of the NHS*, 4th edn. Harlow: Prentice Hall.

Klein, R. (2005) 'A Middle Way for Rationing Healthcare Resources', *British Medical Journal* 330: 1340–1.

Klein, R. (2006) 'The Troubled Transformation of Britain's National Health Service', *The New England Journal of Medicine* 355 (4): 409–15.

Klein, R. (2009) 'Learning from Others and Learning from Mistakes', in T.R. Marmor, R. Freeman and K.G.H. Okma (eds) *Comparative Studies and the Politics of Modern Medical Care*. New Haven, London: Yale University Press.

Klein, R. (2010) 'The Eternal Triangle: Sixty Years of the Centre-Periphery Relationship in the National Health Service', *Social Policy & Administration* 44 (3): 285–304.

Klein, R. and A. Williams (2000) 'Setting Priorities: What is Holding Us Back – Inadequate Information or Inadequate Institutions?', in A. Coulter and C. Ham (eds) *The Global Challenge of Health Care Rationing*. Buckingham: Open University Press.

Kleinke, J.D. (2001) *Oxymorons: The Myth of a U.S. Health Care System*. San Francisco: Jossey-Bass.

Knijn, T. (1998) 'Social Care in the Netherlands', in J. Lewis (ed.) *Gender, Social Care and Welfare State Restructuring in Europe*. Aldershot: Ashgate.

Knowlton, K., M. Rotkin-Ellman, L. Geballe, W. Max and G.M. Solomon (2011) 'Six Climate Change-Related Events in the United States Accounted for About $14 Billion in Lost Lives and Health Costs', *Health Affairs* 30 (11): 2167–76.

Kodate, N. (2012) 'Events, Politics and Patterns of Policy-Making: Impact of Major Incidents on Health Sector Regulatory Reforms in the UK and Japan', *Social Policy and Administration* 46 (3): 280–301.

Konrad, R. (2006) 'E. coli Fears Prompt Recall of Lettuce', *Associated Press*, October 7.

Koop, C.E., C. Pearson and M.R. Schwartz (eds) (2002) *Critical Issues in Global Health*. San Francisco: Jossey-Bass.

Kremer, M. (2005) 'Consumers in Charge of Care: The Dutch Personal Care Budget (PGB) and Its Impact on The Market, Professionals and the Family', unpublished manuscript.

Kreng, V.B. and C.-T. Yang (2011) 'The Equality of Resource Allocation in Health Care under the National Health Insurance System in Taiwan', *Health Policy* 100: 203–10.

Kringos, D., W.G.W. Boerma, A. Hutchinson, J. van der Zee and P.P. Groenewegen (2010) 'The Breadth of Primary Healthcare: A Systematic Literature Review of its Core Dimensions', *BMC Health Services Research* 10: 65.

Kringos, D, W.G.W. Boerma, E. Spaan, M. Pellny, I. Son and A. Korotkova (2009) *Evaluation of the Organizational Model of Primary Care in the Russian Federation. A Survey Based Pilot Project in Two Rayons in Moscow Oblast*. Copenhagen: WHO Regional Office for Europe.

Kroneman, M., W.G.W. Boerma, M. den Berg, P.P. Groenewegen, J. de Jong and E. van Ginneken (2016) 'Netherlands', *Health Systems in Transition* 18 (2): 1–275.

Kroezen, M., G. Dussault, I. Craveiro, M. Dieleman, C. Jansen, J. Buchan, L. Barribal, A.M. Rafferty, J. Bremner, W. Sermeus (2015) 'Recruitment and Retention of Health Professionals across Europe: A Literature Review and Multiple Case Study Research', *Health Policy* 119 (2): 1517–28.

Kroezen, M., L. van Dijk, P.P. Groenewegen and A.L. Francke (2014) 'Knowledge Claims, Jurisdictional Control and Professional Status: The Case of Nurse Prescribing', *PLoS One* 8 (10): 77–9.

Kuhlmann, E. (2006) *Modernising Health Care. Reinventing Professions, the State and the Public*. Bristol: Policy Press.

Kuhlmann, E., I. Bourgeault, C. Larsen and T. Schofield (2012) 'Gendering Health Human Resource Management and Policy', in E. Kuhlmann and E. Annandale (eds) *The Palgrave Handbook of Gender and Healthcare*, 2nd edn. Basingstoke: Palgrave.

Kuhlmann, E., V. Burau, T. Correia, R. Lewandowski, C. Lionis, M. Noordegraaf and J. Repullo, J. (2013) '"A Manager in the Minds of Doctors": A Comparison of New Modes of Control in European Hospitals', *BMC Health Services Research* 13: 246–52.

Kuhlmann, E. and C. Larsen (2015) 'Why We Need Multi-level Health Workforce Governance: Case Studies from Nursing and Medicine in Germany', *Health Policy* 119 (12): 1636–44.

Kuhlmann, E., R. Batenburg and G. Dussault (2015a) 'Editorial. Health Workforce Governance in Europe: Where Are We Going? Special Issue', *Health Policy* 119 (12): 1515–16.

Kuhlmann, E., R.H. Blank, I.L. Bourgeault and C. Wendt (eds) (2015b) *The Palgrave International Handbook of Healthcare Policy and Governance*. Basingstoke: Palgrave.

Kuhlmann, E., P.P. Groenewegen, R. Batenburg and C. Larsen (2015c) 'Health Human Resources Policy: A European Approach', in E. Kuhlmann, R.H. Blank, I.L. Bourgeault and C. Wendt (eds) *The Palgrave International Handbook of Healthcare Policy and Governance*. Basingstoke: Palgrave.

Kuhlmann, E., T. Agartan and M. von Knorring (2016) 'Professions and Governance', in M. Dent, I. Bourgeault, J-L. Denis and E. Kuhlmann (eds) *The Routledge Companion to the Professions and Professionalism*. London: Routledge.

Kuhlmann, E., C.B. Maier, C. Larsen and V. Burau (2017) Skill-mix Innovations and Developments in Primary and Chronic Care Settings: Germany', in M. Wismar *et al.* (eds) *Patients, Peers, Professionals: Skill-mix Innovations and Developments in Primary and Chronic Care Settings*. Brussels: European Observatory for Health Systems and Policy.

Kulkarni, S.C., A. Levin-Rector, M. Ezzati and C.J.L. Murray (2011) 'Falling Behind: Life Expectancy in U.S. Counties from 2000 to 2007 in an International Context', *Population Health Metrics* 9: 16, doi:10.1186/1478-7954-9-16.

Kwon, S. (2011) 'Health Care Financing in Asia: Key Issues and Challenges', *Asia-Pacific Journal of Public Health* 23 (5): 651–61.

Lafortune, G., M. Schoenstein and L. Moreira (2016) 'Trends in Health Labour Markets and Policy Priorities to Address Workforce Issues', in OECD, *Health Workforce Policies in OECD Countries: Right Jobs, Right Skills, Right Places*. OECD Health Policy Studies. Paris: OECD Publishing, http://dx.doi.org/10.1787/9789264239517-en.

Lamm, R.D. (2003) *The Brave New World of Health Care*. Golden, CO: Fulcrum Press.

Lamm, R.D. and R.H. Blank (2007) *Condition Critical: A New Moral Vision for U.S. Health Care*. Golden, CO: Fulcrum Press.

Landwehr, C. and K. Böhm (2011) 'Delegation and Institutional Design in Health-Care Rationing', *Governance: An International Journal of Policy, Administration, and Institutions* 24 (4): 665–88.

Lang, T. and G. Rayner (2005) 'Obesity: A Growing Issue for European Policy?', *Journal of European Social Policy* 15 (4): 301–2.

Langlois, E.V., A. Haines, G. Tomson and A. Ghaffar (2016) 'Refugees: Towards Better Access to Health-care Services', *The Lancet* 387: 319–21.

Lantz, P.M., E. Golberstein, J.S. House and J. Morenoff (2010) 'Socioeconomic and Behavioral Risk Factors for Mortality in a National 19-Year Prospective Study of U.S. Adults', *Social Science and Medicine* 70: 1558–66.

Lantz, P.M., R.L. Lichtenstein and H.A. Pollack (2007) 'Health Policy Approaches to Population Health: The Limits of Medicalization', *Health Affairs* 26: 1253–7.

Lasser, K.E., D.U. Himmelstein and S. Woolhandler (2006) 'Access to Care, Health Status and Health Disparities in the United States and Canada: Results of a Cross-National Population-Based Survey', *American Journal of Public Health* 96: 1300–7.

Lee, K., K. Buse and S. Fustukian (eds) (2002) *Health Policy in a Globalising World*. Cambridge: Cambridge University Press.

Lee, S-Y., C-B. Chun, Y-G. Lee, Y-G. and N.K. Seo (2008) 'The National Health Insurance System as One Type of New Typology: The Case of South Korea and Taiwan', *Health Policy* 85 (1): 105–13.

Leeder, S.R. (1999) *Healthy Medicine: Challenges Facing Australia's Health Services*. St Leonard's, NSW: Allen & Unwin.

Leiber, S., S. Greß and M.-S. Manouguian (2010) 'Health Care System Change and the Cross-Border Transfer of Ideas: Influence of the Dutch Model on the 2007 German Health Reform', *Journal of Health Politics, Policy and Law* 35 (4): 539–66.

Leichter, H.M. (1991) *Free to be Foolish: Politics and Health Promotion in the United States and Great Britain*. Princeton, NJ: Princeton University Press.

Leiter, A.M. and E. Theurl (2009) 'The Convergence of Health Care Financing Structures: Empirical Evidence from OECD-countries', *The European Journal of Health Economics* 13 (1): 7–18.

Leone, C., R. Young, D. Ognyanova, A.M. Rafferty, J.E. Anderson and G. Dussault G (2016) Nurse Migration in the EU: A Moving Target? *EuroHealth* 22 (1): 7–9.

Levy, B.S. and V.W. Sidel (2007) *War and Public Health*. New York: Oxford University Press.

Levy, B.S. and V.W. Sidel (2009) *Social Injustice and Public Health*. New York: Oxford University Press.

Lewis, J. (2001) 'Older People and the Health–Social Care Boundary in the UK: Half a Century of Hidden Policy Conflict', *Social Policy and Administration* 35 (4): 343–59.

Lewis, J. (2005) *Health Policy and Politics: Networks, Ideas and Power*. Melbourne: IP Communications.

Lewis, S.J. and S.R. Leeder (2009) 'Why Health Reform?', *Medical Journal of Australia* 191 (5): 270–2.

Light, D. (1995) 'Countervailing Powers: A Framework for Professions in Transition', in T. Johnson, G. Larkin and M. Saks (eds) *Health Professions and the State in Europe*. London: Routledge.

Lijphart, A. (1999) *Patterns of Democracy*. New Haven, CT: Yale University Press.

Lim, J. and V.D. Joshi (2008) 'Public Perceptions of Healthcare in Singapore', *Annals Academy of Medicine* 37 (2): 91–5.

Lim, M.-K. (2004) 'Shifting the Burden of Health Care Finance: A Case Study of Public–Private Partnership in Singapore', *Health Policy* 69: 83–92.

Lim, W.T.L. (2006) 'Development of Medical Informatics in Singapore: Keeping Pace with Healthcare Challenges', paper presented at the Asia Pacific Association for Medical Informatics meeting, October 27–29, 2006, Taipei, Taiwan, http://www.apami.org/apami2006/papers/wlim(sg).pdf.

Lin, V. and H. Zhao (2015) 'Health Policy Reform in China', in E. Kuhlmann, R.H. Blank, I.L. Bourgeault and C. Wendt (eds) *The Palgrave International Handbook of Healthcare Policy and Governance*. Basingstoke: Palgrave.

Lin, V. and P. Robinson (2005) 'Australian Public Health Policy in 2003–2004', *Australia and New Zealand Health Policy* 2 (7), www.anzhealthpolicy.com/content/2/1/7.

Lin, Y-J., W-H. Tian and C-C. Chen (2011) 'Urbanization and the Utilization of Outpatient Services under National Health Insurance in Taiwan', *Health Policy* 103 (2–3): 236–43.

Locock, L. (2000) 'The Changing Nature of Rationing in the UK National Health Service', *Public Administration* 78 (1): 91–109.

Loewenberg, S. (2015) 'The World Bank under Jim Kim', *The Lancet* 386: 324–7.

Loh, C.H. (2009). 'Use of Traditional Chinese Medicine in Singapore Children: Perceptions of Parents and Paediatricians', *Singapore Medical Journal* 50 (12): 1162–8.

Long, A-J. and P. Chang (2012) 'The Effect of Using the Health Smart Card vs. CPOE Reminder System on the Prescribing Practices of Non-Obstetric Physicians during Outpatient Visits for Pregnant Women in Taiwan', *International Journal of Medical Informatics* 81: 605–11.

Loo, M.V.H., J.P. Kahan and K.G.H. Okma (1999) 'Developments in Health Care Cost Containment in the Netherlands', in E. Mossialos and J. Le Grand (eds) *Health Care and Cost Containment in the European Union*. Aldershot: Ashgate.

Lowi, T.A. (1972) 'Four Systems of Policy, Politics and Choice', *Public Administration Review* 32: 298–310.

Lu, J.-FR. and W.C. Hsiao (2003) 'Does Universal Health Insurance Make Health Care Unaffordable? Lessons from Taiwan', *Health Affairs* 22: 77–88.

Lundsgaard, J. (2004) 'Consumer Direction and Choice in Long-Term Care for Older Persons, Including Payments for Informal Care: How Can It Help Improve Care Outcomes, Employment and Fiscal Sustainability?', *Health Working Papers No. 20*. Paris: OECD.

Lyon, D. and M. Gluckmann (2008) 'Comparative Configurations of Care Work across Europe', *Sociology* 42 (1): 101–18.

Maarse, H. and A. Paulus (2003) 'Has Solidarity Survived? A Comparative Analysis of the Effect of Social Health Insurance Reforms in Four European Countries', *Journal of Health Politics, Policy and Law* 28 (4): 585–614.

Maarse, H. and R. Ter Meulen (2006) 'Consumer Choice in Dutch Health Insurance after Reform', *Health Care Annals* 14: 37–49.

Maarse, J.A.M. (1997) 'Netherlands', in M.W. Raffel (ed.) *Health Care and Reform in Industrialized Countries.* University Park, PA: Pennsylvania State University Press.

Maarse, J.A.M. and P.P. Jeurissen (2016) The Politics and Policy of the Long-term Care Reform 2015 in the Netherlands', *Health Policy* 120: 241–5.

Mabbett, D. and H. Bolderson (1999) 'Theories and Methods in Comparative Social Policy', in J. Clasen (ed.) *Comparative Social Policy.* Oxford: Blackwell.

MacIntyre, C.R. (2011) 'Public Health and Health Reform in Australia', *Medical Journal of Australia* 194 (1): 38–40.

Mackenbach, J. P. and McKee, M. (2015) 'Government, Politics, and Health Policy: A Quantitative Analysis of 30 European Countries', *Health Policy* 119 (10): 1298–1308.

Mackenbach, J.P., I. Stirbu, A-J.R. Roskam, M.M. Schaap, G. Menvielle, M. Leinsalu and A.E. Kunst (2008) 'Socioeconomic Inequalities in Health in 22 European Countries', *The New England Journal of Medicine* 358: 2468–81.

Mackey, T.K. and B.A. Liang (2012) 'Lessons from SARS and H1N1/A: Employing a WHO–WTO Forum to Promote Optimal Economic-Public Health Pandemic Response', *Journal of Public Health Policy* 33: 119–30.

Mackey, T.K. and B.A. Liang (2013) 'A United Nations Global Health Panel for Health Governance', *Social Science & Medicine* 76: 12–15.

Maciosek, M.V., A.B. Coffield, T.J. Flottemesch, N.M. Edwards and L.I. Solberg (2010) 'Greater Use of Preventive Services in U.S. Health Care Could Save Lives at Little or No Cost', *Health Affairs* 29 (9): 1656–60.

Maher, J.M., S. Fraser and J. Wright (2010) 'Framing the Mother: Childhood Obesity, Maternal Responsibility and Care', *Journal of Gender Studies* 19 (3): 233–47.

Maier, C.B. (2015) 'The Role of Governance in Implementing Task-shifting from Physicians to Nurses in Advanced Roles in Europe, US, Canada, New Zealand and Australia', *Health Policy* 119 (12): 1627–35.

Maier, C.B. and L.H. Aiken (2016) 'Task-shifting from Physicians to Nurses in Primary Care in 39 Countries', *European Journal of Public Health*, doi: http://dx.doi.org/10.1093/eurpub/ckw098.

Maier, C.B., J. Buchan, M. Wismar, D. Ognyanova, E. Girasek, E. Kovacs and R. Busse (2014) 'Monitoring Health Professional Mobility in Europe', in J. Buchan, M. Wismar, I.A. Glinos and J. Bremner (eds) *Health Professional Mobility in a Changing Europe: New Dynamics, Mobile Individuals and Diverse Responses.* Observatory Studies Series 32. Copenhagen: WHO.

Majerol, M., V. Newkirk and R. Garfield (2015) 'The Uninsured: A Primer – Key Facts about Health Insurance and the Uninsured in the Era of Health Reform', http://www.kff.org/uninsured/report/the-uninsured-a-primer-key-facts-about-health-insurance-and-the-uninsured-in-the-wake-of-national-health-reform/.

Marcum, Z.A., J.E. Bellon, J. Li, W.F. Gellad and J.M. Donohue (2016) 'New Chronic Disease Medication Prescribing by Nurse Practitioners, Physician Assistants, and Primary Care Physicians: A Cohort Study', *BMC Health Services Research* 16: 312.

Marmor, T.R. and J. Oberlander (2011) 'The Patchwork: Health Reform, American Style', *Social Science and Medicine* 72: 125–8.

Marmor, T.R. and C. Wendt (2011a) 'Introduction', in T. Marmor and C. Wendt (eds) *Reforming Healthcare Systems. Volume 1. Ideas, Interests and Institutions.* Chelthenham, UK: Edward Elgar Publishing Ltd.

Marmor, T.R. and C. Wendt (eds) (2011b) *Reforming Heathcare Systems.* Chelthenham, UK: Edward Elgar Publishing Ltd.

Marmor, T.R. and C. Wendt (2012) 'Conceptual Frameworks for Comparing Healthcare Politics and Policy', *Health Policy* 107: 11–20.

Marmor, T.R., R. Freeman and K.G.H. Okma (2005) 'Comparing Perspectives and Policy Learning in the World of Health Care', *Journal of Comparative Policy Analysis* 7 (4): 331–48.

Marmor, T.R., R. Freeman and K.G.H. Okma (2009a) *Comparative Studies and the Politics of Modern Medical Care.* New Haven, CT: Yale University Press.

Marmor, T.R., R. Freeman and K.G.H. Okma (2009b) 'Comparative Policy Analysis and Health Care: An Introduction', in T.R. Marmor, R. Freeman and K.G.H. Okma (eds) *Comparative Studies and the Politics of Modern Medical Care.* New Haven, London: Yale University Press.

Marmot, M. and R.G. Wilkinson (eds) (1999) *Social Determinants of Health.* Oxford: Oxford University Press.

Marmot, M., S. Friel, R. Bell, T.A.J. Houweling and S. Taylor (2008) 'Closing the Gap in a Generation: Health Equity through Action on the Social Determinants of Health', *The Lancet* 372 (9650): 1661–9.

Marrelli, T.M. (2011) *Handbook of Home Health Standards*, Revised Reprint. Maryland Heights, MO: Mosby.

Marshall, T. (2003) 'The Silent Revolution: Recent Developments in the Organisation of General Medical Practice in New Zealand', *Business Review* 5 (1): 1–8.

Martin, J. and G. Salmond (2001) 'Policy Making: The "Messy Reality"', in P. Davis and T. Ashton (eds) *Health and Public Policy in New Zealand.* Auckland: Oxford University Press.

Martin, R. and A. Conseil (2012) 'Public Health Policy and Law for Pandemic Influenza: A Case for European Harmonization?', *Journal of Health Politics, Policy and Law*, doi: 10.1215/03616878-1813854.

Martineau, T. and A. Willetts (2006) 'The Health Workforce: Managing the Crisis Ethical International Recruitment of Health Professionals: Will Codes of Practice Protect Developing Country Health Systems?', *Health Policy* 75: 358–67.

Masis, D.P. and P.C. Smith (eds) (2010) *Health Care Systems in Developing and Transition Countries: The Role of Research Evidence (Global Development Network).* London: Edward Elgar.

Matcha, D.A. (2003) *Health Care Systems of the Developed World: How the United States' System Remains an Outlier.* Westport, CT: Praeger Publishers.

Matsuda, R. (2013) 'The Japanese Health Care System', in S. Thomson, R. Osborn, D. Squires and M. Jun (eds) *International Profiles of Health Care Systems, 2013.* New York: The Commonwealth Fund.

Matsushige, T., T. Tsuisui and M. Otaga (2012) '"Mutual Aid" beyond Formal Institutions: Integrated Home Care in Japan', *Current Sociology* 60 (4): 538–50.

Matsushita, Y., N. Yoshiike, F. Kaneda, K. Yoshita and H. Takimoto (2004) 'Trends in Childhood Obesity in Japan over the Last 25 Years from the National Nutrition Survey', *Obesity Research* 12: 205–14.

Maynard, A. and K. Bloor (2001) 'Our Certain Fate: Rationing in Health Care', Office of Health Economics Briefings Page, https://www.ohe.org/publications/our-certain-fate-rationing-health-care.

McClellan, M. and D. Kessler (1999) 'A Global Analysis of Technological Change in Health Care: The Case of Heart Attacks', *Health Affairs* 18 (3): 250–5.

McConahy, K. (2002) 'Food Portions Are Positively Related To Energy Intake and Body Weight in Early Childhood', *Journal of Pediatrics* 140 (March): 340–7.

McDonald, R. (2012) 'Restratification Revisited: The Changing Landscape of Primary Medical Care in England and California', *Current Sociology 60 (4):* 441–55.

McDonald, R. (2015) 'Financial Incentives and the Governance of Performance', in E. Kuhlmann, R.H. Blank, I.L. Bourgeault and C. Wendt (eds) *The Palgrave International Handbook of Healthcare Policy and Governance.* Basingstoke: Palgrave.

McGinnis, J.M., P. Williams-Russo and J.R. Knickman (2002) 'The Case for More Active Policy Attention to Health Promotion', *Health Affairs* 21 (2): 78–93.

McGivern, G., G. Currie, E. Ferlie, L. Fitzgerald and J. Waring (2015) 'Hybrid Manager-Professionals' Identity Work, the Maintenance and Hybridization of Professionalism in Managerial Contexts', *Public Administration 93: 412–32.*

McIntosh, E., P. Clarke, E.J. Frew and J.J. Louviere (2010) *Applied Methods of Cost-benefit Analysis in Health Care.* New York: Oxford University Press.

McKie, J., J. Richardson, P. Singer and H. Kuhse (1998) *The Allocation of Health Care Resources: An Ethical Evaluation of the 'QALY' Approach.* Aldershot: Dartmouth.

McKinley, J.B. and L.D. Marceau (2012) 'From Cottage Industry to a Dominant Mode of Primary Care: Stages in the Diffusion of a Health Care Innovation (Retail Clinics)', *Social Science & Medicine* 75 (6): 1134–41.

McKinney, C.J. (2016) 'TTIP and the NHS', https://fullfact.org/europe/does-ttip-mean-privatisation-nhs.

McMichael, A.J. and E. Lindgren (2011) 'Climate Change: Present and Future Risks to Health, and Necessary Responses', *Journal of Internal Medicine*, doi: 10.1111/j.1365-2796.2011.02415.x.

McMichael, C., J. Barnett and A.J. McMichael (2012) 'An Ill Wind? Climate Change, Migration, and Health', *Environmental Health Perspectives* 120: 646–54.

McMurray, R. (2011) 'The Struggle to Professionalize: An Ethnographic Account of the Occupational position of Advanced Nurse Practitioners.' *Human Relations* 64 (6): 801–22.

McNeill, A, L.S. Brose, R. Calder, S.C. Hitchman, P. Hajek and H. McRobbie (2015). *E-cigarettes: An Evidence Update: A Report Commissioned by Public Health England.* UK: Public Health England.

McPake, B. (2002) 'The Globalisation of Health Sector Reform Policies: Is "Lesson Drawing" Part of the Process?', in K. Lee, K. Buse and S. Fustukian (eds) *Health Policy in a Globalising World*. Cambridge: Cambridge University Press.

McRae, I., L. Yen, J. Gillespie and K. Douglas (2010) 'Patient Affiliation with GPs in Australia: Who Is and Who Is Not and Does it Matter?', *Health Policy* 103: 16–23.

Meagher, G. and M. Szebehely (2013) 'Long-Term Care in Sweden: Trends, Actors and Consequences', in C. Ranci and E. Pavolini (eds) *Reforms in Long-Term Care Policies in Europe*. New York: Springer Science & Business Media.

Means, R., S. Richards and R. Smith (2003) *Community Care: Policy and Practice*, 3rd edn. Basingstoke: Palgrave.

Mechanic, D. (1994) *Inescapable Decisions: The Imperatives of Health Care*. New Brunswick, NJ: Transaction.

Mechanic, D. and D.D. McAlpine (2010) 'Sociology of Health Care Reform: Building on Research and Analysis to Improve Health Care', *Journal of Health and Social Behavior* 51 (s): s147–s159.

Medicare Payment Assessment Commission. (2011) 'A Data Book: Health Care Spending and the Medicare Program', http://medpac.gov/-documents-/data-book.

Mehta, K.K. and C. Briscoe (2004) 'National Policy Approaches to Social Care for Elderly People in the United Kingdom and Singapore 1945–2002', *Journal of Aging and Social Policy* 16 (1): 89–111.

Mello, M.M, A. Chandra, A.A. Gawande and D.M. Studdert (2014) 'National Costs of The Medical Liability System', *Health Affairs* 29 (9): 1569–77.

Merçay, C., J-C. Dumont and G. Lafortune (2016) 'Trends and Policies Affecting the International Migration of Doctors and Nurses to OECD Countries', in *Health Workforce Policies in OECD Countries: Right Jobs, Right Skills, Right Places*. OECD Health Policy Studies. Paris: OECD Publishing, http://dx.doi.org/10.1787/9789264239517-en.

Mernagh, P., K. Coleman, J. Cumming, T. Green, J. Harris, D. Paech and A. Weston (2011) 'Cost-Effectiveness Analysis of Public Health Interventions to Prevent Obesity in New Zealand', *Value in Health* 14 (7): A382.

Merson, M.H., R.E. Black and A.J. Mills (2011) *Global Health*, 3rd edn. New York: Jones and Bartlett Publishers.

Milio, N. (2000) *Public Health in the Market: Facing Managed Care, Lean Government, and Health Disparities*. Ann Arbor, MI: University of Michigan Press.

Miller, E.A., M. Booth and V. Mor (2008) 'Meeting the Demographic Challenges Ahead: Toward Culture Change in an Ageing New Zealand', *Australia and New Zealand Health Policy* 5 (5): 5–16.

Mills, A., S. Bennett, S. Russell and N. Attanayake (eds) (2001) *The Challenge of Health Sector Reform: What Governments Must Do?* Basingstoke: Palgrave.

Mills, S.Y. (2001) 'The House of Lords Report on Complementary Medicine: A Summary', *Complementary Therapies in Medicine* 9 (1): 34–9.

Ministry of Health and Social Affairs (2001) 'Towards Public Health on Equal Terms', Fact Sheet no. 3. Stockholm: Ministry of Health and Social Affairs.

Mitchell, A.D. (2010) 'Australia's Move to the Plain Packaging of Cigarettes and Its WTO Compatibility', *Asian Journal of WTO and International Health, Law and Policy* 5: 405–25.

Mladovsky, P., D. Srsivastava, J. Cylus, M. Karanikolos, T. Evetovits, S. Thomson and M. McKee (2012) *Health Policy Responses to the Financial Crisis in Europe*. Copenhagen: World Health Organization.

Mlakar, J., M. Korva, N. Tul, M. Popović, M. Poljšak-Prijatelj, J. Mraz, M. Kolenc, K. Resman Rus, T. Vesnaver Vipotnik, V.F. Vodušek, A. Vizjak, J. Pižem, M. Petrovec and T.A. Županc (2016). 'Zika Virus Associated with Microcephaly', *The New England Journal of Medicine*. doi: 10.1056/ NEJMoa1600651.

Modrek, S., D. Stuckler, M. McKee, M. Cullen and S. Basu (2013). 'A Review of Health Consequences of Recessions Internationally and a Synthesis of the US Response During the Great Recession', *Public Health Reviews* 35 (1): 1–33.

Moeller, D.W. (2011) *Environmental Health*, 4th edn. Cambridge: Harvard University Press.

Mokdad, A.H., J.S. Marks, D.F. Stroup and J.L. Gerberding (2004) 'Actual Causes of Death in the United States, 2000', *Journal of the American Medical Association* 291:1238–45.

Mooney, G. (2009) 'Is It Not Time for Health Economists to Rethink Equity and Access?', *Health Economics, Policy and Law* 4: 209–21.

Moran, M. (1999) *Governing the Health Care State: A Comparative Study of the United Kingdom, the United States and Germany*. Manchester: Manchester University Press.

Moran, M. (2000) 'Understanding the Welfare State: The Case of Health Care', *British Journal of Politics and International Relations* 2 (2): 135–60.

Moran, M. and B. Wood (1993) *States, Regulation and the Medical Profession*. Cheltenham: Edward Elgar.

Moreira, L. and G. Lafortune (2016) 'Education and Training for Doctors and Nurses: What's Happening with Numerus Clausus Policies?', in *Health Workforce Policies in OECD Countries: Right Jobs, Right Skills, Right Places*. OECD Health Policy Studies. Paris: OECD Publishing, http://dx.doi. org/10.1787/9789264239517-en.

Morris, S., N. Devlin, D. Parkin and A. Spencer (2012) *Economic Analysis in Healthcare*. New York: Wiley.

Mossialos, E. and J. Le Grand (eds) (1999) *Health Care and Cost Containment in the European Union*. Aldershot: Ashgate.

Mossialos, E., M. Wenzel, R. Osborne and D. Sarnak (eds) (2016) *International Profiles of Healthcare Systems*. New York: Commonwealth Fund.

Moszczynski, W. (2008) 'Why Britain Needs Polish Migrants', *Telegraph*, 3 April.

Moynihan, R. (2016) 'Caution! Diagnosis Creep', *Australian Prescriber* 39 (2): 30–1.

Muennig, P.A. and S.A. Glied (2010) 'What Changes in Survival Rates Tell Us about U.S. Health Care', *Health Affairs* 29 (11): 2105–13.

Muiser, J. and G. Carrin (2007) 'Financing Long-term Care Programmes in Health Systems: With a Situation Assessment in High-, Middle- and

Low-income Countries', *Discussion Paper No 7*. WHO: Geneva, http://www. who.int/health_financing/documents/dp_e_07_6-longtermcare.pdf.

Murray, C.J.L. and D.B. Evans (2003) 'Health Systems Performance Assessment: Goals, Framework and Overview' in C.J.L. Murray and D.B. Evans (eds) *Health Systems Performance Assessment: Debates, Methods, and Empiricism*. Geneva: World Health Organization.

Musgrave, F.W. (2006) *The Economics of U.S. Health Care Policy: The Role of Market Forces*. New York: M.E. Sharpe.

Musgrave, P., R. Zeramdini and G. Carrin (2002) 'Basic Patterns in National Health Expenditure', *Bulletin of the World Health Organization* 80 (2): 1–17.

Nadash, P. and Y.-C. Shih (2012) 'Introducing Social Insurance for Long-term Care in Taiwan: Key Issues', *International Journal of Social Welfare*, doi: 10.1111/j.1468-2397.2011.00862.x.

Nancarrow, S. and A. Borthwick (2016) 'Interprofessional Working for the Health Professions: From Fried Eggs to Omelettes?', in M. Dent, I.L. Bourgeault, J-L. Denis and E. Kuhlmann (eds) *The Routledge Companion to the Professions and Professionalism*. London: Routledge.

Nathan, S.A., E. Develin, N. Grove and A.B. Zwi (2005) 'An Australian Childhood Obesity Summit: The Role of Data and Evidence in "Public" Policy Making', *Australia and New Zealand Health Policy* 2 (17), www. anzhealthpolicy.com/content/2/1/17.

National Center for Health Care Statistics (2012) *Chartbook on Trends in the Health of Americans*. Washington, DC: Government Printing Office.

National Contract for Public Health (2001) *National Contract for Public Health. Declaration of Intent to Cooperate. 2001–2003*. Leiden, 22 February, www. minvws.nl/documents/Health/natcontract.pdf.

National Health Care for the Homeless Council (2011) 'Homelessness and Health: What's the Connection?' www.nhchc.org.

National Health Insurance Administration (2015) *National Health Insurance Statistical Profile, 2009*. Taipei: Ministry of Health and Welfare (in Chinese).

National Health Service (2008) 'Statistics on NHS Stop Smoking Services in England, April to September 2007 (Q2-Quarterly Report)', www.ic.nhs.uk/ pubs.sss07q2.

National Health Service (2015) 'Smokefree NHS. Are E-cigarettes Safe to Use?' http://www.nhs.uk/news/2015/08August/Pages/E-cigarettes-95-per-cent-less -harmful-than-smoking-says-report.aspx.

National Institute for Health Care Spending (2012) 'The Concentration of Health Care Spending', http://www.nihcm.org/pdf/DataBrief3%20Final.pdf.

National Rural Health Association (2009) 'Recruiting Rural Doctors', *Policy Brief*, May, http://www.ruralcenter.org/recruitment.

Navarro, V. (1999) 'Health and Equity in the World in the Era of "Globalization"', *International Journal of Health Services* 29 (2): 215–26.

Navarro, V. and L. Shi (2001) 'The Political Context of Social Inequalities and Health', *International Journal of Health Services* 31 (1): 1–21.

Navarro, V., C. Borrell, J. Benach, C. Muntaner, A. Quiroga, M. Rodriquez-Sanz, N. Verges, J. Guma and M.I. Pasarin (2003) 'The Importance of the Political and the Social in Explaining Mortality Differentials among the Countries of the OECD, 1950–1998', *International Journal of Health Services* 33 (3): 419–94.

NBC News (2006) 'Study: Child Obesity to Soar Worldwide', www.nbcnews.com/id/11694799/#.WMNfVX_uMfI.

New Zealand Core Services Committee (1992) *The Core Debate: How We Define the Core*. Wellington: National Advisory Committee on Core Health and Disability Support Services.

New Zealand Medical Association (2013) *NZMA Strategic Plan 2011–2016*, https://www.nzma.org.nz/__data/assets/pdf_file/0011/17498/NZMA-strategic-plan-2011-2016-Aug-2013-.pdf.

New Zealand Ministry of Health (2003) *Achieving Health for All People: A Framework for Public Health Action for the New Zealand Health Strategy*. Wellington: Ministry of Health.

New Zealand Ministry of Health (2008) *Annual Report, 2008*. Wellington: Ministry of Health.

New Zealand Ministry of Health (2009) 'Primary Health Organisations (PHOs)', http://www.moh.govt.nz/moh.nsf/indexmh/phcs-pho.

Newman, C. (2014) 'Time to Address Gender Discrimination and Inequality in the Health Workforce,' *Human Resources for Health* 12: 25.

NHS England (2015). 'Proton Beam Therapy', www.england.nhs.uk/commissioning/spec-services/highly-spec-services/pbt/.

Noguchi, H. and S. Shimizutani (2005) 'Supplier-Induced Demand in Japan's At-Home Care Industry', *ESRI Discussion Paper Series* 148: 1–131.

Nolte, E. and C.M. McKee (2011) 'Measuring the Health of Nations: Updating an Earlier Analysis', *Health Affairs* 27: 58–71.

Nolte, E., S. Ettelt, S. Thomson and N. Mays (2008) 'Learning from Other Countries: An On-call Facility for Health Care Policy', *Journal of Health Services Research Policy* 13 (2): 58–64.

Nomura, K. and K. Gohchi (2012) 'Impact of Gender-based Career Obstacles on the Working Status of Women Physicians in Japan', *Social Science & Medicine* 75 (9): 1612–16.

Norval, M., R.M. Lucas, A.P. Cullen, F.R. de Gruijl, J. Longstreth, Y. Takizawa and J.C. van der Leun (2011) 'The Human Health Effects of Ozone Depletion and Interactions with Climate Change', *Photochemical and Photobiological Sciences* 10: 199–225.

Nyman, J.A. (2008) 'American Health Policy: Cracks in the Foundation', *Journal of Health Politics, Policy and Law* 32 (5): 759–83.

O'Dowd, A. (2016) 'UK Could Turn to India for New GP Recruitment Drive', *British Medical Journal* 353: i2091

OECD (1987) *Financing and Delivering Health Care: A Comparative Analysis of OECD Countries*. Paris: OECD.

OECD (2005a) *OECD Health Project*, www.oecd.org/document/28/0,2340,en_2649_37407_2536540_1_1_1_37407,00.html.

OECD (2005b) *The OECD Health Project: Long-term Care for Older People*. Paris: OECD.

OECD (2006) *OECD Health Data 2006. A Comparative Analysis of 30 Countries*. Paris: OECD, Version: 26 June.

OECD (2008a) *OECD Health Data 2008*. Paris: OECD.

OECD (2008b) *The Looming Crisis in the Health Workforce*. Paris: OECD.

OECD (2009) 'Health at a Glance 2009: OECD Indicators', http://www.oecd. org/health/health-systems/44117530.pdf.

OECD (2011) *Health at a Glance 2011: OECD Indicators*, OECD Publishing, http://dx.doi.org/10.1787/health_glance-2011-en.

OECD (2012) *OECD Health Statistics* (database). Paris: OECD, doi: 10.1787/ data-00349-en.

OECD (2013) 'Smoking', in OECD Factbook 2013: *Economic, Environmental and Social Statistics*, OECD Publishing, http://www.oecd-ilibrary.org/ economics/oecd-factbook_18147364.

OECD (2015) *Health at a Glance*. Paris: OECD.

OECD (2016a) Health statistics, http://stats.oecd.org/index. aspx?DataSetCode=HEALTH_STAT.

OECD (2016b) *Health Workforce Policies in OECD Countries: Right Jobs, Right Skills, Right Places*. OECD Health Policy Studies. Paris: OECD Publishing, http://dx.doi.org/10.1787/9789264239517-en.

Ohnuki-Tiernev, E. (1984) *Illness and Culture in Contemporary Japan: An Anthropological View*. Cambridge: Cambridge University Press.

Okamoto, K. (2001) *Public Health of Japan 2001*. Osaka: National Institute of Public Health.

Okma, K.G.H. (2008) 'Commentary. Learning and Mislearning across Boarders: What Can we (not) Learn from the 2006 Health Care Reform in The Netherlands? Commentary on Rosenau and Lako', *Journal of Health Politics, Policy and Law* 33 (6): 1057–71.

Okma, K.G.H. (2001) *Health Care, Health Policies and Health Care Reforms in the Netherlands*. International Publication Series Health, Welfare and Sport no. 7. The Hague: Ministry of Health, Welfare and Sport.

Okma, K.G.H. and L. Crivelli (2009) *Six Countries, Six Reform Models: The Healthcare Reform Experience of Israel, The Netherlands, New Zealand, Singapore, Switzerland and Taiwan: Healthcare Reforms 'Under the Radar Screen'*. Singapore: World Scientific Publishing Company.

Okma, K.G.H., T.-M. Cheng, D. Chinitz, L. Crivelli, M.-K. Lim, H. Maarse and M.E. Labra (2010) 'Six Countries, Six Health Reform Models? Health Care Reform in Chile, Israel, Singapore, Switzerland, Taiwan and The Netherlands', *Journal of Comparative Policy Analysis: Research and Practice* 12 (1–2): 75–113.

Olafsdottir, S. and E. Bakhtiari (2015) 'Citizenship and Healthcare Policy', in E. Kuhlmann, R.H. Blank, I.L. Bourgeault and C. Wendt (eds) *The Palgrave International Handbook of Healthcare Policy and Governance*. Basingstoke: Palgrave.

Olivares-Tirado, P., N. Tamiya, M. Kashiwagi and K. Kashiwagi (2011) 'Predictors of the Highest Long-term Care Expenditures in Japan', *BMC Health Services Research* 11: 103–16.

Oliver, T.R. (2011) 'Health Care Reform as a Halfway Technology', *Journal of Health Politics, Policy and Law* 36 (3): 603–9.

Ono, T., M. Schoenstein M, and J. Buchan (2016) 'Geographic Imbalances in the Distribution of Doctors and Health Care Services in OECD Countries', in *Health Workforce Policies in OECD Countries: Right Jobs, Right Skills,*

Right Places. OECD Health Policy Studies. Paris: OECD Publishing, http://dx.doi.org/10.1787/9789264239517-en.

Or, Z., C. Cases, M. Lisac, K. Vrangbaek, U. Winblad and G. Bevan (2010) 'Are Health Problems Systemic? Health Reforms under Beveridge and Bismarck Systems', *Health Economics Policy and Law* (5): 269–93.

Orellana-Barrios, M.A., D. Payne, Z. Mulkey and K. Nugent (2015) 'Electronic Cigarettes: A Narrative Review for Clinicians', *The American Journal of Medicine*. doi:10.1016/j.amjmed.2015.01.033.

Øvretveit, J. (1998) *Comparative and Cross-cultural Health Research*. Abingdon, UK: Radcliffe Medical Press.

Ozegowski, S. and L. Sundmacher (2012) 'Ensuring Access to Health Care – Germany Reforms Supply Structures to Tackle Inequalities', *Health Policy* 106: 105–9.

PAHO – Pan American Health Organization (2012) *Health in the Americas: 2012 Edition, Regional Outlook and Country Profiles*. Washington, DC: PAHO.

Palmer, G.R. and S.D. Short (2000) *Health Care and Public Policy: An Australian Analysis*, 3rd edn. Melbourne: Macmillan.

Panopoulou, E. and T. Pantelidis (2011) 'Convergence in Per Capita Health Expenditures and Health Outcomes in the OECD Countries', *Applied Economics*, doi: 10.1080/00036846.2011.583222.

Papanicolas, I. and J. Cylus (2015) 'Comparison of Health Systems Performance,' in E. Kuhlmann, R.H. Blank, I.L. Bourgeault and C. Wendt (eds) *The Palgrave International Handbook of Healthcare Policy and Governance*. Basingstoke: Palgrave.

Paris, V., M. Devaux and L. Wei (2010) 'Health Systems Institutional Characteristics: A Survey of Twenty-Nine OECD Countries', *OECD Health Working Paper No. 50*. Paris: OECD.

Pavolini, E. and E. Kuhlmann (2016) 'Health Workforce Development in Europe: A Matrix for Comparing Trajectories of Change in the Professions', *Health Policy* 120 (6): 654–64.

Pavolini, E. and C. Ranci (2013) 'Reforms in Long-term Care Policies in Europe', in C. Ranci and E. Pavolini (eds) *Reforms in Long-term Care Policies in Europe*. Basingstoke: Palgrave.

Pavolini, E. and H. Theobald (2015) 'Long-term Care Policies', in E. Kuhlmann, R.H. Blank, I.L. Bourgeault and C. Wendt (eds) *The Palgrave International Handbook of Healthcare Policy and Governance*. Basingstoke: Palgrave.

Peckham, S. and M. Exworthy (2003) *Primary Care in the UK*. Basingstoke: Palgrave.

Peckham, S., M. Exworthy, M. Powell and I. Greener (2008) 'Decentralizing Health Services in the UK: A New Conceptual Framework', *Public Administration* 86 (2): 559–80.

Pelone, F., M.L. Specchia, M.A. Veneziano, S. Capizzi, S. Bucci, A. Mancuso, W. Ricciardi and A.G.de Belvis (2012) 'Economic Impact of Childhood Obesity on Health Systems: A Systematic Review', *Obesity Reviews* 13 (5): 431–40.

Penno, E., R. Gauld and R. Audas (2013) 'How are Population-based Funding Formulae for Healthcare Composed? A Comparative Analysis of Seven Models', *BMC Health Services Research* 13: 470.

Perry, N. (2012) 'A Smoke-free Country? New Zealand Taxes Aim for It', http://www.cnsnews.com/news/article/smoke-free-country-new-zealand-taxes-aim-it.

Peters, B.G. (1998) *Comparative Politics: Theory and Methods.* Basingstoke: Macmillan.

Peterson, C.L. (2006) *Alternatives for Modeling Results from the RAND Health Insurance Experiment.* Washington, DC: Congressional Research Service.

Pfau-Effinger, B. (2004) *Development of Culture, Welfare State and Women's Employment in Europe.* Aldershot: Ashgate.

Pitts, S.R., E.R Carrier, E.C. Rich and A.L. Kellermann (2010) 'Where Americans Get Acute Care: Increasingly, It's Not at Their Doctor's Office', *Health Affairs* 29 (9): 1620–9.

Plochg, T., N. Klazinga and B. Starfield (2009) 'Transforming Medical Professionalism to Fit Changing Health Needs', *BMC Medicine* 7: 64.

Pocock, N.S. and K.H. Phua (2011) 'Medical Tourism and Policy Implications for Health Systems: A Conceptual Framework from a Comparative Study of Thailand, Singapore and Malaysia', *Globalization and Health* 7: 12–24.

Pollack, H.A. (2011) 'Prevention and Public Health', *Journal of Health Politics, Policy and Law* 36 (3): 515–20, doi:10.1215/03616878-1271189.

Porter, M.E. and E.O. Teisberg (2006) *Redefining Health Care: Value-Based Competition on Results.* Cambridge, MA: Harvard Business School Press.

Portier, C.J., T.K. Thigpen, S.R. Carter, C.H. Dilworth, A.E. Grambsch, J. Gohlke, J. Hess, S.N. Howard, G. Luber, J.T. Lutz, D.M. Wolcock and M.R. Meador (2010) *A Human Health Perspective On Climate Change: A Report Outlining the Research Needs on the Human Health Effects of Climate Change.* Research Triangle Park, NC: Environmental Health Perspectives/National Institute of Environmental Health Sciences.

Post, E.S., A. Grambsch, C. Weaver, P. Morefield, J. Huang, L.-Y. Leung, C.G. Nolte, P. Adams, X.-Z. Liang, J.-H. Zhu and H. Mahoney (2012) 'Variation in Estimated Ozone-Related Health Impacts of Climate Change due to Modeling Choices and Assumption', *Environmental Health Perspectives*, http://dx.doi.org/10.1289/ehp.1104271.

Powers, B.W. and S.K. Chaguturu (2016) 'ACOs and High-Cost Patients', *The New England Journal of Medicine* 374: 203-5.DOI: 10.1056/NEJMp1511131

Powell, M. and M. Anesaki (2011) *Health Care in Japan.* New York: Routledge.

Pratt, B. and B. Loff (2012) 'Health Research Systems: Promoting Health Equity or Economic Competitiveness?', *Bulletin of the World Health Organization* 90: 55–62.

Public Health England (2015) 'E-cigarettes: A New Foundation for Evidence-based Policy and Practice', www.gov.uk/government/uploads/system/uploads/attachment_data/file/454517/Ecigarettes_a_firm_foundation_for_evidence_based_policy_and_practice.pdf.

Quah, E. and T.L. Boon (2003) 'The Economic Cost of Particulate Air Pollution on Health in Singapore', *Journal of Asian Economics* 14 (1): 73–90.

Quah, S.R. (2003) 'Traditional Healing Systems and the Ethos of Science', *Social Science and Medicine* 57 (10): 1997–2012.

Quesnel-Vallée, A., E. Renahy, T. Jenkins and H. Cerigo (2012) 'Assessing Barriers to Health Insurance and Threats to Equity in Comparative Perspective:

The Health Insurance Access Database', *BMC Health Services Research* 12: 107, http://www.biomedcentral.com/1472-6963/12/107.

Radin, B.A. (2010) 'When is a Health Department not a Health Department? The Case of the US Department of Health and Human Services', *Social Policy and Administration* 44 (2): 142–54.

Raffel, M.W. (ed.) (1997) *Health Care and Reform in Industrialized Countries.* University Park, PA: University of Pennsylvania Press.

Rahman, M.A., N. Hann, A. Wilson and L. Worrall-Carter (2014) 'Electronic Cigarettes: Patterns of Use, Health Effects, Use in Smoking Cessation and Regulatory Issues', *Tobacco Induced Disease* 12 (1): 21. doi:10.1186/1617-9625-12-21.

Rahman, M.A. (2015) 'E-Cigarettes and Smoking Cessation: Evidence from a Systematic Review and Meta-Analysis', *PLOS ONE* 10: e0122544. doi:10.1371/journal.pone.0122544.

Rainham, D. (2007) 'Do Differences in Health Make a Difference? A Review for Health Policymakers', *Health Policy* 84 (2–3): 123–32.

Ranade, W. (ed.) (1998) *Markets and Health Care: A Comparative Analysis.* London: Longman.

Ranci, C. and E. Pavolini (eds) (2013) 'Reforms in Long-Term Care Policies in Europe', New York: Springer Science & Business Media.

Ranson, M.K., M. Chopra, S. Atkins, M.R. Dal Poz and S. Bennett S (2010) 'Priorities for Research into Human Resources for Health in Low- and Middle-income Countries', *Bulletin of the World Health Organization*, 88: 435–43.

Raphael, D. and T. Bryant (2006) 'The State's Role in Promoting Population Health: Public Health Concerns in Canada, USA, UK, and Sweden', *Health Policy* 78: 39–55.

Rasanathan, K., E.V. Montesinos, D. Matheson, C. Etienne and T. Evans (2011) 'Primary Health Care and the Social Determinants of Health: Essential and Complementary Approaches for Reducing Inequities in Health', *Journal of Epidemiology and Community Health* 65: 656–60.

Rechel, B. (2015) 'Health Policy Reform in the Countries of the Former Soviet Union', in E. Kuhlmann, R.H. Blank, I.L. Bourgeault and C. Wendt (eds) *The Palgrave International Handbook of Healthcare Policy and Governance.* Basingstoke: Palgrave.

Rechel, B., M. Suhrcke, S. Tsolova, J.E. Suk, M. Desai, M. McKee, D. Stucklerc, I. Abubakar, P. Hunter, M. Senek and J.C. Semenza (2011) 'Economic Crisis and Communicable Disease Control in Europe: A Scoping Study among National Experts', *Health Policy* 103: 168–75.

Reese, P.P., A.L. Caplan, R.D. Bloom, P.L. Abt and J.H. Karlawish (2010) 'How Should We Use Age to Ration Health Care? Lessons from the Case of Kidney Transplantation', *Journal of the American Geriatric Society* 58: 1980–6.

Reeves, A., M. McKee, S. Basu and D. Stuckler (2014) 'The Political Economy of Austerity and Healthcare: Cross-national Analysis of Expenditure Changes in 27 European Nations 1995–2011', *Health Policy* 115: 1–8.

Reibling, N. and Wendt, C. (2012) 'Gatekeeping and Provider Choice in OECD Healthcare Systems', *Current Sociology* 60 (4): 489–505.

Reich, M.R. and K. Takemi (2015) 'Introduction and Overview for Governing Health Systems', in M.R. Reich and K. Takemi, K (eds) *Governing Health Systems: For Nations and Communities around the World*. Boston MA: Lamprey & Lee.

Reisman, D.A. (2006) 'Medisave and Medishield in Singapore: Getting the Balance Right', *Savings and Development* 2: 189–215.

Reisman, D.A. (2009) *Social Policy in an Ageing Society*. Cheltenham, UK: Edward Elgar.

Reuters (2005) 'Expert Sees Obesity Hitting U.S. Life Expectancy', http://preventdisease.com/news/articles/020205_obesity_lifespan.shtml.

Reuters (2006) 'Hospitals Prepare for Growing Ranks of Obese', 6 June.

Reynolds, C. (2011) *Public and Environmental Health Law*. Annandale, NSW: Federation Press.

Rhee, J.C., N. Done and G.F. Anderson (2015) 'Considering Long-term Care Insurance for Middle-income Countries: Comparing South Korea with Japan and Germany', *Health Policy* 119: 1319–29.

Rice, T., Rosenau, P., Unruh, L.Y., Barnes, A.J., Saltman, R.B. and van Ginneken, E. (2013) United States of America: Health System Review. *Health in Transition* 15 (3): 1–431.

Rimmer, A. (2016a) 'BMA Urges Government to Return to Junior Contract Negotiations', *British Medical Journal* 353: i1983.

Rimmer, A. (2016b) 'Doctors Slam Junior Contract for Discrimination against Woman', *British Medical Journal* 353: i1915.

Rix, M., A. Owen and K. Eagar (2005) '(Re)form with Substance? Restructuring and Governance in the Australian Health System 2004/05', *Australia and New Zealand Health Policy* 2 (19), http://www.anzhealthpolicy.com/content/2/1/19.

Roberts, M.J. (2015) 'Equity in Health Reform', in E. Kuhlmann, R.H. Blank, I.L. Bourgeault and C. Wendt (eds) *The Palgrave International Handbook of Healthcare Policy and Governance*. Basingstoke: Palgrave.

Robine, J.M., S. Cheung, S. LeRoy, H. Van Oyen, C. Griffiths and J.M. Michel (2008) 'Death Toll Exceeded 70,000 in Europe during the Summer of 2003', *Les Comptes Rendus/Série Biologies* 331: 171–8.

Rodwell, J. and A. Gulyas (2013) 'The Variety of Primary Healthcare Organisations in Australia: A Taxonomy', *BMC Health Services Research* 13: 130–6.

Rom, O., A. Pecorelli, G. Valacchi and A.Z. Reznick (2014). 'Are E-cigarettes a Safe and Good Alternative to Cigarette Smoking?' *Annals of the New York Academy of Sciences* 1340 (1): 65–74. doi:10.1111/nyas.12609.

Ros, C.C., P.P. Groenwegen and D.M.J. Delnoij (2000) 'All Rights Reserved, or Can We Just Copy? Cost Sharing Arrangements and Characteristics of Health Care Systems', *Health Policy* 52 (1): 1–13.

Roslund, G. (2014) 'The Medical Malpractice Rundown: A State-by-State Report Card, *Telemedicine Magazine*, http://epmonthly.com/article/the-medical-malpractice-rundown-a-state-by-state-report-card/

Ross, E. (2003) 'WHO Links SARS to Three Small Mammals', *Associated Press News Story*, 23 May.

Rostron, B. (2011) 'Smoking-attributable Mortality in the United States', *Epidemiology* 22 (3): 350–5.

Rothgang, H. (2010) 'Social Insurance for Long-term Care: An Evaluation of the German Model', *Social Policy & Administration* 44 (4): 436–60.

Rothgang, H., M. Cacace, L. Frisina, S. Grimmeisen, A. Schmid and C. Wendt (2010) *The State and Healthcare. Comparing OECD Countries.* Basingstoke: Palgrave Macmillan.

Rovere, M. and B. Barua (2012) 'Opportunity for Health Reform: Lessons from the Netherlands', *Fraser Forum*, October, https://www.fraserinstitute.org/sites/default/files/fraserforum-september-october-2012.pdf.

Rubin, E.J., M.F. Greene and L.R. Baden (2016) 'Zika Virus and Microcephaly', *The New England Journal of Medicine* 374 (10): 984–5.

Rudin, S., D.W. Bates and C. MacRae (2016) 'Accelerating Innovation in Health IT', *New England Journal of Medicine* 375: 815-17, doi: 10.1056/NEJMp1606884.

Rummery, K. and M. Fine (2012) 'Care: A Critical Review of Theory, Policy and Practice', *Social Policy & Administration* 46 (3): 321–43.

Russell, J., T. Greenhalgh, E. Bryne and J. McDonnell (2008) 'Recognizing Rhetoric in Health Care Policy Analysis', *Journal of Health Services Research Policy* 13 (1): 40–6.

Russell, L.B. (2007) 'Prevention's Potential for Slowing the Growth of Medical Spending', Washington, DC: National Coalition on Health Care, http://www.ihhcpar.rutgers.edu/downloads/RussellNCHC2007.pdf.

Sabik, L.M. and R.K. Lie (2008) 'Priority Setting in Health Care: Lessons from the Experiences of Eight Countries', *International Journal for Equity in Health* 7 (4): 1–13.

Sade, R.M. (2007) 'Ethical Foundations of Health Care System Reform', *Annals of Thoracic Surgery* 84: 1429–31.

Sage, W.M. and R. Kersh (eds) (2006) *Medical Malpractice and the U.S. Health Care System.* Cambridge, MA: Cambridge University Press.

Saitta, D., G.A. Ferro and R. Polosa (Mar 2014). 'Achieving Appropriate Regulations for Electronic Cigarettes', *Therapeutic Advances in Chronic Disease* 5 (2): 50–61.

Saks, M. (2002) *Orthodox and Alternative Medicine: Politics, Professionalization, and Health Care.* London: Sage.

Saltman, R. and E. van Ginneken (eds) (2013) 'United States of America: Health System Review', *Health Systems in Transition* 15 (3): 1–467.

Saltman, R.B. (1997) 'Convergence versus Social Embeddedness. Debating the Future Direction of Health Systems', *European Journal of Public Health* 7 (4): 449–53.

Saltman, R.B. (1998) 'Health Reform in Sweden: The Road Beyond Cost Containment', in W. Ranade (ed.) *Markets and Health Care: A Comparative Analysis.* London: Longman.

Saltman, R.B. (2002) 'Regulating Incentives: The Past and Present Role of the State in Health Care Systems', *Social Science and Medicine* 54 (11): 1677–84.

Saltman, R.B. (2012) 'The Role of Comparative Health Studies for Policy Learning', *Journal of Health Politics, Policy and Law* 7 (1): 11–13.

Saltman, R.B. (2015) 'Healthcare Policy and Innovation', in E. Kuhlmann, R.H. Blank, I.L. Bourgeault and C. Wendt (eds) *The Palgrave International Handbook of Healthcare Policy and Governance*. Basingstoke: Palgrave.

Saltman, R.B. and V. Bankauskaite (2006) 'Conceptualizing Decentralization in European Health Systems: A Functional Perspective', *Journal of Health Economics, Policy and Law* 1: 127–47.

Saltman, R.B. and S.-E. Bergman (2005) 'Renovating the Commons: Swedish Health Care Reforms in Perspective', *Journal of Health Politics, Policy and Law* 30 (1): 253–76.

Saltman, R.B., A. Rico and W. Boerma (eds) (2006) *Primary Care in the Driver's Seat? Organizational Reform in European Primary Care*. Maidenhead: Open University Press.

Samuelson, M., P. Tedeschi, D. Aarendonk, C. de la Cuesta and P.P. Groenewegen (2012) 'Position paper of the European Forum for Primary Care. Improving Interprofessional Collaboration in Primary Care: Position Paper of the European Forum for Primary Care', *Quality in Primary Care* 20: 303–12.

Sassi, F., M. Devaux, M. Cecchini and E. Rusticelli (2009) 'The Obesity Epidemic: Analysis of Past and Projected Future Trends in Selected OECD Countries', *Health Working Papers No. 45*. Paris: OECD.

Sauerland, D. (2009) 'The Legal Framework for Health Care Quality Assurance in Germany', *Health Economics, Policy and Law* 4 (1): 79–98.

Schäfer, W., M. Kroneman, W. Boerma, M.v.d. Berg, G. Westert, W. Devillé and E.v. Ginneken (2010) 'The Netherlands Health System Review', *Health Systems in Transition* 12 (1): 1–198.

Schlander, M. (2010) *Health Technology Assessments by the National Institute for Health and Clinical Excellence: A Qualitative Study*. Berlin: Springer.

Schmid, A. and R. Götze (2009) 'Cross-national Policy Learning in Health System Reform: The Case of Diagnosis Related Groups', *International Social Security Review* 62 (4): 21–39.

Schmid, A., M. Cacace, R. Götze and H. Rothgang (2010) 'Explaining Health Care System Change: Problem Pressure and the Emergence of "Hybrid" Health Care Systems', *Journal of Health Politics, Policy and Law* 35 (4): 455–86.

Schneider, M-J. (2016). Introduction to Public Health, 5th edn. New York: Jones and Bartlett Publishers.

Schneider, U., G. Sundström, L. Johannson and M.A. Tortosa (2016) 'Policies to Support Informal Care', in C. Gori, J-L. Fernández and R. Wittenberg (eds) *Long-term Care Reforms in OECD Countries: Successes and Failures*. Bristol: Policy Press.

Schoen, C., R. Osborn, M.M. Doty, M. Bishop, J. Peugh and N. Murukulta (2007) 'Toward Higher-Performance Health Systems: Adults' Health Care Experiences in Seven Countries', *Health Affairs* 26 (6): w717–34.

Schoenbaum, S.C., C. Schoen, J.L. Nicholson and J.C. Cantor (2011) 'Mortality Amenable to Health Care in the United States: The Roles of Demographics and Health Systems Performance', *Journal of Public Health Policy* 32: 407–29.

Schoenstein, M., T. Ono and G. Lafortune (2016) 'Skills Use and Skills Mismatch in the Health Sector: What Do We Know and What Can Be Done?', in *Health Workforce Policies in OECD Countries: Right Jobs, Right Skills, Right*

Places. OECD Health Policy Studies. Paris: OECD Publishing, http://dx.doi.org/10.1787/9789264239517-en.

Schroeder, S.A. (2007) 'We Can Do Better: Improving the Health of the American People', *New England Journal of Medicine* 357: 1221–8.

Schut, F.T. and B.V.D. Berg (2010) 'Sustainability of Comprehensive Universal Long-term Care Insurance in the Netherlands', *Social Policy & Administration* 44 (4): 411–35.

Schwartz, F.F. and R. Busse (1997) 'Germany', in C. Ham (ed.) *Health Care Reform: Learning from International Experience*. Buckingham: Open University Press.

Schwartz, M.D. (2011) 'Health Care Reform and the Primary Care Workforce Bottleneck', *Journal of General Internal Medicine* 27 (4): 469–72.

Scott, C.D. (2001) *Public and Private Roles in Health Care: Experiences from Seven Countries*. Buckingham: Open University Press.

Scott, W.G., H.M. Scott and T.S. Auld (2005) 'Consumer Access to Health Information on the Internet: Health Policy Implications', *Australia and New Zealand Health Policy* 2 (13), www.anzhealthpolicy.com/content/2/1/13.

Seedhouse, D. (1991) *Liberating Medicine*. Chichester: Wiley.

Semansky, R., C. Willging, D.J. Ley and B. Rylko-Bauer (2012) 'Lost in the Rush to National Reform: Recommendations to Improve Impact on Behavioral Health Providers in Rural Areas', *Journal of Health Care for the Poor and Underserved* 23 (2): 842–56.

Sexton, S. (2001) 'Trading Health Care Away? GATS, Public Services and Privatisation', www.thecornerhouse.org.uk/pdf/briefing/23gats.pdf.

Sheaff, R. (2013) 'Plural Provision of Primary Medical Care in England, 2002–2013', *Journal of Health Services Research and Policy* 18 (2 Suppl): 20–8.

Sheffield, P.E. and P.J. Landrigan (2011) 'Global Climate Change and Children's Health: Threats and Strategies for Prevention', *Environmental Health Perspectives* 119 (3): 291–8.

Sheldon, G.F. (2011) 'The Evolving Surgeon Shortage in the Health Reform Era', *Journal of Gastrointestinal Surgery* 15: 1104–11.

Shih, F.-L., S. Thompson and P. Tremlett (eds) (2009) *Rewriting Culture in Taiwan*. New York: Routledge.

Shortt, J. (2004) 'Obesity: A Public Health Dilemma', *AORN Journal* 80 (6): 1069–76.

Singapore Ministry of Health (1995) 'Traditional Chinese Medicine', *Report of the Committee on Traditional Chinese Medicine*, October.

Singapore Ministry of Health (2008) Singapore: Singapore Ministry of Health, https://www.moh.gov.sg/content/moh_web/home.html.

Singapore Ministry of Health (2016). 'Manpower Statistics', www.moh.gov.sg/content/moh_web/home/statistics/Health_Facts_Singapore/Health_Manpower.html.

Skinner, J.S., D.O. Staiger and E.S. Fisher (2006) 'Is Technological Change in Medicine Always Worth It? The Case of Myocardial Infarction', *Health Affairs* 25: w34–w47.

Skolnick, R. (2011) *Global Health 101*. Burlington, MA: Jones and Bartlett.

Smith, J. and N. Mays (2007) 'Primary Care Organizations in New Zealand and England: Tipping the Balance of the Health System in Favour of Primary Care?', *International Journal of Health Planning and Management* 23: 3–19.

Smith, P.C., A. Anell, R. Busse, L. Crivelli, J. Healy, A.K. Lindahl, G. Westert and T. Kene (2012) 'Leadership and Governance in Seven Developed Health Systems', *Health Policy* 106: 37–49.

Smith, R.D. and K. Hanson (eds) (2012) *Health Systems in Low- and Middle-Income Countries: An Economic and Policy Perspective.* New York: Oxford University Press.

'Smoking in Taiwan' (2012) http://en.wikipedia.org/wiki/Smoking_in_Taiwan.

Stanhope, M. and J. Lancaster (2011) *Public Health Nursing: Population-Centered Care in the Community*, 8th edn. Maryland Heights, MO: Mosby.

Stanton, G.T. (2003) 'How Marriage Improves Health', www.divorcereform.org/mel/abetterhealth.html.

Stanton, M.W. and M.K. Rutherford (2005) 'The High Concentration of U.S. Health Care Expenditures', *Research in Action Issue* 19. AHRQ Pub. No. 06–0060. Rockville, MD: Agency for Healthcare Research and Quality.

Starfield, B. (2000) 'Is US Health Really the Best in the World?', *Journal of the American Medical Association* 284 (4): 483–5.

Starfield, B., J. Gervas and D. Mangin (2012) 'Clinical Care and Health Disparities', *Annual Review of Public Health* 33: 89–106.

Starr, P. (2011) *Remedy and Reaction: The Peculiar American Struggle over Health Care Reform.* New Haven, CT: Yale University Press.

Steinberg, E.P. and B.R. Luce (2005) 'Evidence Based: Caveat Emptor!', *Health Affairs* 24 (1): 80–93.

Stone, D. (1999) 'Learning Lessons and Transferring Policy across Time, Space and Disciplines', *Politics* 19 (1): 51–9.

Straits Times (2000) 'Singapore's Health System is Best in Asia', 21 January.

Strand, L.B., S. Tong, R. Aird and D. McRae (2010) 'Vulnerability of Eco-environmental Health to Climate Change: The Views of Government Stakeholders and Other Specialists in Queensland, Australia', *BMC Public Health* 10: 441–50.

Stukel, T.A., F.L. Lucas and D.E. Wennberg (2005) 'Long-term Outcomes of Regional Variations in Intensity of Invasive vs. Medical Management of Medicare Patients with Acute Myocardial Infarction', *Journal of the American Medical Association* 293: 1329–37.

Sullivan, L.W. (1990) 'Healthy People 2000', *New England Journal of Medicine* 323: 1065–7.

Swedish Medical Association (2016) Sveriges Läkarförbund, EFMA members, http://legeforeningen.no/efma-who/members/national-medical-associations-representing-both-member-organisations-and-observers/sveriges-lakarforbund-swedish-medical-association/.

Syrett, K. (2003) 'A Technocratic Fix to the "Legitimacy Problem"? The Blair Government and Health Care Rationing in the United Kingdom', *Journal of Health Politics, Policy and Law* 28 (4): 715–46.

Syrett, K. (2008) *Law, Legitimacy and the Rationing of Health Care.* Cambridge: Cambridge University Press.

Taiwan Ministry of Health and Welfare (2013) 'Statistics and Trends in Health and Welfare 2013,' p. 135. Chinese.

Talbot, L. and G. Verrinder (2010) *Promoting Health: The Primary Health Care Approach.* Chatswood, NSW: Churchill Livingstone Australia.

Tamiya, N., H. Noguchi, A. Nishi, M.R. Reich, N. Ikegami, H. Hashimoto, K. Shibuya, I. Kawachi and J.C. Campbell (2011) 'Population Ageing and Wellbeing: Lessons from Japan's Long-term Care Insurance Policy', *The Lancet* 378 (9797): 1183–92, doi: 10.1016/S0140-6736(11)61176-8.

Tan, A.S.L. (2011) 'An Approach to Building the Case for Nutrition Policies to Limit Trans-Fat Intake – A Singapore Case Study', *Health Policy* 100: 264–72.

Tanner, L. (2006) 'U.S. Newborn Survival Rate Ranks Low', *Associated Press*, 5 May.

Tashobya, C.K., V. Campos da Silveira, F. Ssengooba, J. Nabyonga-Orem, J. Macq and B. Criel (2014) 'Health Systems Performance Assessment in Low-income Countries: Learning from International Experiences', *Globalization and Health* 10 (5): doi:10.1186/1744-8603-10-5.

Tatara, K. and E. Okamoto (2009) 'Japan: Health System Review', *Health Systems in Transition* 11 (5): 1–164.

Tay, J., F.N. Yeuk, J. Cutter and L. James (2010) 'Influenza A (H1N1-2009) Pandemic in Singapore: Public Health Control Measures Implemented and Lessons Learnt', *Annals of the Academy of Medicine Singapore* 39: 313–24.

Taylor, S. (2009) 'Wealth, Health and Equity: Convergence to Divergence in Late 20th Century Globalization', *British Medical Bulletin* 91: 29–48.

Taylor, V.H., C.M. Curtis and C. Davis (2010) 'The Obesity Epidemic: The Role of Addiction', *CMAJ* 182 (4): 327–8.

Taylor-Gooby, P. and L. Mitton (2008) 'Much Noise, Little Progress: The UK Experience of Privatization', in D. Béland and B. Grand (eds) *Public and Private Social Policy. Health and Pension Policies in a New Era*. Basingstoke: Palgrave Macmillan.

Tenbensel, T., J. Cumming, T. Ashton and P. Barnett (2008) 'Where There's a Will, Is There a Way? Is New Zealand's Publicly Funded Health Sector Able to Steer Towards Population Health?', *Social Science and Medicine* 67: 1143–52.

Tenbensel T., S. Eagle and T. Ashton (2012) 'Comparing Health Policy Agendas across Eleven High Income Countries: Islands of Difference in a Sea of Similarity', *Health Policy* 106 (1): 29–36.

Teo, P., A. Chan and P. Straughan (2003) 'Providing Health Care for Older Persons in Singapore', *Health Policy* 64 (3): 399–413.

Thacker, S.B., D.F. Stroup, V. Carande-Kulis, J.S. Marks, K. Roy and J.L. Gerberding (2006) 'Measuring the Public's Health', *Public Health Reports* 121: 14–22.

The Lancet (2006) 'Rationing is Essential in Tax-Funded Health Systems', *The Lancet* 368 (9545): 1394.

Theobald, H. (2003) 'Welfare System, Professionalisation and the Question of Inequality', *International Journal of Sociology and Social Policy* 23 (4/5): 159–85.

Theobald, H. (2012) 'Combining Welfare Mix and New Public Management: The Case of Long-term Care Insurance in Germany', *International Journal of Social Welfare* 1–10.

Theobald, H. and S. Hampel (2013) 'Radical Institutional Change and Incremental Transformation: Long-Term Care Insurance in Germany', in C. Ranci and E. Pavolini (eds) *Reforms in Long-term Care Policies in Europe*. Heidelberg, New York: Springer.

Theobald, H. and E. Ozanne (2016) 'Multi-level Governance and Its Effects in Long-term Care Policies', in C. Gori, J-L. Fernández. and R. Wittenberg (eds) *Long-term Care Reforms in OECD Countries: Successes and Failures.* Bristol: Policy Press.

Thomas, R.L. (2011) 'Convergence: It's What's Next in Healthcare IT', *Healthcare Financial Management* 65 (1): 130–2.

Thomas, S.L., S. Lewis, J. Hyde, D. Castle and P. Komesaroff (2010) 'The Solution Needs to be Complex: Obese Adults' Attitudes about the Effectiveness of Individual and Population Based Interventions for Obesity', *BMC Public Health* 10: 420, http://www.biomedcentral.com/1471-2458/10/420.

Thomson, S. and A. Dixon (2006) 'Choices in Health Care: The European Experience', *Journal of Health Services Research Policy* 11 (3): 167–71.

Thomson, S. and E. Mossialos (2008) 'Medical Savings Accounts: Can They Improve Health System Performance in Europe?', *EuroObserver* 10 (4): 1–4.

Thomson, S., E. Mossialos and R.G. Evans (2009) *Private Health Insurance and Medical Savings Accounts: Lessons from International Experience.* Cambridge: Cambridge University Press.

Thomson, S., R. Osborn, D. Squires and M. Jun (eds) (2013) *International Profiles of Health Care Systems, 2013.* New York: The Commonwealth Fund.

Thorpe, K.E., C.S. Florence, D.H. Howard and P. Joski (2004a) 'The Impact of Obesity on Rising Medical Spending', *Health Affairs,* 20 October.

Thorpe, K.E., C.S. Florence and P. Joski (2004b) 'Which Medical Conditions Account for the Rise in Health Care Spending?', *Health Affairs,* 25 August.

Thrasher, J.F., M.C. Rousuc, D. Hammond, A. Navarro and J.R. Corrigane (2011) 'Estimating the Impact of Pictorial Health Warnings and "Plain" Cigarette Packaging: Evidence from Experimental Auctions among Adult Smokers in the United States', *Health Policy* 102: 41–8.

Tirado, F., A. Gómez and V. Rocamora (2015) 'The Global Conditions of Epidemics: Panoramas in A (H1N1) Influenza and Their Consequences of One World Health Programme', *Social Science & Medicine* 129: 113–22.

Tompa, E., A.J. Culyer and R. Dolinschi (2008) *Economic Evaluation of Interventions for Occupational Health and Safety.* New York: Oxford University Press.

Tomson, G. and O. Biermann (2015) Health Policy in Low-income and Lower Middle-income Countries in Southeast Asia', in E. Kuhlmann, R.H. Blank, I.L. Bourgeault and C. Wendt (eds) *The Palgrave International Handbook of Healthcare Policy and Governance.* Basingstoke: Palgrave.

Trappenburg, M. and M. De Groot (2001) 'Controlling Medical Specialists in the Netherlands: Delegating the Dirty Work', in M. Bovens, P. t'Hart and B.G. Peters (eds) *Success and Failure in Public Governance. A Comparative Analysis.* Cheltenham: Edward Elgar.

Trydegård, G-B. (2000) *Tradition, Change and Variation: Past and Present Trends in Public Old-Age Care.* Dissertation. Stockholm: Department of Social Work, University of Stockholm.

Tsai, J.C-H., W-Y. Chen and Y-W. Liang (2011) 'Nonemergent Emergency Department Visits under the National Health Insurance in Taiwan', *Health Policy* 100: 189–95.

Tsiachristas, A., B. Hipple-Walters, K.M.M. Lemmens, A.P. Nieboer and M.P.M.H. Rutten-van Mölken (2011) 'Towards Integrated Care for Chronic

Conditions: Dutch Policy Developments to Overcome the (Financial) Barriers', *Health Policy* 101 (2): 122–32.

Tsiachristas, A., I. Wallenburg, C.M. Bond, R.F. Elliot, R. Busse, J. van Exel, M.P Rutten van Mölken, A. de Bont and the MUNROS team (2015) 'Costs and effects of new professional roles: Evidence from a literature review', *Health Policy*, doi: http://dx.doi.org/10.1016/j.healthpol.2015.04.001.

Tuohy, C.H. (2012a) 'Reform and the Politics of Hybridization in Mature Health Care States', *Journal of Health Politics, Policy and Law* 37 (4): 611–32.

Tuohy, C.H. (2012b) 'Shall We Dance? The Intricate Project of Comparison in the Study of Health Policy', *Health Economics, Policy and Law* 7 (1): 21–3.

Turnock, B.J. (2011) *Public Health: What It Is and How It Works*, 5th edn. New York: Jones and Bartlett Publishers.

Twaddle, A.C. (1999) *Health Care Reform in Sweden, 1980–1994*. London: Auburn House.

Twaddle, A.C. (ed.) (2002) *Health Care Reform around the World*. Westport, CT: Auburn House.

Twigg, J. (1989) 'Models of Carers: How Do Social Care Agencies Conceptualise Their Relationship with Informal Carers?', *Journal of Social Policy* 18 (1): 53–66.

Ubel, P.A. (2001) *Pricing Life: Why it's Time for Health Care Rationing*. Cambridge, MA: MIT Press.

Ueda, H., F. Armada, M. Kashiwabara and I. Yoshimi (2011) 'Street Smoking Bans in Japan: A Hope for Smoke-free Cities?', *Health Policy* 102: 49–55.

UNAIDS (2010) *Report on the Global AIDS Epidemic*, www.unaids.org/globalreport/documents/20101123_GlobalReport_full_en.pdf.

UNAIDS (2012) Press Release, 20 November, http://www.kff.org/news-summary/unaids-report-shows-progress-due-to-unprecedented-acceleration-in-global-aids-response/.

Unal, B., J.A. Critchley, D. Fidan and S. Capewell (2005) 'Life-years Gained from Modern Cardiological Treatments and Population Risk Factor Changes in England and Wales, 1981–2000', *American Journal of Public Health* 95: 103–8.

UNDESA (2015) 'Trends in International Migrant Stock: The 2015 Revision', http://www.un.org/en/development/desa/population/migration/data/index.shtml.

UNFPA (2009) *Facing a Changing World: Women, Population and Climate*. New York: UNFPA.

United States Department of Health and Human Services (2001) *The Surgeon General's Call to Action to Prevent and Decrease Overweight and Obesity*. Washington: US Government Printing Office.

United States Department of Health and Human Services (2004) 'HHS Announces Revised Medicare Obesity Coverage Policy', http://archive.hhs.gov/news/press/2004pres/20040715.html.

United States Department of Health and Human Services (2005) *National Guideline for Overweight and Obesity in Children and Adolescents: Assessment, Prevention, and Management*. Washington, DC: US Government Printing Office.

U.S. Department of Health and Human Services (2014) *The Health Consequences of Smoking – 50 Years of Progress: A Report of the Surgeon General*. Atlanta, GA: DHHS.

United States Environmental Protection Agency (2009) 'Climate Change – Health and Environmental Effects', https://www.epa.gov/climatechange.

Valente, T.W. (2002) *Evaluating Health Promotion Programs*. New York: Oxford University Press.

Van den Berg, M.J., D.S. Kringos, L.K. Marks and N.S. Klazinga (2014) 'The Dutch Health Care Performance Report: Seven Years of Health Care Performance Assessment in the Netherlands.' *Health Research Policy and Systems* 12 (1), doi:10.1186/1478-4505-12-1.

Van Ginneken, E. and B.H. Gray (2015) 'European Policies on Healthcare for Undocumented Migrants', in E. Kuhlmann, R.H. Blank, I.L. Bourgeault and C. Wendt (eds) *The Palgrave International Handbook of Healthcare Policy and Governance*. Basingstoke: Palgrave.

Van Wave, T.W., F.D. Scutchfield and P.A. Honore (2010) 'Recent Advances in Public Health Systems Research in the United States', *Annual Review of Public Health* 31: 283–95.

Verspohl, I. (2012) *Health Care Reforms in Europe. Convergence towards a Market Model?* Baden-Baden: Nomos Verlagsgesellschaft.

Volkow, N.D. and C.P. O'Brien (2007) 'Issues for DSM-V: Should Obesity Be Included as a Brain Disorder?', *American Journal of Psychiatry* 164: 708–10.

Von Lengerke, T. and C. Krauth (2011) 'Economic Costs of Adult Obesity: A Review of Recent European Studies with a Focus on Subgroup-specific Costs', *Maturitas* 69 (3): 220–9.

Vrangbaek, K., R. Robertson, U. Winblad, H.v.d. Bovenkamp and A. Dixon (2012) 'Choice Policies in Northern European Health Systems', *Health Economics, Policy and Law* 7: 47–71.

Vujicic, M., S.E. Weber, I.A. Nikolai, R. Atun and R. Kumar (2012) 'An Analysis of GAVI, the Global Fund and World Bank Support for Human Resources for Health in Developing Countries', *Health Policy Plan* 27 (8): 649–57.

Wagner, A.K., A. Johnson Graves, S.K. Reiss, R. LeCates, F. Zhang, D. Ross-Degnan (2011) 'Access to Care and Medicines, Burden of Health Care Expenditures, and Risk Protection: Results from the World Health Survey', *Health Policy* 100: 151–8.

Wagstaff, A. (2007) 'Health Systems in East Asia: What Can Developing Countries Learn from Japan and the Asian Tigers?', *Health Economics* 16: 441–56.

Wallace, R.B. (2007). *Public Health and Preventive Medicine*, 15th edn. Columbus, OH: McGraw-Hill.

Walton, M., J. Waiti, L. Signal and G. Thomson (2010) 'Identifying Barriers to Promoting Healthy Nutrition in New Zealand Primary Schools', *Health Education Journal* 69 (1): 84–94.

Wang, K.Y-T. (2011) 'Child Care and Elder Care Arrangements in Taiwan', *Journal of Comparative Social Welfare* 27 (2): 165–74.

Wang, Y.C., K. McPherson, T. Marsh, S.L. Gortmaker and M. Brown (2011) 'Health and Economic Burden of the Projected Obesity Trends in the USA and the UK', *The Lancet* 378 (9793): 815–25.

Watson, M.C. and J. Lloyd (2016) 'Editorials: Government Changes Are Jeopardising Public Health', *British Medical Journal* 352: i1662.

Watson, E.A. and J. Mears (1999) *Women, Work and Care of the Elderly.* Aldershot: Ashgate.

Weale, A. (1998) 'Rationing Health Care', *British Medical Journal* 316: 410–26.

Weber, M. (1949) *The Methodology of the Social Sciences.* New York: Free Press.

Weissert, C.S. and W.G. Weissert (2002) *Governing Health: The Politics of Health Policy.* Baltimore: The Johns Hopkins University Press.

Wells, D.A., J.S. Ross and A.S. Detsky (2007) 'What is Different about the Market for Health Care?', *Journal of the American Medical Association* 298 (23): 2785–7.

Wen, C-P., S-P. Tsai and W-S. Chung (2008) 'A 10-Year Experience of Universal Health Insurance in Taiwan: Assessing the Health Impact and Disparity Reduction', *Annals of Internal Medicine* 148 (4): 258–67.

Wendt, C. (2014) 'Changing Healthcare System Types', *Social Policy & Administration* 48 (7): 864-82.

Wendt, C. (2015) 'Healthcare Policy and Finance', in E. Kuhlmann, R.H. Blank, I.L. Bourgeault and C. Wendt (eds) *The Palgrave International Handbook of Healthcare Policy and Governance.* Basingstoke: Palgrave.

Wendt, C. and J. Kohl (2010) 'Translating Monetary Inputs into Health Care Provision: A Comparative Analysis of the Impact of Different Modes of Public Policy', *Journal of Comparative Policy Analysis: Research and Practice,* 12 (1): 11–31.

Wendt, C., T.I. Agartan and M.E. Kaminska (2013) 'Social Health Insurance without Corporate Actors: Changes in Self-regulation in Germany, Poland and Turkey', *Social Science and Medicine* 86: 88–95.

Wendt, C., L. Firsina and H. Rothgang (2009) 'Healthcare System Types: A Conceptual Framework for Comparison', *Social Policy and Administration* 43 (1): 70–90.

Werkö, L., J. Chamova and J. Adolfson (2001) 'Health Technology Assessment. The Swedish Experience', *Eurohealth* 7 (1): 29–31.

West, R., E. Beard and J. Brown (2015). 'Electronic Cigarettes in England – Latest Trends', *Smoking in England,* www.ecigclick.co.uk/e-cig-research/trends-in-electronic-cigarette-use-in-england/.

Wharam, J.F. and N. Daniels (2007) 'Toward Evidence-Based Policy Making and Standardized Assessment of Health Policy Reform', *Journal of the American Medical Association* 298 (6): 676–79.

White, C. (2011) *The Personal Touch – The Dutch Experience of Personal Health Budgets.* London: Health Foundation.

WHO (1946) 'Preamble to the Constitution of the World Health Organization as Adopted by the International Health Conference', New York, 19–22 June, 1946; signed on 22 July 1946 by the representatives of 61 States, and entered into force on 7 April 1948.

WHO (1978) *Primary Health Care - Report of the International Conference on Primary Health Care.* Alma Ata, Health for All Series No 1. Geneva: WHO.

WHO (1981) *Global Strategy for Health for All by the Year 2000.* Geneva: WHO.

WHO (1996) 'Traditional Medicine', Fact Sheet no. 134, September. Geneva: WHO.

WHO (2000) *The World Health Report 2000. Health Systems: Improving Performance*. Geneva, World Health Organization.

WHO (2003) *Moving towards a Tobacco-free Europe: The European Report on Tobacco Control Policy, 1997–2002*. European Ministerial Conference for a Tobacco-free Europe. Copenhagen: WHO.

WHO (2008a) *Health for All, All for Health Workers*. Geneva: WHO.

WHO (2008b) 'Climate Change and Human Health', http://www.who.int/globalchange/en/.

WHO (2008c) *WHO Report on the Global Tobacco Epidemic, 2008: The MPOWER Package*. Geneva: WHO.

WHO (2008d) Primary Health Care: Now More Than Ever. Geneva: WHO.

WHO (2009a) *Global Database on Body Mass Index*. Geneva: WHO.

WHO (2009b) *WHO Report on the Global Tobacco Epidemic, 2009: Implementing Smoke-free Environments*. Geneva: WHO.

WHO (2010a) 'Climate Change and Health', Fact Sheet No. 266, http://www.who.int/mediacentre/factsheets/fs266/en/.

WHO (2010b). *User's Guide to the WHO Global Code of Practice on the International Recruitment of Health Personnel*. WHO: Geneva.

WHO (2012a). Health Workforce Governance and Leadership Capacity in the African Region, *Human Resources for Health Observer 9*: 1–24.

WHO (2012b) 'Obesity and Overweight', Fact Sheet No. 311, www.who.int/mediacentre/factsheets/fs311/en/index.html.

WHO (2012c) 'HIV/AIDS, Data and Statistics', www.who.int/hiv/data/en/.

WHO (2012d) 'The Labour Market for Human Resources for Health in Low- and Middle-income Countries', *Human Resources for Health Observer* 11, www.who.int/hrh/resources/Observer11_WEB.pdf.

WHO (2015a). *Draft Global Strategy on Human Resources for Health: Workforce 2030*. Copenhagen: WHO, http://who.int/hrh/resources/globstrathrh-2030/en/.

WHO (2015b). *Core Health Indicators in the WHO European Region. 2015 Special Focus: Health Human Resources*. Copenhagen: WHO, http://www.euro.who.int/__data/assets/pdf_file/0019/290440/Core-Health-Indicators-European-2015-human-resources-health.pdf?ua=1.

WHO (2015c). *Nurses and Midwives: A Vital Resource for Health*. Copenhagen: WHO.

WHO (2016a) 'Electronic Nicotine Delivery Systems and Electronic Non-Nicotine Delivery Systems (ENDS/ENNDS)', http://www.who.int/tobacco/industry/product_regulation/eletronic-cigarettes-report-cop7/en/.

WHO (2016b). 'WHO Global Strategy on Human Resources for Health: Workforce 2030', http://who.int/hrh/resources/globstrathrh-2030/en/.

WHO Public Health and Environment Department (2011) *Gender, Climate Change, and Health*. Geneva: WHO.

WHO Regional Office for Europe (2003a) *European Environment and Health Committee*, http://www.euro.who.int/en/health-topics/environment-and-health/pages/european-environment-and-health-process-ehp/governance/european-environment-and-health-committee.

WHO Regional Office for Europe (2003b) 'Global Change and Health', http://www.euro.who.int/__data/assets/pdf_file/0009/91098/E81923.pdf.

WHO Regional Office for Europe (2003c) 'National Environmental Action Plans', http://www.euro.who.int/__data/assets/pdf_file/0005/109877/EUR_ICP_CEH_212A.pdf.

WHO Regional Office for Europe (2004) Declaration. Fourth Ministerial Conference on Environment and Health, 23–25 June 2004. Budapest, (EUR/o4/5046267/06). Copenhagen: WHO, Regional Office for Europe.

WHO Regional Office for Europe (2006) *European Charter on Counteracting Obesity*. Copenhagen: WHO Regional Office for Europe.

Wilkinson, R.G. (1997) *Unhealthy Societies: The Afflictions of Inequality*. London: Routledge.

Wilkinson, R.G. and K.E. Pickett (2006) 'Income Inequality and Population Health: A Review and Explanation of the Evidence', *Social Science and Medicine* 62 (7): 1768–84.

Williams, A. (1997) 'Rationing Health Care by Age: The Case for', *British Medical Journal* 314: 820–2.

Williams, B.O. (2000) 'Ageism Helps to Ration Medical Treatment', *Health Bulletin* 58 (3): 198–202.

Williams, I., S. Robinson and H. Dickinson (2011) *Rationing in Health Care: The Theory and Practice of Priority Setting*. Bristol, UK: Policy Press.

Wilsford, D. (1994) 'Path Dependency, or Why History Makes It Difficult, but Not Impossible to Reform Health Systems in a Big Way', *Journal of Public Policy* 14 (3): 285–306.

Winkelmann, R, (2009) 'Unemployment, Social Capital, and Subjective Well-Being', *Journal of Happiness Studies* 10 (4): 421–30.

Winkleby, M.A., D.E. Jatulis, E. Frank and S.P. Fortmann (1992) 'Socioeconomic Status and Health: How Education, Income, and Occupation Contribute to Risk Factors for Cardiovascular Disease', *American Journal of Public Health* 82 (6): 816–21.

Wipfli, H. and G. Huang (2011) 'Power of the Process: Evaluating the Impact of the Framework Convention on Tobacco Control Negotiations', *Health Policy* 100: 107–15.

Wismar, M., C. B. Maier, I. A. Glinos, G. Dussault and J. Figueras (eds) (2011) 'Health Professional Mobility and Health Systems. Evidence from 17 European Countries', *Observatory Study Series No. 23, European Observatory on Health Systems and Policies*, WHO Regional Office for Europe, Copenhagen.

Wismar, M., I.B. Glinos and A. Sagan (eds) (2017) *Patients, Peers, Professionals: Skill-mix Innovations and Developments in Primary and Chronic Care Settings*, Brussels: European Observatory for Health Systems and Policy.

Wissenschaftsrat (2012) Empfehlungen zu hochschulischen Qualifikationen für das Gesundheitswesen. Köln: Geschäftsstelle des Wissenschaftsrats.

Withrow, D. and D.A. Alter (2011) 'The Economic Burden of Obesity Worldwide: A Systematic Review of the Direct Costs of Obesity', *Obesity Reviews* 12 (2): 131–41.

Wittenberg, R. (2016) 'Demand for Care and Support for Older People', in C. Gori, J-L. Fernández and R. Wittenberg (eds) *Long-Term Care Reforms in OECD Countries: Successes and Failures*. Bristol: Policy Press.

Witz, A. and E. Annandale (2006) 'The Challenge of Nursing', in D. Kelleher, J. Gabe and G. Williams (eds) *Challenging Medicine*, 2nd edn. London: Routledge.

Wong, M. (2003) 'WHO Removes Hong Kong from SARS List', *The Associated Press*, 23 June.

World Factbook (2016), https://www.cia.gov/library/publications/resources/the-world-factbook/geos/rp.html.

Worldwide Market for the Clinical Management of Obesity, 2007–2015 (2007) Report #825. MedMarket Diligence.

WP7 Joint Action on Health Workforce Planning and Forecasting (2016). *WP7 Report on Circular Migration of the Health Workforce*. Leuven: Catholic University of Leuven.

Wrede, S. (2012) 'Nursing: Globalization of a Female-gendered Profession', in E. Kuhlmann and E. Annandale (eds) *The Palgrave Handbook of Gender and Healthcare*, 2nd edn. Basingstoke: Palgrave.

Wütscher, F., F. Breyer, H. Kliemt and F. Thiele (eds) (2010) *Rationing in Medicine: Ethical, Legal and Practical Aspects*. Berlin: Springer.

Yang, C-M. (2010). 'The Road to Observer Status in the World Health Assembly: Lessons from Taiwan's Long Journey', *Asian Journal of WTO & International Health Law and Policy* 5 (2): 3311–54.

Yoshikawa, A., J. Bhattacharya and W.B. Vogt (eds) (1996) *Health of Japan: Patients, Doctors, and Hospitals under a Universal Health Insurance System*. Tokyo: University of Tokyo Press.

Youde, J. (2012) *Global Health Governance*. Cambridge UK: Polity Press.

Zheng, Z. (2014) 'Acupuncture in Australia: Regulation, Education, Practice and Research', *Integrative Medicine Research* 3: 103–10.

Zhu, X, A.L. Carlton and A. Bensoussan (2009) 'Development in and Challenge for Traditional Chinese Medicine in Australia', *Journal of Alternative and Complementary Medicine* 15 (6): 685–8.

Zuckerman, S., T.A. Waidmann and E. Lawton (2011) 'Undocumented Immigrants, Left Out of Reform, Likely to Continue to Grow as Share of the Uninsured', *Health Affairs* 30 (11): 1997–2004.

Zwillich, T. (2001) 'Medical Technologies May Drive Up Health Costs', *Reuters News Service*, 6 March.

Index

352

Printed by Printforce, the Netherlands